Substance Abuse

Information for School Counselors, Social Workers, Therapists, and Counselors

Gary L. Fisher
University of Nevada–Reno

Thomas C. Harrison
University of Nevada–Reno

Allyn and Bacon
Boston • London • Toronto • Sydney • Tokyo • Singapore

*To our children, Colin Fisher, Aaron Fisher, and Iain Harrison,
and Tom's wife Elizabeth*

Senior Editor: Ray Short
Executive Marketing Manager: Steve Dragin
Senior Production Administrator: Marjorie Payne
Editorial Assistant: Christine Suitila
Cover Administrator: Suzanne Harbison
Composition/Prepress Buyer: Linda Cox
Manufacturing Buyer: Aloka Rathnam
Editorial-Production Service: Chestnut Hill Enterprises, Inc.

Copyright 1997 by Allyn & Bacon
A Simon & Schuster Company
Needham Heights, Massachusetts 02194

Library of Congress Cataloging-in-Publication Data
Fisher, Gary L.
    Substance abuse : information for school counselors, social
workers, therapists and counselors / Gary L. Fisher, Thomas C.
Harrison.
    p. cm.
Includes bibliographical references and index.
ISBN 0-205-16447-1 (pbk.)
    1. Social work with narcotic addicts—United States   2. Social
work with alcoholics—United States.   3. Narcotic addicts—
Counseling of—United States.   4. Alcoholics—Counseling of—United
States.   5. Narcotic habit—United States—Prevention.
6. Alcoholism—United States—Prevention.   I. Harrison, Thomas C., (date).
II. Title.
HV5825.F566   1996
362.29—dc20   95-26504
                                            CIP

Printed in the United States of America

10 9 8 7 6 5 4 3   00 99 98 97

Contents

Preface

We teach in a counseling department that offers training in school counseling, marriage and family therapy, college student development, mental health counseling, and school psychology. Our department requires that all students take a course titled, "Substance Abuse Counseling," which is a misnomer since the goal of the course is to familiarize students with the alcohol and other drug field including basic pharmacology, conceptualizations of alcohol and other drug problems, assessment, models of treatment, prevention, family issues, etc.

In teaching this course, we reviewed many textbooks. Many were focused primarily on the pharmacolgy of alcohol and other drugs. Others were oriented towards the person who wanted to work in alcohol and other drug treatment. Some espoused a narrow orientation to understanding addiction. We never found a book designed for the mental health professional in generalist settings that included all information that we believe to be necessary and that presented a balanced view of addictions. So, we wrote one.

In Chapter 1, we give a rationale regarding the need for mental health professionals (school counselors, social workers, marriage and family therapists, mental health counselors, rehabilitation counselors) to have this information and an overview of the topics covered in this book. Both of us have done most of our clinical work in generalist settings (schools, private practice, community mental health centers, universities) and have used our experiences to select these topics. In contrast to mental health professionals who work in alcohol and other drug treatment, our clients have ranged from those with no alcohol or other drug problems to those who have been in numerous treatment programs (and everything in between). We hope that this results in a balanced presentation of some controversial areas.

While writing, we have tried to keep in mind the common complaints of our students about textbooks. To illustrate the application of concepts, we have included many examples from our clinical experiences. We attempted to maintain interest by minimizing the traditional "stilted" style and personalizing more. Let us know if this has worked to make the text interesting and accessible.

As with any effort such as this, many people contribute to the final product. Graduate students Gary Pregal and Katie Swanson spent many hours in the library finding that elusive reference. Susan Malby-Meade, another graduate student and former English teacher, double-checked references, edited, and indexed the book. We appreciate their efforts immensely.

Nancy Roget, faculty member in the Addiction Training Center at the University of Nevada, Reno, reviewed the Relapse Prevention and Legal and Ethical Issues chapters and gave some valuable feedback. Her background in addiction treatment was invaluable. Graduate students, Frank Tirado and Priscilla Wu and their cohorts reviewed the chapter on diverse populations and added the "inside story" to help make the various population descriptions authentic.

In spite of her best efforts, our friend and colleague, Cheri Dunning, could not teach the senior author to use "affect" and "effect" correctly, nor could she effect change in the second author's use of the words, "how come" instead of the word "why". However, she patiently made these and other corrections while reading each chapter of this book. We are indebted to her for support, assistance, and for remembering to save everything on the hard drive.

Most of all, we thank Elizabeth Harrison, Tom's wife, for reading each chapter as a potential student. As a marriage and family therapist, she provided an essential viewpoint in preparing this book. She often re-adjusted her schedule on very short notice and patiently tolerated our anxieties, particularly near deadlines.

Chapter 1

The Role of the Mental Health Professional in Prevention and Treatment

It has become almost trite to recite the problems related to the use of alcohol and other drugs[1] in our society. Various statistics are reported in newspaper articles, surveys, and research studies that become mind-numbing with the array of graphs, percentages, and dollar amounts in the billions. It is not our purpose to contribute to the data avalanche in an effort to convince you that the abuse of alcohol and other drugs causes a variety of serious problems in our country. If you are reading this book, you are probably in a training program to prepare for a career in one of the helping professions and, one hopes, you have some awareness of the severity of this problem. On the other hand, our experience in training mental health professionals has taught us that there is a need for a framework to understand the extent to which alcohol and other drug issues affect not only the lives of those individuals you will be working with, but your own lives as well and the so-

---

[1]As is the case with many areas in the helping professions, terminology can be confusing. In this book, we will use the term *alcohol and other drugs* to clearly indicate that alcohol is a drug and to avoid having the reader omit alcohol from any discussion about drugs. If tobacco is relevant to a discussion, we will generally refer to "alcohol, tobacco, and other drugs." We will use the phrase *illegal drugs* when discussing issues that do not involve drugs such as alcohol and tobacco.

The use of terms such as *alcoholism, drug addiction, chemical dependency,* and *substance abuse* can also be problematic. In Chapter 2, we will give some definitions of terms used in the field, and, in Chapter 5, we provide the criteria to diagnose certain alcohol and other drug conditions. However, since these terms are used in this chapter, you should think of *alcoholism* as an addiction to the drug alcohol. *Drug addiction* refers to addiction to drugs other than alcohol. *Chemical dependency* includes addiction to alcohol and other drugs. *Substance abuse* means that there has been individual or societal problems as a result of alcohol and other drug use. After reading Chapters 2 and 5, you should have a more useful understanding of these terms.

ciety in which we live. Therefore, allow us to provide this framework with a few facts.

We recently listened to a speech by an official of the Center for Substance Abuse Treatment (of the U.S. Department of Health and Human Services) who stated that there are three current epidemics in the United States: substance abuse, AIDS, and violence. Substance abuse is a major cause of the other epidemics. David Smith, the founder of the Haight-Ashbury Free Clinics in San Francisco, estimated that there are 13 million alcoholics in the United States (Smith, 1986). The National Institute on Drug Abuse (NIDA) conducts a yearly survey on the use of all drugs, legal and illegal, in the United States. In 1988, 7.3% of all individuals above the age of 12 reported using an illegal drug in the past month. In the young adult age group (18–25), 17.8% reported use in the previous month (NIDA, 1990). There were 419,000 deaths caused by the use of tobacco in the United States in 1990 (Sacramento Bee, 1993) and approximately 100,000 deaths yearly as a result of alcohol (Wicker, 1987).

With regard to communicable diseases such as AIDS, 32% of adult AIDS cases and 35% of pediatric AIDS cases are attributable to intravenous (IV) drug use (Center for Substance Abuse Treatment, 1993). IV drug users are spreading the AIDS virus at a faster rate than any other group (see Chapter 14).

The relationship between crime, violence and substance abuse can be established simply by examining statistics with regard to alcohol. The National Institute on Alcohol Abuse and Alcoholism reported that 50% of all homicides were alcohol related; 50% of rapists, 77% of child abusers, and 72% of robbers had been drinking immediately before the crime was committed (National Institute on Alcohol Abuse and Alcoholism, 1980).

Obviously, illegal drugs are also related to violence and crime. A Department of Justice study found that 13% of convicted offenders committed crimes to obtain money to buy illegal drugs. Twenty-five percent of violent crimes were committed by individuals under the influence of illegal drugs, and 23% of inmates were incarcerated because of illegal drug activities (Associated Press, 1991). Of the homicides occurring in New York City in 1988, 53% were estimated to be drug related (Goldstein, 1989).

Finally, according to the U.S. Bureau of Justice Statistics (1992), approximately one-half of individuals who were in state prisons for committing violent crimes reported that they were under the influence of alcohol or other drugs at the time of the offense.

We risk contributing to the data avalanche to illustrate that the abuse of alcohol and other drugs is like a tree with many branches. The trunk is alcohol and other drug abuse but the branches are the multitude of other problems caused by or related to alcohol and other drugs. To avoid totally clogging your mind with statistics and/or completely depressing you before you read the rest of this book, we neglected to describe other branches of the tree such as the astronomical health care costs, decreased work productivity, excessive school truancy and work absenteeism, and detrimental effects on partners, children, and fetuses resulting from alcohol and other drug abuse. However, these and other branches exist and are the concern of all helping professionals.

The Need for Generalist Training

A few years ago, your senior author was asked by a local school district to conduct an independent psychological evaluation of a 14-year-old student who was a freshman in high school. The young man's parents were dissatisfied with the school district's evaluation of their son and had asked for another opinion. The youngster was failing most of his classes and was skipping school frequently. The parents were quite sure that their son had a learning disability that would explain his difficulties. The district's school psychologist had tested the student and not found a learning disability. The school counselor had suggested that there may be an emotional problem and recommended family counseling. In addition, a weekly progress check was initiated at school so the parents could be kept informed of assignments and homework that their son needed to complete. They had also hired a tutor. However, none of these interventions seemed to be helping, so the independent evaluation was requested.

In reviewing the test information, no indications of a learning disability were found. An alcohol and other drug assessment (which will be discussed in Chapter 5) was conducted and there was evidence that the young man was using alcohol and other drugs on a daily basis. The parents said that they allowed their son and his friends to drink in their home because they believed that this would prevent them from using "drugs" and from drinking and driving. The parents were defensive about their own alcohol and other drug use and rejected suggestions that the cause of their son's problems could be related to his alcohol and other drug use. A couple of months later, there was a request for the young man's records from an alcohol and other drug treatment program. He was referred to the program following an arrest for stealing alcohol from a convenience store.

Your junior author was supervising a master's student who was in a marriage and family therapy internship. The intern had been seeing a family of four (mom, dad, and two children, aged 3 and 9) who were referred to our university counseling clinic by Children's Protective Services. A child abuse report had been filed at the 9-year-old's elementary school because of bruises on the youngster's face. The father explained that he had slapped his son because of his frustration with the boy's behavior and "back-talking." The parents complained of frequent conflicts related to parenting techniques and family finances. The intern had developed an intervention plan that included referring the parents to a parent education program and working with the family on "communication skills" including "I-messages" and conflict resolution procedures. The intern was frustrated because the parents had failed to follow through on the parent education classes and had not made much progress in improving their communication patterns. It was suggested that the intern assess the alcohol and other drug use of the parents and she did so at the next session. The mother and father had a heated argument about the father's drinking behavior. They did not show up for their next appointment and, when the intern called, the mother said that they were discontinuing counseling because the father said it was a waste of time.

We regularly consult with a social worker in private practice. One of her clients is a woman in her early 30s who sought counseling for "depression" related to a series of failed relationships. The woman had been married twice. Her first husband was an alcoholic and the second was a polydrug abuser. She had been living with a man for two years who was in recovery from cocaine addiction. However, she found out that he had been having numerous affairs during their relationship. The woman, who has a master's degree, could not understand why she continued to become involved with these kind of men. She felt that there must be something wrong with her because the men in her life needed alcohol, other drugs, or other women. Her father was an alcoholic and verbally abusive, and she had also been sexually molested by her paternal grandfather.

In the three situations described, the "helping professionals" (school psychologist, school counselor, marriage and family therapy intern, social worker) were not involved in substance abuse treatment, but they needed information and skills in the alcohol and other drug field to perform their job functions in a competent manner. Your two authors between them have worked in schools as teacher and school psychologist, in a mental health clinic, in a university athletic department, and in private practice. We currently train school counselors and marriage and family therapists, as well as substance abuse counselors. We have found that the frequency of alcohol and other drug-related problems is so pervasive in the helping field that the lack of training in this area would result in inadequate preparation for mental health professionals.

It would be unreasonable to expect all helping professionals to have the same set of skills as substance abuse counselors. We don't expect substance abuse counselors to be able to plan educational interventions or to do family therapy. Similarly, school and mental health counselors, social workers, and marriage and family therapists do not need to be able to monitor detoxification or to develop treatment plans. However, all mental health professionals will encounter individuals who need assessment and treatment for alcohol and other drug problems and clients who are having problems as a result of relationships with individuals with alcohol and other drug problems. Included in the related problems that mental health professionals (school counselors, mental health counselors, rehabilitation counselors, psychologists, social workers, and marriage and family therapists) will encounter are children who have been fetally affected by parental alcohol and other drug use, the psychological impact on children and adults who live or have lived with caretakers who abuse alcohol and other drugs, and the intrapersonal and interpersonal problems of individuals who are in relationships with people who abuse alcohol and other drugs. Many of you have read about fetal alcohol syndrome, adult children of alcoholics, and codependency, which are included in these "related" problems. All of these issues will be discussed in this text (see Chapters 11 and 12).

We hope that you are convinced that mental health professionals need training in the alcohol and other drug field, not only to identify those clients who need further assessment and treatment but for the multitude of related problems that all mental health professionals will encounter on a regular basis. As with many areas in the mental health field, there are differing views on the causes and treatment of alcoholism and drug addiction based on the variety of disciplines concerned with these problems and the philosophical orientation of different individuals.

Philosophical Orientation

Jerome is a 47-year-old African-American man who had been arrested for a DUI (driving under the influence). It was his third DUI and he had previously been in an alcohol treatment program. There had been previous arrests for writing bad checks and spousal abuse. He was unemployed and dropped out of school in the tenth grade. An assessment revealed a long history of alcohol and other drug use beginning at age 12. Jerome's mother was an alcoholic and he was raised by his grandmother. He does not know his biological father.

Jerome's problem may be viewed in different ways by different professionals, depending on their training and experiences. A sociologist may focus on the environmental and cultural factors that modeled and encouraged alcohol and other drug use. Some psychologists might attend to the fact that Jerome experienced rejection by his biological parents that led to feelings of inadequacy. The use of alcohol and other drugs might be seen as a coping mechanism. A physician might be impressed by the family history of alcoholism and hypothesize that Jerome had a genetic predisposition for chemical dependency. A social worker may think that Jerome's unemployment and lack of education resulted in discouragement and consequent alcohol and other drug use. A criminal justice worker may see his behavior as willful misconduct and believe that punishment is necessary.

These differing views of the causes and treatment of Jerome's problem are not unusual in the mental health field. However, what is unique in the alcohol and other drug field is that many drug and alcohol counselors, others involved in the treatment of chemically dependent people, and many people who are recovering from alcohol and other drug problems believe that Jerome has a disease that has affected him mentally, physically, socially, emotionally, and *spiritually*. This spiritual component separates alcohol and other drug problems from other mental health problems and has had implications for the understanding and treatment of alcohol and other drug problems. One implication is that methods to attend to the spiritual aspect of treatment (e.g., Alcoholics Anonymous) are a common component of treatment. Another implication is that there are many individuals involved in the treatment of alcohol and other drug problems who do not have formal training as counselors but who are "in recovery" and hold a fervent belief in a particular orientation to treatment. This belief may not be based on scientific evidence but on their own experience and the experience of other recovering individuals. This phenomenon is similar to an individual's religious beliefs that cannot (and should not) be disputed by research since the beliefs are valid for that individual. Clearly, the potential for disagreement and controversy exists when scientific and spiritual viewpoints are applied to the same problem, which has certainly been the case in this field.

In Chapter 3, we will discuss the different models of addiction and will thoroughly discuss the "disease concept" of chemical dependency. Our point here is that we believe that the alcohol and other drug field requires an openness on the part of the mental health professional to a wide variety of possible causes of alcohol and other drug problems and a multitude of methods by which people recover from these problems. We have worked with people who discontinued their use of alcohol and other drugs without any treatment, individuals who stopped after walking into a church and "finding Jesus", clients and students who swear by AA, and people who have needed a formal treatment program.

If you work in a treatment program, you tend to see people who have experienced many life problems related to alcohol and other drug use. It is easy to develop a viewpoint about chemical dependency based on these clients' experiences. It is important to remember that treatment providers do not see those people who modify or discontinue their alcohol and other drug use through methods other than formal treatment.

This book is written from the perspective of the mental health professional working in a generalist setting rather than from the perspective of a substance abuse counselor in a treatment setting. Therefore, we will provide the type of information we believe all mental health professionals need in the alcohol and other drug field to work effectively in schools, community agencies, and private practice, rather than providing all the information needed to work as a substance abuse counselor in a treatment setting. We want to provide a balance in the types of viewpoints that exist in this field so that you can understand these perspectives. We will describe the popular literature in certain areas (e.g., adult children of alcoholics) and contrast this with research in the area so that you can understand that clinical impressions and research do not always match. Finally, we want to communicate our belief that it is not advisable to adopt universal concepts of cause and treatment in this field. In other areas of mental health treatment, we encourage practitioners to assess a client and to develop treatment strategies based on the individual and group characteristics of the client. The same rules should apply in the alcohol and other drug field.

Attitudes and Beliefs

Close your eyes for a minute and visualize an alcoholic. What did your alcoholic look like? For most people, the alcoholic is a white male, middle aged, who looks pretty seedy. In other words, the stereotypical skid row bum. Did you visualize somebody that looks like Betty Ford, the former first lady? Did you visualize one of your professors? Did you visualize a professional athlete?

Attitudes and beliefs about alcoholics and drug addicts have an effect on the mental health professional's work. Imagine that you are a mental health counselor and a well-dressed middle-aged woman comes to see you complaining of symptoms of depression. If you hold false beliefs about alcoholics, such as that they must be dirty and drunk all the time, you might fail to diagnose the Betty Fords of the world. The senior author tells his students in his substance abuse class about his own alcoholism to dispute stereotypes about the educational level and employment of alcoholics.

To help students understand their own attitudes about alcoholics and drug addicts, we have our students attend an Alcoholics Anonymous (AA) or Narcotics

Anonymous (NA) meeting as a class assignment. We encourage you to do this as well (if you do go to a meeting, make sure you attend an "open" meeting [see Chapter 8]). In addition to acquiring a cognitive understanding of this type of support for alcoholics and addicts, students report interesting affective reactions that provide information about their attitudes. For example, many students report that they want to tell others at the meeting that they are there for a class assignment and that they are not alcoholics. Our response is that unless you believe that alcoholism or drug addiction is simply a condition that some people develop and has nothing to do with morals or a weak will, you would not care if you were mistakenly identified as alcoholic or drug addicted. If you do care, you must believe that alcoholics and drug addicts have some type of character flaw. This realization helps many potential mental health professionals modify their attitudes and beliefs about alcoholism and drug addiction.

A second type of affective reaction that students report is surprise with the heterogeneity of the group. At most meetings, they see well-dressed businessmen and women, young people, blue-collar workers, unkempt people, articulate individuals, and people obviously impaired from their years of using alcohol and other drugs. Seeing such a variety of people tends to destroy any stereotypes the students may have.

Although we believe that potential mental health professionals may hold any belief system they want, the belief that alcoholism or drug addiction is due to a moral weakness or a character flaw may have a detrimental effect on providing or finding appropriate help for those with alcohol and other drug problems. For example, imagine that you are a marriage and family therapist and that you are seeing a couple in which one partner is drinking excessively. You believe that changing heavy drinking to moderate drinking is largely a matter of will power and desire, and you communicate this to the drinking partner. If this individual is addicted to alcohol, your belief system will be incompatible with this client's reality. Your client may experience shame because he or she is not strong enough or anger at your lack of understanding. Resistance and termination are frequent outcomes, and the client fails to get the proper help. Therefore, if you do believe that excessive alcohol and other drug use is largely due to moral weakness or character flaws, you would be well advised to refer these cases to others.

Denial, Minimization, Projection, and Rationalization

Imagine (or maybe you don't have to imagine) that you are in love with someone you believe to be the most wonderful person in the world. You cannot imagine living without this person and firmly believe that you need this person to survive. Your mother sits you down one day and tells you that you must no longer associate with this person. She tells you that this person is destroying your life, that you have changed since becoming involved with this person, and that all your family and friends believe that you need to break off the relationship before something terrible happens to you. How would you react? You might tell your mother that she is crazy and that all her complaints about this person are untrue (denial). Perhaps you acknowledge that your person does have some little quirks, but they really don't bother you (minimization). You tell your mother that she and the rest of your family and friends are really jealous because they do not have someone as wonderful as you (projection) and that you may have changed but these changes are for the better and long overdue (rationalization).

We use this analogy so you can develop an empathic understanding of what many alcohol and other drug addicted individuals experience. Obviously, the person in this case is the individual's drug of choice. The addicted individual may be seen as having an intimate and monogamous relationship with alcohol or other drugs and believe that he or she needs the drug to function and survive. In the same way that people deny that a relationship has become destructive, the addicted individual may deny that alcohol or other drugs have become destructive in spite of objective evidence to the contrary. The defense mechanisms of denial, minimization, projection, and rationalization are used so that the person does not have to face a reality that may be terrifying: a life without alcohol or other drugs.

While we know that it may be easy for you to intellectually understand these concepts as applied to alcoholic and other drug-addicted people, we have found it useful for our students to have a more direct experience with their own use of defense mechanisms. At the first class session of our substance abuse class, we ask the students to choose a substance or activity and abstain from this substance or activity for the semester and that the first thing that popped into their heads and was rejected because it would be too hard to give up is the thing they should choose. Students usually choose substances such as alcohol, coffee, chocolate, or sugar, or activities such as gambling (we live in Nevada where gambling is legal) or watching television. Some choose tobacco and an occasional courageous student will choose an illegal drug. The students record their use of the defense mechanisms through journal entries and write a paper about the experience at the end of the semester.

If you are wondering whether some students "blow off" the assignment and just make up the material in their journals and papers, the answer is "of course". When the assignment is given, this issue is discussed. The students are told that they can do anything they want to; the instructor will never know the difference. However, there is some reason for potential mental health professionals to take a close look at themselves if they are unwilling to abstain from a substance or activity for 15 weeks, particularly when mental health professionals will be encouraging clients to abstain from alcohol or other drugs for a lifetime.

We encourage you, our reader, to examine your own use of denial, minimization, projection, and rationalization, particularly in regard to your own use of alcohol and other drugs. Mental health professionals are not immune to alcohol and other drug problems and are just as likely to use these defense mechanisms as anyone else is. As you read the rest of this book, take some time to examine your own substance-using behavior. If there is a problem, this would be the ideal time to get some help. This would certainly be preferable to becoming one of the many impaired professionals who may cause harm to their clients and themselves.

Helping Attitudes and Behaviors

Although we have encountered many mental health professionals with alcohol and other drug problems, we have found that a more pervasive problem may be the potential mental health professionals who gravitate to the helping professions because of unresolved issues in their lives. Although there may be a sincere desire to help others, these potential mental health professionals may actually be unhelpful to clients. For example, in our counselor education program, we find that many of our students are adult children of alcoholics. Now, that is no problem in and of itself. In fact, as we will discuss in Chapter 11, many adult children of alcoholics have the same or fewer problems than other adults. However, being raised by one or more alcoholic caretakers may lead to certain characteristic ways of behaving that could have implications for a mental health professional's effectiveness. For example, a graduate student in marriage and family therapy whom we will call Debbie (we are changing all of the names of students and clients we are using in this book to protect anonymity) decided to pursue a career in the helping professions because everyone told her that she was easy to talk to and was a good listener. Debbie said that she was one of those people to whom total strangers immediately told their life stories.

Debbie was raised by her biological parents, both of whom were alcoholics. Within her family, she had developed a method of behaving that would minimize the probability of conflict developing. She did most of the cooking and cleaning at home, took care of her younger siblings, and worked very hard at school. Debbie reported being in a constant state of anxiety due to her worry that she had "missed" something that would send one of her parents into a rage.

In hindsight, it is easy to see that Debbie developed a false belief that she could control her parent's moods and behavior by making sure that everything was perfect at home and by her achievements at school. It is not unusual for children raised by alcoholic caretakers to develop a role designed to divert attention away from the real problem in the family. (Again, this will be discussed in detail in Chapter 11.) However, the development of this childhood role had implications for Debbie's work as a marriage and family therapist. We noticed that she was quite hesitant to confront clients and that she seemed very uncomfortable with conflict. Debbie had more than the usual anxiety for a student when counseling and brooded excessively when her clients did not immediately feel better. Clearly, the characteristic ways Debbie had learned to behave as a child were having a detrimental effect on her development as a marriage and family therapist in spite of the fact that people found her easy to talk to.

Another of our graduate students in counseling, Patricia, was taking our substance abuse counseling course. She failed her midterm examination. Patricia came to see the instructor and explained that the content of the course generated a great deal of emotion for her since her parents were alcoholics and she had been married to a drug addict. Because of these emotions, she said that she had difficulty concentrating on the lectures and the reading material and in following through on class assignments (students were required to attend an Alcoholics Anonymous and an Alanon [for family members of alcoholics] meeting). The instructor communicated his understanding that the course could have that impact on people with history and experiences in the substance abuse area and suggested that Patricia drop the course (he offered a passing withdrawal) and pursue counseling for herself. Patricia chose to avoid working on these issues, she stayed in the course, and failed.

Since most of you who are reading this text are graduate students, this may strike you as rather harsh. However, consider the alternative. Let's say that the instructor had offered his understanding and allowed Patricia to remain in the course without dealing with these issues and passed her. Would Patricia be able to work effectively with individuals and families in which there were alcohol or other drug problems, with adult clients who were raised by chemically dependent caretakers, or with clients living with alcohol- or other drug-abusing partners? In an attempt to avoid these problems, she might do a poor job of assessment, or she might ignore the signs and symptoms of alcohol or other drug problems. Or she might ignore or fail to inquire about substance abuse in the family of origin or in the current family of her clients. In short, we believe that her unwillingness to face these problems would result in her being a less-effective counselor.

What about Debbie? Her excessive anxiety and concern with her performance prevented her from objectively looking at her clients and her own counseling behaviors. Debbie's fear of conflict resulted in an unwillingness to confront her clients, which limited her effectiveness. Fortunately, Debbie was receptive to feedback and suggestions. She did some work on her own issues, and she has become a fine marriage and family therapist.

This discussion is not meant to discourage those of you who are adult children of alcoholics, are in recovery from an alcohol or other drug problem, or have lived or are living with a chemically dependent person from pursuing your careers. It is our experience that most people who want to become helping professionals have a need or desire to help people that is based on family of origin issues that may adversely affect their work. This is certainly the case with both of us. It is not a problem if you enter a training program in one of the helping professions because of your own need to be needed. It is a problem if you avoid examining your own issues and fail to take steps to resolve these issues in order to avoid ineffective (or in some cases, harmful) work with clients.

In this particular field, we find helping professionals who cannot work effectively with clients because of their own alcohol and other drug use or their experiences with alcohol and other drug use in their families of origin and/or with partners. In the rest of this book, we will attempt to provide you with information that will enable you to deal effectively with the direct and indirect problems resulting from alcohol and other drug use that social workers, school counselors, mental health counselors, marriage and family therapists, and other helping professionals will encounter. However, all of this information will be useless if your own use patterns or issues are unresolved and if they impact your work. Since denial is so pervasive, we encourage you to seek objective feedback regarding the necessity to work on your own use of alcohol or other drugs or on other issues and, if necessary, to choose a course of action with professional assistance. But please, for your own benefit and for the benefit of your future clients, don't choose to avoid.

Overview of the Book

In our choice of chapter topics and the orientation of each chapter, we have tried to maintain a primary goal of providing useful information in the alcohol and other drug field to general mental health professionals. Therefore, Chapter 2 (Classification of Drugs), Chapter 3 (Models of Addiction), Chapter 7 (Treatment of Alcohol and Other Drug Problems), and Chapter 8 (Twelve Step and Other Types of Support Groups) are overviews of these topics. We have attempted to provide enough detail about treatment and Twelve Step groups to reduce any myths about these activities and to allow mental health professionals to make informed referrals. Issues that usually provoke some controversy among generalists (e.g., the disease concept, relative dangers of different drugs, etc.) are also discussed.

In several chapters, we have attempted to integrate the role of the mental health professional in working with clients with alcohol and other drug problems with the specialist in the field. In Chapter 5 (Assessment and Diagnosis), Chapter 6 (Intervention), Chapter 9 (Employee Assistance Programs and Student Assistance Programs), and Chapter 13 (Relapse Prevention), our goal is that you will understand the types of alcohol and other drug services that mental health professionals in generalist settings provide.

Chapter 10 (Families), Chapter 11 (Children from Chemically Dependent Families), Chapter 12 (Codependency), and Chapter 15 (Other Addictions) involve issues related to alcohol and other drug problems. In many instances, mental health professionals may work with clients with these problems. In each of these chapters, we have attempted to provide sufficient depth of coverage so that you will have a conceptual framework to understand the relationship of these topics to alcohol and other drugs and to understand the implications for treatment.

Chapter 4 is an in-depth discussion of multicultural issues in the alcohol and other drug field. As with all mental and other health-related topics, it is essential to understand both individual and group characteristics of clients. The cultural context of alcohol and other drug use is of crucial importance in both prevention and treatment. We have chosen to highlight its importance by devoting a chapter to the topic rather than integrating multiculturalism into each chapter. Therefore, we encourage you to maintain an awareness of diversity issues as you read the remaining chapters.

At the beginning of this chapter, we mentioned the AIDS epidemic. The relationship between HIV/AIDS and substance abuse is discussed in Chapter 14. Our inclusion of a chapter on this topic reflects the increasing need for awareness among all mental and other health professionals regarding transmission and prevention of this disease.

Having only one chapter on prevention (Chapter 16) does not imply that the subject is unimportant. Indeed, if prevention efforts were more successful, there would be less need for the rest of this book. Clearly, school counselors and school social workers must be well informed about effective prevention approaches. However, successful prevention involves all aspects of a community, and all helping professionals must be involved. We are particularly interested in increasing your awareness of our perverted public policy regarding the marketing of legal drugs (alcohol and tobacco) and its effect on prevention efforts.

The final chapter in this book involves confidentiality and ethics (Chapter 17). In teaching a substance abuse counseling class to mental health generalists, we have found nearly universal ignorance of the fact that almost all mental health professionals are bound by federal confidentiality regulations. Students often perceived this topic as "dry." However, we have seen the consequences of lack of awareness of confidentiality regulations. So, please have the stamina to wade through this chapter and remember (if your instructor follows the order of the chapters) it is nearly the end of the term.

We need to mention two issues about writing style so you understand what we are trying to do in this book. First, there are many examples from clinical cases included. We both maintain clinical practices and believe that such cases can illuminate concepts and increase interest. Second, the tone of our writing may be less scholarly than you are accustomed to. We have taught many university courses and have used a lot of text books. We also were students for a *long* time. From these experiences, we found that many text books were marvelous, nonpharmaceutical methods to induce sleep. Although accurate and scholarly, the stilted style was often a barrier to acquiring information. It has been our intention to make this book accurate and informative but with a lower probability of causing drowsiness. Let us know if it worked.

Chapter 2

Classification of Drugs

As we noted in Chapter 1, this textbook is designed for the mental health professional (e.g., school counselor, mental health counselor, rehabilitation counselor, social worker, marriage and family therapist) who will encounter alcohol and other drug problems with their clientele but who, generally, will not provide treatment for these problems. Therefore, the goal of this chapter is to provide an overview of the drugs (including alcohol and tobacco) that are most often abused and drugs that are used in the treatment of some mental disorders. However, a thorough understanding of the pharmacology of drugs and related issues (e.g., medical management of overdose, use of psychotropic medications in the treatment of mental disorders) would require far more attention than one chapter can offer. Also, information in this area changes rapidly as a result of research. For example, there is no medication that has been found to be effective in significantly reducing cocaine craving. However, there is considerable research in this area. By the time you read this book, there may be pharmacological management of cocaine withdrawal that does not currently exist. We are including an additional reading list at the end of this chapter if you want to acquire more comprehensive information on the topics discussed. In addition, we encourage you to develop contacts with alcohol and other drug treatment providers who are likely to remain current with regard to research in this area. This will reduce the probability that you will pass along misinformation or outdated information to your clients.

Different methods exist that are used to classify drugs (Jacobs & Fehr, 1987). We will use the method that classifies drugs by their pharmacological similarity. Drugs exist that do not fit nicely into one classification, and these will be noted. For each drug classification, we will mention the common drugs contained in the classification and some common street names, the routes of administration, major effects, signs of intoxication, signs of overdose, tolerance, withdrawal, and acute and chronic effects. First however, we will present information on the federal schedule of drugs, some simple definitions of terms that will be helpful in understanding the rest of the chapter, and a brief discussion of the concept of "dangerousness."

Comprehensive Drug Abuse Prevention and Control Act

In 1970, the Comprehensive Drug Abuse Prevention and Control Act (often referred to as the Controlled Substances Act) was passed by the U.S. Congress. As part of this law, drugs are placed in one of five "schedules," with regulatory requirements associated with each schedule. Schedule I drugs have a high potential for abuse, no currently accepted medical use in treatment in the United States, and a lack of a safe level of use under medical supervision. Drugs on Schedule I include heroin, Quaalude, hallucinogens, and marijuana. Schedule II drugs also have a high abuse potential and can lead to psychological or physical dependence. However, these drugs have an accepted medical use in treatment. These drugs include narcotics other than heroin, cocaine, amphetamines, and PCP. As you can probably surmise, the criteria for the other schedules involve less abuse potential, increased medical uses, and less likelihood of psychological and physical dependence.

As you will see from our discussion of the classification of drugs, the way some drugs are classified is clearly illogical. For example, benzodiazepines such as Valium and Xanax are Schedule IV drugs, with part of the criteria for inclusion being that the drugs have a lower abuse potential than drugs on Schedules I, II, and III. In reality, these drugs have a much greater abuse potential than does marijuana, a Schedule I drug. However, the inclusion of a drug on a certain schedule is related to public policy, which will be discussed in Chapter 16. For example, the reclassification downward of a drug such as marijuana would be politically unpopular, and the reclassification of benzodiazepines upward would be resisted by the manufacturers of these drugs.

The Concept of Dangerousness

Related to the preceding discussion of schedules of drugs is the concept of the inherent dangers of certain drugs. Tobacco, alcohol, and other drugs are not safe to use. There are acute and chronic dangers, and these dangers vary by drug. For example, there is little acute danger from the ingestion of a glass of wine by an adult. The acute danger of shooting cocaine is far greater. Chronic use of any drug (including alcohol) has an increased risk but the danger of smoking one pack of cigarettes a day for 40 years is greater than the dangers from drinking one can of beer a day for 40 years. Danger is also related to the method used to administer a drug. Smoking a drug or injecting it produces the most rapid and intense reaction, while ingesting a drug generally produces effects with longer duration, although less intensity. Snorting drugs is in between but has more similarities to smoking and injecting than ingesting. Although any method of administration may be dangerous both acutely and chronically, smoking or injecting drugs tends to result in the most acute problems since these routes of administration rapidly introduce the drug to the bloodstream and, subsequently, to the brain. Also, smoking drugs causes damage to the respiratory system, and the intravenous use of drugs may cause serious problems including abscesses, blood clots, allergic reactions to the substances used to "cut" the drug, and communicable diseases such as hepatitis and AIDS.

It is certainly important that you understand the acute and chronic effects of different drugs and the addictive potential of tobacco, alcohol, and other drugs. However, it is essential that you understand that any of the psychoactive drugs we discuss in this chapter can be used in an addictive manner. You will learn that hallucinogens are not physically addicting in the sense that body tissues require these drugs for normal functioning. However, this does not imply that people are immune from serious problems resulting from the use of hallucinogens. Alcohol is clearly an extremely dangerous drug in spite of the fact that many people use the drug without problems. Marijuana is not as acutely or chronically dangerous as cocaine, but that does not mean it can be used safely. We have worked with clients who have serious life problems from marijuana use. This is not a sermon to "Just Say No." It is a caution to avoid concluding that you can direct clients away from some drugs to other drugs, and a caution to avoid using your own experience with alcohol and other drugs as a basis for determining which drugs are safe and which are dangerous.

Definitions

Terminology in the alcohol and other drug field can be confusing. One author may have a very specific meaning for a particular term while another may use the same term in a more general sense. An analogy might be the use of the term *neurotic* in the mental health field. While one professional may use this term when referring to some very specific disorders, another may use it to describe a wide variety of mental health problems. However, there is no universal agreement about how some of these terms should be used. Therefore, the following definitions should assist you in understanding this chapter and the rest of the book, but you may find differences in definitions as you read professional and popular literature in the alcohol and other drug field.

> *Addiction:* Compulsion to use alcohol or other drugs regardless of negative or adverse consequences. Addiction is characterized by psychological dependence (*see below*) and, often (depending on the drug or drugs) physical dependence (*see below*). As we will discuss in Chapter 15, the term *addiction* is sometimes applied to behaviors other than alcohol and other drugs (e.g., eating, gambling).
>
> *Alcoholism:* Addiction to a specific drug: alcohol.
>
> *Chemical dependency:* A term used to describe addiction to alcohol and/or other drugs and to differentiate this type of addiction from nonchemical addictions (e.g., gambling).
>
> *Dependence:* A recurrent or ongoing need to use alcohol or other drugs. Psychological dependence is the need to use alcohol or other drugs to think, feel, or

function normally. Physical dependence exists when tissues of the body require the presence of alcohol or other drugs to function normally. All psychoactive drugs can produce psychological dependence and many can produce physical dependence. Dependence will also be defined in Chapter 5, based on the criteria in the Diagnostic and Statistical Manual of Mental Disorders, Fourth Edition (DSM-IV) (American Psychiatric Association, 1994), to diagnose alcohol and other drug dependency disorders.

Intoxication: State of being under the influence of alcohol or other drugs so that thinking, feeling, and/or behavior are affected.

Psychoactive drugs: Natural or synthetic chemicals that affect thinking, feeling and behavior.

Psychotropic drugs: Chemicals used to treat mental disorders.

Substance abuse: The continued use of alcohol and/or other drugs in spite of adverse consequences in one or more areas of an individual's life (e.g., family, job, legal, financial). Abuse will also defined in Chapter 5 according to the criteria in the DSM-IV.

Tolerance: Requirement for increasing doses or quantities of alcohol or other drugs in order to create the same effect as was obtained from the original dose. Tolerance results from the physical or psychological adaptations of the individual. *Cross tolerance* refers to accompanying tolerance to other drugs from the same pharmacological group. For example, tolerance to alcohol results in tolerance to minor tranquilizers such as Xanax, even when the individual has never used Xanax. Reverse tolerance refers to a condition in which smaller quantities of a drug produce the same effects as did previous larger doses.

Withdrawal: Physical and psychological effects that occur when a drug-dependent individual discontinues alcohol or other drug use.

Central Nervous System Depressants

Central nervous system (CNS) depressants (also referred to as *sedative-hypnotics*) depress the overall functioning of the central nervous system to induce sedation, drowsiness, and coma. The drugs in this classification include the most commonly used and abused psychoactive drug, alcohol; prescription drugs used for anxiety, sleep disturbance, and seizure control; and over-the-counter medications for sleep disturbance, colds and allergies, and coughs. In general, CNS depressants are extremely dangerous. In 1990, there were 100,000 deaths caused by alcohol in the United States, the third leading cause of death (McGinnis & Foege, 1993). Alcohol in combination with other depressants accounted for nearly one-third of drug abuse-related emergency room episodes in 1992 and 39% of deaths resulting from drug overdose (Substance Abuse and Mental Health Services Administration, 1994).

Drugs in This Classification

Alcohol is the most well-known CNS depressant because of its widespread use and legality. The alcohol content of common beverages is beer, 3 to 6%; wine, 11 to 20%; liqueurs, 25 to 35%; and liquor (whiskey, gin, vodka, etc.) 40 to 50%. The "proof" on alcohol beverages is computed by doubling the alcohol content. Therefore, a bourbon that is described as "90 proof" is 45% alcohol. It is important to remember that the amount of alcohol in one beer is about the same as the amount of alcohol in one mixed drink. The alcohol in beer is simply contained in a larger amount of liquid.

Barbiturates are prescription drugs used to aid sleep for insomniacs and for the control of seizures. These drugs include Seconal (reds, red devils), Nembutal (yellows, yellow jackets), Tuinal (rainbows), Amytal (blues, blue heaven), and Phenobarbital. There are also nonbarbiturate sedative-hypnotics with similar effects but with different pharmacological properties. These include Doriden (goofballs), Quaalude (ludes), Miltown, and Equinil. Being a Schedule I drug, Quaalude cannot be legally prescribed in the United States.

The development of benzodiazepines or minor tranquilizers reduced the number of prescriptions for barbiturates written by physicians. These drugs were initially seen as safe and having little abuse potential, a view that has proved to be inaccurate. The benzodiazepines are among the most widely prescribed drugs and include Valium, Librium, Dalmane, Halcion, Xanax, and Ativan.

Finally, certain over-the-counter medications contain depressant drugs. Sleep aids such as Nytol and Sominex, cold and allergy products, and cough medicines may contain scopolamine, antihistamines, or alcohol to produce the desired effects.

Routes of Administration

Obviously, alcohol is administered by drinking. Some over-the-counter medications are also in liquid form. The barbiturates, nonbarbiturate sedative-hypnotics, and minor tranquilizers come in pill form. As with many psychoactive drugs, liquid forms of the drugs are produced and administered by injection.

Major Effects

The effects of CNS depressants are related to the dose, method of administration, and tolerance of the individual, factors that should be kept in mind as the effects are discussed. At low doses, these drugs produce a feeling of relaxation and calmness. They induce muscle relaxation, disinhibition, and a reduction in anxiety. Judgment and motor coordination are impaired, and there is a decrease in reflexes, pulse rate, and blood pressure. At high doses, the person demonstrates slurred speech, staggering, and, eventually, sleep. Phenobarbital and Valium have anticonvulsant properties and are used to control seizures. The minor tranquilizers are also used to control the effects from alcohol withdrawal.

Overdose

Alcohol overdose is common. We refer to this syndrome as being "drunk". The symptoms include staggering, slurred speech, extreme disinhibition, and black-outs (an inability to recall events that occurred when the individual was intoxicated). Generally, the stomach goes into spasm and the person will vomit, helping to eliminate alcohol from the body. However, the rapid ingestion of alcohol, particularly in a nontolerant individual, may result in coma and death. This happens most frequently with young people who participate in drinking contests.

As these drugs depress the central nervous system, overdose is extremely dangerous and can be fatal. Since the fatal dosage is only 10 to 15 times the therapeutic dosage, barbiturates are often used in suicides, which is one reason they are not frequently prescribed. It is far more difficult to overdose on the minor tranquilizers. However, CNS depressants have a synergistic or potentiation effect, meaning that the effect of a drug is enhanced as a result of the presence of another drug. For example, if a person has been drinking and then takes a minor tranquilizer such as Xanax, the effect of the Xanax may be dramatically enhanced. This combination has been the cause of many accidental deaths and emergency room visits.

Tolerance

There is a rapid development of tolerance to all CNS depressant drugs. Cross tolerance also develops. This is one reason why overdose is such a problem. For example, Bob, a very heavy drinker, is quite anxious and is having difficulty sleeping. He goes to his physician with these symptoms. The physician does not ask about his alcohol use and gives him a prescription of Xanax. Bob follows the directions and takes one pill. However, because he is tolerant to alcohol, he is also cross-tolerant to Xanax and the pill has no effect. He can't sleep so he takes three more pills and has a glass of brandy. The synergistic effect of these drugs results in a coma.

The tolerance that develops to the CNS depressants is also one reason that the use of the minor tranquilizers has become problematic. People are given prescriptions to alleviate symptoms such as anxiety and sleep disturbance that are the result of other problems such as marital discord. The minor tranquilizers temporarily relieve the symptoms but the real problem is never addressed. The person continues to use the drug to alleviate the symptoms, but tolerance develops and increasing dosages must be used to achieve the desired effect. This is a classic paradigm for the development of addiction and/or overdose.

Withdrawal

The withdrawal syndrome from CNS depressants can be medically dangerous. These symptoms may include anxiety, irritability, loss of appetite, tremors, insomnia, and seizures. In the severe form of alcohol withdrawal called delirium tremens (DTs), additional symptoms are fever, rapid heartbeat, and hallucinations. People can and do die from the withdrawal from these drugs. Therefore, the detoxification process for CNS depressants should include close supervision and the availability of medical personnel. Chronic, high dosage users of these drugs should be discouraged from detoxifying without support and supervision. For detoxification in a medical setting, minor tranquilizers can be used, in decreasing dosages, to reduce the severity of the withdrawal symptoms.

The dangerousness of withdrawal from CNS depressants is one reason why supervised detoxification is needed. In addition, supervision and support are usually required because the withdrawal symptoms are unpleasant and rapidly alleviated by using CNS depressants. For example, a 47-year-old man decides that he has been drinking too much and wants to quit. He doesn't tell anyone and is going to "tough it out". Although he doesn't have any medically dangerous symptoms, he is anxious, irritable, and has trouble sleeping. His family, friends, and co-workers remark about how unpleasant he is, and he is quite uncomfortable. He has a few drinks and finds that the symptoms are gone. Very rapidly, he is drinking heavily again.

Acute and Chronic Effects

In terms of damage to the human body and to society, alcohol is the most dangerous psychoactive drug (tobacco causes far more health damage). Alcohol has a damaging effect on every organ system. Chronic effects include permanent loss of memory, gastritis, esophagitis, ulcers, pancreatitis, cirrhosis of the liver, high blood pressure, weakened heart muscles, and damage to a fetus including fetal alcohol syndrome and fetal alcohol effect (see Chapter 11). Other chronic effects include family, social, occupational, and financial problems. Acutely, alcohol is the cause of many traffic and other accidents and is involved in many acts of violence and crime. The yearly monetary cost to the United States attributable to alcohol is estimated to be more than $70 billion (Inaba & Cohen, 1989).

Certainly, the other CNS depressants can cause the same acute problems that are the result of injury and accident and chronic effects on the individual and family due to addiction.

Central Nervous System Stimulants

CNS stimulants affect the body in the opposite manner as do the CNS depressants. These drugs increase respiration, heart rate, motor activity, and alertness. This classification includes highly dangerous, illegal substances such as crack cocaine, medically useful stimulants such as Ritalin, drugs with relatively minor psychoactive effects such as caffeine, and the most deadly drug used, nicotine. Cocaine was mentioned in 46% of the drug abuse-related deaths reported through the Drug Abuse Warning Network (137 medical examiner facilities in 38 metropolitan areas) and in 40% of the drug abuse-related emergency room episodes (Substance Abuse and Mental Health Services Administration, 1994).

Drugs in This Classification

Cocaine (coke, blow, toot, snow) and the freebase or smokeable forms of cocaine (crack, rock, base) are the most infamous of the CNS stimulants. Cocaine is found in the coca leaves of the coca shrub that grows in Central and South America. The leaves are processed and produce coca paste. The paste is, in turn, processed to form the white hydrochloride salt powder most of you know as cocaine. Of course, before it is sold on the street, it is adulterated or "cut" with substances such as powdered sugar, talc, arsenic, lidocaine, strychnine, or methamphetamine. Crack is produced by mixing the cocaine powder with baking soda and water and heating the solution. The paste that forms is hardened and cut into hard pieces or rocks. The mixing and heating process removes most of the impurities from the cocaine. Therefore, crack is a more pure form of cocaine than is cocaine hydrochloride salt powder.

Amphetamines are also CNS stimulants, and one form in particular, methamphetamine, is a major drug of addiction. The amphetamines include Benzedrine (crosstops, black beauties), Methedrine or methamphetamine (crank, meth, crystal), and Dexedrine (Christmas trees). There are also nonamphetamine stimulants with similar properties such as Ritalin and Cylert (used in the treatment of attention deficit-hyperactivity disorder) and Preludin (used in the treatment of narcolepsy). These drugs are synthetics (not naturally occurring), and the amphetamines were widely prescribed in the 1950s and 1960s for weight control.

Some forms of CNS stimulants are available without a prescription and are contained in many substances we use on a regular basis. Caffeine is found in coffee, teas, colas, and chocolate as well as in some over-the-counter products designed to help people stay awake (e.g., No Doz, Alert, Vivarin). Phenylpropanolamine is a stimulant found in diet-control products sold over-the-counter (e.g., Dexatrim). These products are abused by individuals who chronically diet (e.g., anorexics).

Although it has no euphoric properties, nicotine is the highly addictive stimulant drug found in tobacco products. In 1990, 419,000 people died as a result of their use of tobacco (MacKenzie, Bartecchi, & Schrier, 1994). This is four times as many deaths as resulted from alcohol. By a wide margin, nicotine is the most deadly drug we will discuss. Ironically, it is not only legal, it is marketed. We will mention this contradiction in public policy in Chapter 16.

Routes of Administration

With CNS stimulants, every method of administration is possible and utilized. Caffeine is consumed in beverage form, but it is also eaten (e.g., chocolate) or taken in pill form (e.g., No Doz). Nicotine is obviously smoked but can be chewed (chewing tobacco, nicotine gum) or administered through a skin patch. Cocaine and amphetamines can be snorted, smoked, injected, and ingested.

Major Effects

The uses of CNS stimulants have an interesting history. Many of you know that Sigmund Freud wrote "Uber Coca," which described the use of cocaine to treat a number of medical problems. Originally, Coca-Cola contained cocaine. In the 1980s, cocaine was depicted in the popular press as a relatively harmless drug. Amphetamines were used in World War II to combat fatigue and were issued by the U.S. armed forces during the Korean War. These drugs have a long history of use by long-distance truck drivers, students cramming for exams, and women trying to lose weight.

As with most of the psychoactive drugs, some of the CNS stimulants (cocaine and amphetamines) have a recreational use. The purpose is to "get high," or to experience a sense of euphoria. Amphetamine and cocaine users report a feeling of self-confidence and self-assurance. There is a "rush" that is experienced, particularly when cocaine is smoked and when cocaine and methamphetamine are injected. The high from amphetamines is generally less intense but longer acting than cocaine.

CNS stimulants result in psychomotor stimulation, alertness, and elevation of mood. There is an increase in heart rate and blood pressure. Performance may be enhanced with increased activity level, one reason why athletes use CNS stimulants. These drugs also suppress appetite and combat fatigue. That's why people who want to lose weight and people who want to stay awake for long periods of time (e.g., truck drivers) will use amphetamines.

Overdose

CNS stimulants stimulate the reward center of the brain. The most powerful of these drugs result in the body's not experiencing hunger, thirst, or fatigue. There is no built-in satiation point, so humans can continue using cocaine and amphetamines until there are no more or they die. Therefore, the compulsion to use, the desire to maintain the high, and the unpleasantness of withdrawal make overdose fairly common. There may be tremors, sweating and flushing, rapid heart beat (tachycardia), anxiety, insomnia, paranoia, convulsions, heart attack, or stroke. Death from overdose has been widely publicized because it has occurred with some famous movie stars and athletes. However, far more people experience chronic problems from CNS stimulant addictions than from overdose reactions.

Tolerance

There is a rapid tolerance to the pleasurable effects of cocaine and amphetamines and the stimulating effects of tobacco and caffeine. If you drink five or six cups a day of combinations of coffee, tea, and colas, you probably know this with regard to caffeine. You will find that if you stop using caffeine for a couple of weeks and then start again, the initial doses of caffeine produce a minor "buzz," alertness, and/or restlessness.

The rapid tolerance to the euphoric effects of cocaine and amphetamines leads to major problems with these drugs. The pleasurable effects are so rewarding, particularly when the drugs are smoked or injected, that the user is prone to compulsively use in an effort to recapture the euphoric effects. When injected or smoked, the effects are enhanced but of relatively short duration. Continual use to achieve the high leads to rapid tolerance. The user is then unable to feel the pleasure but must continue to use the drug to reduce the pain of withdrawal.

A sensitization or reverse tolerance can occur, particularly with cocaine. In this instance, a chronic user with a high tolerance has an adverse reaction (i.e., seizure) to a low dose.

Withdrawal

Unlike the withdrawal from CNS depressants, the withdrawal from these drugs is not medically dangerous. However, it is extremely unpleasant. If you have an addiction to caffeine and want to get a small taste of the withdrawal from CNS stimulants, discontinue your use of caffeine. The symptoms you can expect include a chronic headache, irritability, restlessness, and anxiety. You may have trouble sleeping and concentrating.

The withdrawal from cocaine and amphetamines is called "crashing." The severe symptoms usually last two to three days and include intense drug craving, irritability, depression, anxiety, and lethargy. However, the depression, drug craving, and an inability to experience pleasure may last for several months as the body chemistry returns to normal. Suicidal ideation and attempts are frequent during this time, as are relapses. Recovering cocaine and amphetamine addicts can become very discouraged with the slow rate of the lifting of depression, and, therefore, support is very important during this time.

If you have been or are addicted to nicotine, you probably have experienced the unpleasant withdrawal symptoms during attempts to quit (we are assuming that nearly everyone addicted to nicotine has tried to quit or has succeeded). Enhance the severity of your experience dramatically, and you may be able to achieve an empathic understanding of the withdrawal syndrome for cocaine and amphetamine addicts.

Acute and Chronic Effects

As previously stated, the acute effects of CNS stimulants can be dramatic and fatal. These include heart attacks, strokes, seizures, and respiratory depression. However, the results of chronic use cause the most problems. The addictive properties of these drugs is extremely high. Individuals with addictions to cocaine and amphetamines spend a tremendous amount of money to obtain drugs, and they encounter serious life problems related to their addiction. Also, there is an increased risk of strokes and cardiovascular problems, depression, and suicide in chronic users. Symptoms of paranoid schizophrenia can occur. If cocaine or amphetamines are snorted, perforation of the nasal septum can occur. Injection of CNS stimulants has the same risks as injecting other drugs (e.g., hepatitis, AIDS). Since these drugs suppress appetite, chronic users are frequently malnourished.

If you are smugly saying to yourself that the only CNS stimulant you use is caffeine, see the caffeine-induced disorders that are described in the DSM-IV (see Chapter 5). Also, caffeine may precipitate panic attacks in individuals predisposed to panic disorders, and the drug may be detrimental to some heart patients (Julien, 1995). A woman who is considering having a baby should reduce caffeine intake, and pregnant and breastfeeding women are advised to abstain (Julien, 1995).

Clearly, the chronic effects of nicotine addiction are damaging to health. The number of health-related problems, deaths, and days of work missed due to the chronic use of tobacco products is astounding.

Opioids[1]

The opioids are naturally occurring (opium poppy extracts) and synthetic drugs that are commonly used for their analgesic (pain relief) and cough-suppressing properties. Opium was used by early Egyptian, Greek, and Arabic cultures for the treatment of diarrhea since there is a constipating effect to this drug. Greek and Roman writers such as Homer and Virgil wrote of the sleep-inducing properties of opium, and recreational use of the drug in these cultures did occur (Julien, 1995). Morphine was isolated from opium in the early 1800s and was widely available without prescription until the early 1900s when the nonmedical use of opioids was banned. However, as Julien (1995) states,

> *The use of opioids is deeply entrenched in society; it is widespread and impossible to stop. The pharmacology of the opioids should be discussed like that of any other class of psychoactive drugs that have pleasurable effects, produce tolerance and physiological dependence, and have a potential for compulsive misuse. Emotional reactions and extensive legal efforts will probably fail to eradicate the recreational use of these drugs. Also, the opioids will continue to be used in medicine because they are irreplaceable as pain-relieving agents. In addition, the profound effects of opioids on the central nervous system . . . induce an enormous potential for compulsive abuse—a liability that is likely to resist any efforts at total control (p. 239).*

Heroin accounted for 39% of drug-induced deaths from overdose and 11% of drug abuse-related emergency room episodes in 1992 (Substance Abuse and Mental Health Services Administration, 1994).

Drugs in This Classification

The opioids include opium, codeine, morphine, heroin (smack, horse), Vicodin, Dilaudid, Percodan, methadone, Darvon, Demerol, Talwin, and LAAM (long-acting methadone).

---

[1]We will use the term *opioid* to refer to any natural or synthetic drug that has an analgesic (pain relieving) effect similar to that of morphine. The terms *opiate, narcotic,* and *analgesic* are also used to describe this classification of drugs.

Routes of Administration

We are familiar with many of these drugs in the pill or liquid form when used for pain relief or cough suppression. When used illicitly, the opioids are used intravenously, but this is also a route of administration when these drugs are used medically for pain relief. Heroin, which is used only illicitly, can be snorted or smoked in addition to the common intravenous method. As the danger of disease from dirty needles has been widely publicized, alternative routes of administration for heroin have become more popular. Opium has been smoked for centuries.

Major Effects

Opiods have medically useful effects including pain and cough suppression and constipation. Obviously, there is also a euphoric effect that accounts for the recreational use of these drugs. These drugs can produce nausea and vomiting and itching. A sedating effect occurs, and the pupils of the eyes become constricted.

Methadone or Dolophine is a synthetic opioid that does not have the dramatic euphoric effects of heroin, has a longer duration of action (12 to 24 hours compared with 3 to 6 hours for heroin), and blocks the symptoms of withdrawal when heroin is discontinued. This is the reason for the use of methadone in the treatment of opioid addiction (see Chapter 7). The action of LAAM has an even longer duration.

Overdose

Death from overdose of injectable opioids (usually heroin) can occur from the direct action of the drug on the brain resulting in respiratory depression. Death can also occur from an allergic reaction to the drug or to substances used to cut it, possibly resulting in cardiac arrest. Overdose of other drugs in this classification may include symptoms such as slow breathing rate, decreased blood pressure, pulse rate, temperature, and reflexes. The person may become extremely drowsy and lose consciousness. There may be flushing and itching skin, abdominal pain, and nausea and vomiting.

Tolerance

Frequency of administration and dosage of opioids is related to the development of tolerance. Tolerance develops rapidly when the drugs are repeatedly administered but does not develop when there are prolonged periods of abstinence. The tolerance that does develop is to the euphoric, sedative, analgesic, and respiratory effects of the drugs. This tolerance results in the individual's using doses that would kill a nontolerant person. The tolerant individual becomes accustomed to using high doses, which accounts for death due to overdose in long-time opioid users.

Cross-tolerance to natural and synthetic opioids does occur. However, there is no cross-tolerance to CNS depressants. This fact is important, because the combination of moderate to high doses of opioids and alcohol or other CNS depressants can (and often does) result in respiratory depression and death.

Withdrawal

When these drugs are used on a continuous basis, there is a rapid development of physical dependence. Withdrawal symptoms are unpleasant and uncomfortable but are rarely dangerous. The symptoms are analogous to a severe case of the flu with running eyes and nose, restlessness, goose bumps, sweating, muscle cramps or aching, nausea, vomiting, and diarrhea. There is significant drug craving. These symptoms rapidly dissipate when opioids are taken, which accounts for relapse when a person abruptly quits on his or her own ("cold turkey"). When the drugs are not available to the dependent individual, the unpleasant withdrawal symptoms also result in participation in criminal activities in order to purchase the drugs.

Acute and Chronic Effects

As we have already stated, there is an acute danger of death from overdose from injecting opioids, particularly heroin. Also, the euphoric effects of opioids rapidly decrease as tolerance increases, and, as this tolerance occurs, the opioid use is primarily to ward off the withdrawal symptoms.

Compared with the chronic use of CNS depressants, chronic use of the drugs themselves is less dangerous to the body. However, the route of administration and the life-style associated with chronic opioid use clearly has serious consequences. Obviously, there is the risk of communicable disease from the intravenous use of opioids and sharing needles. The life-style of heroin addicts often includes criminal activity to secure enough money to purchase heroin. Women may participate in prostitution, which adds the associated risks of diseases and violence. Nutrition is frequently neglected. However, those individuals who have been involved in methadone maintenance programs for long periods of time do not experience negative health consequences from the use of methadone.

Hallucinogens

Many of the hallucinogens are naturally occurring and have been used for thousands of years. Some have been (and are currently) used as sacraments in religious rites and have been ascribed with mystical and magical properties. Today, many types of hallucinogens are synthetically produced in laboratories. Some of the hallucinogens became very popular in the 1960s and 1970s, with a drop in use in the 1980s. Recently, there has been some resurgence of use. For example, the percent of 12th graders who reported using a hallucinogen in the previous twelve months was 11.2% in 1975 (first year data is available). There has been a gradual decrease to the mid-to-high 5% through 1992. However, in 1993, 7.4% reported use (Johnston, O'Malley, & Bachman, 1994).

Drugs in This Classification

As Julien (1995) points out, this classification comprises a group of heterogeneous compounds. Although there may be some commonality in terms of effect, the chemical structures are quite different. The hallucinogens we will discuss include LSD (acid, fry), psilocybin (magic mushrooms, shrooms), morning glory seeds (heavenly blue), mescaline (mesc, big chief, peyote), STP (serenity, tranquility, peace), MDA (ecstasy), and PCP (angel dust, hog). PCP was developed as a veterinary anesthetic, primarily for use with primates.

Routes of Administration

Hallucinogens are usually swallowed. For example, LSD may be put on a sticker, stamp, or sugar cube. Psilocybin is eaten. However, hallucinogens can also be snorted, smoked, or injected. PCP is often sprinkled on a marijuana joint and smoked.

Major Effects

These drugs produce an altered state of consciousness, including altered perceptions of visual, auditory, olfactory, and/or tactile senses and an increased awareness of inner thoughts and impulses. Common sights and sounds may be perceived as exceptionally intricate and astounding. In the case of PCP, there may be increased suggestibility, delusions, and depersonalization and dissociation. Physiologically, hallucinogens produce a rise in pulse and blood pressure.

Overdose

With the exception of PCP, the concept of "overdose" is not applicable to the hallucinogens. For example, Julien (1995) reports that the lethal dose of LSD is 280 times the normal dose. "Bad trips" or panic reactions do occur and may include paranoid ideation, depression, undesirable hallucinations, and/or confusion (Julien, 1995). These are usually managed by providing a calm and supportive environment. An overdose of PCP may result in acute intoxication, acute psychosis, or coma. In the acute intoxication or psychosis, the person may be agitated, confused, excited, and may exhibit a blank stare and violent behavior. Analgesia (insensibility to pain) occurs that may result in self-inflicted injuries and injuries to others when attempts are made to restrain the individual.

Tolerance

Tolerance to the hallucinogenic properties of these drugs occurs, as well as cross-tolerance between LSD and other hallucinogens. No cross-tolerance to cannabis has been demonstrated. Tolerance to PCP has not been demonstrated in humans (American Psychiatric Association, 1994).

Withdrawal

There is no physical dependence that occurs from the use of hallucinogens although psychological dependence, including drug craving, does occur.

Acute and Chronic Effects

A fairly common and well-publicized adverse effect of hallucinogens is the experience of flashbacks. Flashbacks are the recurrence of the effects of hallucinogens long after the drug has been taken. Reports of flashbacks more than five years after taking a hallucinogen have been reported although abatement after several months is more common.

With regard to the effects of LSD in particular, Julien (1995) states:

> Whether long-term, frequent, high-dose use of LSD results in discernible damage to the brain has not been determined, but it is generally agreed that occasional use of LSD does not induce physical damage.... Even though some users experience psychological dependence, most persons eventually cease taking LSD and return to less potent drugs. Thus, despite the extreme potency and unusual psychedelic effects of LSD, the social use of other psychoactive drugs that have potent behavioral-reinforcing properties (such as alcohol, nicotine, cocaine, amphetamine, and the opioids) should cause more concern (p. 318).

On the other hand, PCP does result in significant adverse effects. We have already discussed some of these effects. Chronic use may result in psychiatric problems including depression, anxiety, and paranoid psychosis. Accidents, injuries, and violence occur frequently.

Cannabinols

Marijuana is the most widely used illegal drug. Over 23% of adults in the 19- to 32-year range reported using marijuana in the last year, with 12.9% reporting use in the previous month (Johnston, O'Malley, & Bachman, 1993). The earliest references to the drug date back to 2700 B.C. (Julien, 1995). In the 1700s, the hemp plant (Cannabis sativa) was grown in the colonies for its fiber, which was used in rope. Beginning in 1926, states began to outlaw the use of marijuana since it was claimed to cause criminal behavior and violence. Marijuana use became popular with main-stream young people in the 1960s. Some states have decriminalized possession of marijuana although, according to the federal government, it remains a Schedule I drug.

Drugs in This Classification

The various cannabinols include marijuana (grass, pot, weed, joint, reefer, dube), hashish, charas, bhang, ganja, and sinsemilla. The active ingredient is delta-9-tetrahydrocannabinol (THC). Hashish and charas have a THC content of 7 to 14%;

ganja and sinsemilla, 4 to 7%; and bhang and marijuana, 2 to 5%. For simplicity, we will refer to the various forms of cannabinols as "marijuana".

Routes of Administration

Marijuana is usually smoked in cigarette form or pipes. It can also be ingested, normally by baking it in brownies or cookies.

Major Effects

Marijuana users experience euphoria; enhancement of taste, touch, and smell; relaxation; increased appetite; altered time sense; and impaired immediate recall. An enhanced perception of the humor of situations or events may occur. The physiological effects of marijuana include increase in pulse rate and blood pressure, dilation of blood vessels in the cornea (which produces bloodshot eyes), and dry mouth. Motor skills and reaction time are slowed. Intraocular pressure is reduced, a factor which has resulted in the use of THC in the treatment of glaucoma. THC has also been used as an anti-nausea drug for chemotherapy patients.

Overdose

Overdose is unusual because the normal effects of marijuana are not enhanced by large doses. Intensification of emotional responses and mild hallucinations can occur, and the user may feel "out of control." As with hallucinogens, many reports of overdose are panic reactions to the normal effects of the drug. In individuals with preexisting mental disorders (e.g., schizophrenia), high doses of marijuana may exacerbate symptoms such as delusions, hallucinations, disorientation, and depersonalization (Julien, 1995).

Tolerance

Tolerance is a controversial area with regard to marijuana. According to Palfai and Jankiewicz (1991), tolerance is observed in high dosage, chronic users. However, Inaba and Cohen (1989) stated that, "Tolerance to marijuana occurs in a rapid and dramatic fashion" (p. 154). The difference of opinion as to whether tolerance develops slowly or quickly may be due to type of subject studied and various definitions of "dosage". For example, tolerance rapidly occurs in animals but with frequent use of high doses in humans (Witters, Venturelli, & Hanson, 1992). At the least, chronic users probably become accustomed to the effects of the drug and are experienced in administering the proper dosage to produce the desired effects. Cross-tolerance to CNS depressants, including alcohol, has been demonstrated (Palfai & Jankiewicz, 1991).

Withdrawal

A withdrawal syndrome can be observed in chronic, high-dosage users who abruptly discontinue their use. The symptoms include irritability, restlessness, decreased appetite, insomnia, tremor, chills, and increased body temperature. The symptoms usually last three to five days.

Acute and Chronic Effects

Marijuana is certainly not acutely or chronically dangerous when death is the measure of dangerousness. However, the effect on motor skills and reaction time certainly impairs the user's ability to drive a car, boat, plane, or other vehicle, and marijuana use has also been detected in a significant number of victims of vehicle and nonvehicle accidents (Soderstrom, Trifillis, Shankar, & Clark,1988).

Chronic use of marijuana does seem to have an adverse effect on lung function, although there is no direct evidence that it causes lung cancer. Although an increase in heart rate occurs, there does not seem to be an adverse effect on the heart. As is the case with CNS depressants, marijuana suppresses the immune system. Chronic marijuana use decreases the male hormone testosterone (as does alcohol) and adversely effects sperm formation. However, no effect on male fertility or sexual potency has been noted. Female hormones are also reduced, and impairment in ovulation has been reported.

Although marijuana has been reported to cause amotivational syndrome, which is characterized by apathy, loss of goal directiveness, and dulled emotions, no causal relationship has been established (Schwartz, 1987).

Inhalants and Volatile Hydrocarbons

Inhalants and volatile hydrocarbons consist largely of chemicals that can be legally purchased and that are normally used for nonrecreational purposes. In addition, this classification includes some drugs that are used legally for medical purposes. As psychoactive drugs, most of these substances are used mainly by young people, particularly in low socio-economic areas. Since most of these chemicals are accessible in homes and are readily available for purchase, they are easily used as psychoactive drugs by young people who are beginning drug experimentation and by individuals who are unable to purchase other mind-altering substances due to finances or availability.

Drugs in This Classification

The industrial solvents and aerosol sprays that are used for psychoactive purposes include gasoline, kerosene, chloroform, airplane glue, lacquer thinner, acetone, nail polish remover, model cement, lighter fluid, carbon tetrachloride, fluoride-based sprays, metallic paints, and typewriter correction fluids. Volatile nitrites are amyl nitrite (poppers), butyl and isobutyl (locker room, rush, bolt, quick silver, zoom). Amyl nitrite has typically been used in the gay community. In addition, nitrous oxide (laughing gas), a substance used by dentists, is also included in this classification.

Route of Administration

As the name of this classification implies, these drugs are inhaled, a method of administration referred to as "huffing" or sniffing. The industrial solvents and aerosol sprays are often poured or sprayed on a rag and put in a plastic bag. The individual then places his or her head in the plastic bag and inhales rapidly and deeply.

Major Effects

The solvents and sprays reduce inhibition and produce euphoria, dizziness, slurred speech, an unsteady gait, and drowsiness. Nystagmus (constant involuntary movements of the eyes) may be noted. The nitrites alter consciousness and enhance sexual pleasure. The user may experience giddiness, headaches, and dizziness. Nitrous oxide produces giddiness, a buzzing or ringing in the ears, and a sense that the user is about to pass out.

Overdose

Overdose of these substances may produce hallucinations, muscle spasms, headaches, dizziness, loss of balance, irregular heartbeat, and coma from lack of oxygen.

Tolerance

Tolerance does develop to nitrous oxide but does not seem to develop to the other inhalants.

Withdrawal

There does not appear to be a withdrawal syndrome associated with these substances.

Acute and Chronic Effects

The most critical acute effect of inhalants results from the method of administration, which can result in loss of consciousness, coma, or death from lack of oxygen. Respiratory arrest, cardiac arrhythmia, or asphyxiation may occur. Many of these substances are highly toxic, and chronic use may cause damage to the liver, kidneys, brain, and lungs.

Anabolic Steroids

Anabolic steroids are synthetic drugs that are illicitly used to improve athletic performance and increase muscle mass. These drugs resemble the male sex hormone, testosterone. Although some anabolic steroids are approved for use in the United States for medical purposes, the abuse of these drugs led Congress to pass the

Anabolic Steroids Act of 1990. This law regulated the distribution and sale of anabolic steroids and added these drugs to Schedule III of the Controlled Substances Act. In 1993, 2.5% of high school seniors reported steroid use in the previous year (Johnston et al., 1994).

Drugs in This Classification

Anabolic steroids approved in the United States include Depo-Testosterone, Durabolin, Danocrine, and Halotestin. Some veterinary anabolic steroids are illicitly sold for human use and include Finiject 30, Equipoise, and Winstrol. Delatestryl, Testex, and Maxibolan are sold legally only outside of the United States.

Routes of Administration

Anabolic steroids are taken orally or injected. "Stacking" refers to combining oral and injectable steroids.

Major Effects

Anabolic steroids are used medically for testosterone replacement and treatment of muscle loss, blood anemia, and endometriosis. However, the abuse of these drugs by athletes and by those who wish to improve their physical appearance is prompted by the effects of anabolic steroids on muscle strength, body mass, and personality. These drugs increase muscle strength, reduce body mass, and increase aggressiveness, competitiveness, and combativeness.

Overdose

When used illicitly to improve athletic performance or physical appearance, the dosage used is well beyond the therapeutic dose. For example, Brower, Blow, Young, and Hill (1991) found that weight-lifters used from 2 to 26 times the recommended dose of anabolic steroids. Although there is no immediate danger of death or serious medical problems from high dosage levels of anabolic steroids, there are serious complications from long-term use. These effects will be described later in this section.

Tolerance

No evidence of tolerance to anabolic steroids exists.

Withdrawal

Physical and psychological dependence to anabolic steroids does occur, and there is a withdrawal syndrome. The symptoms of withdrawal include depression, fatigue, restlessness, insomnia, loss of appetite, and decreased interest in sex.

Acute and Chronic Effects

For males, atrophy of testicles, impaired production of sperm, infertility, early baldness, acne, and enlargement of the breasts occurs. In females, there are masculizing effects including increased facial and body hair, lowered voice, and irregularity or cessation of menses. There is an increased risk of coronary artery disease due to reduced "good" cholesterol (HDL) and increased "bad" cholesterol (LDL). An association has also been established between oral anabolic steroids and jaundice and liver tumors (Julien, 1995). Mood swings, with periods of unreasonable and uncontrolled anger and violence, have been noted.

Drugs Used in the Treatment of Mental Disorders

Mental health professionals will work with clients who are taking a variety of legally prescribed drugs to treat many mental disorders. These drugs generally have little or no euphoric effects and, therefore, are not used for recreational purposes. However, it is certainly important for helping professionals to have some familiarity with the uses and effects of these drugs.

Drugs Used in the Treatment of Psychotic Disorders

Antipsychotic or neuroleptic drugs are used in the treatment of schizophrenia and other psychotic disorders. These major tranquilizers produce psychomotor slowing, emotional quieting, and an indifference to external stimuli. Although these drugs are called "tranquilizers," the effects are not euphoric or pleasant. Therefore, they are not drugs of abuse. The phenothiazines (Thorazine, Compazine, Stelazine, Prolixin, Mellaril) and nonphenothiazines (Navene, Haldol) control agitation and hallucinations. Disturbed thinking and behavior is reduced. These effects have allowed many schizophrenic individuals to live in noninstitutional settings and to function more effectively. However, if the drugs are discontinued, the psychotic symptoms reappear. The drugs do not produce tolerance or physical or psychological dependence. Acute side effects include a dry mouth and Parkinson-like symptoms such as disordered motor movements, slow motor movements, and underactivity. Chronic effects include repetitive, involuntary movements of the mouth and tongue, trunk, and extremities. Massive overdoses are usually not lethal.

Drugs Used in the Treatment of Affective Disorders

Anti-depressant drugs elevate mood, increase physical activity, improve appetite, reduce insomnia, and reduce suicidal ideation in most depressed clients. They are used for the treatment of acute and chronic depression. There are three types of anti-depressant drugs. The MAO (monoamine oxidase) inhibitors (Marplan, Nardil, Parnate) are used infrequently today because these drugs can raise blood pressure if foods with tyramine (cheeses, herring, chianti wine) are consumed. The tricyclics (Tofranil, Elavil, Sinequan) were widely used as anti-depressants until the development of the "second generation" anti-depressants (Prozac, Wellbutrin, Zoloft). These drugs, although no more effective than the tricyclics, have a more rapid onset of effect and fewer adverse side effects. The tricyclics may take two to three weeks to produce the desired effects, while the newer drugs take about one week. This time difference can be critical with depressed clients. The tricyclics can produce cardiac problems and potentiate the effects of alcohol. Lethal overdoses are also possible. The media has widely publicized claims that Prozac has caused homicidal or suicidal behavior, but no cause-and-effect relationship has been scientifically established. Second generation anti-depressants have also been used in the treatment of obsessive-compulsive disorder and panic disorders.

Lithium is used in the treatment of bipolar disorder. It is an anti-manic, rather than an anti-depressant, drug. Clients who take Lithium must be closely monitored, since high concentrations can cause muscle rigidity, coma, and death.

The treatment of panic attacks has included anti-anxiety agents (benzodiazepines) that were discussed in the Central Nervous System Depressant section of this chapter (Librium, Valium, Xanax, Halcion). However, these drugs are dependence producing and are abused. Nonbenzodiazepines that are used to treat panic disorders but are noneuphoric include Equanil, Atarax, and Buspar.

Drugs Used in the Treatment of Attention Deficit Disorder

Recently, there has been a great deal of attention directed toward children and adults who have attention deficit disorder. This condition may exist with or without hyperactivity and is characterized by distractibility, inability to concentrate, short attention span, and impulsivity. It has been found that Ritalin and Cylert, amphetamine derivatives, reduce many of these symptoms. Ritalin has a rapid onset of effect and a short duration. Cylert is longer acting but also takes longer to work. Both of these drugs are CNS stimulants and can be abused. The use of stimulants to control the symptoms of attention deficit disorder has always seemed paradoxical. However, it may be that this disorder is due to unfocused electrical activity in the brain, and the stimulant drugs may improve the ability of the individual to concentrate and focus. Rather than calming the person down, the affected client is simply better able to focus their energy, concentrate, and reduce attention to extraneous stimuli. This may also reduce the anxiety that often accompanies attention deficit disorder.

Since these drugs are CNS stimulants, there are the associated side effects of appetite suppression, sleep disruption, and growth disturbance when these drugs are continuously used by pre-adolescents. A small number of individuals experience lethargy and emotional blunting. If these symptoms occur, the physician should immediately be contacted to adjust the dose or to prescribe a different drug.

It should also be mentioned that these drugs should not be prescribed to control unruly behavior in children. Attention deficit disorder should be diagnosed only after a careful multi-disciplinary assessment. The best protocol to evaluate the efficacy of medication is a double-blind procedure in which neither the school nor parent is aware when a placebo or active drug has been taken. Behavior should be observed at school and at home and the case manager can then determine whether medication will be helpful.

Additional Reading

Abadinsky, H. (1993). *Drug abuse: An introduction* (second edition). Chicago: Nelson-Hall Publishers.

Avis, H. (1990). *Drugs & life.* Dubuque, IA: Wm. C. Brown Publishers.

Dusek, D. E. & Girdano, D. A. (1993). *Drugs: A factual account* (fifth edition). New York: McGraw Hill.

Inaba, D. S. & Cohen, W. E. (1994). *Uppers, downers, all arounders* (second edition). Ashland, OR: Cinemed Inc.

Inciardi, J. A. & McElrath, K. (1995). *The American drug scene: An anthology.* Los Angeles: Roxbury Publishing.

Julien, R. M. (1995). *A primer of drug action* (seventh edition). New York: W. H. Freeman and Company.

Maisto, S. A., Galizio, M. & Connors, G. J. (1991). *Drug use and misuse.* Orlando, FL: Holt, Rinehart and Winston, Inc.

Palfai, T. & Jankiewicz, H. (1991). *Drugs and human behavior.* Dubuque, IA: Wm. C. Brown Publishers.

Schuckit, M. A. (1984). *Drug and alcohol abuse: A clinical guide to diagnosis and treatment* (second edition). New York: Plenum Press.

Witters, W., Venturelli, P., & Hanson, G. (1992). *Drugs and society* (third edition). Boston: Jones and Barlett.

Chapter 3

Models of Addiction

You may have heard of or remember Charles Manson, the leader of a cult of people who committed some horrible murders in 1969 in California. He ordered his cult members to kill some famous and wealthy people with the hope of creating a race war. Manson is currently serving a life sentence in prison and has been the subject of popular books and periodic media interviews, particularly whenever he has a parole hearing. Manson has been variously described as being possessed by evil spirits, as being the victim of an abusive and violent childhood, as being a sociopath, and as having a chemical imbalance that created a psychosis including delusions of grandeur and persecution. When one reads about Manson, all of these explanations of his behavior seem to make some sense. Certainly, whatever explanation makes the most sense probably depends on a person's values and beliefs, formal and informal training, and experience. However, it is important to critically examine the explanations of the behavior of someone such as Charles Manson, since different explanations have different implications for the proper method to deal with him. For example, if you believe that he is possessed by evil spirits, there may be a spiritual method to treat him (i.e., exorcism). If you accept the explanation that he is a sociopath, then the appropriate method may be firm punishment for his actions. If his behavior is due to his violent and abusive childhood, he may be deserving of our sympathy and in need of therapeutic interventions. Finally, if Manson's behavior is due to a chemical imbalance, then he is not responsible for his behavior and may need medication to manage his condition.

You can see that values and beliefs play a role in whichever explanation you accept. If you believe in evil spirits or possession, this explanation may appeal to you. Formal and informal training will have an effect, since you may have taken some courses in sociology or social psychology and been taught that abusive childhood experiences can result in violent behavior. Maybe you work in law enforcement and have seen directly the victims of brutality, and, from these experiences, you have come to believe that the perpetrators must be lacking in conscience to commit such crimes.

However, it may be that all of these explanations for the abnormal behavior of a Charles Manson have some validity. He may have a spiritual deficit, lack a conscience in the manner in which most of us understand this concept, be influenced by his childhood experiences, and have some form of physiological abnormality. The "amount" of explanation of his behavior may not be equally divided among these factors (they may not have equal weights in explaining Manson's behavior), and it may be necessary to consider a number of different variables in determining the most appropriate course of action. For example, the brutality of the murders, Manson's lack of remorse, and his potential for future violence may lead to a decision to incarcerate a person such as Manson, no matter what the "true" explanations are for his behavior.

The alcohol and other drug field has also been characterized by a variety of explanations for the same behavior. This is certainly not unusual in the mental health or medical field. However, the fervor and inflexibility with which some proponents of certain models of addiction adhere to their models has produced controversy in this field. Furthermore, the use of alcohol and other drugs interests and elicits extensive involvement from the legal system, business, government, the religious community, as well as from the medical and mental health fields. The differing goals and orientations of these disciplines has resulted in sharp differences regarding the explanation of problematic use of alcohol and other drugs. Consequently, the manner in which those people with alcohol and other drug problems are dealt has also been a controversial issue. We will discuss some of the various "models" or explanations of addiction, giving particular attention to the popular "disease concept". Also, we will discuss some cases that illustrate that one explanation alone for addictive behavior may be insufficient.

The Moral Model

The moral model explains addiction as a consequence of personal choice. Individuals are viewed as making decisions to use alcohol or other drugs in a problematic manner and as being capable of making other choices. This model has been adopted by certain religious groups as well as by the legal system. Drunkenness is viewed as sinful behavior by some religious groups (Miller & Hester, 1995), and the use of alcohol is prohibited by certain religions (e.g., the Mormon Church). From this perspective, religious or spiritual intervention would be necessary to change behavior. Several years ago, we conducted an alcohol and other drug workshop for clergy, and the moral model was strongly advocated by many of the members who were present. Many saw acceptance of a particular religious persuasion as the necessary step to overcome alcohol and other drug problems.

A 1988 Supreme Court decision found that crimes committed by an alcoholic were willful misconduct and not the result of a disease (Miller & Hester, 1995). Certainly, the manner in which states deal with drunk driving violations may relate to the moral model. In states where violators are not assessed for chemical dependency and where there is no diversion to treatment, the moral model guides policy.

If excessive alcohol use is the result of personal choice, then violators should be punished.

Not all adherence to the moral model is found in the legal and religious communities. Proponents of the disease concept of chemical dependency (discussed later in this chapter) talk about the "total self-centeredness—the spiritual illness that causes the person to demand 'what I want when I want it' that makes the individual vulnerable to addiction" (Doweiko, 1993, p. 206). The distinction between this viewpoint and that of the legal and religious moral model is that the "spiritual illness" is seen as a *result* of the progressive increase in the use of alcohol and other drugs, while the legal and religious view would postulate that there was a spiritual or character deficit that existed prior to the initiation of problematic use.

Sociocultural and Psychological Models of Addiction

While the moral model explains addiction as a matter of personal choice caused by spiritual or character deficiencies, other explanations of addiction focus on factors that are external to the individual, such as cultural, religious, family, and peer variables or psychological factors. For example, Stanton Peele (1989), in his book criticizing the disease concept of alcoholism, points to the low rate of alcoholism among Chinese and Jewish populations. He provides a cultural explanation for this, since the Chinese and Jews do not disapprove of the use of alcohol but do disapprove of excessive drinking, particularly if it leads to inappropriate behavior. In these groups, young people use alcohol in social or ceremonial situations along with adults, but they also observe the prohibitions against excessive use and perceive the judgments made of those who violate the cultural sanctions regarding alcohol use (Peele, 1989). Cultural acceptance of heavy drinking has also been postulated to account for the high rate of alcoholism among certain groups such as Irish-Americans (Peele, 1984).

While the prohibition against the use of alcohol and other drugs by certain religious groups would seem to limit the number of alcoholics and other drug addicts among members of the group, this is not always the case. Those who believe that the problematic use of alcohol and other drugs is the result of environmental factors point to the moderate use of alcohol among certain religious groups (e.g., Jews) and their corresponding low rate of alcoholism, and they attribute this to the fact that members are taught to use alcohol responsibly. Those who are raised in a religion that prohibits the use of alcohol never observe moderate use and, therefore, if use is initiated, the individual is more likely to use in an excessive manner. Thus, in this conceptualization, the religious prohibition against the use of alcohol may actually contribute to excessive use for those who violate the prohibition or leave the religion.

Regardless of the model of addiction one adheres to, the use patterns and attitudes about alcohol and other drugs of family members and peers is highly related to addiction. Lawson, Peterson, and Lawson (1983) found that 30% of children with alcoholic parents developed alcoholism, compared with 5% of children with moderately using parents and 10% of children with abstaining parents. (These results have been used to support both genetic and environmental explanations of addiction.) Parental use of alcohol and other drugs has been identified as one of the most important factors in early use by adolescents (Barnes, Farrell, & Cairns, 1986), and parental permissiveness toward use is highly correlated with adolescent alcohol and other drug abuse (Johnson, Shontz, & Locke, 1984; McDermott, 1984). Furthermore, proponents of a sociocultural model of addiction believe that certain family environmental patterns predispose children for alcoholism. For example, Lawson (1992) found that disengaged, rigid families who are conflict-oriented and repress the expression of feelings and rigid, moralistic families were more likely to produce alcoholic offsprings. In the effort to identify risk factors for adolescent substance abuse, Hawkins and his colleagues found that family history of alcoholism, family history of criminality or antisocial behavior, family management problems, parental drug use and positive attitudes toward use and friends who use drugs were all predictive of adolescent alcohol and other drug problems (Hawkins, Lishner, & Catalano, 1985; Hawkins, Lishner, Catalano, & Howard, 1986). Having friends who use drugs was among the strongest predictors.

While sociocultural or external factors have been used to explain addiction, psychological explanations of addiction also exist. It is beyond the goals of this text to discuss each of these theories, but we will spend some time on the most widely held psychological explanations of addiction. Perhaps the most accepted view, particularly by those outside the addiction field, is that the problematic use of alcohol and other drugs is secondary to some other psychological problem or condition. The primary psychological problem causes emotional pain, and alcohol and other drugs serve to temporarily relieve this pain. For example, a woman was sexually molested as a child by a relative. She does not tell anyone or her story is not believed and she does not receive any assistance. The woman experiences anger, guilt, embarrassment, and anxiety as a result of the experience and gravitates towards alcohol and other drugs to relieve these uncomfortable feelings. Another example would be the person who suffers from endogenous depression and self-medicates with stimulants to relieve the constant symptoms of depression.

John Bradshaw, the popular author and lecturer, has described compulsive behavior, including alcohol and drug addiction, as a reflection of an individual's effort to escape shame from the family of origin (Bradshaw, 1988). In support of this view, Coleman (1982) found that 33 to 62% of female alcoholics had suffered neglect or sexual abuse in their families of origin.

Related to the view that alcohol and other drug problems are secondary to other psychological problems is the question about whether an alcoholic or addictive personality exists. Clearly, there are alcoholics and drug addicts who seem to be free of any identified psychological problems prior to their problematic use patterns. Proponents of psychological explanations of addiction believe that there may be an "addictive personality" that could be identified and that would explain why individuals with alcohol and other drug addictions often have problems with nondrug addictive behavior (e.g., gambling, food, work, sex) following successful recovery from their drug of choice. However, this effort to identify the "addictive personality" has largely been unsuccessful. As Miller (1995) noted, "alcoholics appear to be as variable in personality as are non-alcoholics" (p. 90). Furthermore, "Although the terms *prealcoholic personality* and *alcoholic personality* have been used, there is little agreement on the identity of alcoholic personality traits or whether they may be the cause or the result of excessive drinking" (Witters, Venturelli, & Hanson, 1992, p. 202, italics in original).

An additional psychological theory that has been used to explain addictive behavior is social learning theory. As a leading proponent of this theory, Alan Marlatt, has stated, "From a social-learning perspective, addictive behaviors represent a category of 'bad habits' including such behaviors as problem drinking, smoking, substance abuse, overeating, compulsive gambling, and so forth." (Marlatt, 1985, p. 9). In this conceptualization, drug use is initiated by environmental stressors or modeling by others and is reinforced by the immediate effects of the drug on the feelings generated by the stressor(s) or by acknowledgement or recognition from models with perceived status. One example would be the case of the sexually molested woman we discussed earlier. From a social learning viewpoint, this woman used alcohol and other drugs to avoid the unpleasant emotions generated by her molestation (environmental stressor). Since there is an immediate (although temporary) relief from these negative feelings, alcohol or other drug use is reinforced. Another typical example would be the individual who uses alcohol to "unwind" after a stressful day at work. Since tolerance to alcohol develops, over time this person must use an increasing amount of alcohol to experience the reinforcing effects of alcohol on tension. A "bad habit" is developed.

The senior author has a vivid recollection of his first experience with alcohol and how modeling contributed to this first experience and subsequent alcohol use. In his house, there was a wide variety of alcohol, and he saw it used daily with few observed negative consequences. One night when he was 12, the author was alone at home and began experimenting with a variety of alcoholic beverages. He became quite ill. Although his parents were upset, there was also a lot of talking about their first experiences with becoming sick from alcohol and some laughter about the situation. He also got a lot of attention from his friends when he told them about the incident. Therefore, in spite of some negative consequences (nausea and parental anger) there was sufficient positive reinforcement to increase the probability of repeated use.

In a social learning model, the sociocultural factors we discussed play a role in determining what type of drug is used, when it is used, and how it is used. For example, social use of alcohol may be acceptable, but drinking alone may be perceived as deviant. Snorting or smoking drugs may be within the behavior parameters of a social group, but intravenous use of drugs may result in ostracism. Furthermore, the psychological state of the person is also important. For example, if a child sees parents use alcohol excessively in social situations, the child may be more likely to see drug use as acceptable in a social situation as a means of creating social comfort and fun. In contrast, imagine that the father in a family isolates himself and drinks in response to negative emotions. The child may see drug use as the appropriate reaction to negative emotions. The psychological state of the individual would be important, since social discomfort might elicit the desire for alcohol or other drugs in the first example, while negative emotions would elicit this desire in the second example.

Eventually, as the individual uses more and more, a physiological state of dependence occurs, and, consequently, withdrawal symptoms are experienced if the drug is removed. The use of the drug to relieve withdrawal symptoms is highly reinforcing, since an immediate and effective reduction or elimination of symptoms occurs (Tarter & Schneider, 1976). The social learning model of addiction has been widely used in the development of relapse prevention strategies, a topic that will be discussed in detail in Chapter 13.

Medical Model of Addiction: The Disease Concept

This popular and controversial model of addiction is credited to E. M. Jellinek, who presented a comprehensive disease model of alcoholism (Jellinek, 1960). This model has become an implicit component of the Alcoholics Anonymous and Narcotics Anonymous programs (Lewis, Dana, & Blevins, 1994) as well as a guiding model for many treatment programs (Kurtz, 1990). The World Health Organization acknowledged alcoholism as a medical problem in 1951, and the American Medical Association declared that alcoholism was a treatable illness in 1956. Following Jellinek's work, the American Psychiatric Association began to use the term *disease* to describe alcoholism in 1965, and the American Medical Association followed in 1966 (Royce, 1989). As with many concepts and theoretical models in the addiction field, the disease concept was originally applied to alcoholism and has been generalized to other drug addictions.

The disease of addiction is viewed as a primary disease. That is, it exists in and of itself and is not secondary to some other condition. This is in contrast to the psychological models discussed earlier in which addictive behavior is seen as secondary to some psychological condition. In Jellinek's (1952) own words:

> The aggressions, feelings of guilt, remorse, resentments, withdrawal, etc., which develop in the phases of alcohol addiction, are largely consequences of the excessive drinking . . . these reactions to excessive drinking—which have quite a neurotic appearance—give the impression of an 'alcoholic personality,' although they are secondary behaviors superimposed over a large variety of personality types . . . (p. 682).

Jellinek (1952) also described the progressive stages of the disease of alcoholism and the symptoms that characterize each stage. The early stage, or prodromal phase, is characterized by an increasing tolerance to alcohol, blackouts, sneaking and gulping drinks, and guilt feelings about drinking and related behaviors. The next stage, the middle or crucial phase, is defined by a loss of control over drinking, personality changes, a loss of friends and jobs, and a preoccupation with protecting the supply of alcohol. The issue of "loss of control" has come to be a central defining characteristic of alcoholism and one of the more controversial aspects of the disease concept. We will examine this issue when discussing criticisms of the disease concept. The late stage, or chronic phase, is characterized by morning drinking, violations of ethical standards, tremors, and hallucinations.

It is important to conceptualize these stages as progressive. In other words, the stages proceed in sequence and, in the disease model of addiction, are not reversed. Therefore, an individual does not go from the middle stage back to the early stage of alcoholism. The rate at which this progression occurs depends upon factors such as age, drug of choice, gender, and physiological predisposition (Royce, 1989). For example, adolescents progress more rapidly than adults, females faster than males, and users of stimulants more quickly than alcohol users (Royce, 1989). Proponents of the disease concept also do not believe that the progression of addiction disease is affected by a period of sobriety, no matter how long the period of sobriety lasts. As David Ohlms, a physician, has stated:

> let's say that Jack or Jane stops drinking. Maybe because of some formal treatment: maybe he or she just goes on the wagon, and there is a prolonged period of sobriety for, say, 10 or 15 or even 25 years. . . . then for some reason, . . . Jack or Jane decides that they can drink again, and tries to return to the normal, social, controlled type of drinking that any non-alcoholic can get away with. But poor alcoholic Jack or Jane can't. Within a short period of time, usually within 30 days, the symptoms that the alcoholic will show are the same symptoms showed when drinking was stopped 25 years before. And usually worse. It's as if the alcoholic hadn't had that 25 years of sobriety, as if they meant nothing. An alcoholic cannot stay sober for awhile and then start over and have early symptoms of alcoholism." (Ohlms, 1983, p. 5).

Consistent with this concept (that the individual with addictive disease does not reverse the progression of the disease even with a prolonged period of sobriety) is the notion that addictive disease is chronic and incurable. That is, if an individual has this disease, it never goes away, and there is no drug or other treatment method that will allow the alcoholic or addict to use again without the danger of a return to problematic use. One implication of this notion is that the only justifiable goal for the alcoholic or addict is abstinence, which is the stance of Alcoholics Anonymous (Bratter, 1985; Ward, 1990). Furthermore, the idea that addiction is chronic and incurable is the underlying rationale for alcoholics and addicts who are maintaining sobriety for referring to themselves as "recovering" as opposed to "recovered" or "cured" (Royce, 1989).

In addition to the idea that abstinence must be the goal for those with addictive disease, there are other implications to the disease concept. First, if addictive disease is progressive, chronic, and incurable, then it is logical to assume that a person with this condition who does not enter "recovery" will eventually die. Death occurs as a result of accidents or the physical effects of alcohol and other drugs over time. However, most of these individuals are not identified as dying from addictive disease. For example, in 1994 a member of the Houston Oiler professional football team was involved in a traffic accident in which his best friend was thrown from the car and killed. The football player was so distraught at the sight of his dead friend that he took a shot gun from his car and killed himself. Both men were well over the legal limit for blood alcohol level. The football player's friend had a blood alcohol level over three times the legal limit. Although we cannot diagnose these men as alcoholics, whether they were or not, their deaths would not be classified as the result of alcohol use. These deaths were a result of a traffic accident and a suicide. However, if the men were indeed alcoholic, a proponent of the disease concept would attribute these deaths to alcoholism. Similarly, consider the individual who, after many years of heavy drinking, develops a liver disease. Eventually, he dies of liver failure. Is the cause of death liver failure or alcoholism? Again, in the disease concept of addiction, these deaths are the result of untreated addiction.

A further implication of the disease concept of addiction is that, if a person has this disease and, for example, the drug of choice of the person is alcohol, the person will continue to exhibit all the symptoms of the disease if they discontinue their use of alcohol and begin to use some other drug. This is true no matter what the drug of choice is. As Royce (1989) stated, "We mentioned the recovered alcoholics who relapse when given a painkiller by the dentist and have seen long-recovered alcoholics whose doctor prescribed tranquilizers after a mild heart attack relapse into alcoholic drinking within three weeks and death in six months" (p. 132). This phenomenon is not restricted to alcohol. "Based on extensive clinical experience, use of any psychoactive drug will usually lead back to use of the primary drug or addiction to the secondary drug (drug switching). I believe the only safe path to follow is complete abstinence from all psychoactive drugs." (McCarthy, 1988, p. 29).

Evidence to Support the Disease Concept

Studies that have examined a possible genetic link in addiction are often cited as support for the disease concept and other biological explanations for addiction. Schuckit, Goodwin, and Winokur (1972) studied alcoholism in half-siblings and found that the best predictor of alcoholism among these subjects was the existence of a shared alcoholic parent. Most studies of twins have also found the existence of a genetic predisposition to alcoholism (Parsian & Cloninger, 1991), and Schuckit (1985) found that adopted children with alcoholic biological parents were more likely to become alcoholics than adopted children with nonalcoholic biological parents. Furthermore, offspring of alcoholics are approximately three to five times more likely to develop alcoholism than offspring of nonalcoholics (Sher, 1991). However, the genetic influence on other drug addiction has received less research attention (Pickens & Svikis, 1988).

There has also been considerable interest in physiological indicators of addiction. For example, in the early 1980s, there was a popular hypothesis of addiction articulated by Ohlms (1983) that proposed that alcoholics produced a highly addictive substance called THIQ through the metabolism of alcohol. THIQ is normally produced when the body metabolizes heroin and is supposedly not metabolized by nonalcoholics when they drink. According to Ohlms, animal studies have shown that a small amount of THIQ injected into the brains of rats will produce alcoholic rats and that THIQ remains in the brain long after an animal has been injected. Therefore, the theory is that alcoholics are genetically predisposed to produce THIQ in response to alcohol, that the THIQ creates a desire for alcohol, and that the THIQ remains in the brain of the alcoholic long after the use of alcohol is discontinued. This would provide a physiological explanation for the fact that recovering alcoholics who relapse quickly return to their previous use patterns. More recent research on genetic causes of alcoholism has focused on some abnormality in a dopamine receptor gene (Blum, Noble, Sheridan, Montgomery, Ritchie, Jagadeeswaran, Nogami, Briggs, & Cohn, 1990) and deficiencies in the neurotransmitter serotonin or in serotonin receptors (Goleman, 1990).

Critics of the Disease Concept

As we said earlier, the disease concept is controversial and not without critics. For example, "because the majority of the treatment programs are based on the disease concept of alcoholism, their lobbying, public relations, and advertising efforts inevitably propagate the disease theme" (Fingarette, 1988, p. 23). Probably, the two most famous critics are Stanton Peele and Herbert Fingarette, both of whom have written books (Fingarette, 1988; Peele, 1989) as well as articles disputing the disease concept of addiction. Some of their arguments will be summarized here.

Since the disease concept is widely attributed to Jellinek, much criticism has been directed at his research, which was the basis for his conclusions about the disease concept. Jellinek's data were gathered from questionnaires distributed to AA members through its newsletter, *The Grapevine*. Of 158 questionnaires returned, 60 were discarded because members had pooled and averaged their responses. Also, no questionnaires from women were used. Jellinek himself acknowledged that his data were limited. Therefore, one might wonder why Jellinek's concept of the disease of alcoholism received such widespread acceptance. One reason is that the disease concept is consistent with the philosophy of AA, which is by far the largest organized group dedicated to help for alcoholics. Secondly, as Peele (1988) noted:

> *The disease model has been so profitable and politically successful that it has spread to include problems of eating, child abuse, gambling, shopping, premenstrual tension, compulsive love affairs, and almost every other form of self-destructive behavior... From this perspective, nearly every American can be said to have a disease of addiction (p. 67).*

Furthermore, Fingarette (1988) accuses the alcohol industry itself of contributing to the public perception of alcoholism as a disease:

> *By acknowledging that a small minority of the drinking population is susceptible to the disease of alcoholism, the industry can implicitly assure consumers that the vast majority of people who drink are not at risk. This compromise is far preferable*

> to both the old temperance commitment to prohibition, which criminalized the en-
> tire liquor industry, and to newer approaches that look beyond the small group di-
> agnosable as alcoholics to focus on the much larger group of heavy drinkers who
> develop serious physical, emotional, and social problems (p. 27, italics in original).

The progressive nature of addiction has also been criticized. George Vaillant (1983),
a proponent of the disease concept, has suggested that there is no inevitable progression of Jellinek's stages of alcoholism:

> The first stage is heavy "social" drinking. . . . This stage can continue asymptom-
> atically for a lifetime; or because of a change of circumstances or peer group it can
> reverse to a more moderate pattern of drinking; or it can "progress" into a pattern
> of alcohol abuse. . . . At some point in their lives, perhaps 10–15 percent of Amer-
> ican men reach this second stage. Perhaps half of such alcohol abusers either return
> to asymptomatic (controlled) drinking or achieve stable abstinence. In a small
> number of such cases . . . such alcohol abuse can persist intermittently for decades
> with minor morbidity and even become milder with time (p. 309).

Similarly, Royce (1989), in describing the patterns and symptoms of alcoholism,
stated, "Even when progression occurs, it does not follow a uniform pattern. The
steps may be reversed in order, or some steps may be omitted. Symptoms progress,
too; something that was minor in an early stage may appear later in a different
form or to a greater degree. . . . Rate of progression varies also" (p. 89). As with Vaillant, Royce takes a favorable position toward the concept of addiction as a disease.

As we have seen, some of those with sympathetic views toward the disease
model of addiction have recognized that the concept of a rigid and inevitable progression of stages is not consistent with reality in working with individuals with
alcohol and other drug problems. However, the issue of "loss of control" has been
a more contentious one. As Fingarette (1988) states, loss of control may be "the central premise of the classic disease concept of alcoholism . . ." (p. 31). Certainly, the
first step of the twelve steps of Alcoholics Anonymous implies this loss of control:
"We admitted that we were powerless over alcohol—that our lives had become unmanageable." (Alcoholics Anonymous, 1981, p. 5).

Several arguments have been advanced to dispute the notion of loss of control.
Fingarette (1988) pointed out that if alcoholics lack control only after first consum-
ing alcohol, then they should have no difficulty abstaining. Obviously, however, alcoholics do have difficulty abstaining. If loss of control exists before the first drink
(which would explain the difficulty in abstaining), it implies a difficulty in exercis-
ing self-control or willpower, which is a much different model of addiction. Furthermore, experimental studies have demonstrated that alcoholics do exert control
over their drinking and that variables such as the amount of effort to get alcohol,
the environment in which drinking occurs, the belief about what is being consumed, rewards, etc., influence how much is consumed by an alcoholic (Fingarette,
1988; Peele, 1989). As one example, Marlatt, Demming, and Reid (1973) divided alcoholics into four groups. One group believed that they were taste-testing three

brands of a vodka-tonic beverage when they were actually drinking tonic water only. A second group believed that they were taste-testing tonic water only, when they were actually drinking vodka and tonic. The third group was correctly told they were drinking a vodka and tonic beverage, and the fourth group was correctly told they were drinking tonic water only. The results showed that it was the alcoholic's belief about what they were drinking that determined the amount they drank and not the actual alcohol content of the beverage they consumed. The alcoholics who expected tonic and got alcohol drank an almost identical amount to those alcoholics who expected and got tonic. Both of these groups drank considerably less than the groups who expected alcohol, and the alcoholics who received and expected alcohol drank nearly the same amount as those alcoholics who expected alcohol but got tonic.

Defenders of the disease concept point out that "experimenters took too literally the idea that one drink always means getting drunk." and "Many research projects set out to disprove the 'one drink' hypothesis in laboratory or hospital settings so artificial and with criteria so wooden that nobody with real experience in alcoholism could take the results seriously" (Royce, 1989, p. 135). Loss of control has been modified to mean that the alcoholic or addict cannot predict the situations in which they will exercise control and the situations in which they will lose control. Therefore, this loss of predictability is thought to define the alcoholic or addict (Keller, 1972). Fingarette's (1988) response is that "This new approach to loss of control so emasculates the concept that it becomes useless in explaining or predicting drinking behavior" (p. 44).

Advantages of the Disease Concept

Perhaps the greatest advantage to the articulation that addiction is a disease has been to remove the moral stigma attached to chemical dependency and to replace it with an emphasis on treatment of an illness. We do not punish a person for having a disease; we provide assistance. In a more functional sense, defining addiction as a disease has also resulted in treatment coverage by insurance companies. Using medical terminology to describe addiction has also led to greater interest in scientific research. Few medical scientists would be interested in investigating the physiological correlates of a lack of willpower or to a moral deficiency. For the individual who has problems with alcohol or other drugs (and for the family as well), the concept of a disease removes much of the stigma and associated embarrassment, blame, and guilt. You would not feel guilty if you were diagnosed with diabetes and, therefore, a person with addictive disease need not feel guilty for having this disease. Persons who believe that addiction is due to a lack of willpower or to a moral deficiency may avoid treatment, since the admission of the need for help is an admission that some character flaw exists. Therefore, an acceptance of the disease concept may make it easier for some people to enter treatment. Another advantage of the disease concept is that it is clearly understandable to people and provides an explanatory construct for the differences in their alcohol and other drug-taking behavior compared with others. To reuse the well-worn analogy with diabetes, it is quite clear to the people with diabetes that they cannot use certain foods in the same manner as those who do not have diabetes. If they do, there will be certain predictable consequences. Knowledge about the disease allows the alcoholic or addict to understand that he or she is physiologically different from others. In the same way that it may be unwise for the diabetic to eat a hot fudge sundae (in spite of the fact that friends may do so without consequences), the alcoholic learns that it would be unwise to drink (in spite of the fact that friends may do so without consequences). Finally, the disease concept has a logical treatment objective that follows from its precepts: abstinence. If you have a physiological condition that results in severe consequences when alcohol or other drugs are used, you can avoid these consequences by abstaining from alcohol or other drugs. If you attempt to use moderately, you will eventually lose control, progress through predictable stages, and suffer the consequences. Since most individuals who seek treatment for alcohol or other drug problems have experienced some negative consequences already, this argument can be compelling.

Disadvantages of the Disease Concept

As the critics of the disease concept have pointed out, the orthodox precepts of the disease concept may not be accurate. There is not an inevitable and completely predictable progression of symptoms and stages nor a consistent loss of control. Therefore, individuals with alcohol or other drug problems who may need some form of intervention or treatment may avoid help since they do not fit the "disease model". For example, we were told by a substance abuse program counselor about an inquiry from a man who's girlfriend thought he had a drinking problem. Although he drank on a daily basis, his use of alcohol had not progressed in the last few years. When asked if he was having any financial, occupational, legal, or family problems, he said that he was not. Now certainly, denial may be at work here, but the point is that the intake counselor did not encourage the man to seek help since he did not fit the classic "disease" characteristics, while the program in which the counselor works is based on this model.

An adherence to the disease model may also result in a purely medical model of treatment:

> While this may have the advantage of motivating physicians to treat the alcoholic in a nonjudgmental way . . . the average American physician is still both reluctant to treat alcoholics and often ignorant about alcoholism. . . . Medical models tend to put the physician in full charge, focus almost exclusively on physical damage, and perpetuate a medical 'revolving door' which is more humane than the drunk tank but equally ineffective for long-range treatment. It implies that nonmedical persons are unable to treat the illness . . . (Royce, 1989, p. 123).

The notion that the disease concept removes the responsibility for his or her behavior from the alcoholic or addict is frequently cited as a disadvantage of this model (e.g., Doweiko, 1993; Royce, 1989). Since the alcoholic or addict is "powerless" over the disease, inappropriate or even criminal behavior may be attributed to the "disease". Relapse may also be blamed on the disease, "If alcoholics come to view their drinking as the result of a disease or physiological addiction, they may be more likely to assume the passive role of victim whenever they engage in drinking behavior if they see it as symptom of their disease . . ." (Marlatt & Gordon, 1985, p. 7). In other words, if an alcoholic believes the disease concept and the AA slogan "one drink away from a drunk," then a slip (return to use) may result in the alcoholic's giving up responsibility for maintaining sobriety and returning to a previous level of use, since the slip is symptomatic of the loss of control. Proponents of the disease concept counter this argument by saying that the addict is not responsible for the disease but is completely responsible for recovery. In addition, court rulings have rarely allowed a defense of addiction for criminal behavior (Miller and Hester, 1995).

A Multivariate Model of Addiction

We want to describe six people we have known or worked with. Each has a history of heavy alcohol or other drug use. Bill, a bartender, was diagnosed as alcoholic at the age of 50. He was drinking over a fifth of whiskey a day. On his own volition, he went to a treatment program that used aversive conditioning techniques (see Chapter 7). At the time he entered treatment, his liver functioning was at about 20% of normal. In other words, if he had continued to drink much longer, he would have died. After completing the program, Bill returned to his job as a bartender. He never attended an AA meeting or returned to the treatment program for follow-up. Bill once said, "I'll drink myself to death rather than go back to that (treatment center) place". In 19 years, he never had a slip or relapse. Bill finally died of lung cancer, because he could not quit smoking.

Marty was a 15-year-old special education student with a diagnosis of learning disability. He was having continual problems with the law due to his use of alcohol. When Marty would consume a small amount of alcohol, he would suffer black-outs and become violent. He went through several in-patient treatment programs but quickly relapsed each time. When he was 20, Marty broke into a house while intoxicated and was discovered by the owner. He stabbed the man to death and is now in prison for life.

Loretta, a 30-year-old woman, was on probation for possession and distribution of methamphetamine. She lived with a man who used drugs and who was physically abusive to her and to her daughter. Another daughter had been removed from her custody. She lost her license to work in her profession due to her felony conviction. Her "boyfriend" had been sent to prison, she had found a job and a new place to live, and she was on the road to regaining custody of her other daughter. However, a random urinalysis by her probation officer came up dirty, and she was placed in an in-patient treatment program as an alternative to prison. Loretta lost her job, home, and custody of her children. Before this relapse, she had been sober for six months and was attending NA meetings.

Marvin, a 63-year-old man, had been a heavy drinker for 40 years. He was retired and relatively healthy. He developed a respiratory illness that required prolonged use of a medication that affected liver functioning. Marvin was told that he could not drink alcohol while taking the medication and that he was to take the medication for one year. It was suggested that his withdrawal from alcohol be medically supervised due to his prolonged and heavy use. Marvin rejected this suggestion, discontinued his alcohol use, and has been clean and sober with no slips for 10 years. He has never attended an AA meeting or any other form of treatment.

Hector, a 30 year old man, began using alcohol and other drugs at the age of 13. He was in street gangs, involved in crimes, and incarcerated as a juvenile. Hector was placed in a drug treatment program at the age of 16 and attended NA meetings after treatment. He remained sober for about six months, at which time he again began to use cocaine, marijuana, and alcohol. At age 23, he married, had a child, and discontinued his heavy use. He continues to use alcohol and marijuana on an irregular basis. Hector is a successful officer in a small company although he cannot read or write at a functional level.

Rebecca is currently 43 years old and has been sober for seven years. She reported that her husband expressed concern about her level of alcohol use prior to their marriage and that she "just decided to stop." Rebecca did not go through any treatment program, nor has she attended any AA meetings. She says that she has problems doing anything on a moderate basis, and, as a result, she has to monitor her eating behavior and work habits. Rebecca says, "I can't eat just a couple of M & Ms. If I start, I'll keep eating until they are all gone." She likes to drink non-alcoholic beer and wine, saying "It makes me feel like a grown-up."

Although we have changed the names of these people, these cases are all real. We are not implying that they are typical or atypical, and we did not include those individuals who completed traditional treatment programs or use AA as a primary method of maintaining sobriety, although we know plenty of people who do so. These cases are meant to illustrate the concept that is well articulated by Pattison and Kaufman (1982):

> *Most scientific authorities in the field of alcoholism now concur that the construct of alcoholism is most accurately construed as a multivariate syndrome. That is, there are multiple patterns of dysfunctional alcohol use that occur in multiple types of personalities, with multiple combinations of adverse consequences, with multiple prognoses, that may require different types of treatment interventions (p. 13).*

Bill, Marty, and Loretta had patterns of use that could well fit within the disease model of addiction. In particular, Marty had a very unusual response to alcohol that certainly would make one suspicious of physiological differences. Bill's progression was very similar to that described by Jellinek (1952), but he responded to a treatment that was quite unlike the traditional models based on the disease concept. Loretta also continued to use in spite of having every reason to stop, which certainly seems like a loss of control.

In contrast, Marvin's drinking remained at a stage that Lewis, et al. (1994) described as heavy, nonproblematic use for many years with no apparent progression. In opposition to what might be expected, he had no physical or psychological problems discontinuing his use when faced with a strong motivation to stop. Hector, who seemed to have serious problems with alcohol and other drugs, reverted to moderate use when he matured and acquired responsibilities for others. His behavior could be explained from a social learning perspective. Rebecca seemed to demonstrate an "addictive personality". She constantly had to be aware of her characteristic of going overboard. Her use of nonalcoholic beer and wine is contrary to what is recommended by most treatment programs, but it works for her.

It's quite natural for treatment providers to develop a concept of addiction based on the clients they come in contact with. Helping professionals who work in substance abuse treatment programs see individuals who have had some pretty serious life problems as a result of their alcohol and other drug use. They are not likely to see individuals who have successfully discontinued their use on their own or through a non-traditional method or to work with clients who interrupt their use patterns before they experience serious life problems. Finally, alcohol and other drug treatment providers do not usually see clients who are heavy users but who do not have life problems as a result of their use. Therefore, it is logical that those professionals who work in the substance abuse treatment field may develop a concept of addiction that is based on a biased sample. This is not to say that the disease concept does not fit many alcoholics and addicts or that traditional treatment approaches and Twelve Step recovery programs are not useful. Certainly, as we illustrated with Bill, Marty, and Loretta, many alcoholics and addicts fit the characteristics of the disease concept, and many, many people have been helped by traditional treatment programs based on the disease concept and utilizing AA and NA. We are arguing that other explanations for problematic alcohol and other drug use and a variety of treatment options should be considered. Interestingly, Jellinek (1960), who is credited with developing the disease concept, identified five different types of problem drinking patterns, only two of which were thought to demonstrate the characteristics of the disease. This seems to be ignored by many disease concept proponents.

People begin alcohol and other drug use on an experimental basis for lots of different reasons. They continue using because there is reinforcement for doing so through a reduction of pain, experience of euphoria, social recognition and/or acceptance, success, etc. Some people progress to abuse and addiction. Why?

It is certainly possible that progression in some people is due to a genetic predisposition and that this genetic predisposition may be understood through physiological differences. It is also plausible that personality characteristics may explain some progression, or that physical or emotional pain may explain some problematic use, or environmental circumstances may provide answers. Any combination of these factors may also be possible. With a certain client, we may find that the reduction of chronic back pain leads to a reduction in alcohol use. Another client (like Hector) may have a change in environmental factors that leads to a change in use. Through therapy, another client may come to a greater self-awareness with regard to personality characteristics, and modification of use may occur. With other clients, reduction of pain, change of environment, and self-knowledge does not affect their use at all. We suggest that mental health professionals, whether or not they work with substance abuse problems, thoroughly assess clients (see Chapter 5), develop multiple hypotheses to explain the client's alcohol or other drug problem based on the assessment, avoid forcing the client to fit a rigid or preconceived notion of addiction, and utilize a variety of treatment methods and interventions (see Chapter 7) evolving from the assessment, hypotheses, and most important, the needs of the client.

Chapter 4

Culturally and Ethnically Diverse Groups

As mentioned in Chapter 3, it is quite natural for treatment providers to develop a concept of addiction based on the clients with whom they come in contact. An important ingredient in this tentative formulation is the treatment provider's possession of a sound theoretical basis of the general nature of addictions. The same holds true when working with individuals and groups of different cultural and ethnic backgrounds. One needs to be well grounded in the understanding of the cultural values of that individual or group so that the formation of tentative hypotheses about alcohol and other drug use, abuse, and addiction are more likely to be accurate. Without sensitivity to cultural differences, providers will likely be ineffective from the outset, because attempts to assess alcohol and other drug involvement will be met with both cultural and therapeutic resistance. This double-whammy will undoubtedly preclude an accurate assessment of any type, let alone that of drug involvement.

For example, a Native American family requested family counseling. The mother and father brought in their two children, aged 6 and 9. The African American counselor, who held a doctorate degree from a prestigious university and enjoyed an excellent reputation in the community, employed confrontation as a therapeutic intervention and preferred brief family therapy approaches. In other words, she preferred to work fast. At the outset of the initial session, the children were moving about the counselor's office at will and, although they were not being loud, their frequent movement did create some distraction in the session. Believing this to be a de-focusing tactic and therefore a part of the problem, the counselor confronted the parents about their apparent lack of control over the children. The counselor did not understand that many Native American families continue to value "noninterference" as a philosophy guiding the upbringing of their children. As a result, the therapist became perplexed when the parents began to overtly and covertly distance themselves from her. An alternative intervention, reflecting cultural sensitivity, could have been, "Please help me understand here. I am noticing that your children seem to keep you two from being able to discuss this issue in-depth. I was wondering about the extent to which your childrens' behavior here is similar to their behavior at home when you are discussing important issues. What are your thoughts on that?" This intervention would likely have led to different results in the session.

The responsibility for the lack of cultural awareness and its impact upon counseling cannot be placed solely upon the shoulders of this very competent counselor. A recent survey of 26 textbooks on the subject of alcoholism published between 1976 and 1989 found only four books giving detailed attention to Native American populations (Young, 1991). Another four books offered a less extensive discussion (averaging three to four pages). Eight books offered "a sentence or two" of information, and ten books made no reference to Native Americans.

Why is there inadequate coverage of these special populations? Perhaps the critical variable concerns the counseling field in general. Required graduate coursework in pluralism is relatively new in the helping profession field, and no consensus has been reached about what is important for helping professionals (Arnold, 1993; Locke, 1990). A second reason relates to the nature of the alcohol and other drug use problem in the general United States population. As was pointed out in Chapter 3, investigators do not always agree upon assumptions and terminology when studying models, incidence, and/or prevalence of alcohol and other drug use. In addition to these limitations, Lex (1987) points out that several methodological problems exist in the current literature on ethnically diverse populations, including African Americans, Asian Americans, and Latino/Hispanic Americans.

For example, to date no large-scale survey of Native Americans' drinking practices or drinking problems has utilized samples from different tribes or communities (Lex, 1987). In general, Native American males are usually the ones included in studies (Lex, 1987). Moreover, Native Americans were not included in the national sample of a broad-based study on patterns and prevalence of alcohol and other drug use in the United States conducted in 1979 (Clark & Midanik, 1982). Thus, a significant data-base was lost for Native Americans.

Similar research concerns exist for African Americans. In spite of the fact that African Americans comprise the largest ethnic minority in the United States, Clark and Midanik (1982) report that relatively little information is available about the drinking patterns, problems, practices, or prevalence of alcoholism among this group. Most of the research on African Americans was conducted in the 1960s and was an outgrowth of the "War on Poverty." Instead of looking specifically at the drinking patterns, the plethora of studies during this period focused upon the sociological and exogenous factors that appeared to contribute to the low economic status of African Americans (Clark & Midanik, 1982). Alcohol was studied only peripherally or incidentally. In addition, Barbara Lex (1985) points out weaknesses in studies on African Americans and alcohol. She maintains that, aside from the fact that most studies focus upon men, there is an inconsistent reporting of data by gender, and very little attention is paid to the rural populations of either gender.

Hence, although alcohol use in this population has been alleged to contribute significantly to their states of mental, physical, and social well-being, the dearth of studies examining these variables allows only for a limited ability to generalize the results to the African American population as a whole.

Other general methodological problems exist in the research on ethnically diverse populations and drug use. There are problems such as (a) the lack of comparable interview schedules, (b) the over-use of retrospective self-reports, (c) the possible over-sampling of persons in stable living conditions (and the coinciding under-sampling of individuals estranged from their families or those estranged through homelessness or institutionalization), and (d) the lack of combining observations and surveys to insure that the meanings of certain questions are understood (Lex, 1985).

This same author also purports that treatment utilization rates, a common method for obtaining data, may not reflect the magnitude of alcohol-related problems in specific groups (Lex, 1985). This lack is due largely to the fact that the decision to obtain alcohol treatment is influenced by such cultural variables as the individual's beliefs about the cause of the problem, their values, and their perceptions of what it means to seek help. One's decision can be especially influenced when there is the perception that barriers to treatment exist. For example, a great deal of paperwork is often required before one can receive in-patient treatment, and this may become a significant barrier to treatment. Another example relates to Native Americans whose adherence to the value of noninterference (i.e., often letting drug abusers make their own decisions about treatment) can lead to a perception of them as "uncooperative." Should this misperception be communicated by the therapist, the Native American client may be reluctant to enter treatment.

Financial considerations also exist and may influence sample size and representation in the research on ethnically diverse populations. In-patient treatment is very expensive and most likely requires some type of insurance benefit. If a client is unemployed, the treatment facility will likely need a mechanism to offer financial aid. If none is available, then alternative treatment plans might include partial hospitalization where transportation may be a problem. Therefore, studies employing service utilization rates may seriously underestimate the prevalence and/or use patterns in ethnically diverse populations.

Based upon the need for cultural relativism, this chapter will present information on Native Americans and Alaska Natives, Asian/Pacific Islanders, African Americans, and Latino and Hispanic populations. For each group, both background information and values appearing to increase or explain risk for substance abuse will be discussed. Concerns for helping professionals when working with members of these populations will conclude the chapter.

Native Americans and Alaska Natives

Native Americans (which include American Indians, Alaska Natives, and Aleuts) have been separated by the United States government into three categories:

(1) federally recognized tribes and bands, (2) nonfederally recognized tribes and bands, and (3) urban Native Americans. The 1.4 to 1.8 million Native Americans live in one of ten major cultural areas: Northeast, Southeast, Plains, Arctic, Subarctic, Northwest Coast, Plateau, Great Basin, California, and the Southwest. These cultural areas are further subdivided into urban or reservation lifestyles. In general, about one-half of Native Americans live in cities, and the other half reside on reservations or other remote, widely separated areas (Lex, 1987).

If you were to spend a moment reflecting upon the differences between the Euro-Americans living in the northeastern United States and the South, or between the southwest and the mid-west, or between California and the rest of the United States, you would begin to see that there are now and always have been vast differences in the ways that people speak, eat, dress, and approach life in general. The Native American populations are no different. Alaska Natives, for example, can be seen as differing along geographic lines that reflect a difference in cultures (Attneave, 1982). Alaskan Eskimos inhabit the coastal areas to the north while the Aleuts occupy settlements along the Aleutian Islands. Fairbanks is the cultural hub for the Athabascan-speaking tribes who reside in the surrounding mountains and valleys. Yet, very different are the coastal tribes who reside on the islands close to Juneau and Ketchikan and along the coast of the Alaskan panhandle. In attempting, then, to summarize and underscore the geographic distribution and variety of Native American cultures, it can be said that, in all probability, most Native Americans living outside of the Southwest would look at the silver and turquoise jewelry of the Southwest Pueblo Indians as being as much an exotic art form as would the non-Native American—regardless of whether they lived in urban centers, on reservations, or in rural settings (Attneave, 1982).

Background

According to Atteneave (1982), there is no Native American or Alaskan Native person today who categorically lives out a traditional lifestyle. All are involved in the non-Native American United States culture to some degree. For example, more than half of the Native American and Alaskan Native populations do not use the reservation as their principle residence. Since urban centers offer different opportunities for work, education, and other endeavors, thousands of Native Americans can be found residing in these urban areas for varying lengths of time.

In the late 1700s, trappers, traders, and frontiersmen introduced alcohol as a social beverage to Native Americans on a widespread scale. Prior to that, little or no use of alcohol existed among Native Americans north of Mexico, with the exception of use for certain ceremonial purposes. For woodland and plains tribes especially, methods of obtaining altered states of consciousness as a means to communicate with the Great Spirit and the spirits of nature was achieved mainly through dancing, fasting, drumming, sleep deprivation, and isolation (Westermeyer and Baker, 1986).

As the concept of Manifest Destiny became the accepted orientation fueling the exploration of the lands to the West, so did alcohol become the most important item exchanged for furs (Chittenden, 1935). With little history to guide alcohol consumption, Native Americans as a group were uncertain about how to view it. Many tribes came to believe that alcohol had magical powers associated with curing disease. Other tribes simply viewed drunken people as unaccountable for their behaviors. It has been stated that perhaps Indians first learned to drink in a binge pattern at the trade fairs where drinking parties often lasted several days, accompanied by games, acts of bravado, and fighting (Westermeyer & Baker, 1986). Still others saw drinking as more social and economic. Although cautioned by leaders to abstain, alcohol was accepted by many Native Americans as a gesture of friendship from the white-skinned traders. Thus, alcohol took on an economic value. Accepting alcohol, even drinking with the Whites, was believed to cement good trade relations.

Many Native American leaders became so disturbed by the spate of drinking among their people that they appealed to government officials for help. Federal intervention finally came in 1832 with the Indian Prohibition Act. This act prohibited the selling or providing of liquor to American Indians. However, it was deemed largely unsuccessful: alcohol was deeply infused into the trading economy and social practices of many tribes by the 1830s creating a demand for the drug. As a result, many Native Americans as well as Whites turned to smuggling alcohol, and they made good profits. Moreover, by the 1830s, Native Americans had learned to ferment alcohol from their plethora of carbohydrate sources. Although the Indian Prohibition Act was ineffective, the United States government did not revoke the law until 1953. In its absence, many Native American leaders remained vigilant about the potentially destructive nature of alcohol, so that currently 69% of all United States reservations are under a self-imposed system of prohibition (Young, 1991). Although Kaufman (1975) reports that Native American youth in certain areas of the Southwest have had epidemics of solvent abuse with high rates of mental retardation, and Winfrey and Griffiths (1983) report that marijuana use and abuse has been widespread among some Native American youth, the Indian Health Service (1977) believes alcoholism to be the most urgent health problem facing Native Americans. Contemporary research in the area does not refute the claim (Hill, 1989).

The Native American relationship with alcohol has also been mitigated by the historical events of forced relocation of tribes, the break-up of Native American families, and the constant harassment from settlers and soldiers. In an attempt to assess the influence of these historical events upon Indian drinking behaviors, as many as 42 theories have been promulgated—the most notable of which is the sociocultural explanation (Young, 1991). This theory maintains that, as a culture, Native Americans are continuing to mourn the loss of their heritage and culture and are reacting to the stresses of acculturation and the demands to integrate into the mainstream of Euro-American society. In this theory, alcohol is seen as salubrious, anesthetizing the pain associated with the multiple losses incurred by Native

Americans. Aside from whatever biophysiological proclivities that exist among Native Americans (and the jury is still out on this issue), the current state of anomie or normlessness is seen as acting to maintain the abuse of alcohol.

It becomes important, then, to examine the values that are purported to be at the heart of this grieving process. Sadly, it will become apparent that Native American values were functional prior to the introduction of alcohol but may have now become seriously problematic in the development of current Indian drinking patterns. The grieving process for the Native Americans and Alaskan Natives thus includes not only mourning the loss of a culture, but mourning the deleterious effects of alcohol upon their peoples.

Values

In spite of the enormous diversity among Native American populations, there are some basic values that are thematic for Native Americans and Native Alaskans. These values focus upon orientation to time, the relationship between humans and the natural world, social relationships, and the concept of "noninterference." Many of these values are held by both Native American and Euro-American cultures, but they usually vary in philosophy or in the emphasis placed upon them.

Time

Attneave (1987) explains that Euro-American culture is concerned with present time in terms of minute-by-minute awareness: What time is it? How much time do I have left? How long will it take me to drive to Long Island? Native Americans and Native Alaskan peoples also view time in the present. However, for them, present time is cyclical or universal rather than linear. Native Americans view present time as it relates to personal rhythms (not unlike the popular notion of biorhythms) and seasonal rhythms that encompass days, months, and even years. Native American life is thus organized in broad context around these various rhythms and not organized by traditional calendars and watches—both of which are seen as external.

For Native Americans, linear time (i.e., digital watch time) is organized around personal bodily needs, work schedules, social times, and times of reflection. Historically, however, linear time was structured around cyclical patterns reflecting seasonal variations in weather and their logical influence on hunting, migrating, and social organization (Attneave, 1987). In the Native American culture of that period, the future was important only as it related to the present need of gathering food resources. One needed to be cognizant of the need to gather materials for shelter during seasonal changes as well as of the need to develop political alliances. During the relocation efforts in the 1830s, the cyclical patterns of time became problematic for the Native American culture and a source of grieving. As the Euro-American population travelled West, they brought with them a view of time vastly different from that of the Native Americans. Receiving wages, producing manufactured goods, and formalized schooling all but overthrew the Indian concept of cyclical time. Moreover, awareness of the rhythms of nature went by the wayside as the relocation of tribes eliminated seasonal migration.

Currently, Attneave (1987) points out that the Native American concept of past time has little or nothing to recommend its revival to the Native American population. The immediate past is measured in one or two generations, and this timeline is filled with a grim and depressing past. The future, no longer anchored to the seasonal variations, remains unknown and unpredictable. In spite of it all, though, it is important to note that today Native Americans will likely have preserved some of their original concept of time and, because of the clash of cultures, some distortions of it as well.

Humans, the Natural World, and Social Relationships

Since the Industrial Revolution, the prevailing view of nature in Euro-American culture is that it is wild and capricious. Therefore, nature is seen as needing to be controlled, and increasing or improving technology is viewed as increasing control over nature. For Native Americans and Native Alaskans, nature cannot be controlled. They advocate the need to understand the natural forces of nature and the need to harmonize with them rather than attempting to control or dominate these forces. Thus, Native American populations aim to surrender control. Surrendering with regard to alcohol meant that if one was going to drink, so be it. But surrendering to the forces of nature is not the same as being passive. Moreover, becoming drunk might be met with temporary ostracism.

Native Americans believe that the group takes precedence over the individual, which may go a long way in explaining the rapid spread of alcohol among earlier Native American peoples. In the past, there was little ability to preserve perishables from season to season. Sharing of food, clothing, and transportation was the norm as well as the necessity. For example, imagine you and a group of friends were camping in the desert during the summer and you had a gallon of milk as your only source of nourishment. You would likely share it immediately with everyone until it was all gone or risk the probability of its spoiling and becoming useless before nightfall. This concept of sharing of goods has existed in the Native American culture for many centuries, so it can be easily seen how, in Native American culture, alcohol would have been passed around until it was gone. For this reason, some consider this idea the underlying explanation for "binge drinking" (Attneave, 1987).

Noninterference

Another source of grieving, and a source of explanation for early Native American alcohol use patterns, revolves around a concept called "noninterference." Although the Native American peoples respected the idea of the group, there was an underlying principle explaining the proper place of the individual. Just as there was respect for the natural forces of nature, there was also respect for the natural unfolding of the potential in each person. "Noninterference" is an academic term used to describe this approach to human behavior (Attneave, 1987). This philosophy allows Native American parents to nurture their children while allowing them to learn from their mistakes. In this process, there is much more emphasis placed upon having the child learning by doing, so the children can learn from their own mistakes. Noninterference is also practiced with the elderly. For example, no matter how senile or ill the elders in the tribe may be, they still retain the right to determine their own course of actions. This notion of allowing one to learn from mistakes may have had a significant impact upon the development of alcohol abuse and alcoholism among Native Americans throughout generations.

Risk Factors for Alcohol and Other Drug Abuse

Sociocultural Factors

As mentioned earlier in the chapter, Andre (1979) found that 75% of all Native American deaths are related to alcohol is some way. Regarding alcohol-related suicides and homicides among Native Americans, it is reported that the rates are comparable to the Euro-American population but twice those of the African American population (Baker, O'Neill & Karpf, 1984). These observations certainly show the Native American population being "at risk." Aside from the sociocultural theories pointing to mourning as a significant risk factor, Westermeyer advances another risk factor. In citing studies that examine drinking patterns among various subgroups of Native Americans, Westermeyer (1991) found differences between Native Americans living in the West and those residing in other geographic locations. Motor vehicle crashes and injuries, usually associated with intoxication, are elevated among Western mountain tribes (Center for Disease Control, 1989). Given that the Western states are significantly larger than other states and the fact that most reservations prohibit the sale of alcohol, those Native Americans living in the West and desiring alcohol have greater distances to travel in order to purchase it. Therefore, Westermeyer (1991) believes that the sheer number of miles involved in procuring alcohol may contribute significantly to the higher incidence of alcohol-related accidents.

Physiological Risk Factors

High rates of abstinence also occur among Native American populations, but this is often overlooked because a gross examination of drinking prevalence appears to support the idea that these populations have a higher alcohol consumption rate than other ethnic groups or subgroups in the United States (Hill, 1989). Upholding this stereotypic view is the popular folklore theory called "firewater." This theory maintains that Native Americans have an inherent weakness for alcohol. Comparative studies examining this theory, however, have failed to show a consistent and significant difference in alcohol metabolism among Native Americans (Westermeyer, 1991). Hence, support for the physiological theory of alcoholism is mixed.

Patterns of drinking behavior were studied by Weisner, Weibel-Orlando and Long (1984), who caution those in the helping profession against making drinking level synonymous with drinking style. For Native Americans, drinking styles are influenced by socioeconomic status, degree of Native American identity, and extent of tribal affiliation. Through their research, these same authors identified "tee-totalers," "serious drinkers," and "White man's drinking" patterns in urban-dwelling Native Americans and offered some interesting profiles of those falling into each category. Teetotalers are seen as comprising two different groups: those who never drink and those former drinkers now abstaining. Older Native American women primarily make up the former group, while older men tend to make up the latter group. The "White man's drinking" patterns were noted in both women and men who were profiled as having "more white collar jobs, higher and more stable incomes, and more formal education" (Weisner, et al., 1984, p. 245). Younger, more often unmarried individuals, and those individuals from lower socioeconomic backgrounds were seen as the "serious drinkers." These individuals were thought to participate less in traditional Native American activities.

Psychological Risk Factors

Psychological risk factors may have important implications for treatment and prevention. Jones-Saumty, Hochaus, Dru, and Zeiner (1983) conducted a seminal study investigating the extent to which the apparent higher incidence of depression in their sample of Native Americans was the cause of or the result of compulsive drinking. In their study, they compared the psychological adjustment and drinking behaviors in one group with one or more first-degree (directly related) alcoholic relatives and a group without a history of familial alcoholism. Results indicated no differences between these groups. A second study by these same authors compared the group of Native Americans with a family history of alcoholism and a group of Caucasians with similar family history. Results indicated a significant difference between these two groups in level of depressive symptoms (Jones-Saumty et al., 1983). The authors conclude that there are differences in psychological adjustment and drinking behavior between these two groups. Although neither group obtained clinical levels of depression, the "consistency of symptoms across two different instruments seems to indicate a prevalence of depressive tendencies within American Indians with a history of family alcoholism" (Jones-Saumty et al., 1983, p. 788). Rather than concluding these differences as categorical, these same authors suggest that "possibly, we have begun to identify some potential areas of risk for American Indian social drinkers in developing an alcohol problem" (p. 789).

Asian Americans

From your reading of the section on Native Americans, it is hoped that you would anticipate the Asian population to be diverse. Numbering about seven million people (United States Bureau of Census, 1990) and reflecting the largest growth rate of all ethnic/racial groups in the United States between 1980 and 1988, the Asian population does share many common cultural and religious traditions. At the same time, however, Asians comprise significantly diverse populations such as Asian Indians (India), Pakistanis, Thais, Filipinos, Vietnamese, Laotians, Cambodians, the Hmong peoples (Highland Laotian), and Pacific Islanders (Hawaiians, Samoans, and those from Guam). The peoples of East Asia include Chinese, Japanese, and Koreans.

Typical Western observers tend to view all East Asians as being very similar—if not the same. Nothing could be further from the truth. Language is the most apparent difference. Yet, the histories of China, Japan, and Korea reveal vastly differing social and economic development. Moreover, once living in the United States, all Asian groups demonstrate significant within-group differences that will become more pronounced in future years.

Virtually all of the world's great religions are represented in this culturally and ethnically diverse group of Asian Americans including Animism, Hinduism, Buddhism, Judaism, Christianity, and Islam. The culturally and ethnically diverse populations presented in this chapter all have conflict as part of their history, and Asian Americans are no different. However, the Asian population is distinctive in that they also have a history of fighting among themselves. This single variable may distinguish Southeast Asians in another significant way: Although Asian Americans (including Southeast Asians) tend to group themselves ethnically, Southeast Asian Americans, especially those living in urban centers, have demonstrated a lack of pulling together due to their history of internal fighting (Burns & D'Avanzo, 1993). The transitions involving acculturation and accommodation will only exacerbate this cultural tension and can increase the risk factor for alcohol and other drug abuse.

Background

Although Islamic laws eschew alcohol, and most Moslem, Hindu, and Buddhists groups avoid alcohol, many Asian cultures do use alcohol in rituals (Shon & Ja, 1982). An example of this is found in the "tribal binge" drinking of Pacific Islanders and in the ceremonial and traditional events in Japan. Drinking in Japan is reported to start as early as age 11, and alcohol use is organized and institutionalized (Tani, Haga, & Kato, 1975). Working men of all ages have their favorite drinking establishment. The more exclusive establishments have a host of taxis and private automobiles to transport their regular customers home. In less prestigious places, friends and companions transport those who drink too much. Oashi and Nishimura (1978) have categorized four types of Japanese drinking: (1) drinking at dinner done mainly by the man to relax after work; (2) drinking to celebrate annual events; (3) drinking with one's friend after work; and (4) drinking at a roundtable after meetings and conventions—usually to lessen communication barriers. Oashi and Nishimura show that the lessening of communication barriers by drinking is important in Japan and that it is acceptable for a subordinate to be very frank with one's boss when either one or both are drunk.

The Chinese not only allow the use of alcohol at social functions, it is virtually pushed on one as a display of hospitality during social functions. However, drunkenness is discouraged. Traditionally, Hong Kong has few drinking-centered establishments, generally restricts the use of alcohol to males, and values drinking alcohol at meals. In Chinese culture, alcohol is often viewed in a somewhat similar fashion to that of the abolitionist in the temperance movement in America's nineteenth century (see section on African Americans). That is, alcohol is associated with lack of restraint, but it is not generally feared that drunkeness will lead to violence. Chafetz (1964) has noted that Taiwanese have well-defined ways of behaving, have strong social sanctions against excessive drinking, and encourage drinking only at meals or at special events. He also found that the Taiwanese have little official concern about alcohol treatment programs due to the overall lack of psychiatric resources and the low level of alcoholism in the dominant Chinese population.

Koreans generally view alcohol as part of their culture in which drinking is for celebrations, mourning, to feel good, and to find friends (Kitano, 1982). Korea is roughly 80% Christian, and this Christian influence may be reflected in Korean males' being sanctioned to drink whenever they wish, while females are often restricted to drinking at celebrations and dances.

Polynesians do not employ guilt as a means to regulate drinking and drunkenness. However, Tongans and Samoans, many of whom are Christian, do seem to use guilt to control the amount of drinking. Drinking to excess is seen as potentially threatening in the Samoan culture. In an early study, Lemert (1964) reported that a large number of Samoan wives had left their husbands because of the heavy drinking of their physically abusing husbands.

Values

When attempting to describe the values held by Asians, the vast within-group differences prohibit any attempt at brevity. What follows are some general descriptions that would more likely apply to recent Asian immigrants and are less likely to describe earlier generations of Asian Americans. Such discrepancies are mostly due to the effects of acculturation.

Family Roles

Most Asian societies are structured with well-defined role expectations. This includes a patriarchal family structure consisting of elders or extended family members and a structure in which children are seen as subordinates. According to Fukuyama and Inoue-Cox (1992), there is a strong sense of "filial piety" and respect for authority, which reinforces obedience and protection of the family name. The father's decisions are beyond reproach and are categorically accepted. The mother nurtures both her husband and her children. Whereas at one time it was socially desirable for the father to be the disciplinarian, the contemporary Asian father is not home as much, so the discipline is essentially left to the mother.

The male is expected to provide for the economic welfare of his family and in so doing is the one upon whose shoulders falls the responsibility for the family's successes or failures. Because the physical appearance of Asians differs significantly from Euro-Americans concomitant with the presence of racial and cultural discrimination toward Asian Americans (Shon & Ja, 1982), Asian men can face extraordinary pressures when attempting to provide financially for their families. Research suggests that it usually takes about ten or more years for them to find economic security (Burns & D'Avanzo, 1993). This length of time and the pressures to succeed increase their risk for alcohol and other drug abuse. Risk for substance abuse also seems to increase with the level of educational attainment for these men—especially for Chinese, Korean, and Japanese men. Chi, Lubben, & Kitano (1989) found consumption rates of alcohol increased with educational attainment.

Shame, especially the idea of "saving face," controls behaviors in the Asian family and is learned early in life. The concept of shame and loss of face involves not only the exposing of one's actions for all to see, but also involves family, community or social withdrawal of confidence and support (Shon & Ja, 1982). Inextricably woven into the value of shame is obligation. Obligation in the Asian/Pacific Islander community contains spoken and unspoken elements of reciprocity, and the greatest obligation is toward one's parents. According to Fukuyama and Inoue-Cox (1992), this is an obligation that cannot ever truly be repaid. Regardless of what the parents may do to the child, the child is still obligated to give respect and obedience to them. The more that Asian children are exposed to Euro-American schools, the more this sense of obligation can come into question and become a source of confusion. The transition will produce a period of anomie for the Asian offspring, and it is during this period of normlessness that they may be at an increased risk for alcohol and other drug abuse.

Communication

Roles also play an interesting and important part in communication for the Asian/ Pacific Islander population. Communication between individuals is governed by such characteristics as age, gender, education, occupation, social status, family background, marital status, and parenthood (Shon & Ja, 1982). These variables influence behavior in terms of who will bow the lowest, who will initiate and change topics in a conversation, which person will speak more loudly, who will break eye contact first, and who will be most accommodating or tolerant. Most of the newly immigrated Asian/Pacific Islanders are likely to want to avoid confrontation, keeping conversations on a harmonious level, and often maintaining self-control over their facial expressions while avoiding direct eye contact. This information is important when assessing for alcohol and other drug problems, because it can work in reverse. If responses from Asian clients appear to upset the professional conducting the assessment, answers may not be given accurately so as to avoid confrontation.

Religion

Beliefs about health and responses to offerings of health care are influenced by religious beliefs in the Asian/Pacific Islander population. For example, Buddhism holds that life is suffering, and suffering emanates from desire. Pain or other suffering is seen as punishment for transgressions in this or previous lives. Alcohol and other drug problems may fall into this context. The notion of pain and suffering may so strongly influence one's beliefs that the likelihood of seeking help for alcohol and other drug problems may be severely diminished (Shon & Ja, 1982). Animism is the idea that evil spirits, demons, or gods have control over one's life. Because of this, the "shaman" may be the primary care giver or helper in situations involving alcohol or other drug abuse. However, Western helpers may be invited to help in the process. Confucianism is prevalent among older Vietnamese and is a moral and ethical code that includes the worshipping of ancestors. Because Confucianism stresses a hierarchical order in both family and social systems, it will be the family elder who would have the final say in decisions involving treatment for alcohol or other drug abuse. As a helping professional, you need to be very careful to demonstrate respect for this individual.

Taoism, which stresses harmony, is also quite prevalent among the Asian population. Burns and D'Avanzo (1993) point out that medically invasive procedures are seen as disrupting harmony. Harmony also plays a significant role in one's intention to seek help. A passive posture toward treatment may be assumed by an individual of Asian or Pacific Islander descent because anything else would disrupt harmony and perfection.

Risk Factors for Alcohol and Other Drug Abuse

Although subject to the same methodological concerns mentioned earlier for Native Americans and other special populations, most studies addressing Asian/ Pacific Islanders' drug use and abuse have shown that, over the course of their lifetimes, members of this population seem to have less drug use in all categories when compared with other groups (Burns & D'Avanzo, 1993). This is due largely to a general pattern of emphasizing family unity, pursuing higher education for better job opportunities, and the value of self-sacrifice in order to give the next generation better opportunities. If drugs are turned to as a means of alleviating stress and pain, the drugs of choice appear to be tranquilizers, marijuana, and pain killers such as morphine, Demerol and Percodan (McLaughlin, Raymond, Murikami, & Goebert, 1987).

The values mentioned above will be mediated by the adjustment patterns of Asian/Pacific Islanders once they enter the United States. The sheer number of immigrants concomitant with the age distribution of this group suggests that these families are in a constant state of transition once they arrive in the United States. The process of acculturation will impact all family members and will differentially affect their risk for alcohol abuse. For example, a newly arrived Asian American homemaker will be confronted with Euro-American values of female independence, assertiveness, achievement, and work. As a result, elder Asian Americans, expecting to be cared for by family members, can experience great shock and loneliness when faced with nursing home care. Such conflicts between newly acquired values and traditional values can place these individuals at risk for alcohol and other drug abuse. Although it is reported that Asian women drink less than their male counterparts (Chi, Lubben, & Kitano, 1989), an earlier study by Gedig and Gedig (1977) did indicate increasing levels of alcohol consumption among Japanese women. A revealing study on Chinese American women found that two-thirds reported they abstained, while none reported heavy use of alcohol (Gordis, 1990). However, young, widowed, and divorced Asian American women and elder Asian Americans are "disproportionately vulnerable to psychosocial stresses and attendant stress-induced problems" (Lee, 1983, p. 531). The effects of such reactions to stress may be seen among Cambodian women of whom Burns and D'Avanzo (1993) found 15% of a sample of Cambodian women residing on the East Coast reporting a family member having drug problems. Over half of that same sample said that they had used a drug for nonmedicinal purposes, such as for relieving the emotional pain of their plight.

Often, in attempting to meet security needs, all Asian family members will seek employment immediately upon arrival in the United States. According to Shon and Ja (1982), the family will often survive in dilapidated housing in order to save enough money to purchase a small business. While the family hierarchy may provide a stabilizing force to deal with the pressures of financial adjustment, youths who are exposed to the parental pressures for high achievement and financial success may fall victim to feelings of isolation and self-blame. To help brace against fear of long-term insecurity, many Asian Americans also work hard to send their children to schools in hopes that they will become high-paid professionals. This value is reflected in the sheer numbers of Asian American youth attending prestigious universities in the United States. However, attempts to further the education of their children can be met with resistance, in that the younger are likely to be attending English-speaking schools while their older siblings and parents may still prefer or use their native language. This would suggest that there might be a bi-cultural splitting within this population in terms of language. Language differences within families can lead to increased levels of stress, thereby increasing individual family member's risk factors for alcohol and other drug abuse.

Moreover, language difficulties in school may preclude the Asian/Pacific Islanders' abilities to fulfill their parents' wishes to excel. This would be especially true for first generation immigrants who came to the United States involuntarily or because of economic hardships faced in their homelands. The sum total of language difficulties and perceived inabilities to meet parental wishes can lead to alienation inside the family (Shon & Ja, 1982). For example, the father's insistence upon obedience may be called into question and, when the father's beliefs are called into question, it may significantly contribute to a breakdown of traditional family structure. The result can be anomie, leaving the youth at risk for drug abuse. Kim (1991) states that, in families where the parents do not speak English, youths often lose filial respect because parents who have a difficult time providing for the family also find it difficult to establish the traditional authoritarian family role structure. As a result, youths are left feeling depressed and alienated, which can lead to alcohol and drug abuse as a means to cope.

African Americans

The role of alcohol in the contemporary African American community varies from that of many other groups. African Americans have culturally acceptable means for achieving spontaneity, sociability, and relaxation. Alcohol, then, is not seen a requisite for a feeling of celebration. In addition, specific drinking patterns of African Americans are found to be somewhat different from those of Euro-Americans. Early ethnographic studies suggest that taverns appear to be social centers for a majority of African Americans who drink (Sterne and Pittman, 1972). As would be true with any group regardless of ethnicity, African Americans who frequent taverns and bars are a group unto themselves and, as you would expect, are regarded as candidates for the underclass in African American culture rather than seen as responsible participants in community life. The exception would be a man who was a weekend tavern drinker and was otherwise a capable wage earner and family man. Women who frequent taverns and bars, however, would likely be socially compromised in the wider African American community.

In general, alcohol is often perceived to be a "party food" and is associated with being palliative, while the potential harmful effects are often overlooked or not understood. Alcohol consumption at parties or other social gatherings has a minor role in terms of setting the mood of gaiety and spontaneity. Therefore, abstaining from alcohol does not mean the person is being staid or a "party pooper."

Many African Americans drink almost exclusively on the weekends—traditionally a time of relaxation, visitation, and celebration. Brand names and the quantity of alcohol drunk reflect status in many African American communities. Several studies also report that African Americans tend to be polar in their use: They either abstain or drink heavily (Bourne, 1973; Harper, 1976; 1978). These authors also report that African Americans begin to drink at an earlier age, to purchase larger containers of alcohol than their Euro-American counterparts, to concentrate their drinking on the weekends, and to share alcohol with relatives and groups of friends. According to Harper (1978), this latter pattern appears to be more likely associated with lack of disposable income than to the atavistic, group-oriented value held by Africans and Native Americans.

The history of the relationship between African Americans and alcohol is engaging. Since the institutionalization of slavery in the early 1600s, a broad social and intellectual climate, known as Enlightenment thinking, has prevailed in American thought and has had a significant impact upon views of alcohol and its relationship to African Americans. So, to understand the history of African Americans and alcohol is to trace the institutionalization of slavery up through the prohibition period in the twentieth century.

Background

Early stereotyping of Africans (who became "African Americans" after the Emancipation Proclamation) and the institutionalization of slavery in the United States led to subsequent fears of slave insurrection and fueled numerous social measures aimed at controlling this population. Aside from legislation rigidly restricting their ability to trade, Africans were also prohibited from using alcoholic beverages. A West Jersey (New Jersey) law of 1685, for example, stated: "Any person convicted of selling or giving of rum, or any manner of strong liquor, either to a negro or Indian, except the stimulant be given in relief of real physical distress is liable to a penalty of five pounds" (Herd, 1982, p. 355). Similar laws were in effect in most of the colonial governments including Maryland, North Carolina, Georgia, Delaware, Pennsylvania, and New England (Larkin, 1965). Rather than being fueled by the fear that drunkenness would lessen their work ethic, the assumptive premise of these laws was based upon the fear that intoxicated slaves would foment rebellion. While the relationship with alcohol and insurrection was presumptive, the manner in which the early African slaves were treated certainly did little to quell the fear of insurrection.

The American Revolution witnessed the abolition of slavery in most of the northern states, but not in the newly formed states of the south. And for southern slaveholders, the discrepancy between the "free north" and the "slave south" exacerbated fears of insurrection. Many new laws were instituted that further restricted the use of alcohol by slaves. However, in spite of laws, the popular views held by slave owners varied on the use of alcohol as a means of controlling Africans. As stated earlier, some believed that prohibiting slaves' use of alcohol would help guard against rebellion. This view was based upon the southern planters' widely held view that alcohol was an important cause of every insurrectionary movement in the United States (Freehling, 1965). Another popular view stood in direct opposition. This view was equally concerned with controlling Africans, but held that the sober, thinking slave was the one who was dangerous and needed the constant vigilance of the owner (Douglas, 1855). Herd (1991) summarized these two views:

> One [view of alcohol] inspired images of force and rebellion, whereas the other suggested images of passivity and victimization. From the former perspective liquor was believed to be a powerful agent of disinhibition capable of unleashing violent and irrational behavior in otherwise civilized people. Hence, alcohol was regarded as a cause of crime and violence, a substance that made people commit barbaric and cruel acts. In the latter view alcohol was believed to be a powerfully addicting substance that forced men to drink and left them weak, slothful, and in a thoroughly degraded condition (p. 357).

What were the views of alcohol held by the Africans themselves? They varied, of course. But interestingly enough, Africans were essentially split on the issue as well. Many regarded drinking as a natural reaction to being held against their will. For example, Stampp (1961) maintains that the consumption of alcohol by slaves was internally motivated as the "only satisfactory escape from the indignities, the frustrations, the emptiness, [and] the oppressive boredom of slavery" (p. 368). According to this view, there was a demand for alcohol by slaves, and Stampp offers a quote from a former slave to corroborate this assertion: To be sober during the holidays "was disgraceful; and he was esteemed a lazy and improvident man, who could not afford to drink whiskey during Christmas" (p. 370). However, during the same period, black and white abolitionists alike maintained that holidays were perhaps the paragon of travesty. To these abolitionists, when slaveowners offered libations to slaves during times of celebration, their intent was anything but to celebrate. They believed that holidays instilled more docile and passive resistance among slaves (Herd, 1991).

The views of alcohol as the enslaver and the disinhibitor, coupled with the Enlightenment philosophy of the time, inspired a spontaneous practice of temperance in the middle nineteenth century. Temperance ideology was focused upon Enlightenment thinking and the role of self-control, since it was this ability to control one's irresistible desires that would free humans to be rational and productive. The temperance movement did not stop there, however. Temperance was seen in a broader scope as a vehicle for freeing the will as well as having significant social implications for freeing slaves. Freedom and self-control meant freedom for all and freedom from all. This included freedom from slavery as well as freedom from alcohol. It is not surprising, then, to see that the northern abolitionists embraced a view of alcohol as the enslaver, and therefore, the enemy. Those southern slave owners who believed in temperance adopted the view that alcohol was the disinhibitor and could unleash dangerous impulses in slaves. In describing the abolitionist view, George Fredrickson (1971) writes

> *What made slavery such a detestable condition was not simply that it created a bad environment; it was a severely limiting condition that was incompatible with the fundamental abolitionist belief that every man was morally responsible for his actions (p. 37).*

For many Africans, intemperance was seen as analogous to promoting slavery. The popularity of abstinence was reflected in the spate of temperance societies and in the periodicals promulgated by Africans at the time. The pledge of the American Temperance Union adopted at a New England temperance convention in 1836 demonstrates the rigid adherence to the value of abstinence:

> *Being mercifully redeemed from human slavery, we do pledge ourselves never to be brought into the slavery of the bottle, therefore we will not drink the drunkard's drink: whiskey, gin, beer, nor rum, nor anything that makes drunk come (n.d., p. 4).*

Curiously, the temperance movement among Africans was less a movement toward curtailing high alcohol consumption among their own than it was part of a larger movement of social reform that marked the era. In fact, estimates of the quantity of consumption by Africans during this period are conflicting. So, it cannot be said that alcohol was the primary motivator for African interest in temperance (Sterne, 1967). Herd (1991) believes the lure of temperance was more a reflection of African abolitionist views on slavery and the lure of Enlightenment thinking that valued the social betterment of all.

At the beginning of the twentieth century, stereotyping and the perceived problems with the African American population had become central to the issue of alcohol reform for southern prohibitionists. Influenced by the Victorian Age and the preoccupation with sexual mores, women and children were now seen as needing protection from the disinhibited African Americans who were being portrayed as sexual perpetrators in the sensationalistic periodicals of the time (Sterne, 1967). The hackneyed views of African Americans spilled over into the disenfranchisement campaigns aimed at controlling both the poor white and African American vote (Herd, 1991). "Whiskey-sodden, irresponsible" African American voters "needed" to be controlled, so many politicians urged restrictive voting rights. The temperance movement, which had advocated freedom, was thus thwarted by restrictions on voting rights, and there was a decline in the movement's popularity among many African American reformists who now saw alcohol regulation as antithetical to the true tenets of the temperance movement (DuBois, 1928). However, Herd (1991) claims that it was at the popular level where the most profound changes in views of alcohol among African Americans of the time took place. A new fascination with a sensual lifestyle overshadowed the now anachronistic temperance movement.

Accompanying this fascination were significant demographic and socioeconomic changes in the African American population. Escaping intense oppression in the south, thousands migrated to the northern "wet" cities, only to find many northern industrialists, especially those resisting the union movement, offering only low-paying jobs—primarily recruiting African Americans as strikebreakers. Many took these jobs, while many others found bootlegging much more profitable than farm and other unskilled labor. Speakeasies and cabarets, emphasizing excitement and sensual pleasure, became the arenas for this new lifestyle. As a result, the views of alcohol among African Americans shifted one hundred eighty degrees: Whereas many African Americans had embraced the temperance movement of one hundred years earlier as a means to demonstrate defiance, intemperance in early twentieth century America was the means to demonstrate defiance against an oppressive and restrictive legal system.

Values

While there is no such thing as "The African American Family," studies on the African American family structure can be used to guide a general understanding of this diverse population.

Family Roles
As you would expect, the roles of males and females in the African American family vary. Historically, the displacement of African Americans from agriculture into service and industrial employment, with little adjustment in the amount of racism, left this group as the "last hired, first fired." Unemployment was always high out-

side of southern agriculture, and out of necessity African American women worked outside the home. As a result, egalitarianism among the genders is more common than not and may be more pronounced in the African American culture than in the Euro-American culture of America. The egalitarian nature of the family structure stands in direct opposition to the stereotypic view that African American households are matriarchal households. Hines and Boyd-Franklin (1982) state that this misperception usually arises because African American women often assume responsibilities in their families that are less frequently taken on by women in Euro-American cultures. The emphasis upon egalitarianism in the African American family also allows for an exchange of family roles so that various members can assume responsibility for the children. Fathers and grandfathers, for example, may provide the primary care of the child while the female works.

In spite of the role flexibility afforded by egalitarianism, stereotypic views of African American males as being irresponsible remains. For example, there is an often misunderstood concept called *peripheralness* cited in the literature that reinforces the hackneyed view of African American families being matriarchal. Simply, peripheralness suggests an absence of participation or interest on the part of African American fathers in their families. A more accurate view of the role of fathers reflects the pressures of providing for the family in a society where job ceilings exist and oppression abounds (Hines and Boyd-Franklin, 1982). These same authors also indicate that the African American father may have to spend an inordinate amount of time and energy trying to provide for the family's basic survival needs, a preoccupation that drains the psychic energy that would otherwise be infused into the family. Faced with both pressures to provide and barriers thwarting their efforts, underemployed and unemployed African American fathers may be at risk for turning to alcohol and other drugs as a means of relieving the pain.

Kinship and Extended Family Bonds

The flexibility of roles in African American culture is also influenced by an atavistic value emphasizing strong kinship bonds. While slavery certainly reinforced this value, its origins can be traced to Africa where Africanian thinking had produced the syllogism, "We are, therefore I am" (Hines & Boyd-Franklin, 1982). Prevalent among many African American families and tied to the value of kinship is a phenomenon known as "child-keeping." Child-keeping occurs when a child is informally "adopted" or reared by other family members who have more resources than the biological parents. Rather than seeing child-keeping as the disruption of the family system, Hines and Boyd-Franklin believe that this occurrence actually elevates the importance of the child. Yet African American children may be subjected to ridicule and ostracism by a mainstream Euro-American culture that fails to recognize and/or appreciate this value—believing instead that the child who is raised by grandparents reflects a broken home. As a result of these misperceptions and other factors, African American children may experience stress at school and can turn to alcohol and other drugs. This is reflected in a study of African American adults between the ages of 18 and 23 living in Harlem. Brunswick (1979) found that the initial use of marijuana, heroin, psychedelics, and alcohol occurred most commonly on the way to school. Brunswick also found that alcohol was the drug used earliest in a sample of African American young adults living in Harlem. Moreover, Brunswick found that 20% of the males in the sample had begun using alcohol by the age of ten, and by the age of fourteen half of the males and 40% of the female drinkers had used alcohol.

Religion

The crucial role of the church in the emancipation of slaves in America is reflected in current views of the importance of a strong religious orientation among many African Americans. In times of slavery, cryptic messages about times and places for escape often came from the pulpit during the church service (Hines & Boyd-Franklin, 1982). Interestingly, these same authors point out that songs sung today in many African American churches often carry the remains of those messages such as "Steal Away" and "Wade in the Water." The power of those messages, hidden in church protocol, and their relationship to emancipation issues should leave no one surprised that some of the most notable contemporary leaders in the African American culture are or were preachers: the Reverend Martin Luther King Jr., the Reverend Jessie Jackson, Malcolm X, and others. Although these individuals are of international stature, the local church is an important vehicle allowing for the emergence of leaders in local African American communities. Free from the oppression that exists in mainstream Euro-American culture, the church allows outlets for creative talents that otherwise might be thwarted. The racism and oppression experienced by low-paying jobs during the week may be offset somewhat by becoming a deacon or trustee on Sunday. Hines and Boyd-Franklin remind us that numerous church activities, such as dinners, trips, singing in the choir, and participation in Sunday School, provide an intricate social life for many African Americans and promote their mental health and a sense of connectedness.

Although church affiliation would be expected to temper African American drinking patterns, African Americans are at a high risk for alcohol-related causes of mortality and morbidity. For example, autopsies conducted at the Los Angeles County-University of Southern California Medical Center between 1970 and 1975 revealed high rates of liver cirrhosis in both African American men (29%) and women (10%) (Lopez-Lee, 1979). A similar study was conducted by Malin, Coakley, Kaelber, Munch, and Holland (1982), who examined mortality data in Baltimore, Chicago, Detroit, Los Angeles, New York, Washington, D.C., and Philadelphia. They found rates of liver-cirrhosis for African Americans to be 44% higher than the rate for Euro-Americans. Attesting to the morbidity issues, Johnson (1975) that the "sickest patients in general hospitals are Black males, Black females, White males, and White females in that order" (p. 278).

Risk Factors for Alcohol and Other Drug Abuse

The results of research on the relationship between African Americans and alcohol and other drugs is mixed. Yet, some trends indicating use are notable. For example, the 1985 National Household Survey conducted by the National Institute of Drug

Abuse found that African American males over 35 are much more likely to use illicit drugs than are a comparable sample of Euro-American males (Brown & Alterman, 1992). According to these same authors, this same trend holds for African American males between the ages of 18 and 34. African American women, as well, were found more likely to have used crack cocaine than has any other racial/ethnic group. Since alcohol abuse does appear to increase disease and decrease life expectancy among this population (Malin et al., 1982), it becomes important to try to understand the risk factors associated with substance abuse in the African American population.

Availability and Geographical Factors

One factor increasing risk is availability. In 1978, Los Angeles had approximately three liquor stores per block in addition to those neighborhood stores offering beer and wine (Parker & Harmon, 1978). Parker and Harmon found the availability of alcohol to be a contributing factor in consumption rates among African Americans. It would appear that residing in inner-cities, where there is a plethora of taverns and liquor stores, is a factor that might increase the risk for alcohol and other drug abuse. However, in an early study, Robins and Guze (1971) refuted the notion that impoverished urban areas were associated with increased alcohol abuse among African Americans. The absence of alcohol-related problems was associated with having come from a stable family background, good performance in school, an absence of juvenile arrests, and a lack of early drug experimentation.

Although impoverished geographical locations may not have been a significant variable in determining alcohol use patterns among African Americans in the 1970s, it may be more of a factor now. Brown and Alterman (1992) reviewed the literature regarding substance abuse in culturally and ethnically diverse populations and found that the risk for substance abuse appears to have increased among individuals residing in impoverished areas. These same authors go on to state that

> *to the extent that many African Americans are and continue to be impoverished and deprived of many of the resources and benefits of our society, we should expect to find greater rates of substance abuse and more severe consequences of drug use (p. 861).*

Developmental Issues

King (1982) asked a rather intriguing question regarding African American drinking patterns: "Why is the consumption of alcohol (3+ drinks per day) most prevalent in the age decades 40–49 and 50–59 among African Americans?" He conducted a search of the literature published between 1977 and 1980 and found that most American men (regardless of ethnicity) go through a transition in the middle years. He postulated that the increase of heavy drinking in African American men during the middle years may be due to frustrated attempts at attaining satisfactory love and work aspirations. In an earlier study, Levinson (1978) had theorized that these years from 30 to 40 may be especially difficult for an African American male who is attempting to match aspirations with achievement. Failing to achieve one's goals can be expressed in depression and dependency, and this is exactly what Steer and Shaw (1977) found in their study of African American alcoholics. These authors believe that, having failed to achieve their dreams, many African American men may turn to alcohol in their early 30s to offset feelings of inadequacy and depression. Adding support to this view is Williams (1986), who points out that unemployment can have a deleterious effect upon drinking behavior in that it is correlated with increased risk of alcohol problems.

Latino/Hispanic Populations

The term *Latino American* is used to describe those persons living in the United States who share a common Hispanic cultural background. The term *Hispanic* refers to Spaniards and Portuguese, while *Latino* includes those known as Chicanos, Cubanos, Puerto Ricans, Latin Americans, and Mexican Americans. Three major groups comprise the Latino population: Mexican Americans, Puerto Ricans, and Cuban Americans. The following section will present information on these groups as well as some information on Central and South Americans. In general, differences between these three groups of people are influenced largely by educational level, socioeconomic status, immigration status, age/generation, rural versus urban residence, country of origin, and degree of acculturation (Torres, 1993).

According to the 1990 Unites States census, an estimated 21.4 million Latinos/Hispanics (8.6% of the total U.S. population) reside in the continental United States and another 3 million live in Puerto Rico. Other untold numbers are living illegally in the United States. The Latino/Hispanic population is the fastest growing segment of the ethnic population, and estimates reveal that by the year 2000 they will comprise the largest minority group in America while becoming the majority population in California (Burns & D'Avanzo, 1993). Of this group, about 62% are Mexican American, 11% are Puerto Ricans, 14% are from Central and South America, 5% are Cuban, and another 8% are classified as "other" (U.S. Bureau of the Census, March, 1990).

Although the Latino/Hispanic dropout rate from school is quite high (e.g., the New York dropout rate ranges between 41 and 80%), a little over 50% of Latinos/Hispanics have four or more years of high school and about 10% have four or more years of college. Burns and D'Avanzo (1993) claim that approximately 90% of this ethnic group reside in urban areas, but there are some interesting differences in immigration patterns and geographic distribution among Cuban Americans, Puerto Ricans, Central and South Americans, and Mexican Americans.

Background

The immigration patterns among Cuban Americans, Puerto Rican Americans, Central and South Americans, and Mexican Americans are varied. Joining the 50,000 Cubans already living in the states were large numbers of Cubans who left during the political unrest of the 1950s. The majority of those leaving were the highly educated, professional/business, and upper-class people (Burns & D'Avanzo, 1993). About 3,000 wealthy Cubans left when Fidel Castro came into power in 1959, and these were joined by another wave of middle-class immigrants who came to the United States in 1960. Finally, in 1980, came a wave of working-class Cubans, some 125,000 strong and made up mainly of African American Cubans (Office of Substance Abuse Programs, 1990). Puerto Rican-Americans have immigrated to the United States mainly for economic reasons in low but steady rates. Central and South Americans represent the most recent Latino/Hispanic immigrants to the United States. Most of these individuals came because of political upheaval in their respective countries. Exact figures of immigrants are unavailable due mostly to their being illegal aliens, but it is known that a majority come from Guatemala, El Salvador, and Nicaragua (Burns and D'Avanzo, 1993). These same authors note that there is a high incidence of post traumatic stress disorder (PTSD) in this group and attribute that to the violence experienced by these individuals in their homelands as well as to the trauma, such as beatings and rape, experienced while travelling to the United States through Mexico. With the exception of those living in the southwestern United States, the majority of Mexican families living in the United States are immigrants.

The presence of Latinos/Hispanics in the southwest region of the United States dates back to the early 1500s. The outcome of the Mexican War (1846–1848), caused by conflict over Texas, witnessed the annexation of Arizona, California, Colorado, New Mexico, Texas, and portions of Utah and Nevada. Along with this annexation came over 75,000 Mexican people who were granted U.S. citizenship (Burns & D'Avanzo, 1993). The Mexican Revolution of 1910 was the cause of another influx of Latino/Hispanic immigrants to the United States. In addition, Burns & D'Avanzo point out that, between World War II and the 1960s, the Braceros Programs allowed for seasonal laborers to enter the country to work in the fields of California, Arizona, Washington, Texas, and the midwest.

Mexican-Americans tend to occupy the southwestern states, with most located in Texas and California. New York and other eastern states have the majority of Puerto Ricans, and Florida has the largest number of Cuban-Americans. In terms of socioeconomic standing, the 1990 median income of Latino/Hispanic households was $22,300 (about $10,000 less than that for non-Latino/Hispanic households) (OSAP, 1990). A final note on the "American Dream": Twenty-six percent of all Latinos/Hispanics live below the poverty level.

Values

As with the other culturally and ethnically diverse populations discussed in this chapter, values indigenous to the Latino/Hispanic culture come into frequent conflict with the Euro-American value system, which can cause distress for the Latino/Hispanic individual and family. Feelings of guilt, self-doubt, and even betrayal can create disharmony within and among Latino/Hispanic families. Similar disruptions can occur when individual family members take advantage of economic or educational opportunities not taken by other family members. Moreover, Gilbert (1978) has alluded to problems that can occur within a family when one member who is well adjusted to the sociological and cultural pressures of bi-culturalism marries one who is less well adjusted.

Familism and Cariño

Traditional Latino/Hispanic families value the family above almost everything else. However, Mexican American families do not necessarily place as much emphasis upon this value. The traditional Latino/Hispanic family is private, which is especially true with problems such as alcohol and other drug abuse (Burns & D'Avanzo, 1993). The family protects the individual and demands loyalty while stressing the importance of family proximity, cohesiveness, and respect (respeto) for parental authority. *Orgullo* (pride), *verguenza* (shame), *confianza* (confidence), *dignidad* (dignity), and *pobre pero honesto* (poor but honest) are typical values in traditional Latino/Hispanic families (Falicov, 1982). However, as Latinos/Hispanics become more acculturated into mainstream Euro-American society, these values become a source of conflict. Joining gangs, where these values operate strongly, becomes one way Latino/Hispanic youths cope with the conflict of values.

Similar to, yet different from, many African American families, Latino/Hispanic families usually live in a nuclear arrangement but do have extended families living nearby. The large size of the family, usually consisting of parents and four or five children, influences the family structure in many ways. Depending upon the degree of acculturation, Latino/Hispanic families value affiliation and cooperation while placing much less value upon confrontation and competition (Falicov, 1982). Moreover, many childrearing concerns such as caretaking, discipline, financial responsibility, companionship, emotional support, and problem-solving are shared. In traditional Latino/Hispanic families, for example, the role of godparents is very pronounced.

The emphasis upon intergenerational and lateral interdependence, however, does not diminish the value of *cariño,* or deep caring for the family, nor does it eliminate the need for strong adherence to a high degree of hierarchical organization in which rules are clearly organized around age and gender. Even though traditionally older male children are given the greatest authority and power, there is an unconditional acceptance of family members and an emphasis upon equality. Parents often provide much nurturance and protection for children and do not push them into achievement when it involves unhealthy competition between family members (Falicov, 1982).

Children also occupy a central role in the marriage. Because *el amor de madre* (motherly love) is seen as a much greater love than romantic love, it is the existence of the children that essentially ties the marriage together. This value is reflected in a relatively lower divorce rate for this population than for their Euro-American counterparts (Burns & D'Avanzo, 1993). Even though children enjoy a central role in the family, their status is lower than that of their parents. It is *respeto* (respect) that maintains the child's status while allowing parents to reinforce a dependence and dutiful posture among their children (Falicov, 1982).

Machismo and Marianismo

Almost everyone is familiar with the hackneyed version of Latino/Hispanic *machismo* or *muy hombre*. According to Falicov, this value dictates the need for males to be strong, brave, protective of their women (mother, sisters, wife), aggressive, sexually experienced, courageous, and authoritarian. The implication is for women to be humble, submissive, virtuous, and devoted to home and children. This value for females is known as *hembrismo* or *marianismo* and underscores the importance of the self-sacrificing mother. *Marianismo* also serves to counterbalance the male value of *machismo* (Stevens, 1973).

In actuality, many Latino/Hispanic men are dependent and submissive, and it is the women who are dominant and controlling (Falicov, 1982). In public, the "self-denial" of the mother is reinforced by the father's insistence that the children obey and help her. Often, however, he is much less involved with the children other than to discipline them, and, upon more than one occasion, the mother may find herself in covert disagreement with him. When this occurs, she may act as a mediator between the children and the father, thus adding more to her central position in the family (Stevens, 1973).

The conflict of values arising between the male need to demonstrate *machismo* and the female value of *marianismo* can create stress for Latino/Hispanic males. Alcohol, the most commonly abused drug among contemporary Latino/Hispanics, did at one time help to build a social structure into their societies. It now appears that drinking alcohol is an accepted way of dealing with stresses of acculturation, and the value of *machismo* tends to strengthen the notion that alcohol is an accepted way of displaying this male value (Stevens, 1973). *Machismo* likely influences younger males to drink more than do their female counterparts, especially in the Mexican American youth population (Bettes, Dusenbury, Kermen, James-Ortiz, & Botvin, 1990).

Risk Factors for Alcohol and Other Drug Abuse

Sociological Risk Factors

As with other culturally and ethnically diverse populations, the resulting tensions involved in acculturation raise the level of risk for alcohol and other drug abuse among the Latino/Hispanic population. Patterns of risk vary across male and female populations and between adults and youth and appear to be influenced by both cultural acceptance of alcohol as well as by role-modeling of drinking behaviors.

Research into Latino/Hispanic youth reveals that this population may be at great risk because of language barriers, lowered self-esteem, dropping out of the educational system, early exposure to substance use and abuse by family members, and because of the daily stresses encountered in living (Bettes, et al., 1990; Gilbert & Cervantes, 1986). Moreover, those Mexican-Americans farm laborers who pick crops change residences constantly as they follow crops. The continuous changing of location disrupts a sense of continuity and can adversely affect farm workers' children, placing them at an increased risk for alcohol and other drug use and abuse.

Other sociological risk factors for substance abuse by Latino/Hispanic youth reflect the problems confronted in the schools. Varying degrees of language proficiency are excessive and can pose serious problems both in seeking and maintaining employment or when children attend English-speaking schools. Limited language proficiency can lead to decreases in self-esteem, thus elevating the risk for abusing substances. For example, in a comparative study of adolescents, it was found that Latino/Hispanic adolescents are at high risk for alcohol abuse, a fact mainly attributed to reports of lowered self-esteem (Bettes et al., 1990).

Role modeling also influences adolescent drinking patterns. For example, Gilbert and Cervantes (1986) report that parental and sibling use of alcohol was seen as the best predictor of alcohol use by young Mexican-American males. In the Puerto Rican community, heavy drinking takes place most often in public and in full view of children. As long as family and social obligations are fulfilled, heavy drinking is widely tolerated (Hispanic Health Council, 1987). In general, the Puerto Rican population views alcohol as a socially approved reward for hard work or achievement and sees alcohol as a means to escape undesirable circumstances. Alcohol use allows for a "manly" activity to be shared while acting as a social facilitator and refreshment and is seen as a way to feel and act as Puerto Rican (Burns and D'Avanzo, 1993). The level of risk for alcohol and other drug abuse is compounded when there exists a clash of values between the dominant Euro-American and Puerto Rican culture.

The influences of acculturation also play an important role in drinking behaviors of Latino/Hispanic youth, but research is conflicting with regards to the effects of acculturation upon the drinking patterns of Latino/Hispanic adult males (Markides, Ray, Stroup-Benham, & Trevino, 1990). For example, Latino/Hispanic high school seniors and first-year college students reported that abusing alcohol was the result of pressures faced in dealing with taking responsibility for their decisions (OSAP, 1990). However, Corbett, Mora, and Ames (1991) found that Latino/Hispanic men who had the greatest consumption of alcohol also reported the greatest amount of acculturation and demonstrated the highest level of education and income. This, together with the fact that these men tended to drink with other men, raises the likely possibility that *machismo* continues to be a significant variable across Latino/Hispanic male development and appears to place this group at an increased risk for substance abuse.

The Latino/Hispanic women who report heavy drinking, however, present themselves in a slightly different socio-cultural pattern. The degree of Euro-American socialization was a factor associated with greater consumption rates among Latino/Hispanic women (Caetano, 1990). Caetano reports that Latino/Hispanic women who declare themselves heavy drinkers are usually employed outside of the home, are more often born in the United States, and report a higher degree of acculturation. However, this same author points out that there is very little heavy drinking reported among Latino/Hispanic women in general, with 70% reporting little or no drinking in a given month. So, most Hispanic women do not drink much, but those drinking heavily are more closely aligned with the values of Euro-American women and are found working outside the home. Single Hispanic females who were the heads of the households reported an increased frequency of alcohol use over those females in dual-headed families (Stroup-Benham, Trevino, & Trevino, 1989). Moreover, Latino/Hispanic women who reported being pregnant and battered used more alcohol than their pregnant, non-battered counterparts (Berenson, Stiglich, Wilkenson, & Anderson, 1991).

Psychological Risk Factors

Bettes et al. (1990) reported that Mexican-American youth were found to have the lowest ratings of internal locus of control when compared with other youth. The perception of being in control may depend upon the degree of acculturation, so that a higher level of internal locus of control would likely reflect increased feelings of social adequacy and environmental mastery. Language deficiencies can severely limit one's sense of personal autonomy and perceived control, which can be reinforced if the Latino/Hispanic individual does not see much hope for economic, social, or educational improvement. The shame associated with economic and educational deprivation can exacerbate lowered feelings of self-worth and put Latino/Hispanic individuals at psychological risk for substance abuse. Moreover, the risk for substance abuse can be heightened when one experiences a conflict of values between one's family members or close friends. For example, in a study of Cuban American women who reported tranquilizer use, Kirby (1989) found that reasons for use included stress resulting from having to balance work with traditional Cuban values (for example, maintaining the household and assuming total responsibility for childcare). These women also reported "extreme conflict" over these stressful roles and used drugs to "soothe nerves."

Helping Culturally and Ethnically Diverse Populations

Issues for the Helping Professionals

Mental health professionals are taught to empathize with their client or clients. Moreover, helping professionals are taught to avoid power struggles and coercive relationships with their clients. Power struggles can come in many forms, and stereotyping is a subtle form of power that can be used to coerce clients of varying cultural and ethnic backgrounds. By labeling a group as having certain characteristics and certain drinking or other drug use patterns, one can create a cognitive paradigm in which to gather and filter information.

Empathy has been popularly defined as "walking in the other person's shoes." Often, when working with clients from cultures other than our own, we have little information about what kinds of shoes they wear, nor do we possess much information about the paths they are walking. Certainly, with some training, mental health professionals can learn to identify how their clients feel in certain situations and can learn to ascertain another's mood. When it comes to assessing alcohol and other drug use, knowledge of another's culture is critical. Because many individual members of these special populations have experienced economic and social oppression, the uninformed helping professional may be cast in the same light as are the bureaucratic institutions.

You, as a mental health professional, should take care to undertake an examination of your own world view regarding culturally and ethnically diverse groups. Ivey, Ivey, and Simek-Morgan (1993) state that your world view is the way that you and your clients make sense of things or make meaning of the world. These same authors go on to say that individuals make idiosyncratic meanings, but these individualized meanings also have universal human qualities. It is critical that you develop an awareness of how race/ethnicity, culture, and gender impact your view of the world. In describing "cultural intentionality," Ivey, Ivey, and Simek-Morgan suggest that mental health professionals (1) need to develop an ability and a willingness to generate additional thoughts, words, and behaviors in an effort to communicate with self and others within a given culture; (2) need to develop an ability to develop alternative thoughts, words, and behaviors in an effort to communicate with a variety of diverse groups across cultures; and (3) need to develop enhanced abilities to formulate plans, act on a variety of possibilities that may exist in a given culture, and reflect on these actions.

Assessment and Treatment Issues

Remember, this book is written for the generalist in the helping field, rather than for a specialist in the field of addictive behaviors. You will likely assess your client for the extent of involvement with alcohol and other drugs then refer him or her to a specialist if needed. In order to make an assessment, mental health professionals must understand how the client's culture views alcohol and other drug use. What may be defined as problematic drug use in a predominantly Euro-American culture may be viewed as normal in a nonwhite culture. For example, an Asian American's frank confrontation with his or her boss when both are drunk is considered appropriate. Therefore, sharing with clients that you suspect a problem with their use of alcohol or another drug without an understanding of acceptable use in their culture may be incorrect. It may also be inappropriate. Your lack of knowledge may discourage the client from seeking further assistance from you or others in the helping services. If a problem did exist, you may have missed an opportunity to help. If there were a serious problem, it may become more serious.

The mental health professional's awareness of differing values is crucial when assessing for alcohol and other drug use and abuse. For example, in assessing Native American youth for alcohol and other drug abuse, it is necessary to examine the family's views toward alcohol. Those older individuals engaging in "serious drinking" patterns will likely have a deleterious effect upon the younger generation. Higher rates of alcoholism in Native American children can be expected when drinking supplants family interactions, celebrations, and other rituals. Mental health professionals can assess the extent of rituals and family interactions and attempt to reinforce their importance. Bi-cultural values will not cause psychological problems for children unless the parent has not resolved this conflict adequately. Children will also be affected by parents whose drinking reflects a bi-cultural lifestyle known as "White Man's drinking."

When working with Native Americans, remember that "Direct confrontation is limited to making sure the individual is aware of the consequences of behavior. Then, it is left to the innate forces within the individual to operate" (Attneave, 1982, p. 70). In terms of treatment, Weisner et al. (1984) point out that involvement in an alcoholism treatment program (either as a patient or as a counselor), membership in a church or Alcoholics Anonymous (AA), and the increased adherence to traditional Native American values appear to be the most significant factors in maintaining abstinence for the "teetotalers" group. Native Americans, as a whole, are active in their recovery from alcoholism and have been working on their addictions since the early 1960s. Many support groups exist on reservations, and traditional rituals such as the sweat lodge, the talking circle, prayer, and intervention by tribal leaders are now commonplace. The federally funded Indian Health Services and other local and state agencies, such as the Billy Rogers Wellness and Recovery Program at the University of Oklahoma, are active organizations helping Native Americans to recovery from alcoholism.

Bachman, Wallace, O'Malley, Johnson, Kurth, and Neighbors (1991) have shown that, in many instances, the Asian/Pacific Islander populations' use of most drugs is about half that of the Caucasian population. Alcohol is the exception. Rates for consumption more closely approximate that of Caucasians, and Burns and D'Avanzo (1993) suggest that if trends continue, it will not be long before drugs become a significant problem. Unfortunately, there is a stigma attached to seeking professional treatment in the Asian/Pacific Islander population, and Sue (1987) points out that these folks are less likely than other groups to seek treatment for alcoholism. If, when assessing Asian/Pacific Islanders, you determine that an individual might benefit from treatment, remember that your suggestions for treatment need to be addressed through the father or elder who will be making the decision for himself or for other family members. Whatever intervention is agreed upon, there needs to be an element of cultural sensitivity and bi-lingualism. There are DUI classes for Asian/Pacific Islanders and AA groups exist for Japanese speaking individuals.

Assessing African Americans for alcohol and other drug abuse varies from that of other culturally and ethnically diverse populations. For example, in assessing a middle-aged African American male who reports drinking heavily at the local tavern with friends on Saturday, mental health professionals might be well advised to suggest that a friend drive him home rather than referring him for assessment and potential treatment. Moreover, Hines and Boyd-Franklin (1982) assert that African Americans are often reluctant to trust the mental health care system. It has been reported that African Americans lack information about the harmful effects of alcohol, are less likely to perceive alcohol as a primary disease requiring treatment, and are less likely to seek treatment (Bourne, 1973; Harper, 1978; 1976). A 1981 study focused upon the drinking practices in two San Francisco

African American neighborhoods found that addiction to alcohol was perceived as a weakness in the will (Lipscomb and Trochi, 1981). Emotional difficulties are often seen as "wages of sin." This view of alcohol and emotional problems might explain why African Americans are more likely to turn to families, friends, ministers, and others in times of crisis, the network of help that generally applies regardless of socioeconomic status. For those African Americans in the lower socioeconomic classes, therapy may be viewed as being for "crazy people." Such a view often causes a significant delay in seeking services (McAdoo, 1979). Accompanying this view can be a tendency for those in the lower socioeconomic class to be suspicious of mental health professionals—especially those who ask too many intrusive questions. Nevertheless, African Americans do seem to be seeking services in greater numbers, and their reasons for seeking help do include alcohol and other drug-related problems.

Traditional values may influence efforts to assess alcohol and other drug use in the Latino/Hispanic population. The traditional concept of *machismo* implies that Latino/Hispanic women are not to drink. Yet they do, and younger Latino/Hispanic women are experimenting with alcohol in greater numbers. Many older women may be reluctant to report substance abuse because of the shame associated not only with their loss of control but also with their violation of tradition. So, when assessing for substance abuse in Latino/Hispanic individuals it is important, if not crucial, to determine the extent of the client's acculturation.

Because of the strong value placed on children, an assessment of alcohol and other drug abuse in the Latino/Hispanic population should include referral to a facility where there is childcare or where frequent visits by children are allowed. Without such a consideration, the Latino/Hispanic woman's fear of losing her children may pose significant barriers to treatment. Initial assessment of drug use by Latino/Hispanic women might focus on the impact of use on the family system, and especially the impact on the children.

Ironically, approaching men through the *machismo* value may prove effective in assessing use. While *machismo* allows for heavy drinking, being a strong family provider is also valued and often stands in direct opposition to excessive drinking behavior. By focusing upon the man's need to be a strong provider and a good role model for his sons especially, the helping professional may be able to help the Latino/Hispanic father determine whether a problem exists. Finally, the Latino/Hispanic population generally is a religious one and includes traditional and nontraditional religious practices with many Cuban Americans and Puerto Ricans following nontraditional practices. Assessment and referrals should include attention paid to services offered by churches and facilities that allow for a variety of religious practices.

Summary

It is hoped that you can begin to see the difficulties encountered when attempting to describe the alcohol and other drug use patterns of a given special population.

The methodological problems alone take on geometrical proportions when you consider the enormous intra-group differences that exist. The cultural differences existing in the Native American and Alaska Native populations are as varied as those in the Hispanic culture in which Puerto Ricans differ from Cuban Americans who differ from Mexican-Americans. The alcohol and other drug use patterns in Japan differ from those in China, which differ from those practiced by some Southeast Asian groups and Pacific Island populations. Moreover, there is a large element in the African American population who abstain from alcohol, and there is a significant element in that same population who drink heavily. As with all the other populations presented in this chapter, research results need to be considered carefully so as to glean an accurate understanding of what is known about a group and to avoid the deleterious effects of stereotyping.

Chapter 5

Assessment and Diagnosis

A few years ago, we were supervising a marriage and family therapy intern in our clinic at the university. The intern had just seen her first client and was eager to show the videotape of her session during supervision. The client was a middle-aged woman whose presenting problem was management of her seven-year-old son. The intern was excited about working with the woman because the intern had experience with a structured program for parenting skills and, therefore, thought that she knew exactly what to do to help. The intern asked a few questions about the discipline techniques the client used and gathered a little information on the family constellation. She then described the type of parenting strategies that they could work on in counseling. In watching the tape of the session, we noticed how anxious the client appeared to be, and it seemed that she was not really absorbing the information the counselor was presenting. We asked the intern whether she were sure that she had identified the correct problem. The intern seemed surprised because the client had clearly stated that she needed help with the discipline of her child and had given many examples that illustrated her difficulties with parenting. As the third session began, the client immediately began to cry and told the intern that she thought she was alcoholic.

If you know anything about the counseling process, you probably can identify several problems with this description of counseling. You might attribute the interns' actions to inexperience and a desire to demonstrate success. However, imagine yourself working as a school counselor or in a community mental health agency. You have an extremely heavy case load and see people for a variety of problems, so you feel pressured to make a rapid determination of the problem and to come up quickly with interventions. When a client comes in with a clear statement of the issue and you are familiar with a course of action, it may not occur to you that there is an unstated problem. You are thinking, "Great. I know how to handle this in only a few sessions. Then I can go on to the next person."

Many clients attribute their problems to something other than alcohol or other drugs or, if concerned about their use, the client may be hesitant to discuss these concerns until they feel comfortable with the mental health professional. For example, a client comes to a mental health center complaining of depression. A recent relationship has ended, and the therapist works with the client on grief and loss. The therapist never finds out that the client is a frequent cocaine user. Or, a high school student makes an appointment with the school counselor supposedly to discuss his schedule, when in reality he wants to talk about his increasing use of LSD but wants to "check out" the counselor first.

In any counseling or helping situation, the best methods to identify the "real" problem are to establish a trusting relationship with clients and to conduct a thorough assessment. In your counseling skills classes, you learn about the facilitative conditions that are necessary to build a trusting relationship (i.e., warmth, respect, positive regard, empathic understanding). Hopefully, you have also learned about the assessment process. In this chapter, we will focus on the assessment that any helping professional can (and should) perform, with an emphasis on the signs and symptoms that would indicate the possible existence of an alcohol or other drug problem. In keeping with the goals of this text, the purpose of this discussion of assessment is to ensure that school counselors, social workers, mental health counselors, marriage and family therapists, rehabilitation counselors, and other helping professionals will *always* consider the possibility of alcohol and other drug problems in the normal assessment process. We believe that the prevalence of alcohol and other drug problems in our society necessitates their consideration as a causal or contributing factor with nearly every client. We are not presenting an assessment protocol specific to alcohol and other drug problems, because this type of assessment would be conducted by those involved in the treatment of alcohol and other drug problems. However, we will describe some of the tests that are used in the assessment process so you will be aware of the advantages and disadvantages of these tools.

We also want to discuss the diagnosis of alcohol and other drug problems. Helping professionals need to be aware of the criteria that are used to determine whether someone is or is not chemically dependent. However, awareness does not imply competence in reaching diagnostic decisions. Assessment is the process of gathering information, and diagnosis is the conclusion that is reached on the basis of the assessment. Therefore, we strongly recommend that you refrain from diagnosis unless you have had thorough training specific to assessment and diagnosis of substance use disorders.

Definitions of Use, Misuse, Abuse, and Dependence/Addiction

For most helping professionals who do not have extensive training in the alcohol and other drug field, it is somewhat difficult to determine whether a client's substance use is or is not problematic. They may rely on personal experience and information (or misinformation) they pick up. For example, a high school counselor gets a call from a parent of one of the students. The young man is 17 years old, came home from a party on Saturday night smelling of alcohol, and admitted to drinking at the party. His parents belong to a religious group that prohibits the use of alcohol, so neither has any experience with alcohol or other drug use. They want to know whether their son has a problem. The high school counselor did her share of experimentation in adolescence but is a moderate user as an adult. She assures the parents that nearly all adolescents experiment and they have nothing to worry about. Is she right?

A simple conceptualization of the distinction between different levels of use can be helpful to the mental health professional in determining the type of intervention that is appropriate for a client. However, these definitions are not appropriate for diagnosis. They simply are a guide for the mental health professional in recommending the course of action for a client.

Nearly everyone uses alcohol or other drugs (including caffeine and tobacco) at some point in their lives. We define *use* as the ingestion of alcohol or other drugs without the experience of any negative consequences. If our high school student had drunk a beer at the party and his parents had not found out, we could say that he had used alcohol. Any drug can be *used* according to this definition. However, the type of drug taken and the characteristics of the individual contribute to the probability of experiencing negative consequences. For example, it is illegal for minors to drink alcohol. Therefore, the probability that our high school student will experience negative consequences from drinking alcohol may be far greater than that probability is for an adult. The chances that an adult will experience negative consequences from shooting heroin are greater than experiencing negative consequences from drinking alcohol.

When a person experiences negative consequences from the use of alcohol or other drugs, it is defined as *misuse*. Again, a large percentage of the population misuses alcohol or other drugs at some point. Our high school student misused alcohol because his parents found out he had been drinking at a party and because it is illegal for him to drink. Many people overuse alcohol at some point, become ill, and experience the symptoms of a hangover. This is misuse. However, misuse does not imply that the negative consequences are minor. Let's say that an adult woman uses alcohol on an infrequent basis. It is her 30th birthday, and her friends throw a surprise party. She drinks more than usual and, on the way home, is arrested for a DUI. She really doesn't have any problems with alcohol, but, in this instance, the consequence is not minor.

You may be wondering about the heavy user of alcohol or other drugs who does not *appear* to experience negative consequences. First of all, remember that these definitions are meant to provide the helping professional with a simple conceptualization as a guide. Second, the probability of experiencing negative consequences is directly related to the frequency and level of use. If a person uses alcohol or other drugs on an occasional basis, the probability of negative consequences is far less than if one uses on a daily basis. However, since we are talking about probability, it is possible that a person could be a daily, heavy user and not experience negative consequences that are obvious to others. We say "obvious" because a person may be damaging his or her health without anyone's being aware of this for a long period of time.

We define *abuse* as the continued use of alcohol or other drugs in spite of negative consequences. Our high school student is grounded for two weeks by his parents. Right after his grounding is completed, he goes to a party and drinks again. He continues to drink in spite of the consequences he experienced. Now, he might become more sneaky and escape detection. However, as we discussed previously, the probability of detection increases the more he uses and, if he does have a problem with alcohol, it is likely that his use will be discovered. As another example, let's go back to the woman who was arrested for a DUI after her birthday party. For people who do not have an alcohol or other drug problem, getting a DUI would be so disturbing that they would avoid alcohol altogether or use only at home. If, a month after the DUI, the woman was at another party or a bar drinking when she would be driving, this is considered abuse.

Addiction/dependence is the *compulsive* use of alcohol or other drugs regardless of the consequences. We worked with a man who had received three DUIs in one year. He was on probation and would be sentenced to one year in prison if he were caught using alcohol. But, he continued to drink. The man was clearly addicted to alcohol, because the negative consequences did not impact his use.

The relationship between the level of intervention and these definitions can be illustrated with our high school student. If the assessment (which will be described in this chapter) indicates that the student "misused" alcohol, he may need to suffer a significant consequence to impress upon him the fact that drinking by minors is illegal and unacceptable. He may also need education about the effects and consequences of alcohol use. Furthermore, the student may also need counseling or social skills training if his use is related to peer pressure or to a desire to fit in. If the assessment indicates that he has been abusing alcohol, a referral to a treatment program or helping professional who specializes in alcohol and other drug problems may be the appropriate intervention. Obviously, if he has been using alcohol in a compulsive manner, referral to a treatment program is appropriate.

Continuum of Use

Although the definitions of use, misuse, abuse, and dependence/addiction provide a rough conceptual framework for the helping professional, it would be erroneous to perceive these categories as discrete. Substance use can more reasonably be viewed as a continuum. Lewis, Dana, and Blevins (1994) present such a continuum with six categories of alcohol and other drug use: (1) nonuse; (2) moderate, nonproblematic use; (3) heavy, nonproblematic use; (4) heavy use associated with moderate life problems; (5) heavy use associated with serious life problems; and (6) substance dependence associated with life and health problems. To integrate our definitions with this continuum, *use* would exist after *nonuse* and before the experience of *life problems*. *Misuse* would occur between *nonproblematic use* and *moderate problems*, and *abuse* between *moderate problems* and *dependence*. Although we might prefer different labels for some categories (i.e., given our definition of *misuse*, the category of *heavy, nonproblematic use* is unlikely), the concept of a continuum can be helpful in understanding the alcohol and other drug use of clients. However, as we discussed in Chapter 3, it would be inappropriate to assume that there is an inevitable progression along the continuum. The mental health professional must conduct a thorough assessment to determine a client's placement on the continuum and then decide on the appropriate intervention given the level of use, life problems, and relevant client characteristics.

Psycho-Social History

We assume that you have taken (or will take) a course in assessment as part of your training program and have learned (or will learn) that a psycho-social history is a critical part of the assessment process, regardless of the client's presenting problem. We want to focus on the information that you would gather on the psycho-social history that may relate to alcohol and other drug use problems. However, a couple of remarks related to assessment in general and the psycho-social history in particular are necessary first.

Assessment is a process that should be on-going during counseling, and a helping professional should be continually gathering information that will assist the client. The psycho-social history is a structured method of gathering information in areas that may relate to the client's difficulties. This method insures that a helping professional rules out possible causal factors. However, a psycho-social history is not an interrogation. A helping professional must use the same facilitative skills in a structured interview as would be used in any counseling situation. Certainly, the nature of a psycho-social history necessitates that the interviewer ask questions. However, if the helping professional asks a series of questions without sensitivity to the client, the relationship may be damaged, and the interviewer may elicit resistance from the client that would hinder the assessment process. The helping professional should tell a client that the purpose of a psycho-social history is to learn as much about him or her as possible so that the best service can be provided. Often, the analogy of a physician gathering a complete health history before seeing a patient makes sense to clients. Also, it is best to begin a psycho-social history with areas that are the *least likely* to be threatening to a client.

Every assessment should consider individual characteristics and group differences of clients and, in Chapter 4, we discussed alcohol and other drug issues specific to various ethnically diverse groups. Although it would be erroneous to make *a priori* assumptions about clients from ethnically diverse groups, the interviewer must be aware of group differences and must account for these differences during the assessment. The notion of cultural relativism discussed in Chapter 4 may be helpful in this regard.

Finally, we know that there are situations in which a complete psycho-social history is impractical. For example, a school counselor is rarely in a position to gather such a history due to time constraints, lack of access to the information, or to the restraints of confidentiality. Parents may not be willing to see the school counselor, or a student may ask that the counselor refrain from contacting parents or teachers. In such cases, the helping professional should gather as much information as possible but should exercise caution in reaching conclusions with incomplete information. While real-world barriers are not excuses for poor practice, these barriers do exist and must be acknowledged. However, helping professionals should make every effort to gather a complete psycho-social history to avoid missing the real problem.

With these parameters in mind, we will discuss the areas to be assessed in a psycho-social history and the signs and symptoms of alcohol and other drug use issues related to these areas. As we stated earlier, the prevalence of alcohol and other drug problems necessitates consideration of these problems as a causal or contributing factor in most client difficulties. However, it would also be an error to believe that all client problems are caused by or related to alcohol and other drugs. If you want to do a competent job of assessment, you should be open to a variety of possible explanations.

Alcohol and Other Drug Use History

We suggested beginning the psycho-social history with an area that is least likely to elicit client resistance and an alcohol and other drug use history would generally not fit this criterion. Therefore, we suggest that you do not begin the interview with this history. However, it certainly is the most direct manner to assess alcohol and other drug problems. Clearly, assessment of substance use problems through direct questions about client use requires honesty and accuracy from the client, but this is true with regard to all areas of the psycho-social history. Certainly, some clients minimize their use, particularly if they perceive a problem. However, it is surprising how often clients report heavy use and do not perceive it as a problem or minimize their actual use when it is excessive compared to others.

Clients should be asked "How much (alcohol, marijuana, cocaine, etc.) do you use?" rather than "Do you use (alcohol, marijuana, cocaine, etc.)?" While the latter question elicits a "yes" or "no," the former question is more open-ended. For example, when one client was asked how much alcohol he used, he said, "Not much. About as much as most guys." Follow-up revealed that this was two to three cases of beer a week.

The interviewer should ask about use in each of the psychoactive drug classifications mentioned in Chapter 2. Don't assume—based on gender, ethnicity, appearance, or other characteristics—that a client is involved only with certain drugs. Also, don't forget to ask about tobacco use. Clients should be questioned regarding quantity of use, frequency, setting (alone, at home, with friends), the methods used to procure their supply (e.g., from friends, purchased, stolen, or in exchange for sex), and the route of administration (e.g., ingestion, snorting, smoking, intravenously). With adolescents, it is helpful to ask what drugs their friends use, particularly if they deny their own use, since having friends who use is predictive of adolescent drug problems (Hawkins, Lishner, Catalano, & Howard, 1986).

The alcohol and drug use history of a client is helpful to determine progression (or lack thereof) on the continuum of use and because age of first use (prior to age

15) is also predictive of later problems (Robins & Przybeck, 1985). With regard to progression, clients who report little or no use should be asked whether there were times when their use was heavy. If so, what occurred to change this pattern—treatment, maturity, life changes, or some other event? If their use is currently heavy, how long has it been at this level? Has there been a gradual or sudden increase in use?

The information in this and other chapters of this book should be helpful to you in determining whether the client's reported use is problematic. However, one simple rule may be helpful. Ask yourself this question, "Does a normal drinker (user) drink (use) as this client does?" To answer this question, you must have some knowledge of "normal" and consider the client's *age, gender, ethnicity,* and other characteristics. For example, you are interviewing a 47-year-old man who suffered a back injury in his construction job and is applying for vocational rehabilitation. He reports drinking a six-pack of beer each night and two cases on the weekend. He has a stable marriage, has never been arrested, and had stable employment until his injury. Does he have a problem? Or, a 20-year-old college junior was found in possession of a quarter ounce of marijuana in his dorm room. He and his friends smoke on the weekend. He does not drink alcohol, and he began his marijuana use last year. You are a college counselor, and you must determine the type of intervention or discipline required. Does he have a problem? Maybe you are a probation officer. One of your clients is a 27-year-old, African-American man who lives in an urban area. He was involved in a fight in a bar and was arrested. He drinks alcohol on Friday and Saturday nights and usually drinks to the point of intoxication. His drinking started at age 18 and he does not use other drugs, except tobacco. Does he have a problem?

Does a normal drinker (user) do what these individuals do? Our 47-year-old beer drinker is a heavy drinker with no reported problems. Based on what you have learned about alcohol in Chapter 2, you should know that this level of alcohol use on a daily basis is not normal. If the man has no other problems at this time (which would be surprising, but possible), he will probably have physical problems from his alcohol use in the future. The situation with the college student and probation client are less clear. They have both experienced problems related to their use of alcohol and other drugs. However, we also must consider the social and cultural context of their use. The probation client may have an alcohol problem or he may have a problem with his social group, expectations for male behavior in his culture, etc. The college student may be using marijuana in a manner that is quite consistent with his social group and does not result in any difficulties, with the exception of the illegality of the drug. The rest of their psycho-social histories may help clarify the extent of their problems.

Family History

A psycho-social interview will always have some focus on the client's current family constellation and family of origin. With regard to alcohol and other drug problems, it is well known that a history of alcoholism or other drug addiction in the family of origin is a risk factor for substance abuse (e.g., Hawkins, et al., 1986). However, it is best to ask the client if there were any problems in the family with regard to alcohol or other drugs rather than asking if the parents were (are) alcoholic or drug addicted. The client may be unable to make such a diagnosis, and a perceived stigma to such labels might make the client hesitant to apply these labels.

A variety of problems in families may be related to alcohol and other drug problems (as well as other problems). These include physical and sexual abuse. Since studies have found that as many as 75% of women in alcohol treatment programs have been sexually molested (Rohsenow, Corbett, & Devine, 1988), this is particularly important to assess with women clients. Other types of family problems including financial difficulties, communication problems, and excessive conflict may be caused by or related to alcohol and other drug use, so these issues should be assessed.

Often clients will report a divorce in the family of origin or current family or the death of a parent or caretaker. The psycho-social interviewer should investigate such events further. For example, a client may say that her parents divorced when she was young because her father was "irresponsible." The interviewer should attempt to determine whether alcohol or other drugs contributed to this "irresponsibility." A parent's death in an automobile accident may have been caused by substance abuse, as well.

The importance of assessing alcohol and other drug use in the family of origin and current family is not restricted to the client's own use. As we will discuss in Chapter 11, children who live in substance-abusing homes and adult children who were raised by alcoholic or other drug-addicted caretakers may have a variety of problems as a result. There is also the whole issue of codependency, which will be discussed in Chapter 12. Although codependency is a controversial issue in the field, it is certainly the case that some individuals are attracted to people with alcohol and other drug problems and tend to repeatedly choose such people as partners. Therefore, a positive family history of alcohol or other drug abuse may help explain the current problems of some clients, even if the clients have no alcohol or other drug use problems of their own.

Social History

When the senior author was in a master's program in school psychology, he was seeing a couple for marriage counseling in the university clinic. One of the wife's complaints was that the husband never wanted to go out or have any friends over. This was quite a change from when they first got together. After fumbling around for several sessions and trying some behavioral contracts to increase their social activity (which didn't work), the husband admitted that he was happier sitting at home with his beer and watching TV. The author, who had no training in the alcohol and other drug field at the time, did not know what to do. His supervisors (who also had no training in the alcohol and other drug field) suggested some ways to make the marriage more exciting so that the husband would be more interested in his wife than in TV and beer. Is it surprising that the couple finally became frustrated with counseling and terminated?

Individuals who have progressed in their alcohol or other drug abuse may go through a gradual change in social activities and relationships. There may be a shift to friends who use in the same manner as the client, while non-using friends are dropped. Parents of adolescents will frequently notice this, although the reason for the change in social groups may not be identified by the parents. Eventually, more and more isolation may occur if the social group does not "keep up."

Clients (or significant others) may report that previously enjoyed activities have been discontinued, which may be attributed to depression in adults and rebellion in adolescents. We worked with an adult who had been an avid snorkler but had greatly reduced his involvement as his alcohol and tobacco use progressed. An adolescent client had been involved in the school band but had dropped out and was spending his spare time playing his guitar in his room as a result of heavy methamphetamine use.

It is also important to assess the client's relationship history for involvement with partners who have alcohol or other drug problems. This may provide some evidence for codependency (see Chapter 12). One of our clients was a woman in her mid 30s who was referred by a state agency for depression following a disabling injury that prevented her from working. She was involved in a 10-year relationship with a polydrug abuser and had previously lived with an addict who had been murdered. Her father was alcoholic. In discussing relationships with this client, we found that she had absolutely no idea that it was possible to have a relationship with a man who did not abuse alcohol or other drugs. In treating this client, the social history was important since a good deal of her depression was related to the fact that she could no longer support herself, and she thought that she would be forever dependent on alcoholic and drug-addicted men.

Legal History

There is nothing very complicated about a client's report of DUIs or arrests for public intoxication or possession or distribution of drugs. However, as we discussed in Chapter 1, there is a relationship between all types of criminal behavior and alcohol and other drug use. Therefore, a client's report of a history of shoplifting, assault, robbery, burglary, and other crimes may indicate alcohol or other drug problems. With adolescents, status offenses such as running away, truancy, curfew violations, and incorrigibility may be symptoms of substance abuse problems. Although this area seems very straightforward in a psycho-social assessment, we find it is the most frequently neglected. This may be due to the interviewer's own hesitancy to ask such questions.

Educational History

This is a particularly important area to assess with adolescents. Hawkins, et al. (1986) found that academic failure and lack of commitment to school were risk factors for adolescent substance abuse. In addition, Karacostas and Fisher (1993) found that a higher proportion of students identified as learning disabled were classified as chemically dependent compared with non-learning disabled students. Finally, Archambault (1992) includes the following signs of adolescent substance abuse: truancy, absenteeism, incomplete assignments, sudden drop in grades, verbal abuse toward teachers or classmates, and vandalism.

With adolescents, it is particularly important to determine whether there has been a change in behavior or academic performance over time. In particular, a change that occurs from the elementary grades to middle or high school may suggest alcohol or other drug involvement. Because school counselors may be gathering information in this area from cumulative files, teachers, and parents, they should be particularly attentive to this issue of change. In addition to the signs noted by Archambault (1992), there may be an increase in suspensions or expulsions, fights, or stealing. Teachers may indicate problems with the student's falling asleep in class, belligerence, or increasing withdrawal.

A retrospective report from adults of these kinds of school problems may indicate past or current alcohol and other drug problems. In addition to inquiring about behavioral and academic issues, the mental health professional should ask whether the client has a history of dropping out of educational programs, including post-secondary institutions.

Educational history can be particularly helpful with a young adult (18 to 25) who is being seen for presenting problems unrelated to alcohol and other drug abuse. For example, we assessed a 24-year-old man who had been hit by a car while riding his bike. Some brain damage had resulted, and the man had requested vocational rehabilitation services. The assessment was to determine his cognitive and academic capabilities. During the psycho-social history, the man reported increasing academic problems in high school although he had graduated. Subsequently, he started and dropped out of college three times. He admitted to being under the influence of LSD when the accident occurred (no one had ever asked him if he was using). He had also begun heavy alcohol and other drug use in his junior year in high school and continued to be a heavy user of alcohol and hallucinogens.

Occupational History

With many adults, work history may indicate more current problems with alcohol and other drugs than an educational history that occurred long ago. However, the same types of issues (poor performance, behavioral, and attitudinal problems) that we discussed regarding school may occur in the work setting. For example, frequent job changes, terminations, and reports of unsatisfactory performance may be noted. For a person who maintained a job for an extended period of time, there may be a report of a gradual progression of deteriorating performance. There may also be frequent absenteeism, moodiness and irritability, uncharacteristic displays of anger, and deteriorating relationships with supervisors and colleagues. For those of you who get involved in employee assistance programs (see Chapter 9), a good indication that an employee may have a substance abuse problem is frequent absence from work on Mondays (perhaps the employee has been involved in heavy use on the weekend and is too hung over or too tired to come to work).

Underemployment may be reported by a client whose alcohol or other drug use has progressed to a problematic level. A client may gradually seek jobs that require less responsibility, skills, or time as their substance use impairs their ability to perform at work, and their alcohol and other drug use becomes the primary preoccupation.

Military history should also be addressed. Alcohol, marijuana, and heroin were frequently abused in Vietnam and many veterans from this era returned to the United States with alcohol and other drug problems. Furthermore, stressful military experiences and the subsequent development of emotional problems may put a veteran at risk for difficulties with alcohol and other drugs.

Medical History

Not only do alcohol and other drugs cause some specific ailments, but people who abuse substances get sick more often. For example, alcohol abuse results in lowered immunity to infection. Also, substance abusers may not be as attentive to nutrition and exercise as those who abstain or use in a nonabusive manner. Furthermore, there is a relationship between substance abuse and injuries caused by accidents that result from impaired judgment, perception, coordination, reaction time, and by violence. Therefore, a medical history that includes frequent illnesses and/or accidents may indicate substance abuse problems.

In Chapter 2, we discussed some of the medical problems associated with the abuse of different drugs. For example, if a client reports a medical history that includes gastritis, peptic ulcers, or a fatty liver, the mental health professional should certainly suspect alcohol abuse. You should also keep in mind that the long-term use of legal drugs (alcohol and tobacco) may result in medical problems in clients who show no other symptoms of substance abuse.

Psychological and Behavioral Problems

When people see a mental health professional, either of their own volition or through some form of coercion, they may not recognize a causal relationship between their presenting problem and substance abuse. For example, a woman came to see us at the insistence of her husband. She had symptoms of depression, and the husband had threatened to leave her if she did not get help. The woman's physician had prescribed an antidepressant, but this had not helped. During the psycho-social assessment, we learned that the woman used alcohol and Valium on a daily basis.

The common problems cited by people seeking assistance from mental health professionals may be due to or exacerbated by alcohol or other drug use. Depression, anxiety, panic attacks, mood swings, irritability, outbursts of anger, problems in sleeping and eating, excessive gambling, sexual dysfunction, etc. may be related to substance abuse. However, we are not implying that all psychological and behavioral problems are due to substance abuse. Certainly, a client could present with any of the problems we have listed and have no substance abuse problem at all. Nor are we saying that, if there is alcohol or other drug abuse, it is always the cause of the client's problems. A client may be highly anxious for some reason and begin to use alcohol or other drugs to relieve the symptoms of anxiety. Even if the client stopped using, he or she would still be anxious if the cause of the anxiety still existed. However, the client's use can become a *contributing factor* to the anxiety and must, therefore, be a focus of treatment.

If your reaction to reading this section is, "You seem to be saying that every problem I might see as a mental health professional could be related to alcohol and other drug use," you get an *A*. That's why we are stressing the assessment of alcohol and other drug use and are providing information on the signs of substance abuse that you may find on taking a psycho-social history. Ruling out substance abuse as a contributing or causal factor can save you and your clients time, frustration, and (often) money. Furthermore, given the frequency of these problems, we believe it is simply an element of good practice.

Signs of Adolescent Substance Abuse

Although many of the areas of the psycho-social history may be useful with adults and adolescents in determining the probability of an alcohol or other drug problem, there are additional signs of adolescent substance abuse. Since adolescents may not have experienced the variety or the severity of life problems as adults have, the typical psycho-social history may not assess some of these signs. However, a careful assessment of adolescents who are experiencing school or home problems is important in order to intervene in the adolescent's use pattern before more serious problems occur.

Fisher and Harrison (1992) described a protocol for the assessment of alcohol and other drug abuse with adolescents who are referred in a school setting. Those of you preparing for careers as school counselors or school social workers might find these procedures useful. As part of this protocol, the authors recommend that assessment procedures involve a careful examination of changes in the adolescent's behavior in a variety of areas. As we discussed in the educational history section of the psycho-social history, these changes may involve a deterioration in academic performance, increased absenteeism and truancy, fighting, verbal abuse, defiance, or withdrawal. In addition, it is important to look at the adolescent's social relationships. There may be less and less involvement with friends who do not use and more involvement with peers who are users. The adolescent may identify with a particular school group that typically uses (i.e., "I'm a stoner"). There may be a decreasing involvement and interest in previously enjoyed activities such as athletics or social groups. Furthermore, adolescents may gravitate toward music and dress that depict alcohol and other drug use in a positive manner or are associated with substance-using adolescents. Adolescents may need money to support their use and turn to stealing, selling possessions, or dealing drugs. In the latter instance, parents and teachers may become aware that the adolescent has a large amount of cash at various times that cannot be adequately explained. Finally, it should go without saying that if an adolescent is in possession or under the influence, a problem exists. It is the severity of the problem that must be assessed.

It is often difficult to differentiate adolescent behavior that may indicate alcohol or other drug problems from normal adolescent behavior. If you tell a group of parents that defiance and changes in friends can be signs of adolescent substance abuse, they may all send their children for drug testing. It is important for a mental health professional who works with adolescents to have a thorough understanding of adolescent development to differentiate "normal" adolescent behavior from unusual behavior and to examine all areas of a psycho-social history as well as the additional signs of adolescent substance abuse. It would be an error to isolate one or two signs and attach undue importance to them. For example, if a lot of kids at school are wearing T-shirts with the insignias of beer companies and a child buys one, this does not mean that he or she is using or abusing alcohol (However, we do encourage everyone to express their disapproval of this type of drug advertising). As with the assessment of any individual, you should consider all the information you gather before making a judgment.

Self-Report Inventories

There are many screening and assessment[1] devices and protocols that have been developed to help a clinician determine if a client has a substance abuse problem. Many of these devices and protocols have been designed for use in substance-abuse treatment programs to determine whether a client is appropriate for treatment and the type of treatment setting and services that would be the most appropriate. It is beyond the objectives of this text to discuss these various devices and protocols, but the interested reader will find reviews of the most frequently used screening and assessment devices and procedures in Jacobson (1989), Cooney, Zweben, and Fleming (1995), and Miller, Westerberg, and Waldron (1995). We will discuss four self-report inventories that are frequently used in both substance-abuse treatment and generalist settings. Since these instruments may be used for diagnostic purposes, they should be used only by professionals who have formal training in assessment and diagnosis and who have specific training in the diagnosis of substance-use disorders. In addition, access to some assessment devices is restricted to certain levels of professional training (e.g., MacAndrew Alcoholism Scale of the MMPI).

---

[1]You should be aware that screening and assessment are different. Screening is usually a brief procedure used to identify individuals with possible problems or who are at risk for developing a problem. Assessment is a more thorough process that should involve multiple procedures and is designed to result in diagnostic, placement, and treatment decisions. The self-report inventories we are discussing are used for screening but also may be part of a thorough assessment.

Also, we want to caution you about self-report inventories in general. Certainly, as a part of a comprehensive assessment, self-report inventories can be useful. However, they are not meant to be used in isolation from other assessment data. Second, there is always a validity issue with any test, and self-report inventories are no exception. Since a self-report inventory is a test in which the client "self-reports," you cannot be sure that the client has responded in a truthful manner. Some tests have scales to detect intentional or unintentional distortions, but these are never foolproof. Also, the assumption is often made that the inventory is measuring what it is supposed to be measuring, and this may not always be the case, as we shall see in the following discussion of self-report inventories.

Michigan Alcohol Screening Test (MAST)

The MAST (Selzer, 1971) is a 24-item inventory of drinking habits that is simple to administer and score. It takes about 10 minutes when self-administered but can also be read to a client. Each item is scored "0" for a nondrinking response or, depending on the item, "1", "2", or "5" for a drinking response. The total possible score is 53. A score of 0 to 4 is considered to be nonalcoholic, 5 to 6 suggests an alcohol problem, 7 to 9 is alcoholism, 10 to 20 is moderate alcoholism, and above 20 is severe alcoholism. Examples of questions on the MAST are: "Does your wife, husband, a parent or other near relative ever worry or complain about your drinking?" (No = 0, Yes = 1), "Are you able to stop drinking when you want to?" (Yes = 0, No = 2), and "Have you ever attended a meeting of Alcoholics Anonymous?" (No = 0, Yes = 5).

Based on this sample of questions, you can see that the MAST would be easy to fake. The content of the questions is obvious and this results in many false negatives (client scores in the nonalcoholic category when there is in fact an alcohol problem). Jacobson (1989) reported that studies using a cutoff score of 5 resulted in a 21 to 34% false positive rate (indication of an alcohol problem when no problem actually exists). He suggested using a cutoff score of 12, which results in a 5 to 8% false-positive rate and a 7 to 12% false-negative rate. Obviously, the test is designed to measure only alcohol problems. It can be given to other family members (who are asked to respond about their perceptions of the client), and the results can be compared with the client's responses.

CAGE

This extremely short and simple screening instrument for alcohol problems was first reported by Ewing and Rouse (1970). The CAGE consists of four questions: each question associated with a letter in the name of the test: Have you ever felt the need to Cut down on your drinking? Have you ever felt Annoyed by someone criticizing your drinking? Have you ever felt bad or Guilty about your drinking? Have you ever had a drink first thing in the morning to steady your nerves and get rid of a hangover (Eye-opener)? Responding "yes" to two or more questions indicates an alcohol problem.

As might be expected from such a brief test with such obvious content, the results of studies evaluating the effectiveness of the CAGE in identifying alcoholics are quite mixed (Cooney, et al, 1995). Therefore, the CAGE should be viewed as a very rough screening and should be followed by further questioning when a respondent gives an affirmative answer to any item (Cooney, et al, 1995; Jacobson, 1989).

MacAndrew Alcoholism Scale of the MMPI

The MacAndrew Alcoholism Scale (MAC) is a special scale of the Minnesota Multiphasic Personality Inventory (MMPI). It was developed by MacAndrew (1965) and consists of 49 of the MMPI items that are all in a forced-choice, true/false format. Generally, the MMPI is computer scored, and a score for the MAC is reported with the other MMPI scales. Jacobson (1989) does indicate that the MacAndrew Scale can be administered separately from the rest of the MMPI and takes about 15 to 20 minutes to administer in this format. In contrast to the MAST, the MAC's content is indirect. In other words, the questions are not directly related to alcohol. This does make the MAC less susceptible to faking. "Unfortunately, the MAC . . . has no construct validity . . . we don't know what it really measures. Some sort of common underlying general addictive propensity has been suggested by the research literature, but this idea remains questionable" (Jacobson, 1989, p. 24). Therefore, although the MAC generates few false negatives, there is a high proportion of false positives (Jacobson, 1989). Furthermore, the scale name implies a focus on alcohol, but Butcher and Keller (1984) state that the MAC is "a measure of an individual's proneness to addiction" (p. 312).

Substance Abuse Subtle Screening Inventory (SASSI), (Miller, 1983)

Cooper and Robinson (1987) have criticized the MAST and the MAC because of "a continual lack of agreement on the most appropriate cutting score" and "the unacceptably high rate of misclassifications that researchers have found with both of these instruments" (p. 180). In addition, as has been previously noted, the content of the MAST is so obvious that it would fail to detect alcoholics who deny a problem (Fisher, Mason, & Fisher, 1976). As Cooper and Robinson (1987) noted

> What is needed . . . is a short, inexpensive assessment tool that can accurately differentiate chemical abusers from social drinkers and general psychiatric clients. In addition, the test would need to be unaffected by denial or attempts at impression management on the part of the client. The Substance Abuse Subtle Screening Inventory . . . was developed by Miller to achieve these ends. (p. 181)

The SASSI combines scales that measure obvious signs and symptoms of substance abuse with questions consisting of subtle attributes and items seemingly unrelated to substance use to categorize the client as "chemically dependent" or "not chemically dependent" (the terminology used in the SASSI). A series of "decision rules" guide the mental health professional in determining which classification fits. According to Creager (1989), the SASSI is being used in general mental health centers, university student health and mental health centers, employee assistance programs, addiction treatment programs, court-ordered substance abuse programs, and psychiatric and various medical programs. The SASSI takes 10 to 15 minutes to administer (self-report responses by the client orally or written or by computer) and takes only a few minutes to score. There is an adult version (ages 18 and above) and an adolescent form, with separate scoring norms by gender for each version. The reading level of the test is supposedly fifth grade, although Kerr (in press) indicates that it is probably higher. A comprehensive manual accompanies the test and training workshops are conducted frequently across the country.

As the SASSI combines attributes of the MAST and MAC and seems to be at the forefront of efforts to make the determination of substance abuse problems more sophisticated and psychometrically sound, some discussion of the scales and decision rules is warranted. Both the adult and adolescent forms of the SASSI have "Face Valid Alcohol (FVA)" (12 items) and "Face Valid Other Drugs (FVOD)" (14 items) scales. (On the original adult version, these scales were called "Risk Prediction Scales".) These scales resemble the MAST in that they consist of behavior directly and obviously related to alcohol and other drug use. For example, items on the FVA scale and FVOD scale respectively are, "Gotten into trouble on the job, in school, or at home because of drinking" and "Spent your spare time in drug-related activities (e.g., talking about drugs, buying, selling, taking, etc.)." These items are scored on a 4-point Likert scale (0 = never and 3 = repeatedly). Clients can be asked to respond to the items for the previous six months or for any time in their lives. Regardless of the form of the test or the gender of the clients, scores of at least 12 for life time or 10 for the previous six months results in a classification of chemically dependent.

The rest of the SASSI consists of true-false items (52 on the adult and 55 on the adolescent form), which are empirically derived to differentiate chemically dependent from nondependent clients. With a few exceptions, these items and the associated scales (described as follows) are not obviously related to alcohol and other drugs.

Obvious Attributes (OAT): This scale purports to measure the client's openness or willingness to admit to symptoms or problems related to substance abuse (e.g., I take all my responsibilities seriously).

Subtle Attributes Scale (SAT): A high score on the SAT scale is supposed to indicate a predisposition for chemical dependency. The personal "style" of the client with a high SAT score would be similar to chemically dependent individuals. The SAT is "critically important...because of its resistance to efforts at concealing problems...[and] is an effort to get at more subtle or pervasive personal patterns or styles than do the other measures" (Miller, 1985, p. 5–9).

Defensiveness (DEF): The DEF was originally called the Denial scale but was changed because it is seen as a measure of test-taking defensiveness rather than denial. A high score may be due to unconscious denial or deliberate attempts to fake. Low scores may indicate feelings of worthlessness and difficulty in accepting positive feedback.

Defensive Abuser vs Defensive Non-Abuser (DEF2): This scale is used in combination with the DEF scale to differentiate defensive responses of a chemically dependent client from defensive responses of a nonchemically dependent client.

In addition, there are two other adult scales. The *Alcohol vs Drug (ALD)* scale is designed to show whether a client prefers alcohol or other drugs, with high scores indicating a preference for alcohol and low scores a preference for other drugs. Miller (1985) gives the example of a client with a high FVA score and a low ALD score. The client may need education with regard to dangers of using other drugs as a substitute for alcohol. The *Family vs Controls (FAM)* scale was designed to determine the similarity of the client to family members of chemically dependent individuals. This was meant to be a preliminary measure of codependency.

On the adolescent form, there are also two additional scales. The *Correctional (COR)* is reportedly a measure of acting-out behavior. A high score matches the responses of adolescents in correctional settings. If an adolescent receives a high score, is not in a correctional setting, and is not classified as chemically dependent on the rest of the SASSI, the adolescent's acting out may be attributed to causes other than alcohol or other drug abuse. A similar scale is in the development stage for the adult version of the SASSI (Miller, 1994). Finally, there is a *Random Answering Pattern (RAP)* scale to detect random responding. This scale consists of items that nearly everyone would answer in the same way (e.g., "People always do the right thing"[2]). Responding to a number of these items in unusual manner indicates random responding or an overt attempt to distort results.

The scoring of the SASSI is quite simple. For the FVA and FVOD scales, the points for each item are added. For the other scales (oral or written administration), a template is used to determine the number of items that the client responds to in the scored direction. A profile form (males on one side and females on the other) is used to plot the client's scores, with raw scores converted to "T" scores (a "T" score is a standard score with a mean of 50 and a standard deviation of 10.). The conversion is computed for you on the profile form. On the same form are a series of "decision rules" that allow the clinician to determine whether the client should be classified as chemically dependent. These rules are progressive, so that if the first rule is negative for chemical dependency, the second rule is examined, and so on. For example, if the client achieves the cutoff score on the FVA or FVOD scales, he or she is classified as chemically dependent. If the cutoff score is not achieved, the clinician examines the scores on the OAT and SAT scales. If the "T" score on either scale is 70 or more (two standard deviations above the mean), the client is classified as chemically dependent. If both scales are below 70, the clinician goes on to the next rule.

---

[2]This item is not an actual item from the SASSI but is meant to illustrate the type of item on the RAP scale.

A review of the SASSI by Kerr (1994) indicates that the test does a fairly good job in identifying chemically dependent individuals. However, the FAM scale does not seem to be a valid measure of codependency. The internal consistency of the scales is low, which may be due to the method used in constructing the scales, but the test-retest reliability is acceptable. In discussing the clinical usefulness of the SASSI, Kerr (1994) states,

> *The SASSI is almost as good as its promotion claims it to be. It seems to have been responsibly developed, and it is clearly created with the practitioner in mind. Its ease of administration and scoring, its clear decision rules and suggestions for interpretation, and informative and carefully written manual all make it very attractive to mental health providers who have difficult and important decisions to make about treatment (p. 251).*

We have used the SASSI extensively and agree with Kerr. However, we would add some precautions. As useful as the SASSI is, a self-report inventory should *not* be used in isolation from other assessment techniques. Because of its ease of administration and scoring, we have found instances in which the SASSI is the *only* assessment technique used. Second, the use of the term *chemically dependent* may tempt mental health providers to diagnose on the basis of the SASSI. As we have previously stated, diagnosis should be made only by mental health providers with formal training and experience in the alcohol and other drug field and should be based on a comprehensive assessment. The fact that there is an adolescent form of the SASSI has made the test attractive to public school personnel. Although this is not a bad thing in and of itself, diagnosis of substance abuse problems is generally beyond the scope of practice of most mental health practitioners in public schools (e.g., school counselors, school social workers, and school psychologists).

For those individuals who are not qualified to diagnose but who wish to use the SASSI as part of an assessment, we suggest that the information from the SASSI be communicated to a client as follows: "Your scores are similar to those people who have alcohol or other drug problems." Whatever other data you have gathered that is consistent with this finding should also be provided. As we have said, the SASSI Institute offers training workshops in the scoring and interpretation of the SASSI, and we would recommend such a workshop before using the SASSI in clinical practice.

Referral

Earlier in this chapter, we gave an example of a high school senior (lets call him Tyrone) whose parents were concerned about an incident of alcohol use at a party. The parents contact you (the school counselor) and ask whether their son has a problem with alcohol. You interview the parents and Tyrone, contact his teachers to find out about his academic performance and behavior, review the cumulative file, and administer a SASSI. Based on the assessment, you have some reasons for concern. Although the parents do not use alcohol or other drugs because of their religious beliefs, the paternal grandfather and an uncle are alcoholic. Tyrone's grades have dropped, which the parents attributed to "senioritis." They have also been somewhat uncomfortable about some kids that Tyrone has been hanging around with. You really didn't know Tyrone before you interviewed him, at which time he was friendly but rather evasive. On the SASSI, he is almost, but not quite, classified chemically dependent based on his DEF and DEF2 scores. What should you do?

There does not seem to be enough evidence of a serious problem to justify a Johnson Model intervention (see Chapter 6). The concepts of motivational interviewing (see Chapter 6) would seem to be more appropriate. However, you may still be unsure about Tyrone's placement on the continuum of use, and you do not have the time to work with him individually. So, you want to refer Tyrone and his parents to someone or someplace outside the school. Certainly, asking colleagues for referral sources is great. However, we want to discuss a few guidelines in making referrals.

If you are unsure about the results of your assessment and want another opinion, you may refer clients to an many alcohol and other drug treatment program that conducts assessments. Often, these assessments are free of charge. However, you should be aware that assessments are a marketing tool of for-profit treatment programs. There may be a tendency for programs to find problems and refer to themselves. Therefore, you have a professional obligation to make sure that you are referring to a program that conducts objective assessments.

You may decide that Tyrone is in the "pre-contemplation stage" (see Chapter 6) and referral to an individual or agency is appropriate. Be sure that your referral source has the training and experience to work with alcohol and other drug-related problems, as it is erroneous to assume that all credentialed mental health professionals have this capability. In some states, licensure as a psychologist, marriage and family therapist, or other mental health professional does not require training in the alcohol and other drug field. Therefore, simply having a license in one of the helping professions does not guarantee expertise in the field.

Each state has an agency to coordinate alcohol and other drug treatment and prevention services. This agency will have a listing of all treatment programs and the services they offer. Generally, the state will have some sort of accrediting process for programs. Most, but not all, states also have a certification or licensing process for alcohol and other drug treatment providers. There should also be a record of complaints and/or sanctions imposed on credentialed counselors or programs. There is no guarantee that licensed or certified professionals or accredited programs will always be competent or that others would not do a good job. However, you are always safest in referring to an accredited program or certified or licensed individual to ensure that some minimum standards have been met and that there is some method of monitoring competence and ethical practice.

Diagnosis

After all our cautions to avoid diagnosis, it might seem contradictory to include a section on this topic. The cautions involve two issues. First, diagnosing a condition not only implies that you understand the criteria for making that particular diagnosis but that you also can differentiate that condition from others. For example, if you diagnose a person as alcohol dependent, were you able to rule out dysthymia, post-traumatic stress disorder, and generalized anxiety disorder? Do any of these conditions exist concurrently? Second, there can be a scope of practice and associated liability issues involved in making a diagnosis. If your training and license or certification do not allow you to diagnose, you are exceeding your scope of practice if you diagnose.

However, many mental health practitioners work in settings that require a diagnosis and either are qualified or have supervision by qualified professionals. Even if you do not diagnose as part of your job, knowing the criteria to diagnose substance abuse or substance dependence is important in your conceptual framework of what constitutes an alcohol or other drug problem. We will provide such a conceptual framework and then discuss the specific criteria for diagnosing "Substance Dependence" and "Substance Abuse" as defined in the Diagnostic and Statistical Manual of Mental Disorders, Fourth Edition (DSM-IV).

The easiest conceptual framework to diagnose an alcohol or other drug problem is "trouble." Someone who has medical, social, psychological, family, occupational, educational, legal, or financial trouble as a result of alcohol or other drug use usually has a problem. However, the easiest framework is not necessarily the most accurate. In the section on "Alcohol and Other Drug Use History" on the psycho-social interview, we gave an example of a 47-year-old man who drinks large quantities of beer. No *trouble* was reported but he has a problem. We worked with a couple in which the husband drank three or four beers a week. The wife thought he was alcoholic because she was raised in a home in which no alcohol was used and she had no framework to understand moderate use. This man had family trouble related to his alcohol use but he was not an abuser or dependent. You can see that there can be exceptions, but, usually, *trouble* equals a problem. It can also be the case that the mental health professional must assist clients in identifying trouble. We recently listened to a woman tell of her family and relationship history. Her grandfather, father, husband, brothers, etc. drank to excess on the weekends, were verbally and physically abusive when intoxicated, and spent a great deal of money on alcohol. She did not know that this behavior was abnormal because it was what she grew up with and observed in her community. Her awareness was stimulated by observations made by a nurse in an emergency room after her husband broke her nose while drunk.

The Diagnostic and Statistical Manual of Mental Disorders (DSM-IV)

The Diagnostic and Statistical Manual of Mental Disorders published its fourth edition in 1994. For those of you unfamiliar with the DSM-IV, the manual contains a list of diagnostic criteria for mental disorders that are the focus of treatment for psychiatrists, psychologists, social workers, mental health counselors, marriage and family therapists, etc. For each disorder, the manual specifies features of the condition, the diagnostic criteria, associated features and disorders, specific culture, age, and gender features, prevalence, course, familial pattern, and differential diagnosis. Mental health professionals who work in agency or private settings use the DSM-IV for diagnosis. All insurance companies that we are aware of require a DSM-IV diagnosis for payment. Many publicly funded agencies also require a DSM-IV diagnosis of clients. Therefore, regardless of your feelings about labeling clients, the use of the DSM-IV is a reality in the mental health field.

For our purposes, the most important part of the DSM-IV (1994) involves the chapter on "Substance-Related Disorders." Included in this chapter are the "Substance Use Disorders" ("Substance Dependence" and "Substance Abuse") and "Substance Induced Disorders" ("Substance Intoxication", "Substance Withdrawal" and a variety of other disorders). We will focus most of this discussion on the Substance-Related Disorders since mental health professionals would generally be involved with diagnoses in this classification.

In the DSM-IV, substance dependence is defined as "a cluster of cognitive, behavioral, and physiological symptoms indicating that the individual continues use of the substance despite significant substance-related problems" (p. 176). You may recall that earlier in the chapter, we gave a working definition of addiction/dependence that specified use of alcohol or other drugs regardless of the consequences. Although more technical language is used, the DSM-IV definition is similar. The diagnostic criteria for substance dependence are as follows:

A maladaptive pattern of substance use, leading to clinically significant impairment or distress, as manifested by three (or more) of the following, occurring at any time in the same 12-month period:

(1) tolerance, as defined by either of the following:

(a) a need for markedly increased amounts of the substance to achieve intoxication or desired effect

(b) markedly diminished effect with continued use of the same amount of the substance

(2) withdrawal, as manifested by either of the following:

(a) the characteristic withdrawal syndrome for the substance (refer to Criteria A and B of the criteria sets for Withdrawal from the specific substances)

(b) the same (or a closely related) substance is taken to relieve or avoid withdrawal symptoms

(3) the substance is often taken in larger amounts or over a longer period than was intended

(4) there is a persistent desire or unsuccessful efforts to cut down or control substance use

(5) a great deal of time is spent in activities necessary to obtain the substance (e.g., visiting multiple doctors or driving long distances), use the substance (e.g., chainsmoking), or recover from its effects

(6) important social, occupational, or recreational activities are given up or reduced because of substance use

(7) the substance use is continued despite knowledge of having a persistent or recurrent physical or psychological problem that is likely to have been caused or exacerbated by the substance (e.g., current cocaine use despite recognition of cocaine-induced depression, or continued drinking despite recognition that an ulcer was made worse by alcohol consumption.

Specify if:

With Physiological Dependence: evidence of tolerance or withdrawal (i.e., either Item 1 or 2 is present)

Without Physiological Dependence: no evidence of tolerance or withdrawal (i.e., neither Item 1 or 2 is present)

Course specifiers

Early Full Remission

Early Partial Remission

Sustained Full Remission

Sustained Partial Remission

On Agonist Therapy

In a Controlled Environment

Notice that the first two criteria, tolerance and withdrawal, are not necessary for a diagnosis of dependence. Remember from Chapter 2 that tolerance is the need for increasing amounts of the substance to achieve the desired effect. This may be difficult to determine in some individuals, and individuals vary considerably in initial sensitivity to alcohol and other drugs. Also, with some drugs (e.g., PCP) tolerance has not been demonstrated. Similarly, withdrawal signs and symptoms are not observed with hallucinogen use. Therefore, tolerance and withdrawal are not necessary or sufficient for a diagnosis of dependence. Criteria 3 through 7 are self-explanatory and involve the compulsivity and *trouble* we have previously discussed in substance dependence.

The diagnosis of substance dependence can be specified as being with or without physiological dependence so that it is clear whether tolerance and withdrawal are present. Also, a description of the status of recovery can be given after none of the criteria for dependence (or abuse) have been observed for at least one month. If the client has been in recovery for 1 to 12 months and none of the criteria for dependence or abuse are met, "Early Full Remission" is specified. If one or more criteria is met but the client cannot be diagnosed as "Substance Dependence" (i.e., does not meet three or more of the criteria), "Early Partial Remission" is specified. "Sustained Full Remission" and "Sustained Partial Remission" are the specifiers when the period of recovery is 12 months or longer. The "partial remission" specifiers are generally used to indicate recovering clients who have had one or more "slips" or returns to use but have not had full-blown relapses (see Chapter 13).

"On Agonist Therapy" and "In a Controlled Environment" are specified so that clients who have a low probability of use due to external circumstances can be identified. For example, if a recovering alcoholic is taking Antabuse (see Chapter 7), the diagnosis would specify "On Agonist Therapy." A recovering opioid addict who is incarcerated for two years has a low probability of use because of being in prison. Thus, "In a Controlled Environment" would be specified.

DSM-IV defines Substance Abuse as "a maladaptive pattern of substance use manifested by recurrent and significant adverse consequences related to the repeated use of substances" (p. 182). Again, this is consistent with the earlier definition of abuse in this chapter as continued use of alcohol and other drugs in spite of negative consequences. The criteria are as follows:

> A. A maladaptive pattern of substance use leading to clinically significant impairment or distress, as manifested by one (or more) of the following, occurring within a 12-month period:
>
>> (1) recurrent substance use resulting in a failure to fulfill major role obligations at work, school, or home (e.g., repeated absences or poor work performance related to substance use; substance-related absences, suspensions, or expulsions from school; neglect of children or household)
>>
>> (2) recurrent substance use in situations in which it is physically hazardous (e.g., driving an automobile or operating a machine when impaired by substance use)
>>
>> (3) recurrent substance-related legal problems (e.g., arrests for substance-related disorderly conduct)
>>
>> (4) continued substance use despite having persistent or recurrent social or interpersonal problems caused or exacerbated by the effects of the substance (e.g., arguments with spouse about consequences of intoxication, physical fights)
>
> B. The symptoms have never met the criteria for Substance Dependence for this class of substance.

You may notice that tolerance and withdrawal are not mentioned in the criteria for abuse and that a pattern of compulsive use is also restricted to "dependence." The criteria for "abuse" emphasizes harmful consequences from repeated substance use. Clearly, if an individual meets the criteria for Substance Dependence, the person could also be diagnosed with Substance Abuse. However, "A diagnosis of Substance Abuse is preempted by the diagnosis of Substance Dependence" (p. 182).

Following the general criteria for Substance Dependence and Substance Abuse, there are descriptions for dependence and abuse for a variety of substances including alcohol, amphetamines, cannabis, cocaine, hallucinogens, inhalants, opioids, phencyclidine (PCP), sedative, hypnotic, or anxiolytics, and other or unknown substances (e.g., anabolic steroids, nitrite inhalants (poppers), nitrous oxide (laughing gas)). A short discussion is included on the unique characteristics of the particular drug in relationship to the criteria for dependence or abuse. In addition, there is dependence for nicotine (but not abuse) and polysubstance dependency, defined as dependence on three or more groups of drugs. Caffeine is included for Caffeine-Induced Disorders (e.g., Caffeine Intoxication, Caffeine-Induced Anxiety Disorder, Caffeine-Induced Sleep Disorder) but there are no classifications for dependence and abuse.

DSM-IV contains a variety of Substance-Induced Disorders. As the name implies, these are mental disorders caused by the use of alcohol and other drugs. They may be associated with abuse or dependence. For example, Substance Intoxication "is the development of a reversible substance-specific syndrome due to the recent ingestion of [or exposure to] a substance . . .[with] clinically significant maladaptive behavioral or psychological changes associated with intoxication [e.g., belligerence, mood liability, cognitive impairment, impaired judgment, impaired social or occupational functioning]." (p. 183). Substance Withdrawal "is the development of a substance-specific maladaptive behavioral change, with physiological and cognitive concomitants, that is due to the cessation of, or reduction in, heavy and prolonged substance use." (p. 184). Substance-induced disorders other than intoxication and withdrawal are included elsewhere in the DSM-IV and are referenced under the appropriate substance. These include Substance-Induced Delirium, Substance-Induced Persisting Dementia, Substance-Induced Persisting Amnestic Disorder, Substance-Induced Psychotic Disorder, Substance-Induced Mood Disorder, Substance-Induced Anxiety Disorder, Substance-Induced Sexual Dysfunction, and Substance-Induced Sleep Disorder. For example, there are 12 Alcohol-Induced Disorders listed in DSM-IV.

Summary

It is important for mental health professionals to be aware of the signs and symptoms of alcohol and other drug problems and to be able to identify these signs and symptoms through the normal assessment process. This identification will prevent mental health professionals from missing the real problem. But first, mental health professionals must learn to differentiate alcohol and other drug use, misuse, abuse, and addiction/dependence. A thorough psycho-social history is one of the best means to identify alcohol and other drug problems. Self-report inventories may also be useful, although the reliance on client self-reporting may affect the validity of the assessment. The Substance Abuse Subtle Screening Inventory is a self-report inventory that is designed to overcome this issue.

Once a mental health professional suspects an alcohol or other drug problem, appropriate referral may be necessary. There is a professional obligation to ensure that referrals given to clients have the proper license or certification and the expertise to work with alcohol and other drug-impacted clients.

Mental health professionals are discouraged from diagnosing without the proper training, experience, and supervision. However, diagnosis is often necessary in many professional settings. The DSM-IV provides the diagnostic criteria for substance abuse and substance-dependence disorders as well as substance-induced disorders.

Chapter 6

Intervention

Sara is a high school counselor. One day, two students come to see her to discuss their concerns about their friend Marlow. The students describe a progression of marijuana and LSD use. Marlow is frequently under the influence at school and is selling methamphetamine to support his use pattern. Sara contacts Marlow's teachers who describe absenteeism, failure to complete assignments, and sleeping in class. She calls Marlow's home and talks to his mother. The mother is a single parent who says that Marlow's father is an alcoholic who rarely has contact with the family. She tells Sara that she is also concerned about Marlow's drug use but feels completely helpless to do anything about it. In the past, she has tried to get Marlow to go to a treatment program for an assessment but he refuses. What should Sara do?

Miguel is a marriage and family counselor who works for a community mental health center. He sees a family who was referred by a child protection case worker after an incident of physical abuse of the 10-year-old son was reported by the school. After one session, the father does not return to counseling. The mother describes an increasing pattern of alcohol use and verbal and physical abuse by the father. He has had a DUI in the last month and she is concerned that he will be fired from his job. When the mother tries to talk to the father about his alcohol use, he becomes angry and leaves the house. What can Miguel do about this situation?

Angelica is a social worker who works in an employee-assistance program with a large corporation. One of the vice presidents comes to her to discuss his concerns about the deteriorating job performance of one of the managers. The manager's behavior has become unpredictable. He seems to function well one day and the next day is irritable and even explosive. The manager was rude to an important client and yelled at one of the secretaries in front of other employees. One of the manager's friends has told the vice president that the manager is a frequent cocaine user. Angelica meets with the manager who tells her that he has been under a great deal of stress in his job and that the rumors of his drug use were started by jealous colleagues. How should Angelica handle the situation?

It would be convenient if mental health professionals could learn to identify potential alcohol and other drug problems in their clients, present the client with this information, refer the client to treatment, and move on to something else. Unfortunately, in most cases, this does not reflect reality. To help you understand the reasons for this reality, you must have an empathic understanding of the importance of alcohol and other drugs to the alcoholic/addict. Therefore, we will restate a metaphor from Chapter 1. Think about the most important person in your life. Imagine that one day, a friend comes up to you and says, "(the person you care most about) is no good for you. You need to get rid of him/her right now and never see him/her again." We don't think that your response would be, "You're right. I've been thinking the very same thing. I'll go home right now and tell him/her that it's over." It is much more likely that you would defend this person and your relationship, tell your friend to mind his own business, and leave.

Many alcoholics/addicts have developed a relationship with their drugs of choice that they believe to be critical to their functioning and of primary importance to their lives. Just as you may have difficulty imagining yourself being happy without this most important person, alcoholics/addicts may not be able to imagine functioning without their drugs of choice. Of course, problems do develop in relationships, and there may come a time when the problems outweigh the perceived importance of the relationship. Similarly, alcohol or other drug users may start to have problems as a result of their use and might not experience the euphoria that was once a part of the relationship with their drug(s). In the three situations that are described at the beginning of the chapter, you might question the relationship metaphor. After all, the people described in these situations are having significant problems in their lives as a result of their alcohol and other drug use. Surely, you think, they can see the harm that alcohol and other drugs are having on them and those around them. If this occurs to you, we would ask whether you have ever been "in love" with someone and, when the relationship ended, you looked back and wondered what you ever saw in the person. If anyone criticized your lover or your relationship while you were "in love," you probably responded that no one could possibly understand the depth of your feelings and the intensity of the relationship. Although in hindsight, you may now believe that the relationship was unhealthy, at the time any objective data to support this perception was ignored. Think about the alcoholic/addict as being "in love" with their drugs of choice.

The reality is that people often do not acknowledge the harm that a relationship is having in their lives, or, if the harm is acknowledged, the person may be reluctant to abandon the relationship. The old saying "Love is blind and lovers cannot see" applies to human relationships as well as the relationship people can have with alcohol and other drugs. Many authorities in the field attribute this "blindness" to the psychological defense mechanism of denial. We will discuss denial later in this chapter. An alternative explanation is that people are fearful of abandoning a relationship that, while harmful, is familiar. For example, there is considerable interest in the fact that women who leave abusive relationships frequently return to the relationship (Griffin, 1993). One explanation is that the women have no other concept of relationships, and, although the abuse is unpleasant, they are at least familiar with the "rules" and are afraid of the alternatives. The alcoholic/addict may be aware of the undesirable consequences of addiction but be immobilized by the fear of living without alcohol/drugs.

Whatever the explanation, the mental health professional still faces a problem: a client with alcohol or other drug problems and an unwillingness to change. What can be done? In the rest of this chapter, we will describe two models of motivating an alcohol or other drug-affected person to enter treatment. The first model was developed by Vernon Johnson in the 1970s and has been called simply, "Intervention". Following the description of this model, we will recreate the dialogue from an actual intervention. The second model, an alternative to the Johnson style of intervention, is "Motivational Interviewing" described by Miller and Rollnick (1991).

Definition of Intervention

Before describing these two models, it would be useful to have a common definition of *intervention*. According to Anderson (1987), intervention is the process of stopping someone who is experiencing the harmful effects of alcohol or other drugs. Given this definition of intervention, an adolescent who is busted by his parents for using alcohol at a party, is grounded for a month, and stops using because the consequences outweigh the benefits, has received a successful intervention. Similarly, if a teenage girl stops smoking after listening to information about the harmful effects of smoking, the educational information can be considered an intervention.

In the alcohol and other drug field, intervention has come to mean specific procedures for motivating a person to enter treatment. In the remainder of this chapter, we will describe these procedures. However, we want you to see that intervention procedures can interrupt alcohol and other drug use long before serious problems are experienced. Many of these procedures will be described in Chapter 16, "Prevention".

The Johnson Model of Intervention

> It is a myth that alcoholics have some spontaneous insight and then seek treatment. Victims of this disease do not submit to treatment out of spontaneous insight—typically, in our experience they come to their recognition scenes through a buildup of crises that crash through their almost impenetrable defense systems. They are forced to seek help; and when they don't, they perish miserably (Johnson, 1973, p. 1).

Rationale for the Johnson Model

Vernon Johnson, the founder of the Johnson Institute associated with the Minnesota Model of treatment (see Chapter 7), described the process of intervention that has been widely used in motivating alcoholics/addicts[1] to seek treatment. Johnson wrote two books, *I'll Quit Tomorrow* (Johnson, 1973) and *Intervention: How to Help Someone Who Doesn't Want Help* (Johnson, 1986), describing this process.

As the above quote indicates, the Johnson intervention is based on the disease model of addiction. The quotation indicates the need to forcefully motivate the alcoholic to enter treatment because the alternative is death. The Johnson intervention has come to be seen as a dynamic, emotionally charged, confrontation by significant persons in the alcoholic's/addict's life.

The major reason for the need for forcefulness in the Johnson intervention model is "the almost impenetrable defenses of the victims of the disease, which were organized into highly efficient 'denial systems'" (Johnson, 1973, p. 3). These denial systems are often used to explain the difficulty of motivating alcoholics/addicts to seek treatment (Twerski, 1983). Therefore, as Anderson (1987), stated "its [intervention's] major function is to counteract denial" (p. 178). In other words, because alcoholics/addicts are in denial with regard to the harm that alcohol and other drugs are causing in their lives, it is necessary to disrupt this denial through dramatic means. As Johnson so emphatically stated, death is the evitable outcome if this denial system is not disrupted:

> *It became clear to us that it was not only pointless but dangerous to wait until the alcoholic hit bottom. The crises everybody was trying to help him avoid could actually be employed to break through his defenses, by an act of intervention that could stop the downward spiral toward death. We came to understand that crises could be used to creatively bring about intervention (Johnson, 1973, p. 3).*

The rationale of the Johnson model of intervention is to break through the denial system of the alcoholic/addict by confronting the alcoholic/addict with the crises that he/she has caused. This confrontation is done by significant persons in the alcoholic's/addict's life. Through this confrontation, it is hoped that the intervention process will "raise the bottom." In other words, Johnson felt that the "bottom" for the alcoholic was death. This is quite dramatic, and other disease-concept proponents would not be quite so emphatic. However, the "bottom" would be extremely serious (e.g., injury, health problems, loss of family), and those who care about the alcoholic/addict would be anxious to avoid the bottom." The confrontational intervention would serve to precipitate a crisis in the life of the alcoholic/addict that was not life-threatening or otherwise seriously damaging but that would result in treatment. This is the concept of "raising the bottom."

To raise the bottom, Johnson believed that the alcoholic/addict needed a clear view of reality as presented by the significant persons in the alcoholic's/addict's life:

---

[1] For purposes of discussion in this section, we will refer to the person who is the focus of attention in the intervention as "alcoholic/addict". From Chapter 5, you know that this label requires appropriate professional diagnosis.

By "presenting reality", we mean presenting specific facts *about the person's behavior and things that have happened because of it. "A receivable way" is one that the person cannot resist because it is* objective, unequivocal, *and* caring Johnson, 1986, p. 61, italics in original).

Although the Johnson intervention is confrontational, it should not be confused with attacking. Furthermore, Johnson believed that the intervention process was a demonstration of caring by those willing to participate:

In an intervention, confrontation means compelling the person to face the facts about his or her chemical dependency . . . It is an attack upon the victim's wall of defenses, not upon the victim as a person. . . . an intervention is an act of empathy rather than sympathy. You agree to take part in it out of the deep concern you feel for the chemically dependent person (Johnson, 1986, p. 62, italics in original).

The Johnson Intervention Process

In his books, Johnson outlines the specific procedures for conducting an intervention. Although Johnson (1986) wrote a book designed to enable the lay person to organize and implement an intervention, we believe that a mental health professional is nearly always needed. As we describe the intervention process, you will see why we hold this opinion.

First of all, there must be two or more persons involved in the intervention "who are close to the victim and have witnessed his or her behavior while under the influence" Johnson, 1986, p. 66). The reasons for having two or more people are to support those confronting the alcoholic/addict, to emphasize the seriousness of the situation to the person, and to dispute attempts by the alcoholic/addict to dismiss or discount the events of any one person. Clearly, someone must determine the composition of the intervention team—usually the person or people who have instigated the intervention. Participants may include spouses or lovers, children, parents, employers, teachers, or friends. Individuals who are seen as being influential in the life of the alcoholic/addict would be valuable participants. It is sometimes the case that those people who are the most intimately involved with the alcoholic/addict are not helpful in the intervention because of their emotional closeness to the alcoholic/addict and consequent inability to refrain from nonproductive interactions during the intervention. In addition, Johnson suggested that each person on the intervention team be educated about the disease concept.

Each participant in the intervention develops a list of specific incidents of alcohol or other drug-related behavior and describes the effect that each incident had on the participant. Specificity is important to avoid generalized statements that can be disputed (i.e., You're always drunk") and to objectify the process as much as possible. For example, an employer might say, "Last Wednesday night when we took our clients out to dinner, you had a lot to drink and your voice got loud and you got into an argument with one of the clients. They decided not to do business with us, and I was embarrassed and upset." Although it is important for participants to relate the effect of the alcohol/drug-related behavior on them, the tone should be nonjudgmental. These are simply statements of fact. Because the intervention may become quite emotional, it is suggested that participants write down the specific events so that they can remember them during the intervention.

Each participant must also decide what action he or she will be willing to take if the alcoholic/addict refuses treatment. The actions must be serious enough to have an impact and the participant must be willing to follow through. Thus, spouses and lovers may decide to leave the relationship, employers to terminate, or friends to disengage. Obviously, if the intervention does not result in the person's seeking treatment and if participants do not follow through on their actions, it will be extremely difficult to intervene in the future.

Someone on the intervention team must do some homework and determine the treatment options available, the cost of treatment, availability of insurance, and other hurdles such as job and family responsibilities. All of these details must be cleared up before the intervention so that all the alcoholic/addict has to say is "yes." In the first intervention the senior author participated in, he neglected to contact the treatment program to make sure there was room on intervention day. The alcoholic said "yes" but when they arrived at the program, it was full! (Fortunately, space was available two days later). Therefore, someone must check to be sure that all treatment alternatives are open on the day of the intervention.

Given all the aspects of the intervention process we have mentioned, preparation is essential. The intervention team must meet on several occasions to rehearse the intervention and role play possible scenarios. The order in which people will speak should be predetermined. Someone must be assigned the responsibility of getting the alcoholic/addict to the intervention and getting him or her there sober. The team needs to discuss methods to achieve this. Often, deception is used, since the alcoholic/addict would refuse to attend if the true purpose of the intervention were known. Participants need to be prepared for the emotional reaction of the alcoholic/addict. He or she may become angry when the purpose of the intervention is revealed. He or she may simply leave.

When the alcoholic/addict arrives at the intervention, the facilitator (who should be a mental health professional, in our opinion) tells the alcoholic/addict that the people in the room are there because they care and are concerned. The facilitator tells the alcoholic/addict that the people want to describe what they have been seeing. The alcoholic/addict is asked to listen to each person and will then have an opportunity to talk. Each participant (in the pre-determined order) expresses love, caring, and/or concern and describes the specific incidents he or she has prepared. The final participant, who should be the most influential, begins the discussion of what is being asked of the alcoholic/addict (that is, treatment). The facilitator will usually need to contribute to the discussion of available treatment options, should intervene when the alcoholic/addict interrupts with arguments or rationalizations, and may need to remind the alcoholic/addict just to listen until everyone has finished. The facilitator should also intervene when nonproductive interactions occur between a participant and the alcoholic/addict.

Because of the complexity of the intervention process and the dynamics involved, we strongly suggest that a trained mental health professional conduct the actual intervention. We believe that it is important for one member of the intervention team to be "detached" from the alcoholic/addict and that the group process that occurs would best be handled by a mental health professional. Of all the counseling-related activities in which we have been involved, the Johnson model interventions rank as the most emotionally charged. Even the preparation can be difficult, since participants are asked to make difficult decisions about the actions they will take if the alcoholic/addict does not agree to treatment. The role playing can also be emotional. For all these reasons, we suggest that mental health professionals participate in several interventions before "going solo."

Effectiveness of Intervention and Coercive Treatment

You've heard the old saying that you can lead a horse to water but you can't make him drink (irony unintended). If Johnson model intervention does result in the alcoholic/addict's going into treatment, will treatment be effective? (The issue of treatment effectiveness is discussed in Chapter 7.) However, with regard to coercive measures, Matuschka (1985) stated that "treatment which carried a coercive element has been shown to have a higher cure ratio than treatment without a coercive element" (p. 209). Furthermore, Collins and Allison (1983) analyzed data on 2,200 clients who were legally coerced to enter treatment and found that those clients stayed in treatment longer than others and did at least as well in treatment as those who entered voluntarily.

This seems to indicate that coercion may work. However, how often does intervention result in the person entering treatment? Royce (1989) stated that, "Properly done, interventions succeed 97 percent of the time in getting a person into treatment..." (p. 234). With all due respect to Dr. Royce, either we have worked with very different populations or he knows something we don't. With middle-aged men who have received at least one DUI, have minor liver impairment, and are facing the loss of $60,000-per-year middle-management jobs, we have had high success rates with interventions. However, with 16-year-old pot users, no criminal history, and only teachers, parents, and counselors at the intervention, the success rate has been considerably lower than Dr. Royce's.

In all seriousness, the age of the client (adolescents seem to be more difficult), the severity of the life problems experienced, and the impact of the participants in the intervention are all factors affecting success. As a generalization, we have found that about one-half of all interventions we have participated in have resulted in the person's going to some type of treatment.

Example of a Johnson Intervention

To illustrate a Johnson model intervention, we have recreated the dialogue from an actual intervention. Of course, names and other identifying information have been altered to insure confidentiality. The client was a 31-year-old woman named Pat.

Her drugs of choice were alcohol and prescription tranquilizers. She began using alcohol and other drugs at age 15 and had a history of sexual molestation (victim) and suicide attempts. Pat lived with her seven-year-old daughter and her mother. In addition to the mother, the other intervention participants were Pat's older sister Denise (36); two family friends (mother and son), Brenda (55) and Eric (30); and Pat's friend Doug (40). Neither Eric nor Doug was romantically involved with Pat. Doug was a frequent companion when Pat was using. No one particular event precipitated the intervention. Because of her increasing concern with the combination of alcohol and tranquilizers, Pat's mother initiated the intervention. The participants contacted a counselor who was trained at the Johnson Institute, and the counselor prepared the group and facilitated the intervention. Prior to the intervention, the counselor had two sessions with the intervention team. The intervention occurred at the mother's home, where Pat lived. Denise, who was visiting from out of town, brought Pat to the intervention.

Pat: Oh_____! What is going on? [Turning to Denise.] You _____. How could you do this to me?

Counselor (stands up and takes Pat's hand): Pat, I see that you have an idea of why everyone is here. All I want you to do is sit here [indicates chair next to counselor] and listen to what your friends and family have to say to you. My name is Mary, and I'm here to help them talk to you and help you listen. I know you're probably feeling betrayed and a little scared but can you see that these people are here because they love you?

Pat (sits down, puts her head in her hands): Oh _____.

Mother (tone is analytical and intellectual): Pat, you have been drinking and taking those pills. That is extremely dangerous. Yesterday, you slept until noon and I had to call in sick for you again. Now, you know I love you and I'm worried about you but you are not even taking care of Jessica [daughter]. On Wednesday, you went out and when you came home your eyes were glazed and you went straight to bed and didn't even ask about Jessica. Friday, you didn't go to work because you were too hungover. Now, you know I love you. But, I can't keep paying for all the expenses. You quit school and are working but you don't contribute anything to the house. All your money is spent on drugs and booze. [Pat is staring straight ahead and expressionless).

Brenda (tone is parenting and condescending): Now Pat honey, you've been like family to me and it hurts me to see what this is doing to you and your mother. Your mother has been sweating blood for you and you just keep taking and taking. Like I said, I love you like family and have known you since you were a little girl. You have to stop doing this to yourself. [Pat is still staring straight ahead and expressionless].

Eric (tone is caring and compassionate): Pat, I think you've always known that I care for you a lot. I often hoped that we would be more than friends but being friends is OK, too. I'm scared as_____ about you. I miss you. I miss the times that we spent together. You don't seem to want to do that anymore. Last week, you called me up and asked me to watch Jessica for you. I love being with her but I feel used. You wanted a babysitter so you could go out drinking. You came home at 2:30 when you said you would be home by 12:00. You were so wasted that I don't know how you could walk. Last month, we had a date to go to a movie. You called me up at the last minute and said you didn't feel well. I saw you drive off with Doug an hour later. I know you care about me but I don't drink or drug like you and so I think you don't want to be with me. Remember when we went to the Mink's Den [a bar] for my birthday? I wanted to leave around midnight but you didn't, so you started coming on to some guys and said you wanted to stay. I felt like _____. I just can't be your friend anymore if something doesn't change and that hurts like hell. [Pat is looking at Eric with tears in her eyes].

Denise (crying and looking at the ground): Please don't be mad at me. I love you so much. I know we agreed to always stand together against mom and dad and now I've lied to you. But Pat, I love you and I'm scared. Please don't hate me. You know how much I loved partying with you but things have changed. We used to go out and get wasted and everything was cool. Last month when I came to visit, I couldn't believe how much you drank and you didn't even seem drunk. I wanted to go home after three drinks but you wanted to stay until the bar closed. When I asked you about Jessica, you said, "Oh, mom will take care of her" and acted like you didn't care. You had twice as much to drink as I did and still seemed in better shape to drive than I did. It was never like that before. [*Starts crying harder*] God, this is so hard. I really love you and know you must hate me. I feel so awful.

Counselor (sitting next to Denise and putting her arm around her): Take your time. It's important to say everything. [*Pat is crying hard too.*] Let's wait until Pat can hear you.

Denise continues: When we went out last Thursday, the more you had to drink, the meaner you got to me. That has never happened before. I felt so hurt. You were talking to those guys and kept making fun of me. I wanted to cry. [*Starts crying again.*] We always stuck together. I know I lied to you about this and you probably hate me. But I love you and I know you're hurting yourself. I will do anything for you. Please go to treatment. I'll take you there. I love you. [Crying harder.]

Doug (Pat is crying hard at this point but looks at Doug as he speaks. Doug talks in an unemotional tone.): Man, all this _____ blows me away. I just know we've been partying too hard and we both need to stop.

Pat (still crying): I can't believe you're doing this to me. How can you do this? I thought you were my friends. You two-faced _____ [looking at Denise and Doug].

Counselor: Pat, I can understand how hurt and scared you are. Your friends and family have told you that your drinking and drugging is scaring them, and Denise has told you that you need help. Eric said that he can't continue to be a part of your life if something doesn't change.

Mother (interrupting): Yes, and I'm kicking you out of the house if you don't go to treatment.

Pat: _____ you. You never think about anyone but yourself. You think I want to live with you?

Counselor: I don't think it will help to talk about your problems with your mother right now. That is certainly something that needs work but right now we are talking about your drinking and drug use and the fact that your family and friends see that you need treatment for this problem. The West River Hospital has a treatment program that lasts 28 days. They have an opening and you can go there today.

Pat: I can't do that. It's expensive. What about work? What about Jessica? Maybe I have been drinking too much but it's all the _____ I get from all of you.

Mother: I'm going to pay for the treatment. You keep saying you hate your job and half the time you don't go anyway. With the amount of time you spend with Jessica, she probably won't know you're gone.

Pat: That's what I mean. You are such a _____. I love my daughter. You are always interfering with Jessica and me. We would be just fine if you would butt out.

Counselor: I think we are getting off track. Rachel [Pat's mother], it might be helpful if you could just listen for a while. Pat, will you go to West River?

Pat (looks at Denise): Do you think I should go?

Denise (starts crying): Yes! Please go. I'll take you. Nobody else has to go. We packed your bag. Pat, please? I love you.

Pat (crying, nods her head "yes", and stands up): I'll go. I probably shouldn't be mixing reds and booze.

As often happens in real-life situations, this intervention didn't go exactly as the model we have described. Participants sometimes freeze up. Brenda did not discuss the specific incidents she had prepared and really wasn't much of a factor in the intervention. Doug, who was Pat's major drinking partner, was last because he was thought to be the most influential. After the emotional interaction between Pat and her sister Denise, Doug's input was anticlimatic. Although he did become intimidated by the intensity of the intervention, his specific report was unnecessary. With the exception of Eric, participants did not give ultimatums during their presentations. This was probably wise. The mother simply forgot, and then threw in her ultimatum during the counselor's summary. Pat immediately became defensive and attempted to divert the conversation. Eric's ultimatum was effective because of the sincerity of his presentation. Denise, who had an impact on Pat, did not believe that she could honestly give Pat an ultimatum with regard to their relationship. This does point out the necessity for the facilitator of an intervention to carefully assess the participants and the dynamics involved with the alcoholic/addict rather than stick to a rigid pattern of presentation. Again, we believe that this requires the involvement of a mental health professional.

The counselor wisely refrained from interrupting the process until there was a reason to do so. When the interaction between Pat and her mother threatened to divert the intervention, the counselor intervened. It is common for issues between participants to come up during an intervention, and alcoholics/addicts may use these issues to divert the focus away from their alcohol and other drug use.

You may have noticed that the counselor and the participants refrained from using labels such as "alcoholic." Although Pat could be diagnosed as *alcoholic,* the use of this label would probably have elicited defensiveness and may have resulted in an argument. The purpose of the intervention is to get the individual to treatment, not to gain an admission of alcoholism or drug addiction.

Treatment options were not provided because the counselor and Denise (who had some training in the alcohol and other drug field) believed that Pat's heavy use of tranquilizers and alcohol necessitated a treatment setting in which medically supervised detoxification was available. The one treatment option presented (the name of the hospital is fictitious) was the only detoxification setting in the area.

As we hope you have seen from the intervention dialogue presented, the Johnson Model of intervention is often highly emotional and difficult to manage. This type of intervention may be an option for the mental heath professional in the situations we described at the beginning of the chapter. However, as has been emphasized, we strongly recommend that mental health professionals co-facilitate several interventions with an experienced person before organizing and facilitating a Johnson Model intervention alone.

Motivational Interviewing

An alternative to the Johnson Model of intervention has been developed by William Miller and Stephen Rollnick and described in their book, *Motivational Interviewing: Preparing People to Change Addictive Behavior* (Miller & Rollnick, 1991). While the Johnson Model utilizes a set of procedures to use in a confrontation with the alcoholic/addict, motivational interviewing is a process for assessing a client's readiness to change, and it uses procedures based on this readiness to enhance the probability of change. In motivational interviewing, it is acknowledged that a client may not be ready to benefit from a direct attack on the his/her use of alcohol and other drugs.

Use of Confrontation and Defense Mechanisms

Miller and Rollnick (1991) dispute the commonly held belief that confrontation is necessary for the alcoholic/addict to be motivated to seek treatment:

> Confrontation of (the) harsh variety has been believed to be uniquely effective— perhaps the only effective strategy for dealing with alcoholics and addicts. Yet confrontational strategies of this kind have not been supported by clinical outcome studies. Therapist behaviors associated with this approach have been shown to predict treatment failure.... There is ... no persuasive evidence that aggressive tactics are even helpful, let alone superior or preferable strategies in the treatment of addictive behaviors or other problems (p. 6–7).

Interestingly, Miller and Rollnick (1991) state that the use of aggressive confrontational procedures in the field are a product of practice rather than research. Furthermore, they cite statements by Vernon Johnson and Bill W. (one of the founders of Alcoholics Anonymous) that are inconsistent with confrontational approaches.

However, as we noted in the presentation of the Johnson Model, the use of confrontation to motivate alcoholics/addicts to enter treatment came about because of the "impenetrable defense systems" (Johnson, 1973, p. 1) of the alcoholic/addict. Miller and Rollnick dispute the commonly held belief that alcoholics/addicts are "in denial." In discussing the defense mechanism of denial, they state, "there is not and never has been a scientific basis for the assertion that alcoholics ... manifest a common personality pattern characterized by excessive ego defense mechanisms" (p. 10). Again, the view that alcoholics/addicts have "impenetrable defense systems" is more likely the result of perception on the part of treatment providers than as a result of research. Miller and Rollnick assert that to deny the label of "alcoholic" or "addict" and to resist the associated directives (i.e., enter treatment, abstain) are normal reactions to perceived undesirable characteristics and threats to freedom of choice. These normal reactions are labeled as abnormal by treatment providers and symptomatic of the alcoholics "denial." Furthermore, a confrontational style of interviewing or counseling tends to evoke resistance in clients. When the client resists the confrontation of the counselor, it further confirms the counselor's perception that the client is "in denial." Therefore, it is actually the behavior of the counselor that elicits resistance and denial in the client. According to Miller and Rollnick:

> the purpose of confrontation is to see and accept reality, so that one can change accordingly.... [And] confrontation is a goal in many different forms of treatment for a wide variety of problems.... The question ... is this: What are the most effective ways for helping people to examine and accept reality, particularly uncomfortable reality (p. 13, italics in original).

Stages of Change

Miller and Rollnick (1991) describe the stages of change developed by Prochaska and DiClemente (1982) as a conceptual framework for motivational interviewing. The stages of change are (1) Precontemplation; (2) Contemplation; (3) Determination; (4) Action; (5) Maintenance; and (6) Relapse.

At the precontemplation stage, the individual may not be aware that a problem exists and would generally be surprised to learn that others perceive a problem. A client may need information and feedback at this stage to raise awareness. However, Miller and Rollnick believe that coercion or aggressive confrontation would be counterproductive at this stage. With regard to alcohol or other drug problems, we can imagine a 26-year-old man, named Stan, who has always lived, worked, and played with people who drink and use drugs on a regular basis. He has had one DUI and drinks heavily every day. He begins to date a woman who does not use heavily or frequently, and she talks to him about his use. Stan is genuinely surprised that his girlfriend perceives a problem.

At the contemplation stage, the individual is ambivalent about the problem. He or she has become aware that others perceive a problem and vacillates between considering change and rejecting it. For example, let's say that Stan's girlfriend convinces him to talk to a marriage and family therapist she knows to "get a professional opinion." Stan is interested in pleasing his girlfriend, so he agrees. In the course of the conversation, Stan says things such as "My old man is an alcoholic and I sure don't want to end up like him, but he drank Old Crow and I stick to beer," and "I guess I could slow down but everyone would laugh at me." According to Miller and Rollnick, the techniques of motivational interviewing can be helpful at this stage to tip the balance toward change. However, if the therapist moves to the action stage before the client is ready, resistance may develop.

At the determination stage, the helping professional is presented with a window of opportunity to facilitate client movement toward action. If the opportunity is missed, the client moves back to contemplation. At this stage, the techniques of motivational interviewing may help the client find "a change strategy that is acceptable, accessible, appropriate, and effective" (Miller & Rollnick, 1991, p. 17). If Stan seems to be at the determination stage and talks about "slowing down," the counselor might suggest a short-term "experiment" in which he drinks only nonalcoholic beverages for two weeks and then comes back and discusses the experience.

The action stage is when people intentionally act, with or without assistance, to bring about change. After trying the experiment for two days, Stan goes to a bar with his friends after work. He gets drunk, gets into a fight, and suffers a broken nose and a dislocated finger. He doesn't have any sick leave at work so he loses pay, and his girlfriend tells him that she doesn't want to see him anymore. Stan is too embarrassed to go back to the therapist and admit his failure so he "goes on the wagon" on his own.

In the maintenance stage, the person tries to maintain the change that resulted from his or her actions without relapsing. However, people may need specific skills to maintain a behavior change. Stan does well for three weeks. He doesn't go out at all, and his girlfriend agrees to start seeing him again. They spend their evenings at home watching TV. One Friday, his girlfriend is going to spend the evening with her friends and Stan feels that he is ready to go out with the guys. They go to their favorite bar and Stan orders a coke. His friends start teasing him. At the maintenance stage, Stan needs some skills to deal with this social pressure.

Since Stan does not have these skills, he relapses[2]. (In Chapter 13, we will discuss the strategies of maintaining a behavior change related to alcohol and other drug use and relapse-prevention techniques.) With regard to motivational interviewing, an important issue in the maintenance and relapse stages is for the mental health professional to create an environment in the counseling relationship so that the client feels safe to discuss difficulties in maintaining the behavior change and to report relapses that often occur during the change process. Since Stan's therapist

---

[2] There are differences between slips and relapses that will be discussed in Chapter 13.

was not aggressively confrontational and did not impose a label on him, Stan felt comfortable returning after his relapse. He will again go through the stages of change but, hopefully, Stan will begin at the determination stage and avoid the relapse stage. However, the mental health professional who uses motivational interviewing strategies would recognize that clients often cycle through the stages of change several times.

In the context of the Johnson Model of intervention, it can be seen that a client in the determination or action stage may be amenable to a confrontational intervention. However, if the confrontation is too aggressive in the determination stage, it may alienate the client, and the client may return to the contemplation stage. A client in the action stage would probably be receptive to a Johnson Model intervention. However, we would like to motivate a client to change who is at the contemplation stage, where he or she may not have yet experienced serious consequences of alcohol and other drug use, and we do not want to alienate clients at the determination stage through aggressive confrontation. Motivational interviewing is designed to accomplish these goals.

Working through Ambivalence

As Miller and Rollnick (1991) point out, clients at the contemplation stage of change are normally ambivalent about change.

> *Problem drinkers, addicts, bulimics, and pathological gamblers often recognize the risks, costs, and harm involved in their behavior. Yet they are also quite attached and attracted to the addictive behavior, for a variety of reasons. To complicate the conflict further, they typically are not exactly sure what they should* do *about their situation! They want to drink (or smoke, or purge, or gamble), but they don't want to. They want to change, and they don't want to. (p. 37, italics in original)*

Although this ambivalence is normal, a goal of motivational interviewing is to resolve this ambivalence (hopefully, by choosing change). Certainly, the facilitative conditions for counseling (e.g., empathy, respect and warmth, concreteness, immediacy, and congruence, genuineness, and authenticity) are necessary conditions for change in any counseling situation. In addition, Miller and Rollnick suggest some traps to avoid and counseling techniques to use to resolve client ambivalence.

Perhaps the most common trap that would interfere with client resolution of ambivalence is what Miller and Rollnick call the *confrontational trap.* As the name implies, this trap would relate to our previous discussion of the practitioner's perception of the need to confront the denial of alcohol and other drug-abusing clients. When confrontation is used at the contemplation stage, the helping professional can expect resistance. Rather than appearing ambivalent, the client is seen as resistant and in denial. According to Miller and Rollnick, such denial is predictable. If the client is ambivalent and the practitioner argues for the "there is a problem" side of the ambivalence, the client will argue for the "there isn't a problem" side of the ambivalence.

Additional traps mentioned by Miller and Rollnick are the question-answer trap, in which the client answers a series of closed questions by the mental health professional. Hopefully, you have been taught to avoid this type of interviewing in a basic counseling skills course. There is also the expert trap, in which there is an attempt to fix the problem by exerting expertise. Clients may elicit this from a helping professional in order to remain passive and thus minimize their responsibility for change. The labeling trap involves the attempt to attach a diagnostic label (e.g., alcoholic) to a client. As Miller and Rollnick point out, there is no research evidence that the acceptance of such a label predicts favorable treatment outcome, and, clearly, many people resist such labels. Finally, there are the premature focus trap and the blaming trap. In the former, the mental health professional focuses the client on the alcohol and other drug issue before the client is ready, and, in the latter, the client perceives that blame is being assessed for his or her behavior.

The strategies that Miller and Rollnick suggest for resolving client ambivalence use many of the basic counseling interventions of Carl Roger's Person-Centered Therapy. For example, the use of open-ended questions, reflective listening, affirming and supportive statements, and summarization are all recommended. However, the elicitation of self-motivational statements is the "guiding strategy to help clients resolve their ambivalence. . . . *In motivational interviewing, it is the client who presents the arguments for change.* It is the counselor's task to facilitate the client's expression of these self-motivational statements" (Miller & Rollnick, 1991, p. 80, italics in original,).

Self-Motivational Statements

Miller and Rollnick categorize self-motivational statements as cognitive (problem recognition), affective (statements of concern), and behavioral (intentions to act). Evocative questions can be used to elicit self-motivational statements in any of the categories. For example, "In what ways has your marijuana use been a problem for you?" (problem recognition), "What worries you about your cocaine use?" (statement of concern), and "What would be the advantages of changing your drinking habits?" (intention to act) are examples of evocative questions designed to elicit self-motivational statements.

Miller and Rollnick suggest that clients be asked for both the positive and negative aspects of their alcohol and other drug use as a method to elicit self-motivational statements. Expressions of concern are often elicited when the client lists the negative aspects of use. The client can then be asked to elaborate on these concerns. Related to this technique is asking clients to describe the aspect of their use that concerns them the most, comparing the times that they experienced problems to the present, and imagining what life would be like if they changed their use pattern. The clients can also be asked to examine their goals in life and then to describe how their current use pattern facilitates or hinders their ability to achieve their goals. Finally, Miller and Rollnick suggest that the experienced helping professional may use the technique of paradox to elicit self-motivational statements. As one example of the use of paradox, the counselor and client may engage in a role play in which the counselor takes the side of arguing for the continuation of the present pattern of alcohol and other drug use and the client argues for a behavior change. Paradox techniques should be used judiciously and, again, by experienced mental health professionals.

Working with Resistance

As Miller and Rollnick (1991) note, "Ambivalence does not usually disappear, but only diminishes" (p. 87). The avoidance of traps and the use of techniques to elicit self-motivational statements should be helpful in reducing ambivalence. However, a mental health professional can expect clients to remain ambivalent in spite of these efforts and can also expect that this ambivalence will be demonstrated through client resistance.

A difference between motivational interviewing and some other counseling approaches is a "working assumption of motivational interviewing: that *client resistance is a therapist problem*" (p. 100, italics in original). While many mental health professionals view resistance as a personality characteristic of clients or a symptom of client pathology, Miller and Rollnick argue that the behavior of the helper will usually have an impact on the level of client resistance. In addition, the reduction of client resistance is seen as a favorable outcome of motivational interviewing. The logical extension of this point of view is that helping professionals must change their behavior to reduce client resistance.

> [C]ounselors can change their style in ways that will decrease (or increase) client resistance. It is desirable to evoke low levels of client resistance, because this pattern is associated with long-term change ... (p. 100).

Again, the contrast of motivational interviewing and a Johnson Model intervention should be clear. The Johnson Model is based on the disease concept of addiction, and resistance is due to denial that is a symptom of the disease of addiction. Therefore, it is necessary to "crash through the almost impenetrable defense systems" (Johnson, 1973, p. 1). In motivational interviewing, client resistance is a predictable response to ambivalence. The helping professional's task is to reduce client resistance.

Miller and Rollnick describe four categories of resistance: arguing (challenging, discounting, hostility), interrupting (talking over, cutting off), denying (blaming, disagreeing, excusing, claiming impunity, minimizing, pessimism, reluctance, unwillingness to change), and ignoring (inattention, nonanswer, no response, sidetracking). Although it is not important for the helping professional to categorize the type of resistance, it is important to recognize resistance in order to handle it appropriately.

To illustrate the use of the techniques to minimize resistance that are recommended by Miller and Rollnick, let's look at a client statement and the helping professional's possible responses. The client name was Frank, a 37-year-old, and his drugs of choice were cocaine and alcohol. After Frank's second DUI, he was ordered by the court to attend NA and individual counseling. Based on an assessment, Frank was easily diagnosed as Psychoactive Substance Dependence (see Chapter 5). He recognized that the problems he had were the result of alcohol and cocaine use and was afraid of going to prison, but he resisted the label "alcoholic/addict" and complained about the NA meetings. During the third session with his counselor, Frank said:

> "I hate going to those _____ NA meetings. Man, you should see those people, bikers with tattoos, old needle pushers, bums. And all that God _____. I'm an atheist, man. I'm not like those people. I know I can't drink or do coke any more. If I do, they'll put me away. But I'm no junkie or wino."

Frank's statements are certainly reflective of the denying category of resistance. The first strategy recommended by Miller and Rollnick is simple reflection, a skill that you have probably practiced many times in a basic counseling skills course. A simple reflecting response to Frank would be, "You really feel out of place at NA meetings." This avoids the confrontation trap and provides a sense of empathic understanding to the client that may be helpful in moving the client away from resistance and toward further exploration of the problem.

Amplified and double-sided reflections can also be used to focus on the other side of the client's ambivalence as well. An amplified reflection exaggerates the client's perception of the situation, which may result in the client's talking about the other side when he or she hears how extreme their position sounds. In Frank's case, an amplified reflection might be, "You feel like NA is completely wrong for you. You can't see any similarity between NA members and yourself, and the philosophy is totally wrong for you." The double-sided reflection presents both parts of the client's ambivalence. Such a response to Frank would be, "You don't feel comfortable at NA meetings, but you know you need to stay away from coke and booze."

With some issues that cause resistance, Miller and Rollnick (1991) suggest shifting the focus so that the client does not continue to use the issue as a barrier to movement. In Frank's case, the "God" issue in NA was consistently raised. A "shifting focus" response would be, "You know Frank, I really hear how the 'God' stuff in NA turns you off. You also mentioned that the topic of the meeting last night was forgiveness. What did you think about that?" In using "shifting," it is important that the helping professional clearly reflect an understanding of the client's thoughts and feelings prior to shifting. Again, the helping professional would use this technique when the issue presented is seen as a barrier to the client's moving ahead.

Another approach to working with an issue that causes resistance is to agree with the client but with a twist. In other words, the helping professional concurs with the content of the client's concern but takes the discussion in a slightly different direction. For example, with regard to the God issue, Frank's counselor might say, "You are right. There is a heavy emphasis on spirituality in NA and 'God' is mentioned a lot. In fact, I know some people who go to AA and NA regularly but don't believe in 'God'." The twist in this counselor statement is to motivate Frank to ask about this apparent contradiction, possibly leading to clarification of his resistance to attending NA.

Miller and Rollnick also suggest that the helping professional emphasize the personal choice and control of the client as a method of reducing resistance. Although Frank may dislike NA because of a genuine philosophical difference, the fear of being labeled, or discomfort, his resistance may also be related to the fact that he was ordered by the court to attend. In this case, you might think that Frank actually does not have personal choice or control. Although, theoretically, he could choose not to attend, the consequence of such a choice would be imprisonment, therefore, it would be not be constructive to point out that he has personal choice. However, the counselor could say, "Well, you are court-ordered to go to NA and maybe that is upsetting to you. But, no one can make you believe what you hear at the meetings, and no one can make you listen. That's up to you."

A helping professional can also reduce resistance by focusing on the content of the client's statements but interpreting them in a different manner. This is called *reframing*. Reframing may result in the client's acknowledging a different point of view, especially if the counselor has developed the client's trust by clearly hearing the client's perspective. In Frank's case, a reframing response might be, "When you say 'junkie' and 'wino', I know what you mean. But, think about (name some famous athletes or movie stars who are in recovery). They go to AA or NA, and I think you'd agree that they aren't 'junkies' or 'winos'." I wonder if you just focus on the people at the meeting who fit your stereotype and ignore the others. What do you think?"

Miller and Rollnick also discuss the use of therapeutic paradox to reduce resistance. They recommend the use of such techniques when "all change efforts are met with opposition" (p. 109). The gist of therapeutic paradox is "that the client should continue on as before, without changing, or should even increase the behavior in question" (p. 109). As with the discussion of ambivalence, paradoxical techniques should be used only by an experienced professional because the techniques can be risky.

Transition from Resistance to Change

When ambivalence is largely resolved and resistance has decreased, the client is ready to take action for change. According to Miller and Rollnick, the helping professional will be aware of this transition when the client stops resisting (arguing, interrupting, denying, and objecting), reduces the number of questions asked about the problem, seems more calm and settled, makes more self-motivational statements, asks more questions about change, talks about life after change, and experiments with changes. For the helping professional who is not an alcohol or other drug counselor, this transition may present some dilemmas. Should the client be referred to an alcohol and other drug counselor, to a treatment program, or to recovery groups? Or should the generalist continue working with the client? As with other people problems, helping professionals need to have a clear understanding of which types of alcohol and other drug issues they can handle and which would require referral. We discussed some guidelines for referral in Chapter 5. Based on this information, should a generalist continue to work with Stan? He is young and uses alcohol only. However, he also has had a DUI and drinks heavily every day. Or, does Frank need a formal treatment program? As with many issues in the helping professions, answers are not always clear-cut. You may devise a plan, based on a thorough assessment, that seems reasonable. For example, you work on an action plan with Stan to moderate his alcohol use. You find that he is not successful in using alcohol moderately. This feedback suggests that you need a new plan. Hopefully, you will be acquiring enough information to make good judgments about when to refer and what kind of referrals to make.

Miller and Rollnick discuss the steps in the action phase such as setting goals, considering the options to achieve the goals, and deciding on a plan. We would hope that you will use this framework in your work regardless of whether you see yourself developing action plans for individuals with alcohol and other drug problems. Also, we certainly recommend that you read Miller and Rollnick's *Motivational Interviewing* for more information if this approach to intervention appeals to you.

Conclusion

At the beginning of this chapter, we described three cases in which helping professionals are faced with resistant clients who have alcohol or other drug problems. We'd like you to go back and re-read these situations now and consider which type of intervention you would use. Hopefully, you can see that either the Johnson Model of intervention or motivational interviewing can be used. If Marlow will not come to talk to the counselor, there may not be an option to use motivational interviewing. Miguel might have much better luck with motivational interviewing than with a Johnson Model intervention, since he has already seen the father once and the father responds with anger when confronted. Angelica may have access to the cocaine-using manager and be able to have regular meetings with him. Therefore, motivational interviewing may be her choice.

You can see that the situation may dictate which approach to intervention is chosen. Also, you may find that one approach appeals to you more than another. If confrontation is threatening to you, motivational interviewing may seem more comfortable. If you like quick action, you may have thought that motivational interviewing was too slow an approach. Reactions such as these reflect personal issues that require examination. The fact that confrontation feels threatening is not a good reason to avoid confrontational techniques. Your need for rapid client movement does not justify a rejection of motivational interviewing. The client and the situation should guide you in choosing the most appropriate approach.

Chapter 7

Treatment of Alcohol and Other Drug Problems

In a textbook for helping professionals who are not planning to work in substance abuse treatment, a thorough discussion of treatment may not seem necessary. However, we have found that helping professionals have an almost mystical conception of substance abuse treatment. Once the social worker, school counselor, mental health counselor, rehabilitation counselor, or marriage and family therapist has referred a client for treatment, there seems to be an expectation that the client will return cured. In fact, alcoholics used to say they were going for "the cure" as a euphemism for treatment. This view may be encouraged by the fact that clients often "disappear" (in the case of inpatient treatment) or discontinue other forms of counseling or therapy at the insistence of the substance abuse treatment program. The helping professional may never see the client again, which reinforces the idea that alcoholics and addicts have been cured as a result of treatment.

The questions we are asked most often in teaching helping professionals about the alcohol and other drug field is, "What happens in treatment?"; "What are the specific interventions?"; "Why are so many programs 28 days?"; and "Does treatment work?" Answers to these questions are important for the helping professional, since clients referred for treatment expect that they are being directed toward an appropriate and helpful program. However, treatment programs differ in their orientation, in the specific strategies used, in the settings in which treatment occurs, and in treatment for special populations. We want to acquaint you with these aspects of treatment in order to dispel any mystical views you hold and, most important, so that you can make informed referrals. Also, we will discuss the research on the effectiveness of treatment and suggest a model for matching client needs and treatment strategies. Finally, we think that it is important for you to understand some of the controversial issues in the treatment of alcohol and other drug problems.

What Happens in Treatment?

Approaches to Treatment

As you might expect after reading Chapter 3 on models of addiction, there are different approaches to treatment based on the model of addiction adhered to by the program developer(s). However, there is a growing trend toward more eclectic approaches to treatment (Miller & Hester, 1995) that combine aspects of different treatment models. While this may be good practice, it may also be driven by financial concerns, particularly in for-profit treatment programs. For example, some insurance companies pay for substance abuse treatment only if there is another mental disorder as well. This consideration has resulted in treatment programs' developing "dual diagnosis" programs and using components from all of the treatment approaches we will discuss. Dual diagnosis will be discussed further under controversial issues in treatment.

Perhaps the most well-known and widely emulated approach to treatment is that of the Minnesota Model developed by the Hazeldon Foundation in the 1940s and 1950s. As described by Cook (1988), the Minnesota Model

> is an abstinence orientated, comprehensive, multi-professional approach to the treatment of the addictions, based upon the principles of Alcoholics Anonymous. It espouses a disease concept of drug and alcohol dependency with the promise of recovery, but not cure, for those who adhere to it. The programme is intensive, offering group therapy, lectures, and counselling (p. 625).

The philosophy of the Minnesota Model can be described by four components (Cook, 1988). The first is the belief that clients can change attitudes, beliefs, and behaviors. Famous people who have completed the program, such as Betty Ford, Elizabeth Taylor, and Anthony Hopkins, are used as models to illustrate this belief. Second, the Minnesota Model adheres to the disease concept of addiction. The term *chemical dependency* is preferred to *addiction* or *alcoholism* and is seen as a physical, psychological, social, and spiritual illness. The major characteristics of the disease concept are taught. That is, chemical dependency is seen as a primary disease that is chronic, progressive, and potentially fatal. The focus of treatment is the disease and not secondary characteristics.

The third philosophical component is illustrated by the long-term treatment goals of the Minnesota Model: abstinence from all mood-altering chemicals and improvement of lifestyle. Clients are not considered cured since the disease is incurable. However, through abstinence and personal growth, a chemically dependent individual can be in the process of recovery, "an ongoing, lifelong, process of increasing insight and commitment to change" (Cook, 1988, p. 627). Finally, the Minnesota Model uses the principles of Alcoholics Anonymous (AA) and Narcotics Anonymous (NA) in treatment. While we will devote a large portion of Chapter 8 to AA and NA, at this point it is sufficient to mention that the utilization of AA and NA principles implies a heavy spiritual component to treatment in the Minnesota Model.

Cook (1988) also describes the elements and structure of the Minnesota Model program. A continuum of care including assessment and diagnosis, detoxification, inpatient, therapeutic communities, half-way houses, outpatient, and aftercare has been developed using the Minnesota Model. Group therapy is used and is concerned with present and future behavior as opposed to past causal factors. Groups are often confrontational. The family also receives therapy. Didactic experiences including lectures and video tapes are used to educate clients about the disease of chemical dependency and the consequences of chemical dependency. While the staff is composed of professionals from a number of disciplines (physicians, social workers, psychologists, nurses, and clergy), recovering addicts and alcoholics are also used as counselors. Clients have reading and writing assignments, such as reading the AA Twelve Steps and Twelve Traditions (see Chapter 8) and writing their life histories. Attendance at AA/NA meetings is required, and clients are expected to work through the first three to five steps of AA while in treatment. There may also be work assignments and recreational activities, depending on the treatment setting. Aftercare includes attendance at AA or NA.

In contrast to the disease model of treatment exemplified by the Minnesota Model, behavioral models of treatment use techniques of classical and operant conditioning in the treatment of alcohol and other drug problems. Perhaps the best-known behavioral technique applied to alcohol problems is aversive conditioning which is "designed to reduce or eliminate an individual's desire for alcohol . . . [by] pairing unpleasant stimuli or images with alcohol consumption" (Rimmele, Howard, & Hilfrink, 1995, p. 134). The unpleasant stimuli most widely used are nausea, apnea (paralysis of breathing), electric shock, and various images. Nausea is the oldest and most commonly used of these stimuli, with fairly wide use in the former Soviet Union and in certain hospitals in the United States. The process is to give the client a drug that, when combined with alcohol, produces severe nausea. In a supervised setting, the client is then allowed to drink. In the classical conditioning paradigm, the feeling of severe nausea should quickly become associated with drinking alcohol. Electric shock can also be administered when the client drinks or a drug can be administered that produces apnea when alcohol is consumed. Since these procedures are painful, stressful, and potentially dangerous, careful screening of clients and medical supervision is necessary. As might be expected, there is also a high dropout rate from programs using these techniques. In Chapter 3, we described "Bill", who completed an aversive conditioning program and remained sober for 19 years until his death. Although the treatment was successful, he found the whole experience extremely unpleasant, which was exactly the effect intended. While electric shock can be used in the treatment of addiction to drugs other than alcohol, most references to aversive conditioning are related to the treatment of alcoholism. It may be that drugs that produce nausea or apnea have not been developed for narcotics or stimulants.

Covert sensitization (Rimmele et al., 1995) has major advantages over other forms of aversive conditioning techniques. (This process involves pairing the consumption of the drug of choice with aversive images, such as nausea or negative consequences of alcohol or other drug use.) The advantages are quite obvious. Since the client does not actually experience nausea, electric shock, or apnea, there are no medical dangers. Clients would also be less likely to discontinue treatment, although desensitization may elicit "extraordinarily intense responses in your client" (Rimmele et al., 1995, p. 136). The question of effectiveness of covert desensitization compared with other aversive conditioning procedures and other methods of treatment will be discussed later in this chapter.

There are additional behavioral techniques that have been used in treatment. Pomerleau, Perschuk, Adkins, and Brady (1975) used contingency contracting in which clients made monetary deposits that were forfeited if the client did not complete the treatment program. Behavioral Self-Control Training "consists of behavioral techniques which include goal setting, self-monitoring, managing consumption, rewarding goal attainment, functionally analyzing drinking situations, and learning alternative coping skills" (Hester, 1995, p. 148). These techniques have been used to achieve abstinence or controlled use. (Controlled use, a controversial treatment goal, will be discussed later in the chapter).

Pharmacological procedures are also used in treatment. However, it is rare to find these procedures as the only intervention. Rather, they are usually used in conjunction with other treatment methods. The philosophy of treatment and the treatment setting may also determine whether drugs are used to treat alcohol and other drug problems. One would expect that treatment programs adhering to the disease concept would be adverse to using drugs in treatment. However, Cook (1988) stated that detoxification at Minnesota Model programs may use medication. Treatment programs in non-hospital settings without medical staff obviously should not use drugs in treatment.

Detoxification, the period of time in which a client is withdrawing from alcohol and other drugs, is frequently a time when medication is used. An inpatient, hospital setting would normally be necessary for detoxification using medication. In the detoxification process for alcohol and other CNS depressants, minor tranquilizers such as Valium or Xanax are often used to reduce the danger of seizures and the other uncomfortable and dangerous withdrawal symptoms. Careful medical supervision with a gradually decreasing dosage is necessary, since these minor tranquilizers are in the same drug classification as alcohol (see Chapter 2). The use of drugs in the detoxification from opioids has also been suggested (Matuschka, 1985), and there has been use of nondependence producing drugs in the withdrawal from cocaine (Landry, 1988).

Methadone is widely known for its use in treating opioid addiction. Methadone is a synthetic narcotic with a longer duration of effect than heroin, and ingestion blocks the euphoric effects of opioids. The goal of methadone maintenance is to provide medically supervised dosages to eliminate drug craving in chronic opioid addicts (Dole, 1989). Calahan (1980) recommends careful screening of potential candidates for methadone maintenance and contracting with clients who receive methadone. He suggests that clients be withdrawn from the program if other drug use is detected and that methadone clients be involved in other treatment in addition to methadone.

Antabuse (disulfiram) has been used in conjunction with other forms of alcohol treatment. When Antabuse is taken and alcohol is ingested during the following 24- to 48-hour period, the client experiences facial flushing, heart palpitations and rapid heart rate, difficulty in breathing, nausea, and vomiting (Schuckit, 1984). Since Antabuse takes 30 minutes to work after ingestion, it has been of limited value in aversive conditioning. The client must take Antabuse on a daily basis, and this raises an issue of the need for such medication. If an individual were motivated to take Antabuse daily, it would seem that he or she would probably be motivated to remain abstinent without Antabuse. However, some alcoholics, when tempted to use alcohol, are comforted by the fact that Antabuse will result in an unpleasant reaction if they drink. This awareness often reduces or eliminates the urge to use. Clients who use Antabuse must be warned against using over-the-counter products that contain alcohol, since the Antabuse will cause a reaction from the use of these products.

Nondependence-producing psychoactive drugs, such as those mentioned in Chapter 2, have also been used as adjuncts to other types of treatment. As Rone, Miller, and Frances (1995) noted, with regard to the treatment of alcoholism, there is a "close association between alcohol dependence and other psychiatric problems, such as depression and anxiety, for which psychotropics are clearly a useful form of treatment" (p. 267). However, the model of addiction one believes in may affect the decision to use psychotropic drugs. For example, Powell, Read, Penick, Miller, and Bingham (1987) and Schuckit (1983) believe that a small number of alcoholics (2 to 5%) have primary depression, while many alcoholics demonstrate symptoms of depression that are secondary to their alcoholism. From these authors' point of view, the antidepressants would be rare.

Treatment Strategies and Techniques

In describing the major approaches to treatment, we have already mentioned some of the techniques used in the treatment of alcoholics and addicts. For example, the disease or Minnesota Model uses group therapy, education, Twelve Step meetings, and other strategies as well. In this section, we want to describe the most common procedures that are used in treatment. However, understand that not all of these strategies may be used in all treatment programs, or more or less emphasis may be placed on particular interventions depending on the treatment approach and setting. It is a good idea for helping professionals to contact treatment programs in their areas to determine the exact components of the particular program *before* making referrals.

Morgenstern and McCrady (1992) reviewed the literature in the substance abuse treatment field and identified 35 processes used in treatment. They categorized these processes as general psychotherapy, behaviorally oriented, disease model, or pharmacology. Examples of processes used from a disease model included facilitating the client's spiritual experience in recovery, helping the client accept the disease concept, and facilitating the client's commitment to attend AA meetings, to get a sponsor, and to work the Twelve Steps. Behavioral processes include helping the client understand that problem drinking is a learned behavior, helping the client understand the role of high-risk situations in triggering drinking, and teaching the family new ways of coping with the client's drinking-related behavior. Pharmacological processes were related to administering medications (e.g., methadone).

Clearly, the identification of these processes is not much help in understanding what happens in treatment. How do you "help" or "facilitate?" The only concrete processes are those related to providing medication. Treatment planning and the treatment plan are the methods by which treatment staff determine what the problems are and what to do about them. Any substance abuse treatment program that is accredited by a state or other accrediting body will have individual treatment plans for all clients. That does not mean that all treatment plans in all treatment programs are comprehensive or useful—just that potential for usefulness exists. Treatment planning involves the assessment and diagnosis of the client (discussed in Chapter 5), the actual written treatment plan, and an aftercare plan. While the form and content of the treatment plan may vary from program to program and state to state depending on accreditation requirements, every treatment plan should include a statement of the problem(s), long-term goals, short-term objectives that are measurable, strategies to achieve goals and objectives, and review and target dates.

To illustrate a problem statement, long-term goal, and short-term objective, we asked to look at some treatment plans at one of our local treatment programs (with names deleted, of course). As has been our experience in the past, the only differences we saw in treatment plans were the drugs of choice mentioned in the problem statement and length of client use. Goals, objectives, and strategies were almost identical. This example is certainly representative, although we will discuss the problem of applying the same strategies to every client later in this chapter.

Example of Treatment Plan

Problem Statement: (Client's Name) has used alcohol and cocaine on a daily basis for the last 16 months.

Long-term Goal: (Client's Name) will remain abstinent from all mind-altering drugs.

Short-term Objective: (Client's Name) will remain abstinent from all mind-altering drugs for one month.

Strategies: 1. Attend one AA or NA meeting per day.
2. Attend all program lectures.
3. Participate in two individual counseling sessions per week.

4. Participate in three group counseling sessions per week.
5. Participate in one family counseling session per week.

Let's examine these strategies more closely, along with some that are not addressed on this portion of the treatment plan.

Individual, Group, and Family Counseling

Since you are preparing for a career as a mental health professional, you have had or will have courses in individual, group, and family counseling. Although it is beyond our scope to thoroughly discuss the processes and theoretical approaches to counseling, we believe that an individual who enters a counseling relationship with any client should be trained and credentialed to perform counseling functions. At the very minimum, mental health professionals should possess the facilitative qualities of counseling, such as empathy, respect, warmth, concreteness, immediacy, congruence, and genuineness. While the need for training, credentialing, and facilitative qualities have (hopefully) been drilled into your head making this message seem redundant, these issues are of utmost concern in the substance-abuse counseling field. In most states, substance abuse counselors need only a high school diploma or GED and little, if any, formal training.

While the specific techniques and approaches to counseling used in treatment programs depend on the program's model of addiction and on the training and experience of the counselors, "The general approach of individual and group therapy is the confrontation of the addict's system of denial, combined with counseling designed to help the client learn how to face the problems of daily living *without* using chemicals" (Doweiko, 1993, p. 333, italics in original). The use of confrontation as a therapeutic technique in counseling alcoholics and addicts will be discussed later in the chapter.

Royce (1989) described the counseling models he sees as most useful in counseling alcoholics:

> *Whether group or individual, it seems that the most appropriate psychotherapeutic modes for alcoholics are those that focus on the present and future rather than on the past. Examples are the reality therapy of William Glasser, the existential here-and-now logotherapy of Viktor Frankl, the rational-emotive therapy (RET) of Albert Ellis, and other such nonanalytic therapies.... Psychodrama and role-playing can be very useful under a skilled therapist, because of their appeal to both imagination and emotion. Transactional analysis (TA)... can be useful provided one does not get too involved in analyzing the games people play or think of alcoholic addiction as merely learned behavior that can be easily unlearned (p. 256).*

Ironically, Royce, a disease concept proponent, mentions RET as a useful therapy when this theoretical model has been used in a self-help alternative to AA (Trimpey, 1989). In addition to Royce's suggestions, we would also include the previously discussed use of behavioral techniques of therapy, such as covert desensitization and Behavioral Self-Control Training (Hester, 1995).

Traditionally, group counseling is "often the mainstay of both inpatient and outpatient treatment programs" (Doweiko, 1993, p. 330). However, as Lewis, Dana, and Blevins (1994) point out,

> group work with substance-abusing clients has tended to take one of two avenues: an emphasis on verbal confrontation or an emphasis on didactic presentation of information. These methods are inconsistent with what is known about human behavior change and may lack the very characteristics that make group work effective (p. 127).

In other words, in many treatment programs, group counseling may actually be a confrontation of individuals in the group who are not "working the program" or may be dissemination of educational information. This is considerably different from the group counseling described by Corey (1990) that is probably part of your training program. Lewis et al. (1994) advocate group work designed to develop concrete useable skills and to rehearse these behaviors in the group. In addition, they suggest that group counseling be used to analyze drinking and drug taking behaviors and to develop methods of coping, problem solving, and assertiveness, rather than being focused on gaining client compliance to admit to having a disease.

There has been an increasing use of family counseling in treatment programs. As with group counseling, what is sometimes called family counseling is actually education about the disease concept and the family's role in the disease process. However, family counseling is an essential component of treatment as O'Farrell (1995) explains:

> Many alcoholics have extensive marital and family problems . . . and positive family adjustment is associated with better alcoholism treatment outcomes at follow-up . . . Marital and family problems may stimulate excessive drinking, and family interactions often help to maintain alcohol problems once they have developed. . . . Finally, even when recovery from the alcohol problem has begun, marital and family conflicts may often precipitate renewed drinking by abstinent alcoholics (p. 195).

Conceptually, Kaufman and Kaufman (1992) suggested the following paradigm in working with families of substance abusers:

> Treating the family of a substance abuser is a complicated process. Treatment takes place simultaneously on many levels. In meeting the needs of the family as an entity, the spouse subsystem, the sibling subsystem, and the individual needs of each person in the family must be considered. These three areas must interlock and work in harmony. Teaching and demonstrating effective parenting is an important aspect of treatment. Encouraging families to form positive social networks aids in

> *the total treatment. Part of family therapy is the problem-solving process that occurs. Hopefully, these techniques become internalized so that the family maintains them throughout its lifetime. (p. x).*

Kaufman and Kaufman (1992) provide a compilation of approaches to family therapy with substance abusers including psychodynamic, structural-strategic, multi-dimensional, and behavioral models.

Support Groups

We will thoroughly discuss Twelve Step and other forms of support groups in Chapter 8. However, Twelve Step groups are such a central part of most treatment programs that there must be some mention here of this type of treatment strategy. For example, Adelman and Weiss (1989) stated that Alcoholics Anonymous (AA) is an essential component of an effective inpatient program, while Zimberg (1978) said that outpatient treatment for addiction should include AA. In fact, "virtually all of the many programs that this author has examined throughout the country utilize an Alcoholics Anonymous (AA) or Narcotics Anonymous (NA) twelve-step approach for both in- and outpatient treatment" (Abadinsky, 1993, p. 193), and, in discussing outpatient treatment, Doweiko (1993) stated that

> *Outpatient chemical dependency treatment programs usually adopt a twelve-step philosophy, similar to that used by Alcoholics Anonymous. Some programs include AA meetings in their schedule, although it is more common for the program to require client attendance at either AA or NA meetings in the community (p. 332).*

Again, we will save a discussion of the components and effectiveness of Twelve Step groups for the following chapter. However, the use of Twelve Step meetings as a treatment strategy and the utilization of the Twelve Step philosophy in treatment programs is consistent with the disease model of addiction and, as we have already discussed, with the orientation of the Minnesota Model of treatment.

While AA and NA are recommended for the alcoholic/addict, "family members are encouraged to attend either Al-Anon or Alateen meetings.... This is to introduce family members to the potential support available through Al-Anon or Alateen while the client is still in treatment" (Doweiko, 1993, p. 332–333). For those of you unfamiliar with these groups, Al-Anon is a support group for family members of alcoholics/addicts using the Twelve Step model and Alateen is a similar support group specifically for teenagers who have an alcoholic/addicted parent. Clients and family members may also be referred to ACOA (Twelve Step support for adult children of alcoholics) or CODA (Twelve Step support for codependents).

There are alternative support groups to those that use the Twelve Step model. However, the acceptance of these alternatives in disease-model treatment programs may be resisted. Among these alternative groups are Women for Sobriety, started by Jean Kirkpatrick in 1976; Secular Organization for Sobriety or Save Our

Selves (SOS), originated by James Christopher in 1985; Rational Recovery, begun in 1985; and Many Roads, One Journey, a sixteen-step program developed by Charlotte Kasl in 1991. All of these programs and the reasons why they are resisted by disease-model proponents will be discussed in Chapter 8.

Life-Style Changes

Irrespective of the orientation of the treatment program, treatment strategies designed to bring about changes in the lifestyle of the client are essential. For example, if clients return to the same friends and activities that were a part of their lives prior to treatment, relapse is highly probable. The range of lifestyle changes that must be addressed illustrates the complexity of comprehensive treatment and the need for long-term interventions for alcoholic/addicted individuals. We will discuss some of these strategies for lifestyle change in more detail in Chapter 13, Relapse Prevention, since mental health professionals may be involved in the implementation of many of these strategies. The lifestyle areas that should receive attention for a particular client should be determined during the assessment of the client and should then be included in the treatment plan.

The issue of friends, lovers, family members, and acquaintances is a focus of treatment. If a client has close associations with individuals who use alcohol and other drugs, some difficult and painful decisions must be made. These topics may be discussed in individual, group, and family counseling. In addition, clients may need assistance with social skills in order to enhance their ability to make new friends. Many alcoholic/addicted individuals have relied on the use of alcohol and other drugs to feel comfortable in social situations and/or as a common bond to those with whom they spend time. The difficulty of this particular area can often be clearly illustrated with an adolescent who is told during treatment to avoid contact with friends who use. The adolescent returns to school after treatment and perceives his or her options as returning to a previous social group or having no friends at all. If relapse is to be avoided, the adolescent who is treated for an alcohol or other drug problem clearly needs continued support and assistance to help develop a new social group.

Since many individuals with alcohol and other drug problems have used these substances to avoid negative emotions or to manage stress and pain, alternative methods of dealing with common life problems must also be taught in treatment. Strategies may involve stress management techniques, relaxation procedures, and assertiveness training. The intent of such training is to provide the client with skills to use in situations or in response to situations in which alcohol or other drug use was the only perceived option available. For example, a business executive is treated for alcoholism. He returns to work after treatment and, as happens to everyone, has "one of those days." In the past, he has used alcohol to cope with the stress and tension of work. If the client is not taught alternative methods for managing stress and tension along with techniques to relax that do not involve drugs, relapse is a predictable response.

Other lifestyle areas that may be a focus of intervention include vocational and educational planning, financial planning, living environment, and nutrition. To illustrate how these factors can influence recovery, we will use the case of a client named Romentha who was seen for individual counseling. Romentha's drug of choice was methamphetamine and she was on probation for possession and court-ordered to treatment. After completing an inpatient, 28-day program, she was seen for counseling on a weekly basis. Romentha regularly attended NA meetings and seemed sincerely interested in living a drug-free life. She lived in a small house with 14 people, including her daughter and an abusive, drug-using boyfriend. The house was owned by the boyfriend's parents. When Romentha told the boyfriend that she wished to leave the relationship and the house, he threatened to kill both her and her daughter. He had a history of violence. Romentha had lost her license to work in her trained profession (slot machine mechanic) due to her felony conviction. She was unemployed, had no child care, and was diabetic. When she did not manage her diet and insulin, she would experience severe mood swings.

You can easily see all the areas that required attention, any of which could result in a return to use if ignored. These practical issues in treatment go beyond the model used and are critical determinants in whether a client is able to maintain a drug-free lifestyle. So you won't be kept in eternal suspense, this particular situation had a fairly happy ending (as far as we know today). Romentha's boyfriend was sent to prison for a variety of offenses, and she was able to move in with her brother. A vocational rehabilitation counselor helped her find employment, and a latch-key program through her daughter's school provided child care. Again, the point of this case is to illustrate how vocational guidance, financial planning, living arrangements, and nutritional counseling may all be necessary components of treatment.

Education

Many treatment programs, particularly those using a disease-concept model, use lectures and films to provide clients with information on the disease concept, on family issues in alcohol and other drug use, and on the social, medical, and psychological consequences of alcohol and other drug use. Miller and Hester (1995) discuss the rationale for the use of education in the treatment of alcoholism:

> *U.S. alcohol treatment often includes a series of lectures and films. . . . Implicit in such strategies is the assumption that alcohol problems evolve from deficient knowledge—from a lack of accurate information. When armed with correct and up-to-date knowledge, individuals presumably will be less likely to use alcohol (and other drugs) in a hazardous fashion and to suffer the consequences (p. 4).*

Although the teaching of educational information is a commonly used strategy in treatment, Lewis et al. (1994) have criticized this component of treatment:

> *Many counselors assume, for instance, that "educating clients about alcoholism" is a necessary and possibly even sufficient mechanism for engendering sobriety; yet one would be hard pressed to find real support for the generalization that the*

provision of factual information can be counted on to bring about desired changes in attitude or behavior (p. 18).

(As an aside, it has always been fascinating to us that didactic methods are used to present information to clients in treatment with little or no regard for the learning capacity or learning style of the client. For example, since our own research (Karacostas & Fisher, 1993) has found a higher-than-expected proportion of learning-disabled adolescents with probable alcohol and other drug problems, it would be logical to assess clients to determine the most effective method for imparting information. However, we have found that this is rarely a part of the assessment in treatment programs.)

Aftercare

Although aftercare refers to the interventions and strategies that will be implemented after formal treatment is completed, "'Aftercare' is a misleading term; it should be 'continuing care'" (Royce, 1989, p. 288). This means that aftercare programs are usually continuations of many of the strategies from formal treatment. Aftercare has been well-described by Doweiko (1993):

> *The aftercare program is designated and carried out on the assumption that treatment does not end with the individual's discharge from a formal treatment program. Rather, treatment is the first part of a recovery program that...will continue for the rest of the individual's life. The aftercare component of the treatment plan addressed those issues that should be addressed following the individual's discharge from the rehabilitation program (p. 321).*

The case of Romentha we described above is a good example of how issues that cannot possibly be solved in a month-long treatment program can be carried on in aftercare. Frequently, individual and family therapy will be components of an aftercare program as well as vocational, educational, and financial guidance. Attendance at Twelve Step meetings will usually be mentioned in aftercare plans. Aftercare meetings may be a part of the treatment program, or the client may be referred to a mental health professional for management of the aftercare program. Since the aftercare program is an essential element in relapse prevention, we will discuss this in detail in Chapter 13.

Treatment Settings

The strategies and interventions described can be implemented in a variety of treatment settings. In this section, we will briefly describe these settings and then discuss some of the issues that may determine the type of setting in which a client receives treatment.

Therapeutic Communities

The therapeutic community is a residential environment usually associated with treatment for drugs other than alcohol. As Polich, Ellickson, Reuter, and Kahan (1984) explained, "The goal of therapeutic communities is to resocialize the drug abuser by creating a structured isolated mutual-help environment in which the individual can develop and learn to function as a mature participant" (p. 96). The duration of treatment is typically longer than other types of treatment, usually one year or more. Synanon, one of the earliest and most famous therapeutic communities, expected permanent involvement by clients. The characteristics of therapeutic communities "include social and physical isolation, a structured living environment, a firm system of rewards and punishments, and an emphasis on self-examination and confession of past wrongdoing" (Doweiko, 1993, p. 337). Although therapeutic communities have been effective with some clients who have failed in other treatment environments, the social isolation, extreme level of confrontation, and high drop-out and relapse rates have been criticized (Doweiko, 1993).

Inpatient and Residential Treatment

Although this treatment environment is usually associated with hospitals, this is not always the case. Residential treatment may occur in nonhospital settings. The duration of treatment is shorter than in therapeutic communities, and the social isolation is reduced. Most inpatient and residential programs gradually reintroduce the client to a normal environment through community outings and home passes. These programs generally offer supervised detoxification that may involve medication in a hospital setting or social detoxification (i.e., no medication) in a nonhospital setting. The typical 28-day treatment duration has no research base. It has come about as a result of financial constraints, particularly the willingness of insurance companies to pay for treatment. Inpatient and residential treatment settings have the advantages of 24-hour supervision, the reduced likelihood of clients using while in treatment, highly structured days, and a total immersion in treatment, with removal from the everyday stressors and pressures that may interfere with treatment. The disadvantages of this setting are the expense (a 28-day program in a hospital setting may be well over $10,000) and the artificiality of the environment. In a supervised, structured, and protective setting, a client may have little difficulty maintaining abstinence. In a well-supervised program, there may be no choice. However, the client may have little or no opportunity to practice new behaviors and may develop a false belief in self-efficacy (competence to deal with the environment). The real world may quickly dispel the client's perception of self-efficacy, and relapse results.

Outpatient and Day Treatment

As with inpatient and residential treatment, outpatient and day treatment may occur in a hospital or free-standing clinic such as a mental health center. Day treatment programs may involve the client's going to the hospital but not remaining overnight. Outpatient treatment may be in the evening for several hours, two to four nights a week. These programs are obviously less expensive than inpatient or residential programs, and they allow clients to continue to work and to remain involved with their families while they receive treatment. Clients are immediately able to practice what they learn in the real world. Because the programs are less expensive and intensive, they can also be of longer duration than inpatient and residential programs. However, there are disadvantages to outpatient and day treatment programs as well. The drop-out rate is high (Baekeland & Lundwall, 1975), and a greater opportunity exists for a client to use while involved in treatment. For example, a client may during the weekend and return to the program on Monday with no readily apparent evidence of use. Unless the client admits to use or drug testing occurs, the client's use may never be discovered. Also, clients in outpatient and day treatment programs must have social support systems for maintaining sobriety. If the client's family is not involved in treatment or continues an enabling pattern (see Chapter 10), then relapse is likely. Similarly, the client will have difficulty maintaining sobriety if friends are not supportive of the treatment program.

Choice of Treatment Setting

Klar (1987) discussed the concept of "least restrictive environment" with regard to the appropriate treatment setting. Those of you with a background in special education are familiar with this concept as it relates to placement of students, and the rationale is similar for alcohol and other drug treatment. Clients should be placed in the treatment setting that offers the least amount of restriction, with the highest probability of success, while all the factors identified in the assessment are considered. What are some of these factors? Nace (1987) identified criteria for determining whether outpatient alcoholism treatment was appropriate. These criteria included client motivation, ability to discontinue use, social support, employment, medical condition, psychiatric status, and treatment history. Clients who are poorly motivated to discontinue use (i.e., court mandated) or who admit to a failure to abstain if alcohol or other drugs are available may fail in outpatient treatment. Also, we have already discussed the importance of social support. Employment may be a double-edged sword. While continued employment may strongly motivate a client to succeed in outpatient treatment, the work environment is often a source of stress for people or co-workers might encourage the client to use (i.e., going out for drinks after work). An individual who is unemployed (and, ironically, is probably the least able to afford more expensive inpatient treatment), may be a poor candidate for an outpatient program since the client is not occupied for a large segment of time by a job. Obviously, individuals with medical and/or psychiatric conditions may need more restrictive treatment environments. A person with liver damage may need medical supervision and an environment that insures abstinence. Similarly, a client who is receiving pharmaceutical treatment for a psychiatric condition may (but not always) require inpatient treatment.

Finally, if someone has already failed in outpatient or day treatment, more intensive treatment may be needed.

Unfortunately, all of these factors might not be used in determining the treatment setting for a client. "The person whose insurance will pay only for outpatient chemical dependency treatment will have certain financial restrictions placed on his or her treatment options" (Doweiko, 1993, p. 342). In other words, money and the availability of publicly funded treatment programs, rather than client factors, may determine where a person is placed for treatment.

Treatment and Special Populations

As with any aspect of the helping professions, the individual and group differences of clients must be considered in designing treatment. We have previously introduced you to the concept of client-treatment matching and have focused on the need to tailor treatment to the unique characteristics of the client rather than forcing a client to fit a particular model of treatment or addiction. Similarly, group characteristics are important to consider in treatment. This is not to imply that clients should be stereotyped simply because they are members of a particular age, gender, or ethnic group. However, demographic information may be relevant in understanding the client and in designing appropriate treatment. A comprehensive discussion of the treatment issues for all special populations would be beyond our goals for this book. We do want to acquaint you with some of these issues so you will be informed when directing your clients to treatment.

Ethnically Diverse Populations

The issues with regard to ethnically diverse populations were discussed in detail in Chapter 4, not only in regard to treatment, but to other alcohol and other drug issues as well.

At this point, we want to restate several points specifically with regard to treatment. First, diversity in the treatment population and the staff is clearly beneficial for client comfort and understanding. Second, the attitude of an ethnic group toward alcohol and other drug problems may present a barrier for the individual seeking treatment. For example, Brisbane and Wells (1989) have stated that many African-American communities view alcoholism as immoral or sinful behavior, a view that is clearly incompatible with the disease concept of alcoholism. In this view, the person, not alcohol, is responsible for problems, and the use of alcohol could be controlled if the person so desired. African Americans who hold this view would be less likely to encourage and support family members and friends to seek treatment. This barrier is certainly not unique to African Americans, so many disease model programs include education for the family. Third, the customs, beliefs, and language of the group must be considered in treatment. An obvious example is the barrier presented in treatment for Spanish-speaking clients, when the treatment staff are not bilingual. With regard to Native Americans, Young (1992) stated that

Intervention strategies must begin the realization that Native Americans repre-
sent a diverse population. Treatment modalities that prove effective among one
group of Native Americans may not be useful or appropriate among another
group.... In some cases ... the clinician must be prepared to transcend the so-
called clinical mentality through the use of indigenous healers and Native Amer-
ican health care practices (p. 388).

Elderly

According to Jung (1994), the elderly are underrepresented in alcohol and other
drug treatment programs. This may be due to social and economic barriers to entering treatment or because a problem is not identified by the client or the family.
Abrams and Alexopoulos (1987) found that alcoholism was less likely to be identified in the elderly, "in part because the impairments in social and occupational
functioning attributable to alcoholism in younger people are not as obvious"
(p. 1285) although "more than 20 percent of patients over 65 years old admitted for
a psychiatric hospital could be considered drug dependent" (p. 1286). In addition,
family members may be embarrassed by the behavior of the elderly person, and
this embarrassment may cause the family to avoid bringing the use patterns of the
elderly person to the attention of professionals. Finally, the type of problem that the
elderly person has may be difficult to identify. Whereas alcohol misuse may be
clear, many elderly persons also misuse prescription medications, which may not
be obvious to the family.

As Zimberg (1978) pointed out, the problems of the elderly are often different
from those of younger clients and may require specific attention in treatment. For
example, the elderly client may be experiencing an emotional reaction to retire-
ment, feelings of bereavement from the death of a spouse and/or friends, loneliness, and physical pain from illnesses or age.

Adolescents

The senior author conducted a psychological evaluation of an adolescent in an inpatient treatment program some time ago. During the evaluation, the young man
reported that he (and others, so he claimed) had learned that if they publicly (defined as being in a group) said that they had a disease and were powerless, they
would be released from the program. This young man was quite rebellious (one reason the evaluation had been requested), and he refused to say that he had a disease.
In fact, he told everyone that he had every intention to use again when he got out.

This adolescent's statements are indicative of some of the treatment issues for
adolescents. Adolescents have difficulty relating to a concept of a life-long disease.
They have rarely experienced the same level of life problems resulting from their
alcohol and other drug use as adults have. When they attend AA or NA meetings,
they may hear stories from older adults that have little relationship to their lives
(Fisher & Harrison, 1993). If you have worked with adolescents at all, you probably
know that they can be skilled at saying what they need to say to get what they

want. After working with adolescents with alcohol and other drug problems for some time, we have little doubt that what the young man said was true. Many of the adolescents told the staff what they wanted to hear. Finally, adolescents may reject the idea that life-style change is necessary. Adults who have lost jobs, families, possessions, and have been arrested for DUIs may have little difficulty accepting the need to change their lives. An adolescent who has been busted at school for smoking pot may not feel the same way. Even when the problems have been more significant, it is very difficult to convince an adolescent that he or she needs to change his or her social group. Lawson (1992) has suggested considering the developmental stage of the adolescent in treatment strategies and using alternatives to Twelve Step groups and models when necessary.

Persons with Disabilities

Individuals with sensory (hearing or visually impaired), motor, mental, and learning handicaps can and do have alcohol and other drug problems. For example, Karacostas and Fisher (1993) found evidence that adolescents diagnosed as learning disabled had a higher rate of chemical dependency than did nonlearning disabled peers. Obviously, the nature of the disability may be a factor in the development of the substance abuse problem and is certainly a factor in treatment. For example, we worked with a young man named Stan, who became a quadriplegic at age 24 after an automobile accident. Although he had been an occasional alcohol user before the accident, Stan began heavy use of prescription pain medication, alcohol, and marijuana following his accident. He had extreme difficulty handling his grief regarding his loss of mobility and his increased dependence on others. Clearly, these were important treatment issues. Another of our clients, Lisa, had been blind since birth. To cope with social isolation in high school, Lisa began using a variety of drugs and ended up in a hospital emergency room at age 17 after an overdose. Finding a treatment program that could meet her needs was extremely difficult.

Irrespective of the model of addiction, persons with disabilities have treatment needs that require attention. We have already mentioned the grief that a person may experience, particularly if the disability was acquired later in life. With sensory handicaps, there is the obvious problem of communication. In a program with a heavy educational component, the methods of imparting information must be adapted for the sensory-impaired client. For individuals with learning disabilities, instructional strategies must be modified to accommodate the type of learning disability (Karacostas & Fisher, 1993). Individuals with intellectual handicaps may not be able to grasp abstract concepts and, therefore, may be unable to understand the disease concept. More behavioral interventions may be necessary.

Designing the treatment of persons with disabilities is clearly consistent with the notion of client/treatment matching that we will discuss later in this chapter. Rather than forcing the person to fit a treatment program (which is impossible with persons with disabilities), the treatment program must meet the client's needs. However, the complexity of treatment for persons with disabilities also indicates the need for greater prevention efforts for this population. While there are many prevention programs for nondisabled young people (see Chapter 16), few efforts have been made to design programs for young people with disabilities.

Women

While it seems ironic to talk about half of the population as a special group, most information about treatment has come from studies with predominantly male subjects (Harrison & Belille, 1987). Beckman and Amaro (1984) identified the barriers that may keep women from alcohol and other drug treatment. These include the stigma of identification as an alcoholic or addict, family responsibilities, lack of child care in treatment facilities, inaccurate diagnosis because of professional's stereotypes (belief that alcoholics/addicts are men), and negative reactions of family and friends based on stereotypes about alcoholics/addicts. Once in treatment, "their feelings may run from fear of rape to embarrassment at walking down the corridor in a bathrobe" (Royce, 1989, p. 174).

Women may also have special treatment issues that differ from those of men. For example, Rohsenow, Corbett, and Devine (1988) found that as many as three-quarters of the women in treatment may have a history of sexual abuse that may result in sexual dysfunction or post-traumatic stress disorder. Delayed stress symptoms and sexual dysfunction may precipitate relapse (Wallen, 1990). Additional treatment issues may include self-esteem, perceived powerlessness, and guilt if the woman has used alcohol and other drugs during pregnancy. Due to these special treatment issues, Royce (1989) has suggested all-women treatment groups, at least early in treatment.

Gays and Lesbians

As Cabaj (1992) reported, there is an exceptionally high rate of alcohol and other drug problems in the gay and lesbian population. While the reasons for this high incidence are unclear, biochemical and psycho-social explanations have been proposed (Cabaj, 1992). With regard to treatment, Cabaj (1992) stated that "Homophobia is the major consideration in meeting the treatment needs of gay men and lesbians with substance abuse problems, as well as the proper care and prevention of HIV-related infections" (p. 857). Homophobia may be related to staff attitudes or to the client's own denial and dissociation. With regard to HIV, "Treatment centers and programs may still be frightened to work with HIV-positive individuals . . . or may resist talking about safer sex because it is uncomfortable to talk about such matters or it is viewed as detracting from recovery issues" (Cabaj, 1992, p. 858). Another treatment issue for gays and lesbians involves social isolation "when the gay person has limited contacts who relate to him as a gay person. . . . Staying away from bars or parties may be difficult since they are often the patient's only social outlet" (Cabaj, 1992, p. 858). As we discussed with adolescents, the development of a nonusing social group is an important treatment objective for gays and lesbians.

Treatment Effectiveness

Does treatment work? This issue is complex but extremely important, given the time and expense of alcohol and other drug treatment and the costs to society if people continue abusing alcohol and other drugs following treatment. While numerous studies have examined treatment effectiveness, making sense of the results is difficult because of several underlying problems. Before discussing some of these studies, let's look at some of these problems.

Treatment programs (for the most part) are not designed to scientifically evaluate the aspects of treatment that are most effective. This makes research immediately problematic, since there is no control over the many variables that may affect results. The numerous client variables that may impact treatment effectiveness include age, gender, duration of use, type of substances used, life problems experienced, voluntary or involuntary admission to treatment, prior treatment, client health, psychological problems, criminal activity, level of education, and income. The type of treatment environment (e.g., private, for profit; public, nonprofit; hospital inpatient; free standing outpatient; therapeutic community) may impact effectiveness. To adequately research the effectiveness of a treatment program or treatment approach, a control group is necessary. Ethical (and practical) issues in the random assignment of clients to treatment must be considered when the researcher hypothesizes that one form of treatment is superior to another.

Equally as important to the issues that create barriers to well-designed research are the types of outcomes in effectiveness studies. Is client success defined by program completion, abstinence, length of sobriety, and/or reduction in life problems? What if a client completes a program, relapses, goes to a different program, and then remains abstinent? Was the first program a failure or did it contribute to the client's sobriety later on?

With these problems in mind, let's examine some of the available research. McLellan, Luborsky, and O'Brien (1986) studied three different programs: a VA hospital with inpatient and outpatient services; a private, for profit, inpatient hospital; and a private, nonprofit, inpatient hospital. In the researcher's words,

> *we conclude that substance abuse treatment is* associated with *significant improvement in the problems of addicted patients. Further, these improvements occur not just in the target problems of chemical use, but in the important areas of employment, illegal activity, and psychiatric status. Finally, the nature and extent of these improvements are quite similar across rather diverse treatments and patient populations, thus strengthening the generalizability of this conclusion* (p. 117, italics in original).

McLellan et al. (1986) also found that the typical types of demographic information about clients were not significantly related to treatment outcome. However, the existence of pretreatment psychiatric problems was the best single predictor of follow-up status. Finally, the researchers stated, "our clinical experience and a wealth of research data suggest that treatments that target the reduction and elimination of alcohol and/or drug use without strongly addressing...ancillary problems leave the recovering patient at significant risk for relapse" (p. 118).

Hubbard, Marsden, Rachel, Harwood, Cavanaugh, and Ginsberg (1989) studied 10,000 clients admitted to 41 long-term drug treatment programs between 1979 and 1981. Three types of programs were included: methadone maintenance plus counseling, therapeutic communities, and drug-free outpatient. They concluded that treatment does result in the decreased use of drugs but that abstinence was relatively rare. There was also a decrease in criminal activity. They found no differences in the three types of treatments.

Cook (1988) reviewed a variety of studies examining treatment programs using the Minnesota Model. While acknowledging the methodological problems of these studies and the need for additional research, he concluded that, "Despite exaggerated claims of success, it [Minnesota Model] appears to have a genuinely impressive 'track record' with as many as two-thirds of its patients achieving a 'good' outcome at 1 year after discharge" (p. 746).

Length of treatment was the subject of a study by Charuvastra, Dalali, Cassuci, and Wing (1992). They examined male, veteran, heroin addicts in residential community treatment. The treatment program reduced the stay of patients from one year in 1973 to three months in 1985. Charuvastra et al. (1992) found that, six months after treatment, 26% of the 1973 patients were defined as "failures," while 47% of the 1985 patients were failures. These results were not surprising since, "Given what is known about the importance of length of stay in treatment and the complexity of the recovery process in addiction, there is little likelihood that twenty-eight-day clinics or short-term modalities (one to six months) will yield positive outcomes" (DeLeon, 1990, p. 125).

To determine the relative effectiveness of inpatient versus outpatient programs, Miller and Hester (1986) reviewed 16 studies comparing such programs. They found no significant differences between inpatient and outpatient alcoholism treatment programs on various measures of client improvement. O'Brien, Alterman, Walter, Childress, and McLellan (1990) found similar results in examining African American veterans with cocaine addictions. Although equal levels of improvement were found for inpatient and outpatient treatment, the inpatient completion rate was far greater than in the outpatient program.

Although it is not possible to comprehensively review all treatment effectiveness research, several conclusions can be reached. First, treatment does appear to have a beneficial effect on a variety of client behaviors, including their alcohol and other drug use. The model of treatment may be less important than the attention to a variety of client problems and the length of treatment (longer treatment seems to be superior). The treatment setting does not appear to be a critical variable.

Client-Treatment Matching

As you've read the sections of this chapter on treatment strategies and special populations, we hope that it has occurred to you that there are so many and varied client issues, needs, and characteristics that it does not make sense to talk about alcohol and other drug treatment as if it should be the same for everyone. Unfortunately, in this particular field

> *Few people would argue with the common-sense idea that treatment should be individualized to the needs and characteristics of the clients. If one surveys alcoholism treatment programs with the question, "Do you tailor your treatment to the individual?", nearly all will answer "Yes." Yet many programs still consist of a relatively invariant set of treatment experiences offered to almost all clients.*
>
> *Furthermore, the treatment recommended to a client after evaluation is often determined by the door through which the person walked for assessment. Each program tends to find most clients it evaluates in need of the very kind of treatment it happens to offer (Miller, 1989, p. 261)*

Economics obviously is a factor in the fact that assessment personnel usually refer to the program they work for. At least, that is the case in for-profit treatment when the client has money or insurance. However, the failure of treatment programs to individualize treatment for clients may be related to the knowledge and skills of the treatment staff. Here's an example. We were talking to an alcohol and other drug counselor about one of her clients in an outpatient program. The client had recently been transferred to an inpatient psychiatric hospital after a suicide attempt. He had a history of depression and had been taking an antidepressant medication. The counselor complained of the client's denial of his alcohol and other drug problem and his inability to "admit his powerlessness" and to "work the program" (these are AA slogans). The counselor would not acknowledge the possibility that the client's alcohol and other drug use might be secondary to a major depression.

Only one state currently requires a baccalaureate degree for alcohol and other drug counseling, and most require only a high school diploma or GED (although there are other requirements as well). While we admit to a bias (since we are counselor educators), it does make sense that an alcohol and other drug counselor who knows the addiction field only through minimal training and his or her own experiences would have some difficulty managing other types of mental disorders that may exist concurrently with alcohol and other drug problems. If a counselor's training and experience are limited, he or she would likely force the client to adapt to the counselor's own conceptual framework. Otherwise, the counselor would feel helpless. Perhaps this is the reason that clients are indoctrinated with the notion that they must work on their disease before any other problems can be dealt with. Inadequately prepared alcohol and drug counselors may unconsciously project this idea onto their clients because of their own insecurity with working on issues outside their comfort level. Usually, these counselors are familiar only with the disease model of addiction.

Clearly, we would like to see a comprehensive assessment of client needs and an individualized treatment plan that addresses all relevant client issues. This would necessitate that treatment programs have staff who are trained to handle the types of client problems that require attention. A uniform certification process for alcohol and other drug counselors as well as more community college and university training programs would be helpful in this effort. Fortunately, uniform certification requirements are being worked on by professional organizations such as the National Association of Alcoholism and Drug Abuse Counselors and training centers based in colleges and universities have been funded by the Center for Substance Abuse Treatment.

Special Problems in Treatment

Recovering Individuals as Counselors

The issues raised in client-treatment matching relate to the use of recovering individuals as alcohol and other drug counselors. As Royce (1989) said, "Since the first Yale Plan Clinic in 1944, recovered alcoholics have been a part of most treatment teams, whether or not they belonged to a profession or had a college degree.... The understanding and empathy those workers gained from their own experience as alcoholics has long been recognized as a valuable contribution to the recovery process" (p. 341). However, Miller (1995) stated that, "The effectiveness of counselors has been found to be unrelated to whether or not they are themselves 'in recovery'" (p. 94).

The question is not whether recovering individuals should be alcohol and drug counselors. We believe, as we indicated on the section on client-treatment matching, that the issue is training. The counselor we described in the situation with the depressed and suicidal client was not in recovery. She was poorly trained. An assumption has been made in the field that, if one is in recovery, that attribute is sufficient for effectiveness as an alcohol and drug counselor. However, we would be hard-pressed to find support for the notion that if one has attempted suicide, he or she would be an effective crisis intervention counselor. We have trained many master's level counselors who are in recovery, and we believe that the combination of personal experience and professional training can be dynamic. An individual who is well trained and has good interpersonal skills can be an effective alcohol and other drug counselor, regardless of whether the counselor is in recovery. A person with little or no training and poor interpersonal skills will be ineffective, whether he or she is in recovery or not. What about the individual in recovery with little training and good interpersonal skills? This person might be a natural counselor and can undoubtedly be helpful. Lack of training is simply a factor limiting the type of client issue this counselor should work with. The outstanding natural counselors we have worked with who are in recovery and have returned for formal training have been able to recognize this limitation and have sought assistance to increase their effectiveness.

Confrontation as a Treatment Strategy

The association of confrontation with substance abuse treatment came about from the use of high levels of confrontation in therapeutic communities such as

Synanon. As Lewis et al. (1994) indicated, many alcohol and other drug counselors have come to believe that confrontation is the only skill necessary. Confrontation is seen as the therapeutic technique to break through the alcoholic/addict's denial. However, a hostile, confrontational counseling style has been found to be associated with poor long-term results (Lieberman, Yalom, & Miles, 1973).

The controversy regarding confrontation probably results from the association of this technique with hostility and aggression. In fact, some alcohol and other drug counselors may use confrontation in this manner because that is what they have seen and heard. However, confrontation is simply a matter of pointing out to a client that there is a discrepancy between what he or she says and he or she means, or between what is said and what is done (Ivey, Bradford-Ivey, & Simek-Morgan, 1993). In this context, confrontation is a valuable technique in alcohol and other drug treatment just as it is in other counseling situations. The inappropriate use of confrontation by counselors is a result of poor training and/or poor judgment. Hopefully, if client-treatment matching occurs, a counselor will determine the proper type of confrontation for a particular client and will not assume that all alcoholics/addicts must be confronted in a hostile and aggressive manner.

Dual Diagnosis

The dually diagnosed client has presented some interesting challenges in the substance abuse treatment field. To be dually diagnosed, a client must have an alcohol or drug addiction as well as another mental disorder. Ananth, Vandewater, Kamal, Brodsky, Gamal, and Miller (1989) found that 75% of a sample of psychiatric patients could be diagnosed as substance abusers or addicts. Kofoed, Kania, Walsh, and Atkinson (1986) reported that 21 to 39% of clients who were diagnosed with a substance use disorder also could be diagnosed with another mental disorder.

Traditionally, alcohol and other drug treatment programs would assume that other mental disorders, such as depression, were secondary to the substance abuse problem or that clients with clear psychiatric problems (e.g., schizophrenia) were inappropriate for alcohol and other drug treatment programs. It is true that symptoms of a mental disorder may be secondary to an alcohol or other drug problem. For example, clients who abuse cocaine clearly become significantly depressed in the early stages of recovery. Individuals who abuse methamphetamine may develop symptoms that are indistinguishable from paranoid schizophrenia. Therefore, the true dual diagnosis client may be difficult to accurately diagnose until a period of detoxification or until a very accurate history is available. Also, how should the dually diagnosed client be treated? Should the client be treated first for the substance abuse problem or the psychiatric problem? If the client is treated in a alcohol or other drug treatment program, will the staff be trained to work with the psychiatric problem (and vice versa)?

These issues have resulted in the development of dual diagnosis programs that supposedly can treat both alcohol and other drug problems along with other mental disorders. In such programs, there is a clear need for staff who are trained to work with both alcohol and other drug problems and mental disorders. Unfortunately, in order to attract more patients, some programs are advertised as dual diagnosis and are staffed only by alcohol and other drug counselors. This practice is unethical, giving cause for the mental health professional to check on the training of the staff before referring a client to a dual diagnosis program.

The Use of Medication

In the section of this chapter on treatment approaches, we discussed the use of different medications in the management of detoxification, treatment of alcohol and other drug addiction, and treatment of other mental disorders in alcoholics/addicts. Minor tranquilizers are used to prevent the medically dangerous withdrawal symptoms suffered in the detoxification from CNS depressants. Drugs such as Antabuse and methadone are used to treat alcoholism and opioid addiction, and various nondependence-producing psychoactive drugs are used to treat disorders such as depression and bipolar disorder.

The controversy in this area is probably related to a misinterpretation of AA's position on the use of drugs by alcoholics. Royce (1989) explains this misinterpretation:

> *AA rightly takes a strong stand against substituting one addictive drug for another. Overenthusiasm has trapped some AA members into incautious statements about pills that are not substitute addictions and may be medically necessary for a recovering alcoholic. Thus one sometimes hears horror stories about advice to a heart patient not to take digitalis, a diabetic not to take oral insulin, an epileptic not to take Dilantin, or a psychotic not to take lithium. . . . AA has never approved that kind of advice and in fact strongly disapproves (p. 352).*

It is certainly important for a physician to be made aware of the recovering status of a patient before prescribing pain medication with addictive potential, and alternatives to the use of pain medications are recommended (Royce, 1989). However, recovering persons should not be discouraged from taking medically necessary drugs.

Controlled Use

The question of whether alcoholics can learn to use alcohol in a moderate or nonproblematic manner has been a controversial issue in treatment for some time. In the early 1970s, the Sobells (Sobell & Sobell, 1973) were able to demonstrate that chronic alcoholics could successfully be taught controlled drinking in an experimental setting. Also, reports of the Rand study (Armor, Polich, & Stambul, 1978; Polich, Armor, & Braiker, 1981) indicated that many previously treated alcoholics had been drinking in a nonproblematic manner over a four-year period. The Sobell and Sobell (1973) study has been criticized since few of the alcoholic subjects maintained controlled drinking over an extended period of time (Hester, 1995) and, as Royce (1989) noted, "The Rand report and other studies have been criticized . . . for using too short a time period, taking inadequate care in followup, subjective reporting, small number, sampling fallacies, lack of control group, and employing absurdly artificial settings" (p. 134).

While the debate about controlled use makes for some fascinating reading in the field, largely because it evokes emotional as well as scholarly arguments and because it pits disease concept proponents against others, the practical issues seem more clear cut. It makes very little sense to teach a person to use alcohol in a controlled manner when the person has had numerous, serious life problems and has consistently demonstrated an inability to control alcohol use. If an individual can be diagnosed as having a substance dependence disorder based on the *DSM-IV* (see Chapter 5), controlled use is not a reasonable goal. Even proponents of controlled use recognize that this is not a productive goal for everyone (e.g., Miller & Munoz, 1982). Therefore, treatment programs, particularly if they use a disease model, would oppose controlled use because their clients would usually be classified as alcoholics/addicts.

Who would be a candidate for learning to use in a controlled manner? According to Lewis et al. (1994), "If drinkers are young and healthy, if they have not shown signs of physical dependence on alcohol, if their problem drinking is of recent duration, if they have few life problems associated with alcohol use, and if they object to abstinence, they may do best working toward moderating their drinking" (p. 7). These types of clients would more often be seen by generalist mental health professionals or alcohol and other drug counselors in private practice or working in mental health clinics.

We would advise any alcohol and other drug counselor or mental health professional to be very cautious in working with a client on controlled use. An abstinent client has no risk of problems from use; a client who uses at any level is at risk. However, some clients will resist treatment or drop out of treatment if abstinence is demanded. If such a client fits the criteria described above by Lewis et al. (1994), controlled use might be a treatment goal. Also, there are times when working with a resistant client on controlled use demonstrates to the client that he or she is unable to use in a nonproblematic manner. We worked with a young woman in individual counseling who had experienced a few minor problems as a result of her alcohol, marijuana, and cocaine use and would not agree to abstain. We asked her to set goals regarding her intake for two weeks and then to keep track of her actual use. It became very clear to her that her use was out of control since she almost always exceeded her goal. This resulted in her referral to an outpatient program and successful abstinence for at least one year (the last time we saw her).

Again, we suggest that controlled use be a treatment goal only when other alternatives have been explored and when it is probable that the client will experience more serious problems from an insistence on abstinence. There are various behavioral approaches to teaching controlled use including Behavioral Self-Control Training (Hester, 1995).

Natural Recovery and Dry Drunks

The fact that some people discontinue their problematic use of alcohol and other drugs without treatment has been documented by researchers (e.g., Tuchfield 1981; Sobell, Sobell, & Toneatto, 1991) and is certainly something we have seen in our own experience. The question that is raised is whether the person who becomes abstinent without treatment is recovering or is a *dry drunk*. A dry drunk is defined as a person who "may exhibit any or all the feelings and behavior associated with intoxication although no alcohol is consumed" (Royce, 1989, p. 299). This is not to imply that euphoria is experienced, as can be seen is Royce's (1989) description of the symptoms of the dry drunk: "Shakes, insomnia, stiffness, headaches, and other flu-like symptoms may accompany the irritability, fatigue, depression, hunger, egocentrism, over-reaction, unexplained sadness, aimless puttering or wandering, and a host of negative emotions" (p. 299).

There has been a sense from the treatment community and Twelve Step adherents that people who try to quit drinking or using on their own end up in the dry drunk syndrome. This sense probably arises from the same dynamics that cause treatment providers to view all alcoholics/addicts as having a disease. In other words, if you are a treatment provider or an AA member, when would you see someone who is trying to abstain on their own? You would see this person when he or she was having problems (such as the dry drunk symptoms) and was referred, on their own or by others, to a treatment program or to an AA meeting. It would be logical to conclude that discontinuing use without treatment or Twelve Step support is difficult, if not impossible. However, those who discontinue problematic use without experiencing the dry drunk syndrome do not show up in treatment or at meetings. Sobell et al. (1991) suggested that natural recovery is much more frequent than has been suspected.

Summary

In this chapter, we have attempted to give you a clear picture of the treatment of alcohol and other drug problems. We have discussed the approaches to treatment, treatment strategies and techniques, the settings in which treatment occurs, treatment issues with special populations, research on treatment effectiveness, and some controversial issues in treatment. We hope that we have dispelled any magical notions you have held about treatment and that you see that recovery from alcohol and other drug problems is complex, multi-dimensional, and extends far beyond the time constraints that a client can spend in a treatment program. In addition, we have tried to convince you that there is no one treatment approach, strategy, or setting that is effective for every client. As with any other mental health issue, professionals must thoroughly assess a client and design treatment that considers the clients' characteristics and needs. That is the reason why you, as a potential mental health professional, must make informed referrals to treatment programs that use client/treatment matching. Finally, people with alcohol and other drug problems enter the process of recovery in many different ways. Naturally, the process that is successful for a particular client may be seen by that client as the cure for everyone. However, we would encourage you to view as equally valuable every process that results in a person's freedom from the problems of alcohol and other drug use and a return to a productive life.

Chapter 8

Twelve Step and Other Types of Support Groups

If we were to specify one characteristic of the alcohol and other drug field that differentiates it from other areas in mental health, it would be the role of self-help support groups in treatment. One would be hard-pressed to find another area in which the most common method of intervention is through groups that are organized and led by nonprofessionals. The unique contribution of support groups in the recovery of individuals with alcohol and other drug problems warrants a chapter in this text for several reasons. The first and most obvious reason is that, if you work in the helping professions, you will have clients who have attended, are attending, or have been encouraged to attend some type of self-help support group. Therefore, you need to know about such groups. Second, some inevitable conflict seems to exist between mental health professionals and those who are advocates of self-help support groups that requires discussion. Finally, the proliferation of self-help support groups based on the Twelve Steps has led to considerable confusion with regard to the methods and purposes of these groups. It is estimated that there are over 15 million people participating in 500,000 Twelve Step groups (Hemfelt & Fowler, 1990).

In Chapter 7, we discussed support groups as a component of alcohol and other drug treatment programs. As we noted, Twelve Step groups such as Alcoholics Anonymous (AA) and Narcotics Anonymous (NA) are an essential part of many, if not most, treatment programs. In particular, treatment programs that are disease-model based will almost always require (or strongly recommend) attendance at AA or NA as part of the treatment program and aftercare plan. Family members may be encouraged to attend Al-Anon and teenagers to attend Alateen. There are CODA meetings for codependents and ACOA meetings for adult children of alcoholics. A variety of other Twelve Step groups have developed for group support for other issues: Emotions Anonymous, Overeaters Anonymous, Sexaholics Anonymous, Spenders Anonymous, and Gamblers Anonymous.

Since Twelve Step support groups predominate in the support group area and have generated the most confusion and controversy, we want to thoroughly discuss the origin and elements of this type of group. Because Twelve Step support groups originated with AA, and AA meetings are the most common type of Twelve Step group, we will spend the most time discussing the history, elements, and effectiveness of AA. We will also discuss the advantages and disadvantages of Twelve Step groups. Finally, we want you to be aware of other types of support groups that have developed as alternatives to Twelve Step groups.

The topic of Twelve Step groups can generate emotions in those people who have been or are actively involved in these groups. A person who actively attends a group such as AA and maintains sobriety may be a fervent advocate for Twelve Step groups. An individual who had an unfavorable reaction to this type of group may be a vocal critic. Many of you may have had some personal experience with Twelve Step groups and have strong feelings one way or another. Therefore, before discussing AA, we would like you to keep a couple points in mind. First, Twelve Step groups were not designed as treatment. As you will see from the discussion below, AA groups were developed to support alcoholics who were trying to remain sober. Many people do maintain abstinence with support from AA meetings and never go to a treatment program. As we discussed in Chapter 7, many people remain abstinent without AA and without formal treatment. There is no conflict between formal treatment and AA. Some people do both, some one or the other, and some neither. The fact that many people remain abstinent with support from AA meetings has resulted in some AA members' preaching a philosophy of "AA is the only way." This point of view is not that of AA and is, in fact, contrary to the AA philosophy.

Second, as most of you know, Twelve Step meetings contain many references to "God" and "Higher Power." We will discuss spirituality in Twelve Step groups later in this chapter. However, people tend to have an emotional, as opposed to a logical, reaction to anything that appears to be religious. If you have preconceptions about Twelve Step groups because of the spiritual nature of these groups, try to put them aside as you read this chapter. As a mental health professional, we want you to completely understand a very common type of support group and to know when such groups (or others) may be useful for clients. If you have not attended a Twelve Step meeting before, we strongly encourage you to do so (check to make sure they are open meetings). If Twelve Step meetings have benefited you personally, remember that each client is an individual, and what has worked for you may not work for someone else. The spiritual nature of Twelve Step groups presents some interesting and challenging issues for mental health professionals. However, your primary concern should be to objectively assess the needs of your clients and recommend the interventions that best address those needs. To do so, you must put aside any personal preferences for or against Twelve Step groups and objectively determine whether such groups would benefit your clients.

Alcoholics Anonymous

History of AA

An excellent history of AA is presented by Kurtz (1979). June 10, 1935, is thought of as the birthdate of AA, since that is the date that Bill Wilson, a stockbroker, and Bob Smith, a surgeon, met, and "Dr. Bob" had his last drink.

The sequence of events that brought Bill W. and Dr. Bob, the co-founders of AA, together began with the famous psychiatrist, Carl Jung, and his treatment of Roland H., an alcoholic and an American businessman. Jung had told him that he had done all that medicine and psychiatry could do. Jung suggested that Roland H. needed a spiritual awakening if he were to recover from his alcoholism. Roland H. joined the Oxford Group, a popular nondenominational religious group that sought to recapture the essence of first-century Christianity. Roland H. was able to abstain from alcohol after associating with the Oxford Group, and he convinced a friend, Edwin T., to do the same. Edwin T. was a friend of Bill W. When Bill offered Edwin a drink, Edwin replied, "I don't need it anymore. I've got religion." (Kurtz, 1979, p. 7). Bill W., an agnostic, did not immediately see the implication of Edwin's statement. However, after being admitted to a hospital for detoxification, Bill W. had a spiritual experience. Following his release, he read a book by William James, *The Varieties of Religious Experiences,* which became the foundation of the twelve steps. Bill W. was able to stop drinking and his life improved dramatically. During a business trip to Akron, Ohio, Bill W. had a strong desire to drink after a business deal fell through. He wanted to talk to another alcoholic, so he called an Oxford Group minister and was referred to Dr. Bob, an active alcoholic. Dr. Bob reluctantly agreed to talk to Bill W. They ended up talking for hours. Bill W. had made this contact because he needed to talk to another alcoholic to avoid drinking himself. Through this contact, Bill W. avoided relapsing and Dr. Bob stopped drinking. This was the start of the AA method of alcoholics' talking to other alcoholics in order to remain sober. Bill W. had no plan or desire to change Dr. Bob. He only wanted to maintain his own sobriety.

What AA Is About

The AA preamble, which is usually read at meetings, is a good description of the purpose of AA:

> *Alcoholics Anonymous is a fellowship of men and women who share their experience, strength, and hope with each other that they may solve their common problem and help others to recover from alcoholism.*
>
> *The only requirement for membership is a desire to stop drinking. There are no dues or fees for AA membership; we are self-supporting through our own contributions. AA is not allied with any sect, denomination, politics, organization, or institution; does not wish to engage in any controversy, neither endorses nor pro-*

poses any causes. Our primary purpose is to stay sober and help other alcoholics to achieve sobriety. (AA Grapevine, 1985, p. 1).

AA meetings may be closed (for AA members only) or open. Closed meetings are usually "step" meetings in which members can choose which of the twelve steps to focus on. Open meetings may be "speaker" meetings in which people voluntarily tell their stories (their histories of drinking and recovery) or discussion meetings where a topic is suggested by the meeting chair or a participant. The topics relate to some aspect of recovery or a barrier to recovery, such as "forgiveness," "anger," "humility," or "serenity."

As the AA preamble indicates, the only requirement for membership is a *desire* to stop drinking. Those who relapse are not banned but are offered support in their struggle for sobriety. The bible for AA is the book *Alcoholics Anonymous* (1976), commonly referred to as "The Big Book." Anonymity, a central concept in AA, protects the identities of members and ensures that no one person or persons become spokespeople for AA. To further the ideal of equality among members, meetings' chairs rotate and there are no elected directors. Special committees and service boards are created as needed from AA members.

At AA meetings, you will hear many slogans that are amusing, catchy, or clever and are easily remembered. For example, the famous "One day at a time" is meant to reinforce the concept that sobriety is a day-to-day (sometimes minute-to-minute) process to keep the alcoholic focused on the present as opposed to the future. Other examples include "Keep it simple" (sobriety is a simple process: don't drink), "Let go and let God," and "Get off the pity pot."

When a person speaks at an AA meeting, he or she usually starts by saying, "Hi. My name is (first name of speaker) and I'm an alcoholic." The rest of the participants respond by saying, "Hi, _____." The statement of the speaker acknowledges his or her alcoholism, and the response of the participants indicates acceptance and support. At some meetings, a person may be called upon to speak. One can always say, "Hi, my name is _____, and I pass."

In the introduction to this book, we told you that we require our students to attend an AA or an NA meeting, and the students generally are impressed with the friendliness and encouragement they encounter at the meetings. However, some of the students are concerned with another aspect of AA meetings, which is the "no cross-talk" rule. When someone speaks at an AA meeting, subsequent speakers do not address previous speakers. For example, one of our students was very concerned about a woman at a meeting who was emotionally distraught and disoriented in her speech. The next speaker did not react to the woman at all. As we explained, AA meetings are for support in maintaining sobriety. They are not designed to provide therapy. If cross-talk were allowed, there would be a tendency for nonprofessionals to provide therapy. Also, as Bill W. discovered, he was able to avoid drinking simply by talking about himself to another alcoholic. Input and feedback from Dr. Bob was not necessary and, therefore, is not necessary at meetings.

As a helping professional, you might wonder about the advisability of eliminating feedback from members, since this can be a valuable method of growth. Although feedback does not occur in meetings, members are encouraged to seek a "sponsor". McCrady and Irvine (1989) describe sponsors as follows:

> *A very important part of the AA experience is sponsorship. While anyone who wants to stop drinking can join AA, choosing a sponsor as soon as possible is encouraged as a means of maintaining sobriety. The process of sponsorship involves two alcoholics, one of whom has made more progress in recovery and who shares that experience in an ongoing manner with another who is trying to achieve or maintain sobriety. Some groups offer a temporary sponsor program, which matches a new comer with someone until they are able to meet enough members to make their own choice. The important factor is that a newcomer not be left to flounder without introduction to the program and to each new aspect of recovery as it is experienced for the first time (p. 157).*

The Twelve Steps and the Twelve Traditions

> *A.A.'s Twelve Steps are a group of principles, spiritual in their nature, which, if practiced as a way of life, can expel the obsession to drink and enable the sufferer to become happily and usefully whole.*
>
> *A.A.'s Twelve Traditions apply to the life of the Fellowship itself. They outline the means by which A.A. maintains its unity and relates itself to the world about it, the way it lives and grows. (Alcoholics Anonymous World Services, 1981, p. 15).*

The core of the AA program and the basis of similar groups developed on the AA model are the twelve steps. As a statement in the Big Book indicates, "Rarely have we seen a person fail who has thoroughly followed our path" (p. 58). It is truly astounding that these twelve statements, written more than a half-century ago, have generated the number of adherents, groups, and critics. We will present the twelve steps and comment briefly on them. If desired, you can find a thorough discussion in *Twelve Steps and Twelve Traditions* by Alcoholics Anonymous World Services. Professional analysis of the twelve steps can be found in articles such as Peteet (1993).

The Twelve Steps[1]

1. We admitted we were powerless over alcohol—that our lives had become unmanageable.
2. Came to believe that a Power greater than ourselves could restore us to sanity.

---

[1]The Twelve Steps and Twelve Traditions are reprinted with permission of Alcoholics Anonymous World Services, Inc. Permission to reprint this material does not mean that AA has reviewed or approved the contents of this publication, nor that AA agrees with views expressed herein. AA is a program of recovery from alcoholism *only*—use of the Twelve Steps in connection with programs and activities which are patterned after AA, but which address other problems, does not imply otherwise.

3. Made a decision to turn our will and our lives over to the care of God *as we understood Him.*
4. Made a searching and fearless moral inventory of ourselves.
5. Admitted to God, to ourselves, and to another human being the exact nature of our wrongs.
6. Were entirely ready to have God remove all these defects of character.
7. Humbly asked Him to remove our shortcomings.
8. Made a list of all persons we had harmed, and became willing to make amends to them all.
9. Made direct amends to such people wherever possible, except when to do so would injure them or others.
10. Continued to take personal inventory and when we were wrong promptly admitted it.
11. Sought through prayer and meditation to improve our conscious contact with God *as we understood Him,* praying only for knowledge of His will for us and the power to carry that out.
12. Having had a spiritual awakening as the result of these steps, we tried to carry this message to alcoholics, and to practice these principles in all our affairs.

Let us point out a couple of things about the twelve steps. First, alcohol is mentioned only in Step 1. Steps 2 through 11 are the ways to improve a person's life. You can see how these might be applied to many issues other than alcohol. The focus is on surrender, forgiveness, humility, limitations, and service to others. The influence of the Oxford Group on Bill W. also is clear from these aspects of the twelve steps. As Miller and Kurtz (1994) stated in a fascinating article contrasting AA and models of addiction, "Practice of the 12 steps brings a recovery characterized by growth in character traits such as honesty, humility and patience" (p. 161). In this light, the twelve steps can be conceptualized as a way of living.

The Twelve Traditions[2]
The Twelve Traditions govern the operation of AA. They are as follows:

1. Our common welfare should come first; personal recovery depends upon AA unity.
2. For our group purpose there is but one ultimate authority—a loving God as He may express himself in our group conscience. Our leaders are but trusted servants; they do not govern.
3. The only requirement for AA membership is a desire to stop drinking.
4. Each group should be autonomous except in matters affecting other groups or AA as a whole.
5. Each group has but one primary purpose—to carry its message to the alcoholic who still suffers.

---

[2]*Ibid.*

6. An AA group ought never endorse, finance, or lend the AA name to any related facility or outside enterprise, lest problems of money, property, and prestige divert us from our primary purpose.
7. Every AA group ought to be fully self-supporting, declining outside contributions.
8. Alcoholics Anonymous should remain forever nonprofessional, but our service centers may employ special workers.
9. AA, as such, ought never be organized; but we may create service boards or committees directly responsible to those they serve.
10. Alcoholics Anonymous has no opinion on outside issues; hence the AA name ought never be drawn into public controversy.
11. Our public relations policy is based on attraction rather than promotion; we need always maintain personal anonymity at the level of press, radio, and films.
12. Anonymity is the spiritual foundation of all our Traditions, ever reminding us to place principles before personalities.

The emphasis of the Twelve Traditions is on maintaining anonymity and avoiding controversy, thereby reducing the likelihood that AA will be diverted from its mission. You will not find AA endorsing or criticizing any model of addiction or approach to treatment. There is no AA lobbyist to help pass legislation. AA has no "spokesperson" and does not solicit or accept contributions. No matter what your opinion is of AA, you have to be impressed with the singular focus of AA and its ability to maintain this focus for nearly 60 years.

Elements of AA meetings

Although there may be some variability in what you will hear and see at AA meetings, most open meetings have common elements. By describing these, we are not trying to provide a substitute for actual attendance at meetings. However, when you first go to an AA meeting, it is similar to attending a religious service in an unfamiliar denomination. You are not quite sure when to do what, and you don't want to call attention to yourself. Therefore, by describing these events, we hope you will feel prepared to attend a meeting.

Generally, people socialize for a short time before the meeting starts. Coffee and other beverages are usually available. If the meeting is not advertised as nonsmoking, be prepared for cigarette smoke. People who regularly attend the meeting may introduce themselves to those who are obviously new and offer to sit with a newcomer. Remember, last names are not used.

The meeting chair or secretary will introduce the meeting by saying something like, "Welcome to the Gemini meeting of Alcoholics Anonymous. May we have a moment of silence for those alcoholics who are still suffering." The Serenity Prayer will then be recited, "God grant me the serenity to accept the things I cannot change, courage to change the things I can, and wisdom to know the difference." The AA preamble is read and newcomers (those with fewer than 30 days of sobriety) and out-of-towners are given an opportunity to introduce themselves. Members participate in reading part of Chapter 5 of the Big Book, titled "How It Works," the Twelve Steps, and the Twelve Traditions. The chair then speaks, usually telling his or her story. If the meeting is a discussion meeting, the chair either suggests a topic of discussion or asks for suggestions. If it is a speakers' meeting, the chair asks for volunteers or calls on people to speak. Remember, if you are called upon to speak and do not wish to, you can always say "Pass." It is nice if you say, "Hi, my name is Gary and I pass," but you don't have to. Also, don't be confused by the title "discussion meeting." It really isn't an exchange—rather a series of speakers talking about the meaning of the topic of discussion in their sobriety. As we stated previously, cross-talk is not permitted. After the discussion or speakers, AA-related announcements are made and a basket for contributions is passed around. The chair may sign attendance records for those who are court-ordered to attend. "Chips" are given to those in attendance who have 30, 60, and 90 days of sobriety and those who have "birthdays" (anniversary of sobriety). "A Vision for You" from the Big Book is read, and participants stand in a circle, join hands, and recite the Lord's Prayer. They then say "Keep coming back. It works!" and the meeting is over. Participants usually socialize for a brief period following the meeting.

Research on AA

Two areas of research regarding AA exist that have relevance for the mental health professional. The first has to do with the characteristics of clients who are most likely to affiliate with AA. Emrick (1987) summarized the results of ten studies published since 1976 that examined this issue. According to Emrick,

> More often than not, psychosocial, alcoholism, and treatment variables were found to be either consistently unrelated to membership or to be unrelated in some samples but positively or negatively associated in others. A few variables were consistently related in one direction or another (e.g., dual addiction, use of external supports to stop drinking, and warmth of childhood environment) but firm conclusions about these variables must await more data.... Until specific affiliation characteristics are identified, prudence suggests viewing all alcoholic patients in conventional alcoholism treatment as possible members of AA, while at the same time recognizing that many alcohol-dependent patients recover from their alcohol problems without ever joining the organization (p. 418, italics in original).

The second area of research has to do with the effectiveness of AA on the drinking behavior of members, particularly when compared with other types of interventions. In a thorough review of this research, McCrady and Irvine (1989) conclude

> The data about the effectiveness of AA are mixed. There are no well designed, well-executed treatment outcome studies of AA effectiveness which use contemporary standards for treatment outcome research.... The randomized clinical trials which have been executed find no evidence of AA showing superior effectiveness,

these studies had poor outcomes in general and design and clinical problems, as well as using a limited population. . . . Most studies consistently find an association between AA attendance and positive treatment outcome, suggesting that AA involvement is one factor associated with successful outcome (p. 167–168).

McCrady and Irvine note that research on AA is difficult since variability occurs from one AA group to another and because the anonymity of AA makes it difficult to track members. We would add that the goals of such studies may contribute to a misunderstanding of AA. As we pointed out at the beginning of the chapter, AA is not a form of treatment.

AA and Spirituality

The effectiveness of AA has been related to elements in the group process, ego function development, empathic understanding, disintegration of pathologic narcissism, etc. (Nace, 1992). However, as Miller and Kurtz (1994) point out, "It would be helpful for treatment and research professionals to . . . understand the essential nature of AA as a spiritual program of living" (p. 165). It may be easier to understand why studies on affiliation and effectiveness seem confusing and contradictory if one keeps Miller and Kurtz's point in mind. As Nace (1992) states, "Spirituality is rarely part of the lexicon of the mental health professional . . ." (p. 493). Therefore, the well-intentioned efforts to conceptualize the effects of AA in terms of psychological theories or processes and to research AA through traditional scientific methods may be misguided. As we mentioned at the beginning of the chapter, the broad utilization of a spiritual, self-help program is unique in the helping professions. The mental health professional may need to be flexible in order to gain some understanding of the impact of AA on many recovering alcoholics.

Nace (1992) discusses the spiritual themes of AA: release, gratitude, humility, and tolerance. Release is clearly experienced when the alcoholic no longer feels the compulsion to drink. Gratitude results from the release from compulsion. The alcoholic's powerlessness over alcohol elicits humility, since it is a humbling experience to acknowledge one's inability to handle this drug. The theme of tolerance of differences among people and of one's own shortcomings helps the recovering individual to achieve serenity. If you now reread the Twelve Steps and Twelve Traditions, you can see the themes of release, gratitude, humility, and tolerance in these basic precepts of AA.

Myths Regarding AA

In the minds of many professionals, AA is associated with a particular model of addiction and specific methods of dealing with alcoholics. For example, AA is often associated with the disease concept of addiction (see Chapter 3) and with the need to confront the denial system of alcoholics (see Chapter 7). Miller and Kurtz (1994) compare different models of addiction with AA through AA literature and the writings of Bill W. They conclude that:

AA writings do not assert that: (1) there is only one form of alcoholism or alcohol problems; (2) moderate drinking is impossible for everyone with alcohol problems; (3) alcoholics should be labeled, confronted aggressively or coerced into treatment; (4) alcoholics are riddled with denial and defense mechanisms; (5) alcoholism is purely a physical disorder; (6) alcoholism is hereditary; (7) there is only one way to recover; or (8) alcoholics are not responsible for their condition or actions. These assertions involve outside economic, political, social, moral, legal, and disciplinary issues on which AA takes no stand ... (p. 165).

Other Twelve Step Groups

As we mentioned earlier, many other groups have adapted the twelve steps to areas other than alcohol. Narcotics Anonymous (NA) was founded in 1953. AA and NA are not officially affiliated. However, NA uses the same twelve steps as AA replacing "alcohol" and "alcoholism" with "drugs" and "addiction." From 1983 to 1988, there has been a 600% increase in the number of NA groups (Coleman, 1989). This increase is understandable considering the tremendous rise in illegal drug use in this country since the formation of NA. Since so many people present polydrug problems, the choice of whether to attend AA or NA has become less clear. It is probably best to let clients with polydrug problems (if one of the drugs is alcohol) attend both AA and NA meetings and decide which is most comfortable.

When AA was founded, its members were men. The wives of the members would get together and talk about their problems. Lois W., the wife of Bill W., founded Al-Anon Family Groups in 1954. Royce (1989) describes Al-Anon:

Al-Anon is a recovery program for people who suffer because someone close to them drinks too much. At Al-Anon meetings members learn ... that their own recovery is possible whether or not the drinker seeks help or even recognizes that a drinking problem exists (p. 280).

The twelve steps have been adapted for Al-Anon with Step 1 being an admission that the person is powerless to control the drinking of significant others. Essentially, Al-Anon is self-help for family members of alcoholics. Al-Anon does not advocate that family members abandon the alcoholic or coerce the alcoholic into treatment. Rather, it is a spiritual program that encourages detachment and self-improvement. At Al-Anon meetings, you will find family members living with recovering alcoholics, those living with active alcoholics, and those who have separated from alcoholic family members. Alateen is a component of Al-Anon that was started by a teenager in 1957 and is designed for young people who are living with an alcoholic family member. There is a Big Book for Alateen (Al-Anon Family Group, 1973). In our area, Alateen meetings are held at schools providing these young people with a convenient way to attend and experience the support of others with similar issues. At both Al-Anon and Alateen meetings, you will find participants who are living with or involved with people who have addictions to drugs other than alcohol. We encourage you to attend some Al-Anon meetings so you will have first-hand experience with this type of self-help group.

As we mentioned previously, there are numerous other twelve step groups that focus on a variety of issues and where the twelve steps are adapted for the particular focus of the group. Twelve step groups exist for codependency, adult children of alcoholics, eating disorders, sexual behavior, gambling, spending, and other issues.

Advantages and Disadvantages of Twelve Step Groups

There are some obvious advantages to twelve step groups. First of all, they are free. In the mental health field, this is certainly unique. Second, meetings such as AA are available at a variety of times and places (of course, this depends on the size of the area and the type of meeting). An AA member who is on either a business or pleasure trip can usually find a meeting. Third, at meetings, twelve step participants find a group of people who share similar concerns and problems and who can provide group support. This type of support is helpful to many people and would be difficult for them to achieve on their own. Additionally, a social network is often developed through twelve step meetings. For the recovering person, this is a useful way to make non-using friends. Fourth, the structure and ritual of twelve step meetings may be comforting and helpful to people whose lives have been chaotic and unpredictable. Finally, the spiritual nature of twelve step groups, with its themes of release, gratitude, humility, and tolerance, can be a productive focus for self-improvement and general contentment with life. For one who has experienced excessive guilt, blame, and embarrassment, the spiritual themes can refocus the person on more positive emotions.

The disadvantages of twelve step meetings are usually focused on the differentiation (or lack thereof) between spirituality and religion and the concept of "powerlessness." While twelve step meetings are supposed to be nondenominational, the recital of the Lord's Prayer implies a Christian orientation. Those who are members of other religious groups may be alienated by this prayer. Atheists can certainly have difficulty with the notion of "Higher Power." Even though steps 3 and 11 refer to "God as we understood Him," the notion of Higher Power in twelve step meetings is clearly that of the Judeo-Christian God. However, remember that AA was formed in 1935 when diversity was hardly a predominant concept. In the context of the times, it is a tribute to Bill W.'s openness that "God as we understood Him" was included. Regardless, the rituals of twelve step meetings and the references to God and a Higher Power can be problematic for clients who have negative attitudes and/or experiences with organized religion or those who are not Christian.

As Miller and Kurtz (1994) pointed out, AA does not promulgate the notion that alcoholics are not responsible for their condition or actions. Although the first of the twelve steps contains the word "powerlessness" and the third step involves turning "our will and our lives over to the care of God," Steps 4 through 8 involve taking responsibility for past wrongs and shortcomings. However, critics of twelve step groups and some participants have interpreted Steps 1 and 3 to mean that the twelve step philosophy supports the notion that addicted individuals are not responsible for their actions. Clearly, such a view would be counterproductive for clients.

Additional disadvantages of twelve step groups arise from the individuals involved in such groups rather than from the ideas themselves. As Nace (1992) states, "AA is predominantly a white, middle-class organization consisting of middle-aged married males" (p. 493). This might alienate women, ethnically diverse individuals, and young people. Groups for different demographic groups have developed in response.

Some participants in twelve step groups feel so strongly about the benefits of the program that they denigrate other interventions, such as therapy or psychotropic medications. Again, there is nothing in the AA philosophy that is opposed to other forms of intervention or that preaches that AA is the only way to recovery. However, just as some adherents of religious views misinterpret the doctrines based on their personal characteristics and experiences, some twelve step participants appear dogmatic.

Finally, critics of twelve step groups claim that many people simply switch addictions from alcohol and other drugs to going to meetings. Certainly, attendance at twelve step meetings can interfere with social, family, and occupational functioning, and, if a person continued with constant participation in spite of these consequences, this would constitute problematic behavior. Personally, we would rather see someone constantly attending meetings than committing armed robbery to get money for drugs. However, we have no doubt that compulsive twelve step meeting attendance could be a barrier to mature functioning.

To close this discussion of twelve step groups, we want to re-emphasize our personal view that twelve step meetings should not be confused with treatment. Twelve step groups, with the support they offer and the emphasis on spiritual development, can be an important part of a comprehensive treatment program. Some people maintain sobriety (or whatever behavior change they are focused on) without any other form of intervention or support. Others maintain these changes without ever going to a twelve step meeting. As we said to you in Chapter 3, do a thorough assessment on every client, and (if you are involved in treatment) design treatment strategies designed to meet the client's needs. You will find that many clients can benefit from this type of free, available support group consisting of people with similar problems. Whether the group is a twelve step group or one of the other self-help groups we will now discuss depends on the needs, background, and experiences of the client. The recommendation for a self-help group should not depend on your own preconceptions or stereotypes.

Other Types of Self-Help Groups

Rational Recovery

In 1988, Jack Trimpey began Rational Recovery (RR) as an alternative to AA. RR is based on the Rational Emotive Therapy of Albert Ellis. The basis of the RR program is contained in Trimpey's book, *The small book: A revolutionary alternative for overcoming alcohol and drug dependence* (Trimpey, 1992). In Trimpey's words:

> *In Rational Recovery we have a comprehensive system of self-help wherein the "alcoholic" can quickly come to terms with the central issues of addiction and recovery. As in rational-emotive therapy, RR identifies several specific irrational ideas and beliefs that perpetuate the addictive behavior of alcohol-dependent people, and then RR provides the means to change one's own emotions and behavior (p. 101).*

Trimpey takes 15 "central beliefs about alcoholism" (p. 102) that he calls *irrational* and reframes them according to a rational idea. For example, the irrational belief of the alcoholic's powerlessness over alcoholic cravings and the consequent lack of responsibility for what is ingested is reframed as "I have considerable voluntary control over my extremities and facial muscles" (p. 102). Other examples involve the irrational belief that one drink will lead to "my downfall" (p. 104). The rational response is:

> *. . . as time goes by drinking appears increasingly stupid because of the obvious selfish advantages of sobriety, but, if I ever stupidly relapsed by drinking, it wouldn't be awful because I would very likely recover again—selfishly, guiltlessly, and probably very quickly (p. 104).*

Finally, the idea turning one's life over to a Higher Power is reframed as

> *. . . dependency is my original problem, and it is better to start now to take the risks of thinking and acting independently. I cannot really "be" an "alcoholic", but just a person who has believed some of the central ideas of alcoholism (p. 104).*

RR meetings are free and are led by a coordinator who maintains contact with a mental health professional familiar with the RR program. The meetings last about 1 1/2 hours. Cognitive strategies are used to achieve and maintain abstinence, which is the goal of RR. The compulsive and irrational thoughts that lead to drinking are conceptualized as the "Beast", and participants develop and use a "Sobriety Spreadsheet" to combat the Beast. The Sobriety Spreadsheet contains the irrational beliefs and the associated rational thoughts. Members are encouraged to use the Sobriety Spreadsheet in and out of meetings and to read *The small book*. In contrast to AA, participants openly exchange their views on the issues discussed. In addition, there are no sponsors, and members are discouraged from attending RR meetings for more than one year in order to prevent dependence on meetings. Obviously, spirituality is not a focus of RR.

Galanter, Egelko, and Edwards (1993) surveyed 433 RR members to assess the program's effectiveness. In the largely well-educated and employed sample, 73% of those participants who had attended meetings for three months or more were abstinent for at least 30 days. Fifty-eight percent of those attending for six or more months had at least six months of abstinence.

Many Roads, One Journey

In her 1992 book, *Many Roads, One Journey: Moving beyond the 12 Steps,* Charlotte Davis Kasl argues that issues such as child abuse, sexism, racism, poverty, and homophobia are in opposition to twelve step concepts such as conformity, humility, personal failings, and powerlessness. For example, an adult woman who was sexually molested as a child or has been in an abusive relationship and has a substance abuse problem may find the first of the twelve steps unacceptable. To admit powerlessness over anything may rekindle the feelings of powerlessness in the abusive situations.

Kasl suggests an introductory reading to begin meetings of Many Roads, One Journey. We have excerpted some of the content to illustrate the philosophy of this approach:

> *Our purpose in coming together is to support and encourage each other in our healing from addiction, dependency, or internalized oppression. The only requirement for membership is a desire to maintain sobriety as we each define it. . . . We do not impose our beliefs on others or expect others to tell us the way. . . . Healing is a balance between gentle self-acceptance and a firm commitment to sobriety. We overcome addiction and internalized oppression because we want to honor and enjoy the life we have been given. Healing from addiction and dependency is not about moral worth. We are all sacred children of Creation this moment. . . . We believe that through bonding with others, speaking genuinely from our hearts, forgiving ourselves and others, finding purpose, helping create social change, and accepting the imperfections of life, we will find a sense of fulfillment that we have sought to fill through our addictive and dependent behavior (p. 356–357).*

Kasl has developed sixteen steps for "discovery and empowerment" (p. 337). Some examples of these steps are

1. We affirm we have the power to take charge of our lives and stop being dependent on substances or other people for our self-esteem and security.
2. We come to believe that God/the Goddess/Universe/Great Spirit/Higher power awakens the healing wisdom within us when we open ourselves to that power.
3. We make a decision to become our authentic Selves and trust in the healing power of truth.
4. We examine our beliefs, addictions, and dependent behavior in the context of living in a hierarchal, patriarchal culture (p. 338).

The spiritual nature of the steps is clear although acceptance of alternatives to God is more clearly specified than in the twelve steps. An emphasis is also placed on power*ful*ness, choice, and the relationship of behavior to culture.

Kasl also provides guidelines for Many Roads, One Journey groups. Rather than suggesting a rigid structure and rituals, the groups are more flexible. Kasl does suggest that the purpose of the group be defined, a moderator chosen, and time constraints adhered to. She also suggests a six-week commitment for new members and two-week notice when a member is leaving. Readings of poems, sayings, or other literature are recommended. However, that is the extent of structure suggested, since, as the name Many Roads, One Journey implies and as Kasl writes,

> *Let's weave together, creating a form and a process that builds a foundation for positive change. Instead of one linear model, we can have many circles with many ways, all working toward growth, empowerment, and an ability to appreciate life (p. 371).*

Women for Sobriety

Jean Kirkpatrick found AA meetings to be rigid, dogmatic, and chauvinistic and felt that the meetings increased her desire to drink. She found hypocrisy in AA members' resistance to taking blood pressure medication or using vitamins to control the effects of alcohol withdrawal, and in the heavy use of caffeine and tobacco at meetings. After 28 years of alcoholism during which Kirkpatrick experienced hospitalization, violence, and depression, she founded Women for Sobriety in 1976. According to Kirkpatrick (1990):

> *The Women For Sobriety Program . . . is a product of women's new awareness of self developed through the feminist movement. . . . Through this self-help Program, women take charge of their alcoholism. . . . For women to take full charge of self is a revolutionary concept. For too long, women's health has been governed by persons other than themselves.*
>
> *The Program challenges women to learn their strengths and values, to become aware that they are competent women, that sobriety depends upon the discovery and maintenance of strong feelings of self-value and self-worth which, ultimately, will lead to strong self-esteem. (Preface.)*

She believes that women begin to drink because of frustration, loneliness, emotional deprivation, and harassment, while men drink for power. In her opinion, treatment programs have not been responsive to the needs of women and separate self-help groups are necessary to affirm women's autonomy from men.

Kirkpatrick's program emphasizes a holistic approach to recovery. She emphasizes good nutrition, meditation, and cessation of smoking. Consistent with this philosophy, coffee, sugar, and smoking are not permitted at Women for Sobriety meetings.

Kirkpatrick's thirteen "statements" reflect her view that self-esteem is the "magic building block" (Kirkpatrick, 1986, p. 131) of recovery. Some examples of these statements are

1. I have a drinking problem that once had me.
2. Negative emotions destroy only myself.

3. Happiness is a habit I will develop.
12. I am a competent woman and have much to give to others (p. 251).

In commenting on Kirkpatrick's program, Kasl (1992) writes:

> *Kirkpatrick understands the need for women to have groups of their own that stress choices, the positive power of the mind, imaging, broadening one's perspective, the ability to love, and physical healing. Her approach to self-empowerment through monitoring one's thoughts is well documented in psychological research on cognitive therapy with depression (p. 169).*

Secular Organization for Sobriety/Save Our Selves (SOS)

James Christopher had his last drink on April 24, 1978. He attended AA meetings although "[I] gritted my teeth and said the Lord's prayer; after all, these AA people were *sober* (Christopher, 1988, p. 96, italics in original). In 1985, Christopher published an article expressing his frustration with "AA's religiosity and my belief that the needs of free thinkers are not being met there" (Christopher, 1988, p. 95). In 1986, the first SOS meeting was held, and the program now has more than twenty thousand members (Kasl, 1992).

While Christopher is a firm adherent to the disease concept of addiction, he rejects the notion that spirituality is a necessary component for recovery:

> *My personal thoughts, feelings, and experiences within Alcoholics Anonymous were suppressed on a number of occasions, and AA was not particularly fulfilling or supportive to me as an alcoholic free thinker. I had to "go it alone" for many years. But through it all, I kept my sobriety through prioritizing it on a day-to-day basis. There is no higher power keeping me sober. I make this choice and reacknowledge it daily. No one can do it for me (p. 95).*

As indicated in Christopher's statement, the central component of the SOS program is the "sobriety priority":

> *As a sober alcoholic I must daily recommit, reaffirm, reaccept, resurrender, and reacknowledge my disease and its antidote: the sobriety priority. My priority frees me up for another day of life with all its pain, sorrow, joy, fear, sickness, achievements, failures, and goals, rather than trapping me in my previous subhuman, coma-like addiction to alcohol. Sobriety is assured* only *by prioritizing it daily on a day-at-a-time basis. This keeps my addiction to alcohol under "house arrest" day to day, hopefully lifelong.*
>
> *I have the right to fail in any other area of my life. My sobriety priority is the one exception (p. 51, italics in original).*

Christopher suggests five secular guidelines for sobriety. These include an acknowledgement of alcoholism, choosing to remain sober one day at a time, reaching out to those who have been directly or indirectly effected by the person's alcoholism, working toward self-acceptance, change, and growth, and taking responsibility for providing meaning in life. SOS meetings are 1-1/2 hours long with a different person acting as moderator each week. Often soft, classical music is played and a short selection from secular literature related to alcoholism is read. The group may choose a topic to discuss or have an open discussion. Meetings are closed with a short, humanistic reading. Christopher does suggest an opening for an SOS meeting, which stresses sobriety, personal growth, secularism, and humanism. He also emphasizes that his structure and suggestions may be modified as the group wishes.

Summary

Support groups are commonly utilized in the alcohol and other drug field. Support groups that are organized around the twelve steps of Alcoholics Anonymous are the most popular and have grown from AA to include twelve step groups for other drug addicts, family members, and a variety of nondrug problems. Twelve step support groups involve a spiritual approach to recovery and commitment to the anonymity of members. These two components have resulted in difficulty in researching the effectiveness of twelve step groups. Also, there has been predictable conflict between science and spirituality. Alternatives to twelve step support groups have developed and are available to individuals who are uncomfortable with the twelve step approach. The helping professional is advised to become familiar with all the support group alternatives and to assist clients in finding the type of support group that matches the client's needs and values.

Employee Assistance Programs (EAPs) and Student Assistance Programs (SAPs)

Employee Assistance Programs (EAPs)

Imagine that you are a manager in a sporting goods business. Mr. Eugene Franks is in sales and has been working for you for three years. Recently his sales have dropped off, and it has been rumored that he is going through a nasty divorce. It has also come to your attention that he has been coming to work late over the past several months and has not been servicing some of his more important accounts as well as before. It is well known that Eugene does not drink. No one has come forward to tell you of smelling alcohol on Eugene's breath, nor has anyone reported that he has been drinking on the job. Yet, you have noticed that his eyes are red frequently at work, and his conversations are punctuated with inappropriate laughter. Sometimes he does not seem to be making sense. What are you going to do?

One of the more reliable avenues of intervention would be to request a drug test or urine analysis (UA). To obtain a UA, you would likely need to have Eugene obtain a physician's prescription. The analysis itself would likely be performed by a laboratory with experience in understanding the necessity of an appropriate chain-of-command in collecting the specimen, testing, and reporting the results. The technology used to test a urine sample, mass spectrometry or gas chromatography, is quite sophisticated, so there is a decreased likelihood that the results would indicate a "false positive" (reflecting a "positive" for drug use when in fact it should have been reported as a "negative"). Furthermore, the laboratory performing the test will probably set the significance level at .50 nanograms, which would detect the presence of rather large dosages of the drug but report a "negative" with lesser amounts of the substance. The laboratory would likely be setting the baseline at this level for legal purposes to help insure that the substance was, in fact, present. Next, you determine that a meeting with Eugene is necessary for the purpose of confronting him with your suspicions as well as presenting the procedure for a UA. During the meeting, Eugene appears to be taken aback by the allegations and denies having a problem with alcohol or any other drugs. Although Eugene maintains a reasonable amount of composure, he is upset. When you request that he get a UA, he refuses, saying that he doesn't need one because, "My word ought to be good enough."

Now what do you do? Before you decide on how to proceed further, it is important to fully understand the import of what has just taken place in this example. You have been given a double-edged sword. Do you think he refused because he has something to hide? In other words, having the technology to test for the presence of substances also increases the potential for suspicion when one refuses to participate in the procedure. Eugene already has refused to be tested, so you might immediately think he has something to hide because he does not want to pass a specimen. A "right to privacy act" is involved here, which is covered ostensibly in the Fourth Amendment to the United States Constitution: the protection against illegal search and seizure. Furthermore, there is another implication to this right to privacy: What one does to his or her own body on his or her own time ought to be one's own decision as long as it does not infringe on others' rights or endanger others. Even if Eugene discusses his reasons for refusal (and for purposes of this discussion let's assume that he refuses simply on principle), a shadow of doubt has already been cast simply by his refusal. Imagine the complexities involved if Eugene did have a UA performed, and it came up negative. What would you do then? Apologize? Pretend it didn't happen? Blame the test and continue to suspect?

Let's suppose that Eugene came up positive on the UA. Should you continue to test him randomly? Should you make his employment contingent upon his participation in future random tests? If he refused in the future, would you remind him of the agreement and state that although he may be "clean" you would still like a test? And does all of this suggest that once Eugene has come up positive he might never be able to be trusted again? Or, for that matter, once he tested positive, could he ever be able to refuse again "on principle" and have that rationale accepted? Also, would the same considerations hold for Eugene as for an airline pilot, a public bus driver, an athlete, a teacher, or a counselor?

One final note to this example: What do you think the implications will be for the other employees? How will they be impacted by the possibility of being drug tested? Will it tend to increase or decrease morale?

This is not an unusual example. It occurs every day in a thousands of different companies. Moreover, the complexities presented here are probably more simplified than in actual cases. However, it was cases like Eugene's (although without the sophisticated technology for detection) that helped pave the way for the institutionalization of Employee Assistance Programs (EAPs). In general, employee assistance programs are worksite-based programs designed to help individuals improve their productivity when it becomes impaired by personal concerns. Recent developments in the field of drug use and abuse in the workplace have witnessed the blending of alcohol and other drug-directed programs with programs emphasizing wellness. Thus, in many companies one may see Employee Enhancement Programs that are aimed at helping workers with health, marital, family, financial, legal, emotional, stress, and drug concerns (Engelhart, Robinson, & Carpenter, 1992).

History of Employee Assistance Programs

Although there continue to be complex issues surrounding EAPS, there has been a significant growth of these programs over the past two decades. Initially, the focus of the programs was on alcohol abuse, but recently the focus has been expanded to include all substances. Englehart, Robinson, and Carpenter (1992) point out three events that paralleled the rise of the EAP a little over fifty years ago. First was the founding and growth of AA. At the same time, many medical professionals, some of whom were involved in AA, came forth to the support of those attempting to address drug abuse in the workplace. The third event was World War II. The war and the need for production necessitated the hiring of many employees whose skills were marginal or who were inexperienced. The labor intensive schedules, such as consecutive work shifts, exacerbated the abuse of alcohol in many of these individuals, and eventually alcohol began to affect productivity. "Occupational Alcoholism Programs" (OAPs) were what alcohol-specific programs were called at the time: These were the harbingers to the modern-day EAPs. During the war years, the government funded hundreds of such programs. However, the majority of these programs were closed after the war.

During World War II informal industrial alcoholism programs were developed with the aim of confronting the troubled employee with options to choose treatment, become sober, and improve job performance or face the prospect of losing their jobs. Soon after the war, formalized programs based upon the Yale Center for Alcohol Studies began to rise, so that by the middle of that decade 50 to 60 such programs existed in American industries (Engelhart, Robinson, & Carpenter, 1992). These programs focused upon the detection of drinking in the workplace by looking exclusively for alcohol specific symptoms such as bloodshot eyes, slurred speech, and the smell of alcohol on an employee's breath. In 1965, the National Institute on Alcoholism suggested focusing more on deteriorating job performance as indicative of over-involvement with alcohol rather than focusing exclusively upon the physiological effects (Scanlon, 1986). This new emphasis, along with help from Congress, had a significant impact upon the structure of the modern EAP.

In 1970 the passage of the Hughes Act (Public Law 91-616) mandated the development and maintenance of alcohol programs for federal employees and funded model programs for employees in other states. The EAPs were further influenced by the friendly forces of the National Institute of Alcoholism and Alcohol

Abuse (NIAAA), which in 1971 awarded grants to various state alcohol agencies to train and hire EAP specialists. By 1972, NIAAA funded two occupational program consultants for each state. This greatly enhanced the growth of EAPS. It also created some problems.

Many consultants were recruited from the mental health field, while others were recruited from the alcohol field. The latter advocated the "constructive confrontation" model promoted by Harrison Trice (Trice & Roman, 1978). Constructive confrontation is used to help motivate employees address their problems and to aid them in breaking down their inappropriate denial systems. In this approach, supervisors are required to document deteriorating performance on the job and are asked to confront the employee about the details of the diminished performance. Assistance is then offered through the EAP. However, if the assistance is not accepted, the employee is still notified that improvement on the job will need to take place immediately. Initially, there were some problems with the constructive confrontation method. Ambiguous job descriptions and performance standards contributed to the supervisor's difficulties in being able to document consistently. Therefore, one's ability to use constructive confrontation effectively was mediated in part by the company's philosophy and policies. If no clear standards were promulgated, then managers had little to fall back on when employees demanded a standard or context around which the confrontation was focused. Currently, however, with the help of EAP consultants, attention is being paid to clarifying job descriptions and minimum standards of performance.

Mental health professionals also agreed that identifying and addressing employees' mental health concerns would lead to improved performance but criticized constructive confrontation as being too limited and potentially ineffective. This contingency believed that by taking a broader approach and treating all personal problems equally, employees would be more likely to initiate their own help. Self-referral was preferable because of the potential difficulties in confronting someone whose ambivalence (see "Stages of Change," Chapter 6) or denial about alcohol or other drug abuse was deeply entrenched.

It was thought that employees would be more likely to seek help if the focus emphasized the variety of personal problems encountered by employees. If, in the course of assessment, alcohol or other drug use was found to be problematic, the hope was that ambivalence and denial would be diminished simply because the employee self-referred. In essence, the differences between the two groups of consultants centered on questions of breadth and efficacy. Those in the alcohol field were seen as focusing upon alcohol and other drug abuse almost exclusively. The mental health professionals focused upon a variety of problematic behaviors—some of which did include alcohol and other drugs. The issue of efficacy also demonstrated differing philosophies: Which approach would likely be more successful? A supervisor's confrontation or an employee's self-referral?

In spite of the growing pains, EAPs have enjoyed tremendous growth since 1971. Beginning with four programs in 1940, EAPs grew to six by 1945. There were fifty documented programs by 1950. Then the boom: by 1973, there were 500; 2,400 by 1977; 4,400 in 1980. And by 1990 there were approximately 20,000 EAPs in the United States (Engelhart, Robinson, & Carpenter, 1992).

Philosophy, Standards, and Objectives of the EAP

The philosophy guiding EAPs allows for the detection of need and for the provision of help for problems harmful to workers and their work-related behaviors. While services offered by EAPs vary from company to company, the EAPs have three main objectives for the EAP: (1) The EAP provides employees and their families a broad range of services that can help with job performance; (2) The EAP provides management and labor with resources should an intervention be needed; and (3) The EAP provides a structure by which troubled employees can be identified, assessed, and offered appropriate help (Standards for Employee Assistance Programs, 1990). Moreover, the federal government has identified standards for comprehensive employee assistance programs so that several essential ingredients exist that are common to most programs: EAPs are designed to motivate individuals to seek help, to provide short-term professional counseling assistance and referral, to direct employees toward the most efficacious help possible, and to provide continuing support and guidance throughout the process of problem resolution (Engelhart, Robinson, and Carpenter, 1992).

Roles and Structures

A clear written policy and everyone's familiarity with it are crucial to the success of an EAP. An EAP Advisory Committee is usually the entity formulating the policy, and members of that committee will likely be representatives from various levels of management and labor. Care needs to be taken to insure that the policy is viewed by all as being non-punitive, constructive, and confidential. The procedures for initiating contact with the EAP also need to be articulated, and care should be exercised to distinguish the two categories of referrals: self and administrative referrals. In all cases, the policy needs to outline what everyone can expect from his or her involvement in the EAP and the subsequent consequences that will apply when a referral is made by someone other than the employee.

Models and Services

In the past, some medical departments of larger companies managed alcohol services. However, more recently, EAPs are coming under the auspices of the human resource and personnel departments. As you will see later in this chapter (in the section on Student Assistance Programs), there are internal and external models designed to meet the needs of employees. The internal model is one in which the EAP staff is employed by the organization itself and is housed in the company's facilities. Many problems can be thus be addressed "in-house." Employees requiring more intensive interventions can be referred out for long-term counseling or for residential treatment. An external model is one in which the company contracts with an independent provider for EAP services. The EAP staff is located at the actual service site rather than on the company's premises. Usually, this independent organization contracts out for long-term or intensive treatment but can diagnose and provide on-site short term counseling (e.g., 1 to 3 counseling sessions). In many cases, although dependent upon the specific contract these independent EAPs can also provide on-site supervisor and employee training and education. In companies where the number of employees is too small for an in-house EAP, an employee might be identified to act as a liaison between the company and the independently contracted EAP service provider. A third model, also external, occurs when a company contracts with a social service agency within the community to provide EAP services. This agency could be a local hospital. Finally, unions themselves can provide EAP services, with those employees in more serious situations being referred out for treatment as in the other models. In.this model, both employers and union supervisors can identify employees who may be in need of assistance.

The Process of Helping in the EAP

In order to help individuals, all EAPs emphasize identification and outreach regardless of the model to which a company subscribes. The company executives are responsible for establishing an overall climate of helping. Supervisors are trained in how to document deteriorating work performance, and employees are provided education. There are five phases guiding the EAP process: Early identification is key to how an employee enters the system. Self-referral is preferred. Wrich (1982) has identified five factors believed to enhance the self-referral process: (1) confidentiality of records; (2) free assessment and referral; (3) staff perceived as capable helpers; (4) recognition of the importance of self-referral; and (5) an open and supportive program. Diagnosis and referral is the second component and relates to the method by which an employee's problem is described and evaluated. The actual helping process is the third component and refers to both short and long-term help. The fourth component involves the process by which the employee re-enters the organization and is followed-up. Throughout the process care is maintained to insure adequate record keeping so that both employer and employee are protected.

Eugene's Case

The company would have fostered an environment in which Eugene, should he have had a problem, would self-refer. In his case, he referred himself for help in dealing with his divorce. To enter the system, he would re-read the company's Policy Statement that specifies the telephone number he could call for an appointment. The EAP counselor would then help Eugene assess the nature and extent of his problem. In the assessment, Eugene talked about the difficulties with his divorce. Through motivational interviewing (see Chapter 6), the EAP counselor identified alcohol use as problematic. The EAP counselor might believe that in-patient hospitalization would be the preferred mode of treatment, but after assessing Eugene's ability to pay (in this case, Eugene had no in-patient treatment coverage), the counselor would refer Eugene for out-patient counseling at a local treatment center. Once there, Eugene would agree to the treatment plan, which included UAs only on the condition that the results be confidential. Assured of this, Eugene would resume work and attend counseling sessions twice a week and AA meetings throughout the week. The mental health professional providing the counseling service would be kept abreast of nonconfidential information such as the treatment plan and the length of therapy. The EAP counselor would also establish a working relationship with Eugene so that should diurnal problems arise, they could be addressed more informally at work.

One can see how the EAP can be of immense help to troubled employees. The confidential nature of the program keeps private any information that might inadvertently be leaked to others in the organization. No one in Eugene's immediate work environment may even know of his troubled life, because, with the aid of the EAP his work performance would be satisfactory. With appropriate help, Eugene's difficulties may not even be known by his supervisor. In this manner, Eugene could ask and receive help while continuing to perform his job and could do so without the fear of coercive action taken by his supervisor.

Case Example: The EAP Counselor's Considerations

Peggy Thorn (not her real name) was the EAP counselor in a medium-size company in the west that provided services to 232 employees in an in-house employee assistance program. Mary's (not her real name) supervisor contacted Peggy saying that she had heard that Mary was alcoholic. Several assessment procedures came into focus at that point. Peggy first assessed the source of the referral. She wanted to know what the supervisor's attitudes were regarding alcohol. (This assessment can often be a rather informal assessment and can be undertaken covertly). Another question of concern related to the relationship between Mary and her supervisor: How likely was it that Mary would have been hurt or helped by the attitudes of the supervisor? Was their relationship a solid one? Peggy wanted to know what evidence the supervisor had of Mary's impaired functioning. She also wanted information regarding how long the behavior had been going on and who else has noticed or said something. During the course of the referring process, Peggy was interested in the supervisor's flexibility: Would she be a helpful or harmful agent in approaching Mary? Finally, Peggy thought that she needed to know the supervisor's "timeline" for Mary's improved performance (Peggy was assuming that Mary's alcohol use was affecting her work).

Next were considerations of how to go about notifying Mary about the concerns of her supervisor. Peggy assessed whether the supervisor should handle the first level of intervention. (If she decided that it would be more constructive for the supervisor to make the referral, then Peggy needed to assess how much information the supervisor would require in order to cooperate. Consideration was important because the supervisor's job was on the line as well). In this case, Mary's supervisor was known to be rather recalcitrant, so Peggy decided upon a cooperative approach. Such an approach required finesse on Peggy's part in order to maintain the integrity of the program, to help Mary if she had a problem, and to provide enough information to gain the supervisor's trust while buying enough time for Mary to change.

However, the supervisor, herself, wanted to confront Mary right away because she believed in the moral model of addiction (see Chapter 3) and believed in nipping problems in the bud. In this case, Peggy had a conflict of values with the supervisor. Peggy believed more in the disease model of addiction (also discussed in Chapter 3). Concerned that the supervisor's approach would have exacerbated the problem, Peggy offered to take charge and suggested that she would arrange to talk to Mary immediately about the supervisor's concerns. Peggy gave Mary a call and requested a time that would be convenient for her to come by. Mary sounded scared, so Peggy mentioned that there may be nothing to worry about but did think it would be good to just check things out. She added that it would be in Mary's best interest if she came by as soon as possible.

Mary came to Peggy's office the following day during lunch. She was upset by, but not surprised at, her supervisor's accusations. Mary related that her department had been under a great deal of pressure after changing managers several weeks prior. Mary disclosed that she was not the only one "under the gun," and stated as well that she was a recovering alcoholic with two years sobriety. Mary also related that she had no desire to drink and that she was attending AA three times a week. In the course of Peggy's talk with her, both agreed that some team-building might help morale in the department. But before exploring that issue further, Peggy suggested that it would be in Mary's best interest to go down to the hospital and have a blood alcohol test performed immediately. Peggy told Mary that with the test, she could assure the supervisor that alcohol was not a problem. By having Mary take a blood test, Peggy was able to gain access to the supervisor, whom she now believed was having stress-related problems of her own. Inviting the supervisor in to discuss Mary's test results allowed Peggy the opportunity to help all the parties involved.

The strategy worked. The supervisor was surprised at the test results and, while initially suspicious of the results, did agree with them. Peggy asked the supervisor about Mary' performance and through the use of her counseling skills helped the supervisor begin to see that not only was Mary under pressure, but so were the rest of the department and the supervisor herself. Peggy helped the supervisor brainstorm ideas and offered assistance in putting together some workshops focused on team-building and/or stress-reduction. Initially, this was met with some resistance, but was eventually also agreed upon. By assuring the supervisor that Peggy appreciated her perspicuity in assessing problems, Peggy built on the supervisor's strengths, and she agreed to keep all of this confidential as well.

This example underscores the flexibility of a good employee assistance program. Here, the EAP counselor was a masters-level helping professional trained in counseling, consultation, and in alcohol and other drug abuse. The skills used by Peggy involved assessing a variety of issues related to the problem, including her assessment of the supervisor's disposition, behaviors, needs, and attitudes. Care was also exercised to insure that Mary's integrity was kept intact, that she had a chance to respond, and that she had the opportunity to prove the supervisor wrong by taking a blood test for alcohol. The organization itself benefitted because all employees of that department attended three workshops focusing upon stress-reduction. In this case, hasty assumptions about Mary's use would have had a pronounced and negative impact upon both the supervisor, Mary, and the company itself. There was a problem: the whole department was under stress. The EAP counselor, in this case, addressed the correct problem while allowing the supervisor to save face and Mary to feel empowered after initially feeling insulted. At the same time, the blood alcohol test helped Mary's case, the supervisor's concerns, and any remaining question the counselor had about Mary's use.

The issues involved in EAPs are complex, ranging from questions about the role of the employer in the personal problems of employees to questions regarding the Fourth Amendment of the United States Constitution. The efficacy of EAPs is mediated not only by familiarity with a clearly written policy statement but by one's insurance coverage (or lack of coverage) should expensive treatment be indicated. Self-referral is the ideal, yet the nature of drug involvement is such that ambivalence or denial of the problem is often the major barrier to treatment. Supervisors need to be able to detect lowered job performance. However, supervisors' documentation and involvement can be seen by some as one more area where the employer "has the upper hand," and a feeling of mistrust and power struggles can become protracted. Suspicions about the real agenda of the employer can be called into question. Company morale can be affected. But, in spite of these difficulties, employee assistance programs and employee enhancement programs can be effective. They are continuing to grow in number and scope and will likely be a part of most organizations in the future. What follows is discussion of the school-based version of the EAP.

Student Assistance Programs (SAPs)

Carmen is a high school senior. She is a cheerleader. She is vice-president of the Student Government. She is president of the Math Club. She has been voted the "Most Likely to Succeed" by her senior class. Her boyfriend is the football captain. With her 3.89 GPA, Carmen has received early admission to a prestigious college.

Nathan is a high school sophomore. He does not go to football games. He didn't vote in the student government elections. He doesn't belong to any clubs at school. His appearance is ragged and odoriferous. He has no girlfriend. College is not in his plans. Besides, his 1.07 GPA has him on academic probation, and he will have to attend summer school to pass.

Trisha is in middle school. She is quiet. She is a friend of a friend who is in Student Council. She doesn't belong to any extra-curricular clubs, because "she can't." She dresses in a rather plain clothes. Boys are of interest, but she is not involved with anyone in particular. Grades come fairly easy.

Miguel is also in middle school. He is loud. He does not associate with anyone in student government. School clubs hold no interest for him. He dresses in all black. Girls are no problem. Grades are, although he doesn't seem to care.

Sharneatha is in third grade. She is very popular. Her Mom and Dad are prominent in the community. She always has nice things to wear. She gets good marks on her report card.

These students are as different as can be. They come from varied socioeconomic backgrounds, have different ethnic origins, view school differently, and appear to have varying degrees of self-esteem. Some are viewed as having problems while others appear relatively problem free. What do they have in common? Drugs.

Not all are using, however. Miguel is scared to use because he has experienced his parent's divorce over his mother's drinking and his father's addiction to pain killers. Sharneatha's big sister uses cocaine. Trisha doesn't feel she can compete with her 4.0 GPA, popular, and boisterous sister, so she drinks after school instead of "killing herself." Nathan likes acid because it helps him "think about things." Carmen has had two abortions and is pregnant again. This time she wants to keep the baby, but claims if her father finds out, "he will throw me out of the house in one of his drunken rages."

These stories are sad and true. These students are not atypical. Some students in these examples use and some do not. However, all are involved directly or indirectly in drug-related problems. And all are students.

There is little question about the extent of student-related problems in the schools. Estimates are that 25 to 35% of all students in a given school are affected by their own use or the chemical use of a family member (Anderson, 1993). Yet many debate the extent to which the school can and should become involved. Essentially, the argument for school involvement comes from the theory that enhanced self-esteem leads to enhanced performance in school. However, the counterpoint focuses upon the need for school to be school and the need to educate rather than remediate. Regardless of the side of the fence upon which one finds oneself, the school is the primary institution dealing with children and their families. Moreover, a great deal of drug-related behavior takes place in school or around school activities. For example, a quarter bag of marijuana can be easily sold before school. It can be smoked during lunch off-campus. Students can get together after a football game and drink in their parent's basement. An older brother can pick up his younger brother and friends after school and turn them on to crank. School administrators do not disagree on whether the problem exists. However, they might disagree on how to address the problem.

History of Student Assistance Programs

Since the 1960s, schools have been coming out against drugs in various ways. Initially, the attack was focused upon providing information: Give the students enough information about the harmful effects of alcohol and other drugs, and they will steer themselves clear. This approach alone, however, was inadequate. So, guidance programs aimed at effective decision-making were implemented. The word *drug* was not used, in hopes that resistance to the information would be lowered. This plan, too, had less than efficacious results (McGovern & DuPont, 1991). When peer refusal programs, used in cigarette smoking prevention, also failed to deliver the desired results, schools turned to another prevention model: The Student Assistance Program (SAP), an approach that is gaining wide popularity across the nation.

According to Anderson (1993), schools were faced with three problems prior to the inception of the SAP. To begin with, teachers and school administrators were not trained to identify substance abuse problems. Attempts to identify often left the teacher frustrated because students would not be forthcoming in the admission of problems. Also, the fear of liability if the diagnosis of alcohol or other drug abuse was inaccurate was of concern. Second was the problem of intervention. If able to correctly identify a problem, the teacher or administrator usually lacked the expertise and know-how to intervene. Confidentiality was the third major issue. Confidentiality is extremely important when dealing with at-risk or high-risk behavior (see Chapter 17). Teachers found themselves caught between the institution's needs to protect every student (which might require notification of aberrant behaviors) and the teacher's need to hold information confidential.

Employee Assistance Programs (EAPS) formed the basis for the early SAPS. The initial focus of EAPs was to provide help to those in the workplace who were experiencing alcohol and other drug problems. SAPs initially attempted to duplicate the EAP model by placing a substance abuse specialist in the building. More often than not, these specialists were on loan from community agencies and operated outside of traditional school counseling. The focus of these early SAPs was upon voluntary student referrals. Most of those identified as needing assistance came from homes where there was alcohol abuse or were needing assistance because of their own chemical abuse (Moore and Forster, 1993). During these formative years (1978 to 1987), schools with SAPs initiated a "student assistance team," which processed referrals and helped link the student up with the appropriate help. Because parental involvement was usually low during this period, interventions requiring finances or transportation to meetings or counseling were often thwarted. Hence, support groups such as Alcoholics Anonymous, Narcotics Anonymous, Alateen, and others were formed on site.

Many of the substance abuse problems experienced by students were initially identified as discipline problems by teachers and administrators. As SAPs became more refined in terms of having teachers and administrators carefully document behavior patterns, administrators began to utilize the program as an alternative to discipline. This approach invited parents to become more involved. And with their increased involvement came greater ease in developing remedial programs that involved both schools and community agencies. Parents and students alike were referred to the community resources. Moore and Forster (1993) identified this early period from 1978 to 1987 as being focused upon initiating SAP programs. Later, attempts were made to integrate SAPs into school counseling, and SAPs experienced a concomitant rise into a more professional realm.

The professionalism involved paying attention to program evaluation, improved training of personnel, and more funding support. For example, according to Moore and Forster, approximately $9 million was allotted by the Washington state legislature to improve more than 60 SAPs in that state. On the national level, professional organizations such as The National Association of Leadership for Student Assistance Programs and the National Organization of Student Assistance Programs and Professionals were founded. At this time, some professional journals began publication with primary focus upon substance abuse programs in the schools. This growth toward professionalism has had a positive impact upon the SAPs and has continued to raise new and complex questions involving confidentiality as well as raising turf issues between the SAPs and school counselors. To appreciate these issues, you need to understand how the SAP actually works.

Students Targeted by the SAP

There is no one Student Assistance Program. Rather, SAPs are seen as an umbrella for any and all activities that help students deal with the variety of ways they can be affected by their own drug abuse or by someone else's abuse (Anderson, 1993). This same author has identified six groups of students who can potentially benefit from the SAP: (1) students who are actually chemically dependent (about 5% of the school population); (2) students who abuse alcohol or other drugs (about 15% or more of the student population); (3) students who are affected by others' use of alcohol or other drugs (about 25% of the same population); (4) students who are returning to the school setting from an alcohol/drug treatment program or who are attending school and primary treatment concurrently; (5) nonusing and nonabusing students who mainly need support and help in decisions involving use; and, (6) those students who may be at risk for chemical abuse due to divorce, separation, death and loss, suicide, sexuality issues, child abuse and neglect, or other reasons.

Philosophy of the SAP

The overriding philosophy of the SAPs is that they need to be safe places for students to talk about their concerns for themselves and their family members (McGovern & DuPont, 1991). The concept of *safe* has two important meanings. One meaning naturally concerns the interpersonal environment in which students can feel as though they are understood and not judged. The other meaning concerns confidentiality. The students need to feel as though their problems will not be the subject of discussions in the teachers' lounge. Federal laws limit the sharing of information about drug use (see Chapter 17), yet the nature of many SAPs is that several people will know about the problem. Should the student share information with a school counselor in an individual session, state laws also limit what this counselor can share with others, including parents and teachers. However, parents who become aware of their child's being referred for help may express anger at not being told the actual reasons for the referral. Hence, the gray area involving a safe place and the parents' need to know can often result in conflict. To address this and other issues, two models have been developed: The Core Team Model and the Counselor Model (McGovern & DuPont, 1991).

Student Assistance Program Models

Essentially, the distinction between these two models is structural. The Core Team Model is more integral to the school's activities and function and is often run by a school employee or school counselor. The team links those in need with the broader community support systems. In the Counselor Model, the school contracts with an outside agency to run the SAP. The Counselor Model escapes the administrative structure and direct budgetary reallocations. Also, confidentiality in this model is protected, in that no information can be shared with school personnel without the expressed written consent of the client. Yet, the Core Team model also goes a long way in protecting confidentiality. Written guidelines are instituted that reflect how and when parents should be informed of important information that would aid in the intervention. Certainly there are advantages in both approaches, and the model followed will likely parallel each district's philosophy related to the role and function of the school.

Regardless of which model is used, however, there are expectations of school personnel. Anderson (1993) outlines several of these expectations seen as critical for the success of any SAP. School personnel should report instances of witnessed alcohol/drug abuse. They should also develop clear standards for acceptable student behavior and performance and be alert for unexplained or persistent changes in behaviors or performance. These changes should be documented, and, when patterns emerge, school personnel need to confer with members of the SAP and refer when appropriate. Participation in assessment, interventions, and re-entry meetings is also expected. If the SAP Core Team Model is used, there are additional specific expectations for the school counselor. Among these are the need to acquire training in alcohol and other drug use, the need to assess alcohol and other drug use in each and every interview with students regardless of the presenting problem, and the willingness to refer students to the core team for staffing.

SAP Personnel Roles and Functions

The Core Team usually comprises teachers, school administrators, perhaps concerned members of the community, parents, and school counselors. The Student Assistance Coordinator is typically a school counselor or another member of the pupil services staff. Coordination includes the monitoring of individual students in the program, chairing the site-level core team, evaluating the team's effectiveness, and serving as a liaison between the school site, the community resources, and the district-wide SAP core group. According to Anderson, the Student Assistance Counselor is the school counselor who has received the appropriate training in alcohol and other drug use and abuse and has other special qualifications. Among these qualifications are the need to be seen as particularly trustworthy by the student population and also to be seen as fully supporting the philosophy, policies, and procedures of the SAP. Most often, the role of program coordinator and program counselor are combined. Along with the counselor is the Support Group Facilitator. For this role, anyone who is adequately trained and meets the requirements of the school district can lead support groups making this position either professional or nonprofessional. Finally, in terms of roles, there is the Student Assistance contact person. As with the support group facilitator, the contact person may or may not be a mental health professional. In any case, the position often holds the key to the program because it is this person who fields questions from students interested in the program. What is required for this position is the ability to listen well and to be able to impart information to students in a non-threatening way. In some cases, the contact person can be a student or students.

Program Functions and Structure

Six basic functions are usually performed in the SAP, and three teams insure that the six functions are performed or coordinated. Anderson points out that to be effective *all six* functions need to be performed for any given student across all six targeted groups. The first function is the early identification of those in need. This procedure refers to the process by which a student comes to the attention of the appropriate staff. In effective programs, the sources of these referrals will be the students themselves, school staff, peers, parents, and in some cases the community. The referral is the initial contact with the SAP regardless of what ensues. Then a screening process needs to be designed to assess the nature and severity of the problem. Helpful in this process is the placement of the student into one of the six targeted groups mentioned earlier such as "using," "chemically dependent," "affected others," etc. There is a continuum of assessment. On one end are documented notes made by teachers or other administrators. On the other end is formal diagnosis conducted by a qualified substance abuse counselor. It is important that the school avoid the formal diagnosis while being intimately involved in the less formal assessment procedures (Anderson, 1993). There typically are many individuals involved in the assessment who can also help in distinguishing aberrant from developmentally normal behaviors. Should the need arise, interventions and/or referral to appropriate sources can be implemented. In some cases this intervention can be as simple as getting permission to talk to parents. Naturally, it can also be as complex as a structured intervention process involving many key individuals (see Chapter 6). Fourth is treatment for the problem. The school can provide treatment in almost all of the cases with the exception of intervening with students who need formalized in-patient or extensive outpatient treatment. Fifth, provision of support is made for those needing help in making decisions or changing their lifestyle. According to Anderson, support can range from arranging for the student to talk to a "good listener" or arranging support groups all the way to changing the school climate toward a more supportive environment. Whatever the support, it needs to address the specific needs of the specific student. Finally, an effective SAP needs proper case management. This does not refer to bureaucratic follow-up but rather stresses the need to follow the student throughout the process. Three teams designed to carry out the functions of the SAP are the Core Team, the Screening Team, and the Referral Team.

The Core Team is the primary organizational unit of the student assistance model (according to Anderson) and is involved in the implementation, day-to-day operations, and on-going maintenance of the SAP. Most often, the Core Team is involved in the design of the program and in the formulation of policies and procedures. Evaluation of the program also falls under the purview of the Core Team. Core Team is composed of individuals from the school's administration, the professional counseling staff, and other interested staff members such as teachers and coaches. Although the more formal roles of Counselor/Coordinator, Group Facilitators, and Contact Persons guarantees membership on the Core Team, any interested individual can be a Core Team member.

The Screening Team may consist of the Core Team members, but does not necessarily need to do so. It may be a standing committee convened ad hoc. In many cases, the Screening Team will include a member of the school administration, the school nurse, the attendance officer, and perhaps a professional from a local agency or treatment program. The primary purpose of the Screening Team is to collect the data deemed essential to the student's disposition. This team may meet on a regular basis for on-going review and monitoring of new information.

The Referral Team is also convened on an as-needed basis and will be brought together whenever an intervention is planned. As the names implies, the purpose of this team is to assess the appropriate referral placement for the individual student. Two examples will help you understand how the SAP actually works.

Case Examples

Carmen. Carmen is the high school senior presented at the beginning of this section. She is the cheerleader, the president of the Math Club, and the one who carries close to a 4.0 GPA. She is also the one who is pregnant and frightened that her dad will beat her up if he found out.

Molly was Carmen's friend and was very concerned about her friend's pregnancy. Molly had been in classes where the school counselor presented the SAP, so Molly knew that help was available. She passed Carmen's name on to the SAP contact person who, in turn, passed the information along to the Core Team leader. At the next Core Team meeting Carmen's name was brought up, and her situation was discussed. One of the Core Team members mentioned that she had good rapport with Carmen and was willing to talk to her in order to assess the situation more in depth. After meeting with Carmen, the teacher reported back to the Team. In this example, the report consisted of verifying the facts presented by Carmen's friend Molly. The Team discussed Carmen's situation and made an effort to determine what would be an appropriate course of action. Because of the complexities involved including pregnancy and parental alcohol abuse, the Core Team decided that she might benefit from seeing the school counselor and school nurse for help in dealing with her pregnancy. Since Carmen wanted to keep the baby, the school's homebound teacher would likely have to become involved, and plans were made to apprise him of the situation at the appropriate time. It was also decided to offer a referral for couples counseling for Carmen and her boyfriend. The potential for Carmen and her father to be seen in counseling was also anticipated, so the Team chose to refer to a counselor who was trained in both couple's work and in alcohol and other drug use. Finally, the teacher who was managing Carmen's referral assumed the responsibility to follow-up with the proposed intervention so that Carmen did not "fall through the cracks." Eventually, Carmen had her baby, and as a result of counseling she and her dad became closer, although he continued to drink.

Trisha.   Trisha was handled differently. She is the middle school student who drank after school. Since she hung around with virtually no one, her referral came from her fourth-period teacher who noticed that she was "behaving strangely" and was failing to hand in some assignments. The teacher was uncomfortable in talking directly with Trisha, so he passed along her name to the SAP clerk. The clerk brought up Trisha's referral to the Core Team. This was the third time Trisha's name had come up in the Core Team. All referrals had been for alleged drinking, The same Team member assigned to manage the referral before took on Trisha's referral again. The first task was to begin gathering information from Trisha's other teachers. After two weeks of talking informally with others, the teacher reported back to the Team that, indeed, Trisha's performance was slowly but inexorably dropping off in all her classes. The Team decided to ask one of Trisha's teachers, who was a Core Team member, to make a routine call home just to see how things were going. Trisha's mother shared concern about how withdrawn and volatile her daughter had seemed to be behaving lately. This information, along with the data gathered from her other teachers, led the Team to decide that an intervention was needed. They agreed upon the process and agreed that a referral for formal diagnosis was indicated. Trisha was called out of class. She was unusually defiant, but when confronted with a report of her friend's having seen Trisha drinking in the school bathroom, she broke down and sobbed profusely. At that point, she agreed to go to the local treatment center for an assessment. The referral manager arranged for the evaluation, requested a release of information for the diagnosis and treatment plan, and arranged for Trisha's mother to take her over to the unit. Because Trisha was only 13, her mother was asked to sign a release so that the school counselor could confer with the unit. In the formal evaluation, it was found that Trisha was heavily involved with alcohol. The counselor, however, was reticent to recommend in-patient treatment. Weekly out-patient sessions were agreed upon as was attendance at the school's AA meetings. The drug and alcohol counselor also recommended that Trisha and her mother attend 10 sessions of out-patient counseling together with the aim of improving their relationship. Trisha's referral manager assumed the responsibility for following up on her progress. Sadly, further intervention was required in this case. Trisha was cited three months later with a DUI and for Driving Without a License. She was eventually hospitalized for depression and substance abuse. At last report, Trisha was attending an alternative high school, maintaining sobriety and attending AA and NA meetings weekly.

Summary

Both EAP and SAP programs attempt to deal with individuals who are experiencing problems at work or school. While there may be difficulties and controversies about who should assume the responsibility for help, there is little question that these programs go a long way in at least bringing the issues to the surface. Since each EAP and SAP program is unique, professional helpers need only to be reminded that confidentiality, clarity of policies, and a helping attitude are essential ingredients and will likely be the thematic characteristics of all good programs. The training level for an EAP counselor can vary. Some programs have staff that are in recovery and have no formalized training. Other programs may have a staff of individuals, some of whom may be in recovery, but all of whom have had some formal training. Still other programs can have Masters-level trained staff who specialize in both mental health and alcohol and other drug counseling. Professionalization of programs is on the rise, and.with this will come more refined methods of assessment and intervention.

Chapter 10

Families

In Chapter 1, we discussed a conceptualization of addiction in which the alcoholic or drug addict is in an intimate and monogamous relationship with the drug of choice. Clearly, if the primary relationship is with alcohol or other drugs, other relationships will be adversely impacted, and the effect on the family is particularly dramatic. Investigators in this field have identified a myriad of problems in alcoholic or drug abusing families. For example, Reilly (1992) found that communication in these families is characterized by criticism, complaints, judgments, blame, guilt, and nagging. The family often feels powerless and projects the cause of family problems to outside influences such as peers or neighborhoods (Stanton and Todd, 1992). Kaufman and Kaufman (1992) view the alcoholic family as enmeshed, where the alcoholic or addict functions to bring the family to life and together through the crises he or she perpetuates. Parenting is characterized by inconsistency and a lack of clear rules and limits (Reilly, 1992). Children in these families have been shown to demonstrate more aggression and anti-social behaviors (Jacob, Ritchey, Cvitkovic, & Blane, 1981) as well as more temper tantrums and sibling dissension (Wilson, 1982). Umana, Gross, and McConville (1981) also found that the children tend to "fix" the family by tidying up, intervening as peacemakers, and staying home to prevent parental fighting.

This is not meant to be a comprehensive review of the vast literature related to families in which there is an alcohol or other drug problem. Rather, these examples illustrate the obvious fact that, if a family member has an alcohol or other drug problem, the family will be affected. Individuals living in such families did not need researchers to discover this, as evidenced by the development of Al-Anon in 1954 and Alateen in 1975 (see Chapter 8). Furthermore, comprehensive treatment programs include family education and family therapy as a component of treatment (see Chapter 7). They acknowledged that alcoholism and drug addiction affect each member of the family and that successful recovery necessitates the involvement of the entire family.

As we discussed in Chapter 3, different models of addiction and, predictably, differing conceptualizations occur in families in relation to alcohol and other drug problems. Some may argue that the individual with an alcohol or other drug problem is reflecting dysfunction in the family. Others see the alcohol or other drug problem as the primary cause of family dysfunction. As with other controversies in this field, both conceptualizations are probably true. In some families, dysfunction may be acted out through the abuse of alcohol and other drugs. For example, an adolescent female may use drugs to cope with the emotional trauma of sexual abuse. A fairly functional family may become tumultuous as a result of the father's progressive alcoholism. Regardless of the "chicken before the egg" question, we find that the understanding of families and alcohol and other drug abuse is aided through a family-systems conceptualization.

You should be aware that even the definition of *family* varies across cultures. According to McGoldrick (1989), "family" is a traditional white Anglo-Saxon Protestant definition based upon an intact nuclear family, where lineage is of importance when tracing one's ancestry. According to the same author, the family, in the traditional African-American population, is focused on a wide informal network of kin and community that goes beyond blood ties to include close, long-time friends. The traditional Asian-American family includes the entire family group and all ancestors and all their descendants. Differences in the life cycle of the family also reflect cultural and ethnic differences. For example, McGoldrick states that the traditional Euro-American family begins with a psychological being, and growth and development is measured by the human capacity for differentiation. In the traditional Asian-American family, there is a social being (as opposed to a psychological being), and growth and development is measured by the capacity for empathy and connection.

A great deal of the research into alcoholic families has focused upon the Euro-American population. Yet, as we pointed out in Chapter 4, culturally and ethnically diverse families are at risk for alcohol and other drug abuse. While there is a growing body of literature focusing upon diverse families systems, little information about the effects of alcohol on these family systems and structures has appeared in the literature. In fact, we just received two books on therapy with the alcoholic family that were highly recommended for graduate coursework. Neither of these books or other books we have reviewed contained any information about the effects of alcohol and other drug abuse on culturally and ethnically diverse families. Clearly, however, alcohol and other drug abuse will impact all families regardless of cultural or ethnic origin. In this chapter, we will draw your attention to some areas of these family systems that we believe will be most likely affected.

Family Homeostasis

Regardless of ethnicity, families are dynamic systems and are influenced by changes that occur both within and outside of the family system. The larger social, political, and economic forces exert their influence in the family from the outside, while internal changes such as illness, aging, entering and leaving the family, changes occurring in the workplace, changing geographical locations, and changes in stress levels affect families from within.

Jackson (1957) used the term *family homeostasis* to describe the natural tendency of families to behave in such a manner as to maintain a sense of balance, structure, and stability in the face of change. Significant to the concept of homeostasis is the notion that, as one family member experiences change in his or her life, the entire family will be affected and will adjust in some fashion. Family members can adjust overtly and covertly in an effort to maintain this balance and will exert much effort during times when the balance is threatened. This natural resistance can be both a blessing and a bane: by facing some changes with resistance, families can avoid losing their structures and becoming chaotic systems. However, there will inevitably be times when change requires the family to adjust.

It is during these times that the family, to varying degrees, will need to reorganize its roles, rules, boundaries, and values to create a new balance that fits. If families are too resistant to change, they can become rigid and unable to adjust adequately, and family dysfunction can follow. For example, Ewing and Fox (1968) describe the alcoholic marriage as a homeostatic mechanism that is "established to resist change over long periods of time. The behavior of each spouse is rigidly controlled by the other. As a result, an effort by one person to alter typical role behavior threatens the family equilibrium and provokes new efforts by the spouse to maintain status quo" (p. 87). Alcohol is seen as playing a key role in attempting to maintaining the status quo in alcoholic families.

Wegscheider (1981) believes that in an alcoholic family, members attempt to maintain balance by compulsively repressing their feelings while developing survival behaviors, as well as emotional walls, to ward off the pain associated with the family member's drinking. If drinking is removed from the family system, the family can be thrown into chaos. For example, an alcoholic father who becomes sober may attempt to re-exert his influence as head of the household thus throwing the marriage out of the balance to which it had become accustomed. The mother is no longer needed as a buffer between the children and their father, so she fades into the background as the children begin to address their father directly. The oldest son is no longer the surrogate father and begins acting out his frustration. The relationship between the mother, who has relied upon this son for support, and her son becomes strained as the father cannot hide his jealousy over this relationship. Unless the family can adjust adequately, drinking may be initiated again to re-establish balance.

Roles

Family Roles

We pointed out in Chapter 4 the variety of roles assumed by culturally and ethnically diverse families. Roles are an important part of Euro-American families as well. Role is often defined by the individual's behaviors in performing the rights and obligations associated with a certain position, and usually involves a set of complementary expectations concerning one's own actions as well as the actions with whom one is involved (Shertzer and Stone, 1980). Irrespective of the presence of alcohol, one of the basic principles of family homeostasis is predictable family roles. Through these roles, family members can act out the overt and covert family rules in an effort to maintain homeostasis within the family system. According to Satir (1964), because the marital relationship is the "axis around which all other family relationships are formed" (p. 1), it is the interaction of roles in the marital relationship that influences the character of the family homeostasis.

Although the specific family roles differ among diverse populations and across alcoholic or other drug-abusing families (see Chapter 11), there are generic roles for a man that include his behavior as a man, as a husband, and as a father. A woman's behavior will gravitate toward her being a woman, a wife, and a mother. Children's behavior will develop through the stages of child, adolescent, and adult. As the family develops, other roles will come into play as well. Super (1990) identifies the roles that family members will undertake to varying degrees sometime in his or her life: child, student, leisurite, citizen, worker, spouse, parent, and pensioner. As people move in and out of these various roles, all families experience an imbalance and make attempts to re-establish homeostasis.

Roles can also be further divided into affective and instrumental areas. Instrumental roles are those aimed at addressing the day-to-day human needs. The latter, affective roles, have particular significance in alcoholic or other drug-abusing families. Often in these families, there are individuals who will experience and express certain emotions for the family. For example, the alcoholic who becomes angry and sullen when drunk may be carrying the anger for other family members who have difficulty in expressing this emotion. So, when the alcoholic gets angry, things may finally be said (inappropriately or not) to other family members that might not be discussed otherwise because the sober family members do not overtly express their own hostility. In this example, the anger role is carried by the alcoholic, and the emotions of sadness and helplessness may be carried and expressed by other nonalcoholic family members.

Childhood Roles

Children in families carry two essential roles. One role is that of child. There are also roles within roles in that the child assumes a variety of other roles. For example, many believe that birth order in the Euro-American family affects the child's role in the family and see the oldest child in the family as taking on a dominant role with the second child taking on a more rebellious role. Youngest children are often used to having things done for them and take on a more passive role. While birth order alone does not determine an individual's perception of relationships, it does have an influence.

For alcoholic or other drug abusing families, there is a dearth of data on childhood roles among culturally and ethnically diverse populations. Much of the research on childhood roles is the result of clinical impressions of the Euro-American population and, for the most part, the research has been reported in the popular literature. For example, Black (1981) described the roles adopted by children of alcoholic homes as based upon their perceptions of what they need to do to survive and bring stability to their lives. It was Wegscheider (1981) who described the dysfunctional family roles of "hero," "scapegoat," "lost child," "mascot," and "enabler." The hero or heroine child is often a compulsive high-achiever who, through their accomplishments, defocuses attention from the alcoholism in the family system. Music, sports, and academics are frequent arenas in which the heroes or heroines act out their roles, often at the expense of their own needs. Because they can often excel in one or more undertakings, they create the impression that their family must be quite well adjusted. In our own practice, we have seen many adolescents who are valedictorians, captains of sports teams, cheerleaders, and/or student government officers and who come from homes where alcohol is abused. The scapegoat child is seen as acting out the family problem by demonstrating defiance and irresponsibility. The unconscious or conscious agenda for these children is to create a need for overt parental attention as they attempt to defocus from the problem of alcohol. Lost children are believed to be shy, withdrawn, and require very little attention so that the family does not have to worry about them (Wegscheider, 1981). This child often copes through avoidance that, unfortunately, leaves them isolated from the joys and richness of life, feeling unloved and unworthy of love (Kitchens, 1991; Wegscheider, 1981). The family mascot is the funny and often mischievous child who defuses the tension inherent in alcoholic families. In the classroom, this child may act out as the class clown. The enabler is the person who attempts to protect the alcoholic or drug addict from experiencing the natural and logical consequences of his or her behavior. These roles are seen as survival roles in alcoholic families and are deemed as dysfunctional or maladaptive in that they do not allow children to experience the normal, full range of emotions and behaviors. Wegscheider (1981) believes that the roles assumed by children in homes where alcohol and other drugs are present tend to be fixed or rigid. The result is family dysfunction.

Jenkins, Fisher, and Harrison (1993) studied the rigidity of roles adopted by Euro-American children from alcoholic and nonalcoholic families. The results indicated that the roles were not rigid. That is, over 75% of those coming from alcoholic homes and 60% of those having other problems (death, divorce, or abuse) indicated that they took on more than one role. In that only 30% of the other group (i.e., those reporting no family dysfunction) adopted one or more roles, Jenkins et al. concluded that "some type of dysfunctional or disrupted family history was the best indicator of whether a subject would indicate adopting a dysfunctional role or roles as children" (p. 316). Therefore, these same authors suggest that children from alcoholic families and those from families with other dysfunctions appear to be more similar than different. Interestingly, the most commonly reported role combination was that of hero and the lost child. The authors suggest that the child assuming the hero role may attempt to defocus the problem through high achievement, which would be consistent with Wegscheider's (1981) observations. The adaptation to the lost child role was seen as the child's attempting to avoid having to disclose the pain and family dysfunction when in social relationships or when there was parental conflict (Jenkins et al., 1993). Thus, there is some evidence about the validity of the adoption of childhood roles, but the notion of role rigidity is questionable.

Family Rules

All culturally and ethnically diverse families as well as Euro-American families have overt and covert contracts between their members that operate as rules governing family interactions. Barnard (1981) believes that these rules govern (1) what, when, and how family members can communicate their experiences about what they see, hear, feel, and think; (2) who has permission to speak to whom about what; (3) the extent and manner in which a family member can be different; (4) the manner in which sexuality can be expressed; (5) what it means to be a male or female; and (6) how family members acquire self-worth and how much self-worth a member can experience. In all likelihood, culturally and ethnically diverse families are governed by these same rules. The only differences between these families would revolve around what happens if the rules are broken. For example, a Euro-American family may punish the child who has talked back to his or her parents. An Asian-American family might use shame to correct aberrant behavior.

Black (1981) stated three imperatives or rules that govern alcoholic families: Don't talk; Don't trust; Don't feel. In families where alcohol and other drugs are abused, these rules form the basis for family interactions and for the alliances between individual family members and society at large. An example (in which names have been changed) can help you understand.

Tony, a very successful businessman, was married to Mary, and they had three children: Loretta, Mark, and Donnie whose ages were 16, 15, and 9. Tony was alcoholic, but nobody in the family believed his drinking to be problematic. That was Rule #1: Do not believe that your father has a drinking problem. Every night when he arrived home after twelve hours on the job, the children would come downstairs and greet their father, then allow him to change clothes while their mother would mix their father's usual drink: his favorite scotch with crushed ice. She would have a glass of red wine. The children would leave their mother and father alone to discuss the day. That was Rule #2: Do not disturb your father's ritual. Even when the children had something exciting to talk about that had occurred during the day, they were not to disrupt the ritual until it was time for dinner. Gathered around the table, with Tony nursing his second or third drink or even a beer, the children would then "report" the day to their father. The children were not allowed to leave the table until everyone, including their Dad, was finished. Sometimes, if Tony was drinking a lot, the dinner could last an entire evening. Frustrations about wasting time at dinner were not to be discussed, but, when out of exasperation, they were aired, Tony would most often respond by becoming argumentative, oppressive, threatening, and upon occasion physically abusive. This was Rule #3:

Your father is the head of the household and you must do exactly as he wants. When Tony lost his temper at the table, Mary would jump in to mediate between Tony and the children. Usually, the fighting occurred between Tony and Mark, the oldest son, so Mary usually wound up arbitrating between these two. While they did not like the situation, Loretta and Donnie did appreciate Mark's intervening on their behalf because it allowed dinner to be over. The shouting and threatening behavior created so much chaos that Loretta and Donnie could slip away while Mary, Tony, and Mark were fighting it out. This was Rule #4: Mark is the scapegoat. Two or three times during the week, dinners would proceed in a fashion similar to that just described. Hence, Rule #5: Even when things are unpleasant and could be changed, do not change the family. The weekends were just an extension of the weekdays except on the weekends Tony would play tennis in the mornings rather than spend time with the family and would begin drinking at lunchtime. Often, he would come home drunk or noticeably high from alcohol. If he had had a good game of tennis, his mood would be pleasant; if he played poorly, he was easily agitated. The children knew enough to be gone all day Saturday to avoid whatever might occur, while Mary would do household chores until Tony came home. Because Tony and Mary would usually go out on Saturday night, the children would most often find something to do until they were sure that their dad and mom were out of the house before coming home to eat the meal their mother had prepared for them. On Saturday nights, whoever was home would sit watching television with the lights out, prepared to run to their rooms and feigning sleep at the first sign of their parents' arrival home.

It was Loretta who first asked her mother about her dad's drinking. This occurred after the school counselor had done a guidance unit on alcohol and other drugs during Loretta's fifth-period social studies class. Her mother readily confessed to having similar concerns but told Loretta that her dad worked very hard and everyone should be understanding because he was under a great deal of stress. She told Loretta not to worry and to keep this information between the two of them. Rule #7: Do not talk about your feelings about your dad's drinking problem to anyone.

As Tony's drinking progressed over the next two years, Mark became the focus of his dad's displaced hostility. Mark felt as if he could do nothing right in his father's eyes, and, during his later teen years, began to express his own hostility toward his dad. However, when Mark confronted his dad about how unreasonable he was when he drank, his father would respond by yelling, pointing his finger in his son's face, and would eventually become more angry than his son. Mark learned to back down, swallowing his pride, his feelings, and his lowered sense of self-respect. Gradually, his grades began to drop. In spite of his being a very talented golfer, Mark lost his eligibility to participate in athletics due to his grades. Having lost his friends who were busy participating in after-school sports, Mark fell into a crowd who used alcohol and other drugs, and he began drinking alcohol on the weekends and eventually began using marijuana and cocaine. Loretta continued her attempts to soothe her father's nerves by doing whatever he asked but emotionally removed herself from the family and focused her attentions upon her boyfriend and her grades. She confided in Mark that she couldn't wait to get out of the house. Donnie was his mother's favorite, and Mary did everything she could to protect Donnie from her husband. Donnie was able to escape the direct wrath of his father by keeping quiet, getting straight *A*s, and devoting himself to helping his mother.

What was most confusing to Loretta, Mark, and to some extent to Donnie was how their father could be seen as so successful at work, yet be so different at home. When their father was away on business trips and the discussion about his drinking would come up during dinner, Mary would consistently respond by saying that the children's father loved them very much so they need not worry. When pressed by Loretta and Mark, their mother would usually start crying, saying that she did not know what to do, yet she would balk at suggestions to see a counselor and/or confront their dad. Loretta and Mark would comfort their mother by telling her that she was a good mother and that she did not need to cry because her children loved her. Rule #8: Believe that your mother is helpless and that you need to take care of her.

This example shows how rules are developed and maintained by family members. Nobody was supposed to confront the alcohol problem because "there was no alcohol problem." That their father loved the children was supposed to be enough. There was to be no anger. If that rule were broken, Tony would become more angry than anyone, thereby overpowering the family's anger and sending it back into a repressed state. Eventually the children, especially Loretta and Mark, learned to control their emotions—especially anger, hurt, and fear. The rigidity of the rule, "don't talk, don't trust, don't feel," led to Loretta's desire to leave the family and to never confront her father, so that her father never knew how she really felt. Mark responded to his feelings of helplessness and frustration by internalizing his shame and coming to believe that he was to blame for his father's drinking since he was usually the one who fought with his dad. As a result of his internalized shame, he began using drugs and acted out his helplessness by becoming irresponsible, thus neglecting his own desires and hopes in life. Donnie eventually became the family "hero" by getting exceptional grades and becoming involved in student government. He posed "no threat and no problem" to the family. Mary worked herself to the bone as a mediator between her children and their father, all the while attempting to become the apple of her husband's eye. Her whole life was her family, and the centrality of her position provided her with a sense of meaning in an otherwise unhappy marital situation. Because these family rules were rigid, the family system functioned to maintain itself as best it could, but there were grave consequences. In spite of the severity of the consequences, the family was unable to adjust until Tony's alcohol problem was addressed and the rules changed.

Underlying Family Themes

Reilly (1992) identifies two underlying themes that serve to fuel the interactive patterns of families experiencing drug abuse: impaired mourning and homeostasis collusion. Impaired mourning refers to the family's preoccupation with "issues of attachment and separation, loss and restoration, and death and rebirth" (p. 109). Other research suggests that oftentimes in these families there has been parental death, divorce, or abandonment (Kaufman & Kaufman, 1992) that can leave the family with an inability to transform itself to meet new challenges (Minuchin, 1974; 1992). Because of the strong sense of loss, either through abandonment, death, divorce, rejection, or neglect, concomitant with an inability to transform the experience, children never fully grieve the loss, and the family can become stuck. In the example, Tony's drinking problem precluded his ability to develop a strong attachment to his family. The ensuing abandonment left his children and his wife grieving for a relationship with him. The rules were such that any attempt to work through the grieving process would have been met with severe opposition from Tony. So the children and their mother were left to deal with the problem either indirectly or surreptitiously. As a result, the family was not able to fully grieve the loss of a functional and healthy relationship with their father.

Remember how, in Chapter 4 we discussed the issue of Native American mourning and its impact on the risk factors for alcohol and other drug abuse among this population. Knowing that impaired mourning seems to be characteristic of alcoholic families in general, you can readily see how the issue of impaired mourning may have an additive effect with regard to the Native American family. That is, mourning for their lost culture has been cited as increasing the risk among Native Americans for substance abuse (Young, 1991), and impaired mourning is seen as fueling the dysfunctional interactive patterns among families once alcohol and other drugs are abused in the family. It would seem that mourning, in some form, can be seen as both partly causing alcoholism and helping to maintain the resulting dysfunctional family patterns in the Native American population.

When the whole family becomes stuck or unable to transform itself due to its following of the "don't talk, don't trust, don't feel" rule, as it did in this case example, family collusion can occur (Haley, 1973; Noone & Reddig 1976). Paul (1967) points out that families who have not grieved the losses in the early cycles of their system develop a family style that reflects a lack of empathy, a lack of respect for individuality, and a tenacious and unconscious attempt to hold back the passage of time, with the concomitant need to keep individual family members in a dependent position.

Paul's (1967) study demonstrates how family collusion results from a break in the grieving process and how it reinforces the interactive patterns characteristic of families with alcohol or other drug abuse. In the example, Mark turned to using alcohol and other drugs as a means to identify with his father. Eventually, Mark's problem became the focus of attention for the family, thereby diminishing the centrality of Tony's drinking. Mark gained much power in the family because he became a rallying point around which the family could address issues of his drug abuse. Without that rallying point, Mary might have chosen to leave the marriage. She stayed in order to help the family deal with Mark's problems. Also, the family colluded and remained stuck because they covertly reinforced Mark's drug problems. Loretta would occasionally buy marijuana for her brother and often bought him beer until he became of legal age. When she periodically found drug paraphernalia in her son's room, Mary chose to not confront Mark. And Donnie remained distant from his older brother, although he loved him deeply. While these were all conscious decisions, the family members unconsciously knew that, if Mark's problems were addressed and corrected, Tony's alcohol problems would once again become the focal point of concern as well as reminding each of their shame, grief, and helplessness. To avoid the pain, the family unconsciously colluded to keep Mark the scapegoat and the family member with the problem.

Clearly, the character and extent of family collusion in culturally and ethnically diverse families will be influenced by family values, by values regarding alcohol and other drugs, and by the degree of acculturation among family members. For example, we pointed out in Chapter 4 how Gilbert (1978) had noted the problems occurring in Latino/Hispanic families and Shon and Ja (1982) noted corresponding difficulties occurring in Asian-American families where one well-adjusted partner marries a spouse who is less acculturated. The resulting stresses and feelings of guilt, self-doubt, and betrayal were seen as disrupting family harmony. Alcoholism or other drug abuse in that family would only add to the enormous problems inherent in acculturation. The collusion transpiring in Latino/Hispanic families, African-American, and in Asian-American families could include extended family members who likely live nearby and who probably share in child-rearing, discipline, and problem-solving.

Family collusion might become even more complex when you consider family or cultural values. Recall that Stevens (1973) found that drinking alcohol is an accepted way of dealing with the stresses of acculturation for Latino/Hispanic males, and that the value of *machismo* tends to strengthen that notion. In this example, should the alcoholic family member be a less-acculturated male, then family collusion might include the male members of the immediate and extended family who share a common value of machismo. The resulting collusion might serve to sharpen the differences between male and female family members as well as exacerbating the generic difficulties found in the process of acculturation.

In general, the reciprocal nature of any family system suggests that, as the children impact the parents, new dynamics take place between the parents that in turn affect how the parents relate to their children (Erekson & Perkins, 1989). It is common in the literature on alcohol and other drug abuse to find reports of how the alcoholic has impacted the spouse and/or his or her children. Erekson and Perkins (1989) and Wilson (1982) write about the effects of alcoholism upon the family and suggest that family dysfunction may be both a cause and a result of alcoholism.

Family Subsystems and Boundaries

All families, regardless of cultural or ethnicity diversity, are made up of subsystems and boundaries. For the Euro-American family, there are three essential family subsystems: the marital, the parental, and the sibling subsystems. In Native-American, Asian-American, African-American, and Latino/Hispanic families, the family subsystems would include, to varying degrees, extended family members or other significant individuals. For example, the participation of godparents in the child-rearing practices of many Latino/Hispanic families and its parallel value, known as "child-keeping," seen in many African-American families, might reflect an extended parental subsystem.

The primary subsystem is the marital or couple subsystem made up of the wife and husband. This subsystem is closed in that there are certain duties and primary functions performed only by the married partners (e.g., earning money, managing the home). With the birth of a child, the marital subsystem extends to that of a parental subsystem. Interactions continue between the marital partners, which are aimed at the marriage itself (e.g., having a romantic dinner after the child is asleep) or are carried out between the spouses with an aim toward their parenting (e.g., juggling schedules around to cover child care). A third main subsystem is the sibling subsystem. The number of children, along with their ages, sexes, and interests will suggest the number of potential sibling subsystems. In addition, African-American and Latino/Hispanic families may have sibling subsystems that include cousins.

Rules or boundaries help define these various subsystems. Boundaries are like fences surrounding one's home: They define one's property and regulate the nature and type of interactions between neighbors. In essence, boundaries result from cultural and family values and define who can talk to whom, when one can talk, and what one can talk about. Regardless of cultural or ethnic background, both subsystems and boundaries need to be flexible enough to allow for adjustments to changes brought on either within the family or as a result of outside influences.

Family subsystems need to have the capacity to preserve themselves without becoming isolated from the larger family system. According to Minuchin (1974; 1992) and Erekson and Perkins (1989), boundaries must be clear, and usually families boundaries range from clear-but-overly-rigid boundaries to clear-but-flexible boundaries, to unclear-diffuse boundaries. When Euro-American family members are overly concerned about other family members or are so sensitive to other family members that their own needs and wants go unaddressed, the actual boundaries may be somewhat flexible but will remain unclear or diffuse. Here, a heightened sense of belonging occurs that requires some loss of autonomy by family members (Kaufman & Kaufman, 1992). The loss of autonomy in the Euro-American family is referred to as a family that is enmeshed (Minuchin, 1974). Euro-American parent's not allowing their children to grow up is symptomatic of an enmeshed family system. One example is when these parents continue to financially support their children long after they have left home. Another example can be when parents continually bail their children out of problems that their children created for themselves. However, in the Latino/Hispanic community, the value of "respeto" dictates a type of parent-child dependency, which is seen as a positive force keeping their families together.

Erekson and Perkins (1989) point out that, in Euro-American families where the boundaries are overly rigid, communication across subsystems can be restricted, ignored, and serve to handicap the protective functions of the family.

Emotional (and sometimes physical) distance characterizes these families. Minuchin (1974) refers to this type of rigid family structure as a family that is disengaged. These families are thought to tolerate a wide variety of individual differences while in reality they lack a feeling of loyalty, belonging, or the ability to request support when the need arises (Kaufman & Kaufman, 1992; Minuchin, 1974; 1992).

Our example of Tony and Mary's family reflected a disengaged family where Tony was rather removed from his spouse and his children. The children were not allowed to talk with their father about his drinking problem and so began to disengage and live their lives emotionally distant from other family members. With the onset of Mark's drug use, the disengaged nature of the family made it very difficult to regroup to address the underlying issue that was Tony's alcohol abuse. Nor was the family able to find ways to deal effectively with Mark's drug use. To avoid interacting with her father, Loretta spent all of her available time with her boyfriend. Donnie, despite his strong feelings for his older brother, remained rather aloof from him because he didn't understand or like what his brother was doing. Mary, the mother, was emotionally removed from her husband after years of emotional neglect by him. She tolerated her husband's drinking patterns so that she could avoid conflict and more hurt and pain in their relationship.

The issue of disengagement is clearly culturally biased. In traditional Asian American families, the father is expected to be disengaged. Therefore, the construct of disengagement would not always be an appropriate measure of family unity. An African-American male who works two jobs and is not home much in order to help get his family out of poverty may be labeled as disengaged when, in fact, his disengagement is a healthy adaptation to poverty. Likewise, "el amor de madre" (motherly love), a value highly regarded in Latino/Hispanic families, could be described as enmeshment, but this enmeshment is central to Latino/Hispanic culture and is not seen as dysfunctional behavior.

Where there is alcohol and other drug abuse, all families, regardless of cultural or ethnic background, act as "the fulcrum, the pivot point, the mediator, and the interpreter between its members and their culture" (Reilly, 1992; p. 105). The family thus is seen as having a significant influence upon the socialization of its members. As a social lens, the family screens, filters out, or magnifies social influences from the outside. These influences may be prosocial or antisocial.

Reilly maintains that the disturbed Euro-American family system needs a symptom bearer, and this would be the member who is susceptible to drug abuse. In our example, the symptom bearer was Mark, the eldest son. Reilly (1992) also believes that the family will consciously or unconsciously push this individual into antisocial, drug-abusing values as was reflected in our case example.

The Marital or Couple Subsystem

Jacob, Ritchey, Cvitkovic, and Blane (1981) found that the marital relationship where alcoholism exists reflects communication that is hostile, critical, and disapproving. As alcoholism progresses, the communication between spouses tends to increase in hostility thereby suggesting that there is a growing cycle of hostility and resentment.

Moreover, according to Shields (1989), the partners in a Euro-American marriage where there is alcohol or other drug abuse interact with each other in extremes, and the nature of this interactive pattern is symbiotic. Symbiotic relationships are characterized by an excessive amount of projection, poor psychological boundaries, and the frequent use of blame, resentment, ambivalence, and intense love and hate (Beavers, 1985). Shields also maintains that these couples tend to be either totally in control or totally out of control and that they will either really love their partners or they will really hate them. These couples are usually elated or depressed, emotionally disengaged and distant or emotionally enmeshed. Because each spouse's self-esteem is deleteriously affected by the other's drug abuse, a great deal of inner conflict is usually projected onto the other spouse.

Orford and Guthrie (1976) claimed that the nondrinking spouse may protect the alcoholic, may withdraw from the marriage, may safeguard the family's interests such as keeping the children out of the way, and/or may act out. Erekson and Perkins (1989) caution against rigid adherence to the findings of Orford and Guthrie, although they do maintain that clinical impressions do provide some support for these conclusions. We want to draw your attention to the potential limits of this concept when applying it to culturally and ethnically diverse families. No research has been found that reflects a similar dynamic occurring in these families as that identified by Orford and Guthrie. That is not to say that the nonalcoholic spouse won't withdraw from his or her partner in Asian American or another culturally diverse family. It is to say that we have no supporting evidence for this conclusion.

In terms of homeostasis, the coping styles used by the nonalcoholic maintain the system in that they shield the alcoholic in one way or another from the natural consequences of use. This shielding is known as enabling. The progressive use of alcohol tends to increase the use of these coping patterns, so that alcohol becomes an important part of the subsystem's functioning (James & Goldman, 1971).

Boundaries, usually clearly defined and permeable yet fixed in healthy functioning families, are problematic in alcoholic couples (Erekson & Perkins, 1989). These same authors contend that clinical impressions suggest that boundaries in alcoholic couples are usually either too rigid (disengaged) or too diffuse (enmeshed). Hence, when children enter the system, they too are impacted by the pattern of interactions already established by the spouse (now parent) subsystem. Given these dynamics, one can readily see that the introduction of children into a Euro-American couple subsystem already enmeshed or disengaged and highlighted by anger, fear, resentment, and blame will be carried over in some form to the parent-child subsystem as well as to the sibling subsystems.

The Parent-Child Subsystem

Kaufman and Kaufman (1992) identified structural patterns in families when there is alcohol and other drug abuse based upon the works of Minuchin (1974). Most of their sample was observed for over six months, and the research design included postgroup discussions of patterns. In addition, verbatim transcripts of all sessions were made and were analyzed to confirm initial clinical impressions. Videotapes were produced and were given to a group of experienced clinicians who rated the structural patterns they observed. The sample consisted of 75 families representing eight different ethnic groups (Latino/Hispanic, 23%; Italian, 19%; Euro-American, 18%; Jewish, 13%; African-American, 10%; Irish, 9%; Greek, 1%; and Mixtures, 6%).

Kaufman and Kaufman found that of the 75 families, 88% had enmeshed (un-differentiated boundaries) mother-child relationships and 40% had enmeshed father-child relationships. Forty-two percent of the fathers were considered disengaged while only two mothers were seen as such. The mothers of addicts were seen as enmeshed across all ethnic groups. Seven of thirteen Italian fathers were described as enmeshed as were six of thirteen Jewish fathers. Puerto Rican, African-American, and Euro-American fathers tended to be disengaged. The authors found that while the sample of African-Americans was too small to generalize, "most of the Black families had strong, involved mothers" (p. 39). Categorically, no relationship between the addicted family member and other family members was seen as having clear boundaries.

According to Kaufman and Kaufman, the most frequent enmeshed relationship involved the male addict and his mother. This relationship served to separate the mother from her husband, who retaliated with "either brutality to the addict and/or disengagement from the family" (p. 39). The patterns of father-son brutality were similar across groups, and it made no difference whether the father was enmeshed or disengaged. A covert result of the father-son brutality was that it tended to strengthen the mother-son relationship due to parental ambivalence over discipline practices, thereby creating a vicious and self-defeating cycle. In the Latino/Hispanic families, the mother was often the switchboard through which all communication flowed, while the father was the family spokesperson who made all the decisions. In general, families experiencing alcohol or other drug abuse were found to have mother-daughter relationships characterized as extremely hostile, chaotic, and competitive. In roughly half of the cases, this relationship was severely enmeshed as well. It is important that, when interpreting these results, you keep in mind that terms such as *enmeshment* are culturally biased terms and may not really reflect pathology across all culturally and ethnically diverse families.

The Sibling Subsystem

Siblings do appear to have an influence on adolescent drug use in terms of providing the drug and/or modeling drug behaviors (Kaufman & Kaufman, 1992). Research on the impact of siblings upon sibling drug use has focused on Euro-Americans and has been relegated to male siblings, but one can infer that these dynamics will be operating to varying degrees between sister subsystems and sister-brother subsystems. In addition, sibling subsystems for culturally and ethnically diverse families might include cousins and/or other extended kin. Kaufman and Kaufman note three pathways of sibling influence that tend to lead to sibling drug use. An older brother is linked to his younger brother through the *personality-*

influence mechanism. According to this hypothesis, the older brother's personality impacts the younger brother's personality through identification and modeling and likely leads to common values, attitudes, and behavioral orientation. So, deviance in the older brother is reflected in deviance in the younger brother. *Genetic temperamental connection* is the second pathway reported by Kaufman and Kaufman. This genetic predisposition may account for some of the similarity of values between older and younger brothers. Thus, a genetic link between male siblings may reinforce the personality-influence mechanism. The third pathway in this subsystem is called *environmental reactive mechanism* and refers to the ways in which the brothers are linked through their environment. That is, when the relationship between brothers is characterized by tension, there appears to be an increase in the intrapsychic distress in the younger brother. As a result of that distress, the younger brother may disengage from the relationship and withdraw from responsibility (Kaufman & Kaufman, 1992). In our example, Donnie's distancing from his brother exemplified the environmental reactive mechanism.

In less conflicting relationships, there is an increase in the nurturance, admiration, and sibling identification in the relationship. Thus, male siblings can have a positive influence and can provide some protective factors for the brothers and sisters. When there is a strong relationship, the identification between brothers that results is related to more conventional or less deviant attitudes and values, greater responsibility, less intrapsychic stress, and less drug use in the younger brother (Kaufman & Kaufman, 1992). Moreover, these same authors suggest that sibling risk factors that are known to predispose one to drug use, such as jealousy, lack of affection, and disengaged relationships, can be offset by secure parent-child relationships.

Siblings can often help their sibling addict assert him or herself when the need for help is imminent. Moreover, siblings can provide a welcome relief for the addict in terms of providing an alternative focus for the family so that the exclusive focus upon the addicted sibling becomes less intense.

Stepfamilies: System and Structure

"Stepfamilies may prove to be the traditional American family of the next century" (Anderson, 1992, p. 172). Current estimates reflect that one out of every five children is a stepchild, and demographers anticipate that 45% of American children born in the 1980s will experience a parental divorce and 35% of these children of divorce will live with a stepparent (Glick, 1984).

Stepfamilies have some key inherent differences from other families. Although many of the same problems in stepfamilies also exist in other families, stepfamilies are seen as having psychic and physical boundaries that are more permeable than those in a nuclear family (Anderson, 1992). Emotional bonds or psychic boundaries have to be loose enough to allow for affections to be expressed to both the biological parent as well as to the stepparent. The physical boundaries need to be permeable enough to allow for the revolving door of noncustodial visitation and need to be able to allow for visits of a longer duration, such as coming or leaving for an entire school year. Anderson also identifies the complexities involved in decision making in stepfamilies. Often, there needs to be a coordinated effort of two households in making plans. The stepfamily does not have the history that the nuclear family does, and sometimes children (and their parents) can experience a type of culture shock. Anderson says that this culture shock is "an acute feeling of an unfamiliar, sometimes alien, environment that is very disorienting to their basic sense of what 'my family' is" (p. 174). Because stepfamilies are born out of previous losses due to divorce or death, children (and parents) need to be able to grieve the loss adequately. However, grieving the loss is often painful, and many may be reluctant to do so when it appears that the grieving process may impinge upon the happier times of the current relationship.

According to Anderson, current research into stepfamilies reveals that they often have better marital adjustment than other families do. This is usually because nuclear families may exist for the sake of the children, or at least parents may delay divorce until the children are grown (Kanoy & Miller, 1980). Here, the children are seen as the bonding agent for the parents' decision to delay or rule out divorce. In stepfamilies, the spouses (heterosexual spouses or gay spouses) have already experienced a divorce or death and have chosen to marry in spite of vociferous objections by children. The glue in these cases is the marital bond, not the children. Thus, the children are not held responsible for the parent's decisions. By not being held responsible, differentiation in the family is more likely to occur.

Dunst, Trivette, and Deal (1988) have shown that healthy nuclear families have strong parent-child bonds. This is true regardless of ethnicity. Research consistently underscores the fact that the parent-child subsystem in nuclear families is stronger and more positive than in stepfamilies (Anderson, 1992). It is probably unreasonable to expect the same quality relationship in stepfamilies, but the extent to which stepchildren can form a positive and reciprocal relationship with the stepparent is important. In well-functioning stepfamilies, a strong (but limited in terms of intensity) relationship develops between stepparent and stepchildren (Anderson, 1992). Therefore, when assessing the strength of the stepparent-stepchild relationship for risk factors that might suggest alcohol and other drug abuse, it is important that mental health professionals take this natural limitation into account and not compare the strength of the relationship with that of a nonblended family.

Many family theorists maintain that parent-child coalitions (special bonds) can create family dysfunction (Bowen, 1971; Minuchin, 1992; 1974). In the stepfamily, there will be a structural imbalance in the biological, legal, and developmental ties toward the children that spouses share, which makes fertile ground for parent-child coalitions (Anderson, 1992). Often in dysfunctional stepfamily systems, a biological parent-child coalition will form concomitant with a nonreciprocal or negative relationship between the stepparent and stepchild. With regard to adolescents, the developmental tasks of the family unit as well of the individual can become more complex.

The developmental task of the adolescent is to separate and individuate, and this task can often be difficult in stepfamilies. In order to separate adequately, one must first attach. However, stepfamilies that form during a child's adolescent years are attempting to attach at the same time the adolescent is attempting to separate. Moreover, adolescence is often the time for custodial rights to be renegotiated. For example, a male adolescent might be sent to live with his father during high school or a female adolescent might be sent to live with her mother during the same years. However, due to the inherent difficulties experienced by most families during the child's adolescence, the process of forming new relationships or simply renewing relationships with the biological parent can divide the child's loyalties and present problems in the stepfamily. Whiteside (1989) states, "In this combination of age and family stage, there should be no expectation that the stepparent will be able to assume effective authoritative position directly in relation to the child" (p. 153).

In stepfamilies in which the adolescent is a drug abuser, a destructive pattern involving discipline may evolve (Anderson, 1992). The stepparent may be drawn into the disciplinarian role if the biological parent has been ineffective, and this move can result in marital strife if the biological parent steps in to protect the adolescent. Such a situation certainly reinforces the biological parent-child coalition. When this condition occurs and escalates without interruption, Sager, Brown, Crohn, and Walker (1983) warn of the adolescent extrusion syndrome. According to these authors, the adolescent extrusion syndrome happens when a reciprocating negative interaction escalates into the adolescent's self-imposed banishment from the family or when a command is given for the adolescent to leave. The adolescent can become the scapegoat acting to reinforce the fantasy that, if he or she leaves, the problems will go away. Naturally, extrusion more often occurs in stepfamilies that have a lowered sense of consolidation. In those cases in which the adolescent is abusing alcohol or other drugs, neither the stephousehold nor the biological household may welcome them.

It can be seen that stepfamilies are different in terms of the family developmental tasks. These tasks, if not accomplished, can lead to a higher risk for alcohol and other drug abuse. Although a stepfamily in and of itself is not any more at risk than any other family, the unique characteristics of these families can pose problems if the tasks are disrupted or not addressed.

Helping Families

Treating families with substance abuse problems is a complicated process, and treatment takes place on many different levels (Kaufman and Kaufman, 1992). Primarily, the counselor needs to decide which treatment mode will be the most efficacious. Because the plethora of research suggests that alcoholism and other drug abuse is a family problem, family therapy is often indicated, although not all families will want to be treated.

Steinglass (1987) reports that research on interventions for the family is "still struggling to define the scope and form this intervention should take" (p. 332). Steinglass also states that much of the research on treating alcoholism in families points to the efficacy of treating family members and maintains that participation by the alcoholic or drug abuser in treatment increases significantly when family members are included in the treatment. However, according to Steinglass, most treatment programs utilize a concurrent but independent program for the non-abusing family members and many family treatment programs have been reported to be effective. But, the author maintains, there is little evidence that suggests that clinicians are approaching family alcoholism with a sophisticated sense of family dynamics or family systems principles.

Steinglass's Family Life History Model

Steinglass advances an approach for Euro-American families based upon a family life history model (FLH). In distinguishing the FLH model from a traditional family systems approach, Steinglass emphasizes the importance of differentiating the alcoholic family from a family with an alcoholic member in the diagnostic phase and stresses the significance of identifying the family's developmental stage when designing treatment approaches.

Implications for Diagnosis

According to Steinglass, the Euro-American alcoholic family has a proclivity to reorganize itself in a way that accommodates the needs of the alcoholic as well as manifesting characteristic developmental "distortions" that are secondary to the reorganization of family life around the focal point of alcoholism. In alcoholic families, the entire family has alcoholism in that the behaviors related to alcohol use regulate the family interactions. In contrast, the family with an alcoholic member may not organize itself around alcoholism *per se* and may be able to make transitions and other adjustments that are required. The alcoholic family has a tendency to become stuck, unable to make successful transitions. In discriminating between these two types of families in the diagnostic phase, Steinglass believes that the mental health professional should take a history from the entire family rather than from the individual alcoholic alone. Moreover, he believes that it is crucial to include specific questions about the family's regulatory behaviors and to evoke evidence indicating the extent to which the family's behaviors have been altered in fundamental ways during the periods of the heaviest drinking. Through the family life history, the mental health professional can determine which family type is being presented (the alcoholic family or a family with an alcoholic member) and can also glean information about specific or key areas where alcoholism has had its greatest impact upon the family.

Developmental Implications

The family life history model includes assumptions about the developmental phase of the alcoholic family that are seen as having significant implications for treatment. According to the same author, there are three developmental phases in the alcoholic family: early, middle, and late phase. The family that is in the early developmental phase is seen as reacting to alcoholism as it relates to the family's maturational task of forming a solid family identity. If alcoholism occurs during this phase, the family may be over- or under-reacting to potential problems related to alcoholism. Although this model does not specifically address culturally and ethnically diverse families, you can clearly see how acculturation can influence the maturational task of forming a solid family identity. If alcoholism occurs during the acculturating phase of a newly formed family, this will increase the complexities involved as the family attempts the transition.

If the family's identity has already been established prior to the onset of alcoholism, the family is considered to be in the middle phase. Here, Steinglass believes that the most likely scenario is one in which the family presents a nonalcoholic problem and possibly a "fuzzy but suspicious history of abusive drinking" (p. 335). Often, families in the middle phase will use short-term, rigid, homeostatic mechanisms aimed at incorporating alcoholic behavior as part of the family's problem-solving efforts. For example, John and Mary have been married for five years. In the last two years, John has become alcoholic. Prior to the birth of their daughter last year, both had agreed that, because of John's erratic behavior resulting from his drinking, Mary would be the primary financial provider. The birth of their daughter posed serious questions about childcare and finances. Rather than dealing with the problem of alcoholism directly, John and Mary both agreed that she would continue to provide financially and he would care for their child. Things at home went along fine until John began drinking during the day and his concern and care for their daughter was compromised. The short-term solution to the financial issues raised by John's drinking now became problematic and forced the family to directly confront John's alcoholism.

The late phase alcoholic family is characterized by critical developmental issues centered on the nature of the ongoing relationship between parental and child generations. In these families, there is often the need on the part of other children who may be on the verge of leaving the family to bring some closure upon the alcohol-related issues. For example, a woman whose husband comes from an alcoholic family might want her husband to resolve issues regarding his father's alcoholism before she agrees to have children with him. Another example might involve a request from a husband that his wife "do something" about her alcoholic mother.

Steinglass describes the course of therapy with the typical Euro-American alcoholic family. This same author identifies four stages of therapy. The First Stage focuses upon diagnosing alcoholism and labeling it a family problem. Taking a family history that includes a history of alcoholism is important. The important questions relate to whether the family is an alcoholic family, whether alcoholism is the primary treatment priority, whether family therapy is indicated, and whether an appropriate treatment contract can be agreed upon. The Second Stage focuses upon removing alcohol from the family. According to Steinglass, mental health professionals should take a firm stand on the issue of alcoholism in this stage. A less-than-firm stand on the issue of alcoholism can result in a laissez-faire attitude that might reinforce the drinking behavior. Although this stage can be accomplished in relatively short order, the task of establishing a mutual goal of removing alcohol from the family system can be quite difficult. In any case, the mental health professional should not allow the family to de-focus the issue of alcoholism—even in the face of other compelling issues that may arise. Stage Three focuses upon the void that is left when drinking is stopped. Called the "emotional desert" by Steinglass (p. 343), this stage is highlighted by intense dysphoria for all family members. The family will often feel intense pressure to return to the drinking patterns as a way to re-balance itself. It is during this stage that the mental health professional will need to help the family cope with the loss of alcohol while re-establishing their homeostasis. The Fourth Stage is a resolution phase in which the family will attempt to re-group around a dry alcoholic phase. Family restabilization is the focus in this phase, and the therapeutic work centers on re-creating interpersonal relationships without alcohol. When family reorganization is the primary goal, mental health professionals might find themselves working with the parent or couple subsystem.

Kaufman and Kaufman's Family Types

Four types of Euro-American families will likely present themselves for treatment (Kaufman and Kaufman, 1992). In one family type, members might talk openly about drinking or drugging but are more concerned with other important issues. In these families, drinking or drugging may be present but not to the degree that it is a problem, and helping professionals should focus on the presenting problems but should also attempt to emphasize the possible connection between alcohol and other drug use and other problems in their lives. In the second family type, clues to alcohol and other drug use problems may be present, but the clues are oblique and difficult to discern. In these families, the symptom bearer will probably be the child who could be involved in drug abuse. Other clues may be found in reports of drinking in the parents' families of origin, in parental role reversals, in children's attempts to protect their parents, in children's fears of talking about the family, or when the parents present themselves as overly concerned about teenage alcohol and drug abuse. The mental health professional should focus on the presenting problem and should attempt to infuse drinking or drugging into the presenting issue. The third family type is the one whose members present themselves for therapy after the alcohol or other drug abuser has completed some type of treatment program and is clean and sober. The issues here will likely be rebalancing the family system to avoid a full-blown relapse. Slips (see Chapter 13) are to be expected, so the work of the mental health professional is to help the family anticipate situations in which a slip might occur and help the family to determine effective ways to keep the slip from becoming a relapse. The fourth family type is the one presenting alcohol or other drug abuse as the major problem. In these families, alcohol or other drug abuse is the focus of the family, and the conflict will be quite open and apparent. Mental health professionals may need to take more control of these sessions if emotional reactivity is running too high.

Regardless of which family type presents itself for counseling, mental health professionals need to attend to the spousal subsystem, the parent-child subsystem, and the sibling subsystem. The reason for this is simple: Families will balance themselves. So, mental health professionals need to take into account how interventions impact these critical subsystems, the individual family members, and the family itself so that the re-balancing that inevitably will take place will be beneficial.

Kaufman and Kaufman point to situations in which individual counseling may be the preferred mode of treatment for alcoholic families. They see individual work being done in those situations in which family therapy may be misused to deny personal responsibility, psychopathology of one family member can be prevented by individual work, the parents are psychopathological to the point that helping a child cope with the psychopathology is preferred, a family member is deceitful, individual pathology remains after family intervention, and detoxification or getting the client clean and sober is needed prior to family therapy.

There are many avenues open for helping the alcohol or other drug-abusing client or family. The actively drinking or using family member should be directed to a facility where they can become clean and sober. Abstinence may be just an ideal for some families. Therefore, if the individual does not want to go into treatment, the family members have a decision to make: They can learn to cope better with the abusing family member, which creates a "wet" system, or they can decide to go further into an intervention (see Chapter 6) and attempt to move their family into a "dry" system. In either case, support groups for family members such as Al-Anon, Al-Ateen, and Co-dependents Anonymous (see Chapter 8) can be very effective in many, but not all cases.

Case Example

Alan was referred by his biological mother, Jennifer, a physical therapist, because he had attempted to negotiate a conjoint suicide pact with her. His mother wanted to be present for the first session but did excuse herself after a half hour. At the time of the referral, Alan was a seventeen-year-old, Caucasian high school junior. He was a straight-A student and held the number one ranking in his academic class. He had little or no outside interests or friends to speak of in spite of his being articulate and handsome. He did admit that he wanted to commit suicide at one time but that he was "just depressed right now." The mental health professional did not assess Alan as being in danger at the time of counseling. His biological parents had divorced when Alan was seven, and he and his older brother and mother had lived alone for seven years before she married her current husband, Howie, an alcoholic. Alan's biological father had been diagnosed with bi-polar disorder and that was, according to Jennifer, the reason why she divorced him. John, Alan's older brother, had deserted the family (Alan's words) two years previously to marry a woman whom he had gotten pregnant. According to Alan, nobody in the family liked his brother's wife. Alan did not get along with his stepfather, Howie, and had refused to be adopted by him. Alan related that his mother "hates" her husband but is "too chicken to do anything about it." Jennifer did agree their marriage was "less than ideal" but refuted her son's accusation about her lack of courage saying, "

Sometimes love is not all what you want it to be, but you make the best of it you can." She described Howie as being "completely hands off when it comes to raising Alan."

During the first session, Alan revealed that he had begun to "experiment" with beer and other alcoholic beverages. He "didn't like the taste of beer" or the hangover he got after his first experience with it. "I prefer pot," he said, "because there's no hangover, and I don't want to drink and drive. That's stupid." He also said that he had no problem with either alcohol or marijuana and therefore did not really want to delve into this area. Alan cried twice during the first session, saying that he felt responsible for his parent's divorce and said that he felt as if he were the problem. He said that he was still sad over the break-up with his first girlfriend (also his first sexual experience) a year previously and that he found his female classmates too immature for him.

The mental health professional learned that Alan was very angry with his older brother for leaving him with his mother and her husband "to go it alone." Yet, Alan expressed a great deal of guilt over being angry with John. He was also very angry with his mother whom he described as "stupid" and "spineless." However, he realized that she needed help. "After all," he exclaimed in one session, "who would want to live with a f____head like that?" Eventually, counseling included Alan and his mother for three sessions, and then Alan, his mother, and Howie attended one session. Alan did not really want anyone other than himself to attend counseling but agreed "only after mom said that she wanted to come in with Howie for few times."

The family counseling was highlighted by three remarkable characteristics: John's choice not to attend, Alan's sitting between his mother and her husband, and Jennifer's mixed messages to her son. On the one hand she said that she trusted him implicitly ("After all, he's very responsible"), but she categorically resisted his requests that he not have to call her to inform her of any change of plans when he was out. Howie said very little in the session he attended. He described himself as feeling guilty most of the time and as wishing he and his wife could talk to each other without raising their voices. He disclosed that he knew the marriage was in trouble and wanted it to get back on track but did not know how to go about doing that. He blamed Jennifer for being too lenient. He was unable to return for more sessions because "he had too much work to do." During the only session Howie and Jennifer attended, neither Alan nor Jennifer brought up the issue of Howie's drinking. Nor did Howie. Alan did state that he felt "over-loaded" with family activities but was willing to meet those expectations. This first and only family session also witnessed the family's admonition for John who they saw as "doing so much less than he is capable of doing with his life."

Although Jennifer and Howie did not attend another session together, Alan continued seeing the counselor for several months. Together they eventually identified that Alan was using marijuana to cope with the multiple stresses: being number one in his class, the spoken and unspoken tensions in his home, the feelings of grief for his lost love, his current feelings of social inadequacy, and his wish "to have fun for once." He also came to see how his judgments of females as being too immature for him was not only a protective device but also served to keep him available for his mother. Eventually, he raised his self-esteem, tried out for the basketball team and made it, attended his junior prom with a girl he really liked, and stopped using, saying, "It was never me in the first place. Really, I don't want to be identified as a druggie."

This family presented itself with clues to parental drinking. Alan was the "symptom bearer," but no one was ready to address the implications of Howie's alcohol abuse. After attempts to involve the family in counseling were thwarted, the counselor decided to proceed with individual counseling, believing that helping Alan work on his issues would at least be helpful to him. Numerous dynamics were occurring in this family. The family coalitions were disruptive. As in Mary and Tony's case, this family was also mourning. John had been the identified patient in the family and had served to defocus the family from the real problems they were experiencing. The adolescent exclusion syndrome occurred here when John left the family and was unable to return. The loyalty Alan felt for his older brother was seen in Alan's wanting to create a crisis, through suicidal ideation, to relieve some of the disgust and negative attention directed toward John. But Alan was also very angry with John. This ambivalence created great conflict in Alan, and Alan likely experienced an increase in psychic tension because of the environmental reactive mechanism. Jennifer had felt forced to divorce the boys' biological father "for the sake of the boys." As a result of the poor communication and repressed emotions, this issue had never been addressed, and Alan had assumed the blame for the divorce. Jennifer's loathing for her sons' biological father created tension and divided loyalties in Alan, while his brother, John, removed himself from the home as a means of coping with his feelings. Alan had rejected the disengaged alcoholic Howie, and the couple subsystem was reeling as well from the effects of the enmeshed relationship between Jennifer and Alan that left Howie out in the cold.

He drank to relieve some of his frustration and to punish Jennifer. When he drank, he raged. She would rage back, and Alan would come down to console his mother, further reinforcing the vicious cycle of enmeshment.

Eventually, Alan left home to attend college on the East coast—as far away from his family as possible. Jennifer and Howie divorced after Alan's freshman year. John and his wife and daughter moved into a garage apartment behind his mother's house and lived there free in return for his helping with household maintenance.

Summary

We have presented research on families as it relates to alcohol and other drug abuse, but you must remember that there are many families who will not fit the mold. Dysfunctional families will generally not possess all of the negative traits identified by popular writers and researchers. Each family is unique. However, paying attention to race/ethnicity, family structure, interactive patterns, reciprocal relationships, and subsystems can help guide your assessment of alcohol and other drug abuse and can help in choosing interventions.

Most of the research regarding the impact of alcoholism and other drug abuse on the family system has centered on Euro-American families. However, there is little reason to suspect that the dynamics occurring in alcoholic families of other cultural and ethnic origins depart significantly from that of the Euro-American family. Clearly the ideas of family structure, which include the constructs of homeostasis, family rules, roles, and boundaries, will be influenced by the make-up of the subsystems that operate in all families. The main differences between Euro-American and other families will center on the actual make-up of those subsystems as well as on the differing family values and roles.

Assessment of alcoholism in families can be guided by the works of Steinglass and of Kaufman and Kaufman as well as your being guided by an understanding of the values embraced by the family with whom you are working. Collusion will likely occur in all alcoholic families, but the character and dynamics of that collusion will vary among families of different cultural and ethnic diversity.

$$C \ h \ a \ p \ t \ e \ r \quad \textbf{11}$$

Children from Chemically Dependent Families

In the last chapter, we discussed the impact that alcohol and other drug abuse has on family dynamics. In this chapter, we want to focus on the impact that alcohol and other drug abuse has on young children and on the lives of adults who grew up in homes where substances were abused. Although concern has been shown about the passage of drugs through the human placenta and through the mother's breast milk since the end of the nineteenth century, the 1970s reflected an increasing concern in this area and spawned a spate of research into children of substance-abusing parents.

According to Juliana and Goodman (1992), scholarly writing about the effects of alcohol upon children first appeared in the late nineteenth century with a study on the possible long-term effects of fetal opioid exposure. The popular movement appears to have been initiated by interest in Cork's (1969) book *The Forgotten Children*, which examined 115 school-aged children of alcoholics and found them to be suffering from varied problems such as difficulty in expressing anger and resentment, low self-confidence, and difficulty in initiating and maintaining friendships. El-Guebaly and Offord (1977; 1979) reviewed the early empirical literature on children of alcoholics and attempted to identify problems that members of this group had across their life-spans.

Intense popular interest then ensued with the publication of such books as Sharon Wegscheider's (1981) *Another Chance: Hope and Health for the Alcoholic Family*, Claudia Black's (1981) *It Will Never Happen to Me*, and Janet Woititz's (1983) *Adult Children of Alcoholics*. As a result of these popular writings, a children of alcoholics[1] (COA) movement began (Sher, 1991). The surging interest in COAs and

---

[1]The "Monitoring the Future" study surveys the use of a variety of drug over a respondent's lifetime, annually, in a 30 day period, and daily. Respondents are 8th, 10th, and 12th graders; young adults; and college students. We are only providing a small portion of the reported data.

adult children of alcoholics (ACOAs) has been prolific enough to have spawned a cottage industry. Essentially, the message promulgated in these popular writings is that one should confront one's chaotic childhood and work through the repressed pain (Blau, 1990).

It was, perhaps, this emphasis upon confrontation, the perception of "parent-bashing" (blaming one's parents for one's current problems) and the concomitant popularity of codependency (see Chapter 12) that created a critical backlash to the COA movement. For example, Gierymski and Williams (1986) and others point to the dearth of systematic studies undertaken to establish that COAs and ACOAs and codependency are actual clinical entities. Windle and Searles (1990) and Goodyear (1987) point out that, while problems such as parental inconsistencies, double-bind messages, the covert expression of feelings, shame, mistrust, and roles may be present in ACOAs, these same problems have been reported by other adults as well. These same authors caution against attributing characteristics of adult children exclusively to alcohol and other drug use in their families of origin. In addition, research findings examining ACOAs, which will be discussed in this chapter, have been contradictory (Windle & Searles, 1990). Nevertheless, clinical interventions have been formulated to help adult children of alcoholics, and social policy decisions such as employee assistance programs and student assistance programs (see Chapter 9) stem from the awareness of the impact that alcohol and other drug abuse has upon children, families, and concerned others. Therefore, it is important that mental health professionals be aware of the impact of interpersonal exposure to alcohol and other drug abuse.

Children of Alcoholics (COAs)

Russell, Henderson, and Blume (1985) estimate that there are approximately 6.6 million children of alcoholics (COAs) younger than age 18. The negative impact on children as a result of living in a family in which alcohol or other drug abuse exists has been described in Chapter 10 and will be addressed in this chapter as well. The effects on children will differ because of a number of individual and environmental variables including age of exposure, progression of use, characteristics of the child and the abuser, other family dynamics and events, and more. Therefore, it would be unwise to assume that all children (or adult children) who experienced substance abuse in their families of origin will be similar. The information we will present indicates the problems that have been identified but that are clearly not inevitable.

Children Prenatally Exposed to Alcohol and Other Drugs

Detrimental affects from parental alcohol and other drug use can impact an individual's social and psychological development through adulthood. However, there may also be effects on the fetus that can lead to problems in a variety of areas of growth and development when women use tobacco, alcohol, and other drugs during pregnancy.[2] Some of these problems may remain even if the mother discontinues her use or if the child is raised in a nonusing environment.

The topic of maternal use of alcohol and other drugs has become emotionally charged and has received wide publicity in the popular media. This is particularly true with regard to maternal cocaine use. News stories often show pictures of extremely small, premature babies who seem unusually irritable and unresponsive to the usual methods of comforting infants. Attempts have been made to charge women with child endangerment or child abuse if they use illegal drugs during pregnancy. Reports indicate that these children are highly distractable and unable to learn in school. Due to the emotionally charged nature of this topic, we think it is important to provide some accurate information regarding children who are fetally affected by legal and illegal drugs.

Incidence

A survey of tobacco, alcohol, and other drug use by pregnant women was recently conducted by the National Institute of Drug Abuse (CESAR, 1994). Self-report data were gathered from 2,613 women delivering live-born babies in 52 metropolitan- and nonmetropolitan-area hospitals in the United States in 1992. The most frequently used drugs were tobacco (20.4%) and alcohol (18.8%). Prescription analgesics and sedatives were used by 7.6% and 3.6% of the women, respectively. Marijuana use was reported by 2.9% of the sample and cocaine use, by 1.1%. Any illicit drug use (marijuana, cocaine, methamphetamine, heroin, methadone, inhalants, hallucinogens, or nonmedical use of psychotherapeutic drugs) was reported by 5.5%. Using this data, it was estimated that nearly 221,000 women used illicit drugs during pregnancy, nearly 820,000 smoked and almost 757,000 used alcohol.

Similar to many issues in this field, prenatal exposure to illegal drugs generates a great deal of publicity, but legal drugs cause the most problems. The U.S. Department of Health and Human Services (1990) estimated that up to 30% of infants born to women who are heavy drinkers exhibit signs of fetal alcohol syndrome or fetal alcohol effects. We will define these conditions as well as the condition of children affected prenatally by drugs other than alcohol.

Fetal Alcohol Syndrome, Fetal Alcohol Effect, and Fetal Drug Effect

According to Streissguth, Aase, Clarren, Randels, LaDue, and Smith (1991):

> *Fetal alcohol syndrome (FAS) now is recognized as the leading known cause of mental retardation in the United States, surpassing Down's syndrome and spina bifida. Over 2,000 scientific reports have now appeared, confirming that alcohol is a teratogenic drug capable of producing lifelong disabilities after intrauterine ex-*

---

[2]An exception is the Partnership for a Drug-Free America, a coalition of advertising and media associations who donate their time to produce and direct anti-drug advertising. Unfortunately, the partnership focuses on marijuana, cocaine, and crack and tends to ignore tobacco and alcohol.

posure. Fetal alcohol syndrome does not include all individuals affected by alcohol in utero, but rather it represents the severe end of the continuum of disabilities caused by maternal alcohol use during pregnancy (p. 1961).

Not only is FAS the leading cause of mental retardation in the United States, it is a completely preventable cause of mental retardation. FAS is diagnosed medically according to the following criteria: (1) Known or strongly suspected history of maternal use of alcohol; (2) Prenatal and/or postnatal growth retardation with height and weight generally below the 10%; (3) A characteristic pattern of facial features and other physical abnormalities that may include small eye openings that create an appearance of a wide space between the eyes (short palpebral fissures), flat midface, flat ridges between the upper lip and nose (indistinct philtrum), thin upper lip, folds of skin at the inner corner of the eyes (epicanthal folds), flat nasal bridge, short and upturned nose, small chin, and minor external ear anomalies; and (4) Central nervous system dysfunction that may include mental retardation, small head circumference, learning disabilities, attention deficit disorder with or without hyperactivity, or motor coordination problems (Doctor, 1994; Streissguth, Sampson, & Barr, 1989). Children with FAS do not necessarily have all of the characteristics listed above and the absence of a predominant facial feature (e.g., epicanthal folds) does not rule out FAS. Although FAS is the leading cause of mental retardation in this country, not all FAS children all mentally retarded. Streissguth et al. (1991) studied FAS adolescents and adults and found that 58% of the sample had IQs below 70 (the cutoff for the diagnosis of mild mental retardation).

Burgess and Streissguth (1992) state that Fetal Alcohol Effect (FAE) is not a medical diagnosis but is used to describe children born to mothers with a known history of heavy drinking during pregnancy. These children have insufficient physical characteristics to diagnose FAS but demonstrate central nervous system and/or behavioral problems consistent with FAS. The mother of a child with FAE may not necessarily have drunk less than the mother of a child diagnosed with FAS. Burgess and Streissguth maintain that FAE children may have as severe cognitive problems as FAS children. Finally, according to these same authors, there does not appear to be any safe level of alcohol use during pregnancy to avoid FAE. Even one to two drinks per day or occasional consumption of five drinks can cause problems in the fetus.

The term *crack babies* has been used to describe those infants who experience significant problems at birth and whose mothers smoked crack cocaine during pregnancy. However, no syndrome comparable to FAS has been identified and associated with the use of any specific drug. Most mothers who use illegal drugs are polydrug abusers and often smoke and drink alcohol as well. Frequently, lack of prenatal care and/or nutritional issues may adversely affect the fetus. Therefore, children who were exposed to drugs prenatally and have suffered adverse effects are referred to as fetally drug effected, or FDE.

Although most of the attention in this area has been focused on alcohol and illegal drugs, more women in the National Institute on Drug Abuse survey (CESAR, 1994) reported using tobacco than any other drug. In a review of studies involving pregnant women and smoking, Floyd, Zahniser, Gunter, & Kendrick (1991) indicate that smoking during pregnancy is clearly associated with low infant birth-weight resulting from intrauterine growth retardation. In addition, there is an association between age, smoking, and premature births, with older women having significantly more premature infants if they smoke. Smoking also increases the risk of spontaneous abortion.

Impact of Fetal Exposure to Alcohol and Other Drugs

We do not want to minimize the problems that can result from prenatal exposure to alcohol and other drugs. However, we also do not want you to conclude that all children prenatally exposed will have serious, permanent, learning, behavioral, social, and emotional problems. Those children diagnosed as FAS or identified as FAE have been the focus of attention for some problems and an association has then been made with maternal alcohol use. However, many children who have been prenatally exposed to alcohol have had no identified problems. About 30 to 40% of children prenatally exposed to illegal drugs demonstrate some type of developmental delay (Jackson, 1993), which means 60 to 70% do not. We provide this caveat so that you will not jump to conclusions about a child when you learn that the mother used alcohol or other drugs during pregnancy.

Prenatal exposure to alcohol and other drugs is associated with a variety of problems during gestation, birth, and early development. The fetus is at greater risk for miscarriage and spontaneous abortion. Premature birth, growth retardation, and small head circumference are more common (Doering, Davidson, & LaFauce, 1989). Some infants exposed to cocaine or opiates demonstrate greater irritability and less responsiveness to comfort than other children do (Griffith, 1989; Hayford, Epps, & Dahl-Regis, 1990). There is evidence suggesting that toddlers and preschoolers prenatally exposed to alcohol and other drugs have more difficulty in bonding to caregivers, and those exposed to cocaine are more impulsive and have a greater frequency of language problems (Chasnoff, Griffith, Freier, & Murray, 1992; Griffith, 1990; Rodning, Beck with, & Howard, 1990). As preschoolers, many prenatally exposed children are easily frustrated and distracted, have frequent temper tantrums, and demonstrate information processing problems (Chasnoff et al. 1992).

As we have already indicated, the definitions of FAS and FAE involve some type of central nervous system dysfunction. Mental retardation is common, although it is not inevitable. Other associated problems that impact the academic progress and behavior of these children in school include learning disabilities, attention deficit disorder with or without hyperactivity, and motor coordination difficulty.

Implications for Intervention

Since 1986, the National Association for Perinatal Addiction has been following the developmental progress of more than 300 children exposed to cocaine and, often, multiple drugs. About one-third of these children displayed delays in language development and/or problems in attention and self-regulation (Griffith, 1992). Speech therapy was effective in remediating the language problems of most of the children. Griffith describes the attention and self-regulation problems in terms of a low tolerance for overstimulation and a low frustration tolerance. Inconsistency and other threats to the child's ability to predict the environment increases the child's difficulty in regulating his or her behavior. He suggests withdrawing the child from an overstimulating environment before he or she loses the ability to self-regulate, reducing the stimulation in the environment, and providing a consistent and predictable environment. These are common interventions in the management of attention deficit disordered children and other behavioral disorders.

Doctor (1994) has developed a training curriculum for educators who work with FAS, FAE, and FDE children. She emphasizes that educators should acknowledge the learning and behavioral differences of some of these children and should accommodate for these differences. For example, she suggests that a daily routine be established that minimizes transitions. However, when transitions are to occur, students should be prepared in advance. Teaching strategies should include all sensory modalities whenever possible. When an abstract concept is difficult for a student, it should be made more concrete. Sequencing, repetition, reinforcement, and structure are all emphasized. Again, the instructional and management strategies are not different from those used in working with children with a variety of learning and behavioral problems.

Prenatal exposure to tobacco, alcohol, and other drugs can clearly have a number of adverse effects on the fetus and subsequently result in medical, developmental, cognitive, and behavioral problems. No safe level of use during pregnancy has been established, nor have the long-term effects of prenatal exposure to illegal drugs been clearly established. However, the behaviors and learning deficits that have been observed do not appear to be different from those demonstrated by children with learning disabilities, attention deficit disorder, or other emotional or behavioral problems, nor is it possible to distinguish between problems caused by prenatal exposure to illegal drugs and problems caused by other factors (e.g., abuse, poverty, poor prenatal care) (Jackson, 1993).

Although the problems demonstrated by children prenatally exposed may be serious as Jackson indicated, these problems do not seem different from those of other children not exposed. Common sense should prevail here. Prenatally exposed children did not develop suddenly after media attention was focused on them. They have always existed. Either numbers may be increasing, or our awareness may be increasing. As with many developmental, cognitive, and behavioral disorders, prevention is the most effective cure. Abstinence during pregnancy will ensure that no prenatal exposure occurs. If there is prenatal exposure, early intervention including medical care and a supportive and nurturing environment will reduce the frequency of problems. Even if a child's problems are not identified until reaching school age, appropriate educational intervention may be helpful.

Children Interpersonally Exposed to Alcohol and Other Drug Abuse

Aside from in utero exposure to alcohol and other drug abuse that can result in central nervous system dysfunction, there can be little disagreement that children do experience negative effects as a result of being exposed to the interpersonal and environmental influences of alcohol and other drug abuse in their homes.

Behavioral Problems

Towers (1989) believes that children who grow up in homes where alcohol and other drugs are abused can view themselves as worthless, can feel unimportant as a result of being consistently rejected, and may feel responsible for their parents' substance abuse (Towers, 1989). Around the holidays, especially, elementary school-aged children of alcoholics may become moody and "withdrawn, irritable, and certainly not ready or able to participate with the rest of the class and the teacher in holiday-related lessons and activities" (Towers, 1989, p. 20). Another result may be seen in the young child's expressed defiance toward activities of these kinds. It is thought that reasons for this behavior center on the child's anxiety regarding a family get-together or celebration in which drugs will likely be abused.

Apart from the idiosyncratic behaviors demonstrated during or around holidays, general feelings of alienation can lead children into social isolation and reinforce the child's beliefs that they are socially incompetent. Bennett (1988), in her study of school-aged children of alcoholics, suggests that a lowering of a child's self-concept results from exposure to alcohol and other drug abuse. A child who comes to school having slept little the night before because of anxiety or because of parental fighting or abuse cannot really be expected to perform well. As a result, the child's self-concept can be diminished by repeated failures at learning. A vicious cycle can be born. The result can be that the child feels hopeless, fearful, and lonely. In some cases, the effects can be fateful. For example, Whitfield (1980) estimates that 80% of all adolescent suicides are children of alcoholics. Although this estimate may be spuriously high, his estimate does underscore that parental drug abuse may be a significant co-variant in adolescent suicide attempts.

More often than not and depending upon the child's age when first encountering parental alcohol or other drug abuse, the impact of interpersonal and environmental exposure will be reflected in the school classroom and can affect students' hygiene, concentration, achievement, attitudes toward learning, attitudes towards teachers and others in authority, attitudes toward classmates, attendance, completion of homework assignments, and participation in extracurricular activities and sports (Towers, 1989).

Problematic Academic and Intellectual Functioning

Research suggests that there is consistent impaired academic achievement when COA subjects are administered such standardized measures of achievement as the Peabody Individual Achievement Test (PIAT) and the Wide Range Achievement Test (WRAT). Bennet, Wolin, and Reiss (1988) and Marcus (1986), for example, found that scores obtained from COAs on the PIAT indicated impaired performance relative to non-COAs. The same was not found to be true in Johnson and Rolf's (1988) study utilizing the WRAT. Using a sample of children aged 6 to 18, these authors failed to find differences between COAs and non-COAs. Sher (1991) states that "Childhood academic problems appear to be related to both paternal and maternal alcoholism" (p. 86). He supports this assertion by citing studies conducted by Knop, Teasdale, Schulsinger, and Goodwin (1985), Miller and Jang (1977), and Tarter, Jacob, and Bremer (1989), who found that COAs have greater difficulties in school and are more likely to have to repeat a grade, will more likely fail to graduate from high school, and are referred more often to the school psychologist. Reasons for impaired performance are not clearly understood and may be mediated by other variables resulting from in utero exposure, learning deficits, conduct disorder, motivational problems, or a dysfunctional homelife (Sher, 1991). Hegedus, Alterman, and Tarter (1984) examined achievement test scores and found that scores indicating academic underachievement appeared to be more consistently related to cognitive impairment than to family environment variables or to psychopathology. Because of methodological limitations, Sher (1991) cautions against placing a high degree of confidence in these results.

Implications for Intervention

Counselors and social workers who work in the schools will be faced not only with student-clients who are children of alcoholics but will, as well, be consulting with teachers who attempt to teach these children. Helping teachers become familiar with the symptoms outlined above is important. Teachers need to know basic facts about alcohol and other drug abuse. With some empathic guidance from school counselors and social workers, teachers can emphasize the need to make their classrooms safe havens where students can learn to overcome their difficulties and experience success. As in dealing with children affected by in utero exposure to alcohol and other drugs, school counselors can help teachers emphasize the need for structure in their classrooms where children can learn or reinforce appropriate social skills. Helping teachers see the need for students' healthy expression of feelings, including anger and frustration, and helping teachers see the need for activities that aim at bonding, autonomy, and problem-solving can aid in helping students develop protective factors against drug abuse and can help with students' self-esteem and successes at learning in school.

In a study focusing on peer-led COA support groups, DiCicco, Davis, Hogan, MacLean, and Orenstein (1984) reported that school children may not want to be identified as a "child of an alcoholic" *per se*. So identifying children as such for after-school support groups may diminish the number of participants. In both DiCicco et al. (1984) studies, the authors imply that when such groups avoid the label "COA," the number of participants may increase. Thus, in schools, peer-lead support groups that do not identify themselves as "COA support groups" may be more efficacious than if the label is used. Instead, a group might be called "Concerned Others Group."

Implications of Labeling

Burk and Sher (1990) studied the effect of labeling oneself as a COA. In their study, Burk and Sher (1990) asked adolescents to rate themselves as a "mentally ill teenager," a "typical teenager," or a "teenager with an alcoholic parent" on a series of bipolar adjective pairs. These same authors then asked mental health professionals to watch videotapes of adolescents described as having either an alcoholic father or parents with no known problems and possessing either a high or low degree of social success. In summarizing their studies, Sher (1991) states that they found "strong negative stereotypes associated with the COA label, both from peer group and from mental health professionals" (p. 169).

Aside from the potentially negative consequences of labeling oneself as a "COA" during school-aged years, there may be some positive aspects to the labeling process for Adult Children of Alcoholics (ACOAs). Burk and Sher (1988) reviewed the literature in an attempt to determine the relevance of labeling theory for research on ACOAs. One of the possible benefits of labeling might be raising one's consciousness about the need for help. In addition, labeling oneself as an ACOA allows access to a variety of self-help support groups such as Co-Dependents Anonymous and Al-Anon (see Chapters 8 and 12). Burk and Sher (1988) also suggest that labeling oneself as an ACOA allows for an external attribution to be made that can provide a structure for individuals' insight and understanding into their problems. Kaminer (1990) believes that identifying oneself as an "adult child" begins a recovery process that can lead to a lifestyle of recovery. In the final analysis, the authors of this text believe that, as long as the labeling process allows for continued growth in the individual, it might be beneficial for an individual to subscribe to such labeling. However, to label oneself as an "ACOA" in order to avoid personal responsibility is not helpful and can serve to maintain one's self-deprecation and self-defeating behaviors.

Adult Children of Alcoholics (ACOAs)

While there are over 6 million children of alcoholics younger than age eighteen, there are approximately 22 million ACOAs aged 18 and older (Russell, Henderson, and Blume, 1985). Not all of these individuals will identify themselves as an "adult child of an alcoholic." But, millions of adults do identify with the term and relate this to present dissatisfaction in life. Regardless of the extent to which one subscribes to the concepts of "adult children," this area is a focal point of current research.

Research on ACOAs has focused on three areas. One branch of research, referred to as risk factors for later substance abuse, includes both qualitative and quantitative studies that examine the variables believed to influence ACOA's own drug or nondrug use in adulthood. The quantitative research is aimed at identifying the characteristics that predispose ACOAs to alcoholism, other drug dependence, or other substance-related problems. The qualitative writings in this area are found mainly in popular literature and focus upon identifying the personality characteristics and problematic behaviors that increase an ACOA's risk for choosing a partner with an identifiable substance-abuse problem. A second branch of research focuses on identifying the clinical characteristics of ACOAs—an area that has been addressed largely in popular writings and has gained a broad popular following. The third branch of research centers on attempts to empirically validate the clinical characteristics. As you will see, the current state of these three research venues generally reveals mixed results.

Risk Factors for Later Substance Abuse Problems

Risk factors are essentially variables that leave an individual vulnerable to developing problems. Therefore, risk factors do not demonstrate the presence of problems—only the potential for developing such problems. Research into this area is focused on identifying both mediating variables, which may account for the relationship between parental alcoholism and the eventual development of alcoholism or related problems, and moderating variables, which affect the strength and direction of the relationship between parental alcoholism and alcoholism in one's offspring. An example of a mediating variable is ethanol sensitivity, and it is suggested that one's sensitivity to alcohol mediates one's vulnerability to develop alcoholism. A moderating variable might be the nature of communication in an alcoholic family that is believed to moderate one's vulnerability. So, hypothetically, one's sensitivity to alcohol (ethanol) may mediate or predispose one's vulnerability to developing alcoholism, but this risk or vulnerability will be moderated (strengthened or reduced) by the amount of interpersonally effective communication in the family. It can be seen, then, that the plethora of popular writings devoted to interpersonal effects and personality characteristics are essentially identifying moderating variables. Quantitative research is known to have methodological problems in identifying mediating and moderating variables. Sher (1991) and Windle and Searles (1990) believe these problems are related to sampling (the source, size, and age of the sample), the heterogeneity of groups, identifying inclusion/exclusion criteria for groups, finding adequate control groups, and interpreting the results when two or more measures used with the same individual ACOA reveal differential performances (i.e., when performance on Task A is different from performance on Task B). Moreover, studies comparing ACOA and non-ACOA groups may have other methodological problems. For example, D'Andrea, Fisher, and Harrison (1994) (a study discussed later in the chapter) found that ACOAs were a much more heterogeneous group than Black (1981) had originally postulated. Therefore, a large heterogeneous grouping of "normal ACOA individuals" (i.e., those without serious problems) can washout differences between ACOA and non-ACOA groups.

Clinical Characteristics

Popular writers (see Ackerman, 1983; 1987; Beattie, 1987; Black, 1981; Woititz, 1983) and professional writers (See Cermack, 1986; Brown, 1988; Goodman, 1987) have identified some of the characteristics distinctive to an adult child of an alcoholic. These characteristics are based upon the assumption that children see parental behavior as a reflection of the child's own sense of self-worth (Ackerman, 1983). In general, characteristics of ACOAs are seen as emanating from dysfunctional family systems and include excessive use of denial, all-or-nothing thinking, exaggerated need for control, avoidance of anger and other feelings, avoidance of self-disclosure, lack of trust, and difficulty with intimate relationships (Brown, 1988; Sher, 1991). Cermack (1984) and McKearn (1988) identified depression, isolation, rage, avoidance of feelings, survival guilt, anxiety reactions, sleep disturbances/nightmares, and intrusive thoughts as being symptomatic of ACOAs. As mentioned earlier, these characteristics are essentially moderating variables thought to influence one's vulnerability to developing both intrapsychic and interpersonal problems. The characteristics identified through clinical impressions relate more to one's problems in adulthood that may, but do not necessarily, include substance abuse.

Ackerman (1987) and Woititz (1983) have generated a list of adult problems that are believed to reflect "the most commonly agreed upon personality characteristics found in adult children of alcoholics" (Ackerman, 1987, p. 24).

1. ACOAs guess at what normal is. According to popular authors, ACOAs have spent their whole life in a state of confusion and guess at what it would be like if they had experienced a normal (i.e., nonexposure to alcohol and other drug abuse) childhood.

2. ACOAs have difficulty following projects through to completion. It is believed that, in alcoholic and drug abusing homes, "there are an awful lot of promises" (Woititz, 1983, p. 29) that are not kept. The unkept promises are seen as having had a modeling effect upon the child's abilities to follow through on projects. It is believed that, since children did not see this modeled as adults, they do not have the skills or experience to follow through on their own promises or projects.

3. ACOAs lie when it would be just as easy to tell the truth. Woititz believes that the fundamental lie of a family system affected by alcohol is denial of the problem. To cover up, the alcoholic family lives a life of pretense. The second level of the lie is the one that covers up the alcoholic's behaviors, such as the excuses made by the nonalcoholic parent to the children or by calls to the alcoholic's workplace and lying for the abusing parent. For the ACOA, truth has lost its virtue.

4. ACOAs judge themselves without mercy. In homes where alcohol and other drugs were abused, children grow up constantly being criticized. They introject an image of never being good enough and use it upon themselves to reinforce this negative view of themselves.

5. ACOAs have difficulty having fun, and they take themselves too seriously. Woititz believes that the tone of living in an alcoholic home is one that dampens one's fun and playfulness. "Life [is] a very serious, angry business in alcoholic homes" (p. 38).

6. ACOAs have difficulty with intimate relationships. This difficulty results from the fact that healthy, intimate relationships were not modeled in their homes of origin. (For a more complete understanding of these difficulties, refer to Chapter 12).

7. ACOAs overreact to changes over which they do not have direct control. According to many popular authors, the child in an alcoholic home does not experience much control over his or her life because alcohol or other drug abuse takes

control. Meals and entertainment are planned around drinking, as are family outings and perhaps vacations as well. As a result of needing to take some control over their lives, ACOAs must learn to trust themselves before they trust anyone else. While in one form this would appear to be healthy, ACOAs must also learn to trust themselves *instead of* trusting others. Isolation often occurs as a result of these issues of trust.

8. ACOAs feel different from other people. This notion relates to guessing at normality. That is, ACOAs assume that, when they are in a group with others, they are the only ones who feel awkward. An important feature is that ACOAs will not usually check with other group members to see how they are working through their own awkwardness. This feeling of being different results from living in a home where they need to be concerned with problems rather than simply acting as children and having fun (Woititz, 1983).

9. ACOAs constantly seek approval and affirmation. This relates to the idea that alcoholism in the family resulted in the children's learning to rely upon others for a sense of self-worth. Feeling themselves constantly criticized by their parents diminishes their sense of self-worth, and not receiving approval from parents leaves the child hungering for that deep sense of unconditional approval that never comes.

10. ACOAs are either super-responsible or super-irresponsible. ACOAs are seen as having tried so repeatedly to get approval from their parents that at one point they quit trying because the approval never comes. In this sense, ACOAs do not experience much middle ground in their thinking. They live in a constant fear of being discovered to be as incompetent as they believe they are. To make up for this fear, they will take on a project and do it all themselves, or they will fade into the background and participate very little. ACOAs also are seen as not having a good understanding of their own limitations, so they have a difficult time saying "No."

11. ACOAs are extremely loyal regardless of whether the loyalty is deserved. Woititz (1983) and others believe that "family members hang in long after reasons dictate that they should leave . . . The loyalty is more the result of fear and insecurity than anything else . . . The behavior that is modeled is one where no one walks away just because the going gets rough" (p. 49).

12. ACOAs look for immediate rather than for delayed gratification and are, therefore, impulsive. Related to the concept of broken promises and the modeling of mistrust in their homes of origin, ACOAs manage their anxiety about the future by believing that if they do not get something *now,* they won't get it at all. Because anxiety is fundamental to impulsivity, ACOAs are seen as locking themselves into a course of action without giving serious consideration to alternative behaviors or possible consequences. Many authors writing about ACOAs believe that impulsivity in the adult is an attempt to recapture the part of their lost childhood when they could not be impulsive.

13. ACOAs seek tension and crises; then complain. The family environment for a ACOA is seen as having been one where drinking and other drug binges created a crisis-to-crisis lifestyle. "When things go smoothly, it's even more unsettling than when you're in a crisis. So, it's not surprising that you may even create a crisis" (Woititz, 1983, p. 51).

14. ACOAs avoid conflict or aggravate it but rarely deal with it. ACOAs grow up in homes replete with conflict, but they felt as though they had little control over when, how, where, and under what conditions the conflict would arise. Therefore, as adults, conflict is frightening because it likely remains undifferentiated from what they experienced as children. Some ACOAs will avoid conflict out of fear, while others might promote conflict or become aggressive out of the fear that they cannot trust others. In either case, ACOAs do not work through their conflicts because they did not learn how to do it as children.

15. ACOAs fear rejection and abandonment but reject others. ACOAs are seen having lived in homes where they were emotionally, spiritually, intellectually, and in some cases physically and sexually abandoned. The fear and pain that results creates an anticipation of being rejected as adults. In some cases, ACOAs can reject others before they, themselves, are rejected and re-experience the painful trauma of their childhoods. Some ACOAs reject others because they cannot be trusted.

16. ACOAs fear failure while having difficulty handling success. Failure is an over-riding and salient experience for ACOAs, according to many popular authors. It is likely ACOAs have not differentiated childhood failure from discrete experiences of failure as adults. The result is an ambient feeling of having failed that is reflected in fearing failure itself. Because success is the exception for these individuals, they have leaned not to trust that they can be successful. So, when they experience success, ACOAs tend to diminish their accomplishments out of fear that they really do not deserve to be successful.

17. ACOAs fear criticism and judgment, yet criticize others. Again, undifferentiated fear of criticism and parental judgments from their parents can be reflected in the ACOA's approach to criticism and judgment as an adult. In that what was modeled in their homes was criticism, ACOAs learned to do what their parents did to them: criticize and judge others.

18. ACOAs manage their time poorly and do not set priorities in a way that works well for them. In the popular writings, ACOAs are seen as being somewhat self-sabotaging (Beattie, 1987; Black, 1981; Woititz, 1983). Often, this self-sabotage can be reflected in their work where they wait until the last minute to begin a task that takes more time than was anticipated. Not being able to say "No" also complicates matters for the ACOA in terms of taking on too much work. Being seen as impulsive often affects ACOAs' abilities to take the time necessary to set priorities. As a result, ACOAs can often become disorganized when too much work piles up, and, in the end, the quality of the work may become compromised.

Empirical Research on Clinical Characteristics

Because of the intense popularity of "Adult Child of an Alcoholic" characteristics, many investigators have attempted to empirically validate their existence. However, Fisher, Jenkins, Harrison, and Jesch (1992; 1993) and D'Andrea, Fisher, and Harrison (1994) found many investigations to be helpful to the field but note their methodological limitations. For example, Ackerman (1987) used self-reports to study over 1,000 ACOAs and non-ACOAs. Although he found group differences in 20 adult problems, such as difficulty having fun, constantly seeking approval and affirmation, and difficulty with intimate relationships, no statistical analyses were performed in this study and, therefore, no conclusions can be drawn. Another methodological concern relates to small sample size (e.g., Hibbard, 1989). Moreover, the large majority of studies on ACOAs has been conducted on college students (Berkowitz & Perkins, 1988). This latter concern is significant in that the clinical impressions of ACOAs have been made on adults rather than on college-aged students, and therefore the characteristics may not be valid for a younger, college-aged, population.

In addition, while a majority of studies have used comparison groups of ACOAs and non-ACOAs, these studies may be begging the question. That is, Beidler (1989) and Goodman (1987) have argued that ACOAs may not be a separate field of study at all in that ACOAs may not be different from other adults raised in dysfunctional families. Therefore, a concern is raised about whether ACOAs comprise a distinct group with unique characteristics, and this has received some support in the professional literature. For example, while Wright and Wright (1990) did find some evidence supporting the validity of clinical characteristics of codependency, Fisher et al. (1992) found that ACOAs are "not as codependent as they are described by clinicians or that codependency does not occur more frequently in ACOAs than in other adults" (p. 32). In another study, these same authors found that "the ACOAs in this study were more similar [to] than different [from] other adults who report significant problems in their family or origin" (Fisher et al., 1993, p. 482).

Empirical comparisons between ACOA and non-ACOA populations are vulnerable to further concerns. For example, in studying the ACOA population itself, D'Andrea et al. (1994) found that 44% of ACOAs demonstrated profiles that were free of significant problems. The implications of the study seem to be in direct opposition to Black's (1981) view of ACOAs. Black believes that, if ACOAs neither become alcoholic nor marry an alcoholic, they will have significant problems in adulthood. D'Andrea et al. stated that their findings may explain why some studies comparing ACOAs and non-ACOAs may have failed to find significant differences: The presence of a relatively large "normal" population in ACOAs would essentially mask or eliminate many differences that might exist.

Assessment and Treatment Considerations

Assessment of ACOAs

Berkowitz and Perkins (1988) reviewed the means by which ACOAs have been identified in the professional literature and found that there are both broad and strict definitions of ACOAs. Clinical diagnosis of parental alcoholism reflects the more strict definition while the children's perceptions of parental drinking problems mirrors a broader definition. An example of a broad definition is that used in the Russell, Henderson, and Blume (1985) study in which an ACOA is "any person, adult, or child who has a parent identified in any way as having a significant problem related to alcohol use" (p. 1). According to Berkowitz and Perkins, the more strict definition is likely to exclude many individuals whose parents are alcoholic but who have not been formally diagnosed. The more broad definition, based upon the child's perceptions, may also reflect an inaccurate number of ACOAs because the child may see his or her parents only infrequently or may see his or her parent drink only occasionally.

A detailed instrument is the CAST (Jones, 1985), which stands for *Children of Alcoholics Screening Test.* This is a diagnostic instrument containing 39 items that ask questions related to parental problems with alcohol. In an attempt to demonstrate construct validity for a single-item question asking whether "a parent may have had or may have an alcohol abuse problem" (p. 207), Berkowitz and Perkins compared subjects' responses on the CAST to the subjects' responses to that single question and found that the single question reliably classifies ACOAs.

Others have used simple, single-item questions as well. For example, DiCicco, Davis, and Orenstein (1984) asked whether one had ever wished that either or both of his or her parents would drink less and found that this single item identified ACOAs reliably over time. In another study, Bick (1981) asked subjects whether their parents' drinking caused problems for them and found this single question accurately selected ACOAs. The results of using a single question to classify ACOAs is summarized in Berkowitz and Perkins' study in which they assert that

> *studies suggest that it is possible to identify most adolescents from alcohol-abusing families by using a single, objective question focusing on the child's perception of the parent's drinking and that this method produces prevalence rates similar to those obtained from a more detailed diagnostic instrument such as the CAST [Jones, 1985] and large-scale national surveys"* (p. 207).

Implications for Intervention

Empirical studies on prevention and treatment of ACOAs are significantly lacking (Williams, 1990). Nevertheless, Williams describes two essential goals in intervening with ACOAs. The first goal is to identify and address early symptoms of problem drinking, and the second goal is to identify dysfunctional behaviors and coping skills that may be predisposing risk factors for drinking or other adult problems.

Aside from the mixed results reflected in the empirical research, group settings seem to be preferred for families identified as having alcohol issues (Hawley & Brown, 1981; Morehouse, 1986). ACOAs may benefit from the same support groups that are identified in Chapters 8 and 12, which include "Codependents Anonymous" and "Al-Anon." Other self-help groups, such as "Sex Addicts Anonymous," and "Emotions Anonymous," could be used as well depending upon the identified problem.

The mixed results of empirical studies do not suggest that specific interventions should be identified for ACOAs because it is unclear whether such a group exists whose individual members are significantly different from other adults with dysfunctional family backgrounds. Nevertheless, being associated with alcohol or other drug abuse either directly, as in the case of the alcoholic, or indirectly, as in the case of many ACOAs, has been shown to be problematic. In terms of helping clients, mental health professionals may want to provide information regarding alcohol and other drug use as well as help clients clarify their values about use so that they may make decisions regarding abstention or moderation. Many clients who were raised in homes with alcohol abuse may not identify themselves as ACOAs, so counselors need to be careful about using jargon that may create client resistance. Mental health professionals who use the label "ACOA" may leave their clients with the impression that this is a widely accepted clinical syndrome, but such a posture would be misrepresenting the empirical findings about ACOAs.

Adults who were raised in families with substance abuse, physical or sexual abuse, and/or parental death or divorce do seem different from adults with no such history. Moreover, recall from Chapter 10 that a characteristic of families with alcohol or other drug abuse is unresolved grief. This grief, coupled with poor communication skills and a lack of role modeling on how to express feelings, may leave these clients predisposed to difficulty in trusting the counselor. Because ACOAs may control their emotions and attempt to control others as well, it is advisable that mental health professionals focus on developing a strong and deep rapport with the ACOA client.

Summary

The ACOA movement has, to varying degrees, impacted both professionals and nonprofessionals alike. Although there may be some consternation over the use of the term *ACOA*, and some questions about whether ACOAs are a real entity, there is little question concerning the deleterious effects of alcohol and other drug abuse on children while they remain in their mother's womb. The research into FAS demonstrates that this is the leading cause of mental retardation in the United States. The results of interpersonal exposure to this abuse by parents after one's birth and one's problems in adolescence and adulthood is less clearly demonstrated and, often, results of studies comparing ACOAs and non-ACOAs are mixed.

Nevertheless, there appears to be some merit for you, as a mental health professional, to note the clinical characteristics identified by popular writers who describe ACOAs, because many of your clients may accept the tenets of the popular ACOA literature. An important caveat is that you assess the necessity of labeling a client as an ACOA. It has been demonstrated that this term may act as a deterrent to school-aged children, keeping them from services that could help them. Moreover, clients who refer to themselves as ACOAs, may be avoiding responsibility for their present actions by rationalizing their behavior as emanating from their damaged childhood.

Chapter 12

Codependency

The term *codependency* arrived in our popular nomenclature in the early 1980s. Originally referring to the co-alcoholic (Whitfield, 1984), this notion was broadened through the popular writings of Black (1981), Friel, Subby, and Friel (1984) and others who described a variety of compulsive behaviors. With the possible exception of transactional analysis and the famous phrase, "I'm okay-you're okay" (Harris, 1969), few movements in the mental health field have generated so much popular interest and so much professional controversy as has the codependency movement.

The fields of chemical dependency and mental health were beginning to enjoy a healthy, although somewhat acrid at times, relationship once the notion of the dually diagnosed patient became vogue in professional circles and more routine. However, it was the phenomenon of the dually diagnosed patient that sent shudders down the spine of the community mental health system—administrators and clinicians alike, because this dually diagnosed patient was like the chicken before the egg idea: What caused what? Which was the primary diagnosis? Did the alcohol or other drug problem create the mental disorder or was it the other way around? If patients were active in their addictive behaviors during the time of their entry into the mental health system, what was the proper treatment plan? The very real complications resulting from having a dual diagnosis caused the fear that the financial backbone of community mental health centers would be broken. That a professional could be treating the wrong problem was a good possibility.

One direct result of the numbers of such dual diagnoses was a bringing together of chemical treatment providers and mental health providers under one roof. While not an easy operation in terms of administrative logistics, great strides were made by mental health centers to do exactly that. Staff meetings, which were once held to discuss mental health cases, now included addictions counselors whose training was quite different from that of their mental health colleagues. The friction that resulted was to be expected, because often mental health professionals had to move their offices or generate other concessions in order to make room for their new colleagues. As each group became more familiar with and received direct benefits from the work of the others, issues of turf and prestige gradually gave way to more amiable working relationships. Patients began to receive improved care, and with this came shared respect for each professional group. It appeared that all was well.

Then the chemical dependency field introduced the concept of codependency, and whatever strides had been made in the salubrious relationship between the mental health field and the addiction field turned sour once again. The definition and characteristics of codependency were seen by many mental health professionals as a new name for an old mental health disorder, which once again brought problems of professional boundaries into sharp focus. However, the problem was not only that the chemical dependency field was seen as trespassing onto the field of mental health nor was it only that those in the addictions field were being trained to treat codependency: The problem was more the issue of whether codependency actually existed. And if it did exist, questions about what constituted codependency would become the next cause of battle.

Some of the fiery debate was fueled by differences over the disease concept inherent in the popular views of codependency. Recall that, in Chapter 3 ("Models of Addiction"), one's view of alcoholism as being a disease or nondisease were seen to have profound implications for identification and treatment. Moreover, remember how the discriminating variable casting one into a disease or nondisease orientation essentially revolved around one's view of "loss of control" (with the disease model claiming the centrality of a loss of control). Well, the voracity with which mental health professionals have debated the disease concept has been duplicated in the debate over codependency: Are people responsible for the root of their codependency? In other words, are individuals seen as more responsible for how they manage their impulses rather than being responsible for the impulse itself?

Another source of debate centered on the traits of a codependent person. Does codependency really exist, or is it another name for a diagnosis already identified in the DSM-IV under Borderline Personality Disorder, Dependent Personality Disorder, Post-traumatic Stress Disorder? Is codependency essentially a thematic variation on one of these disorders? Does it simply extend the boundaries of an already established diagnosis so that codependent characteristics lie more along one pole of a continuum in a given disorder? Perhaps the contentious issue surrounds the notion of whether codependency is a progressive disease. All of these issues are important and will be discussed in this chapter. Moreover, the origins of codependency will be presented, and its course and development will be examined. Case examples will hopefully allow you to more readily identify codependent characteristics in your clients as well as help you decide upon a course of treatment.

Definitions of Codependency

Definitions of the term *codependency* are influenced by the degree to which one subscribes to the concept. That is, staunch proponents of the concept may see everyone and almost all of our institutions as codependent. For example, Giermyski and Williams (1986) state that enthusiastic proponents of the concept see codependency

> *as a primary disease present in every member of an alcoholic family, which is often worse than alcoholism itself, has its own physical manifestations and is a treatable diagnostic category. Its presence is recognized in individuals, among institutions, in hospitals as well as judicial and legal systems, in schools and even in the Federal Communications Commissions (FCC). The last two are viewed as afflicted with codependency because schools expel students for drug-related offenses, and the FCC has not yet banned wine and beer commercials (p. 7).*

Cermack (1986) noted that efforts to define codependency have included metaphoric and interpersonal approaches as well as those approaches based upon ego psychology, behaviorism, and combinations of behaviorism and intrapsychic dynamics. For example, Alexander (1985) uses a metaphor to state that "being codependent is like being a life guard on a crowded beach, knowing that you cannot swim, and not telling anyone for fear of starting a panic" (p. 16). More formalized definitions of codependency are found in the interpersonal approaches of Claudia Black (1981) and Sharon Weigscheider-Cruise (1985). Black talks about rules operating in the family structure that prohibit the honest expression of feelings regarding alcoholism and the alcohol-dependent family member. Weigscheider-Cruise discusses codependency in terms of its being a preoccupation and dependence upon another person or object. Examples of codependency include individuals who are in a significant relationship with an alcoholic, those having one or more alcoholic parents or grandparents, and those who grew up in a family where there was systematic repression of feelings. Anne Wilson Schaef (1987) presents a definition that depicts the belief in the progressive nature of codependency. She sees codependency as a disease emanating from an "addictive process" similar to that of alcoholism. This addictive process, unless confronted in much the same manner as alcoholism, can lead to a type of spiritual death—a life aimed at existing rather than thriving, or physical death (Schaef, 1986).

Friel, Subby, and Friel (1984) extended the interpersonal approaches to include codependency and emphasized the impact of such behaviors upon the ego-functioning of individuals. These authors maintain that codependency is an emotional and behavioral pattern of interactive coping resulting from one's protracted exposure to a restrictive environment that does not allow the open or direct expression of feelings about oneself or other family members. For example, children who are consistently told that the mother or father's drinking binges are not problematic, even in the face of drunken rages and subsequent physical abuse, will grow up confused about their reality. Any attempt to talk about the problem when the parents were sober would likely be met with cognitive resistance: "There is no problem." Any attempt to talk about the problem when the parent(s) were drinking is likewise met with physical abuse. Hence, these children often learn to keep their feelings and thoughts about the parents' drinking to themselves. This fear of talking would be introjected and thus carried into one's adult life and relationships.

Charles Whitfield (1989) believes that codependency is a disease of lost self-hood, and that it is the most common type of addiction that people develop. Whitfield (1989) states that codependence develops whenever there is "suffering and/or dysfunction that is associated with or results from focusing on the needs and behavior of others" (p. 19). An intrapsychic approach is reflected in Cermack's (1986) definition in which he sees a codependent person as having a personality disorder based upon an excessive need to control self and others. Other symptoms include neglecting one's own needs, boundary distortions centered on approach/avoidance in intimate relationships, attraction to other individuals demonstrating codependent characteristics, denial, a constricted or restricted emotional expression, low-level and persistent depression, and stress-related physical ailments.

Characteristics of Codependent Individuals

Several authors have advanced codependent characteristics, and, like the definitions, these characteristics range from less formal to more pedantic (see Schaef, 1986; Whitfield, 1984; Kitchens, 1991). Potter-Efron and Potter-Efron (1989) identified eight characteristics of codependence: (1) Fear is indicated by a preoccupation with the problems of others, an avoidance of interpersonal risk, a general mistrust of others, persistent anxiety, and manipulative attempts to change another's behavior—especially drinking behavior; (2) Shame and guilt are characterized by a persistence of shame and guilt about another's behavior, self-loathing, isolation, and an appearance of superiority that masks low self-worth; (3) Prolonged despair relates to a generalized pessimism toward the world and feelings of hopelessness about changing one's current situation. One may also demonstrate a low sense of self-worth that stands in direct opposition to one's actual accomplishments; (4) Anger is often present but may be expressed in a passive-aggressive manner. One may also fear that becoming angry will mean a loss of control. Another characteristic of anger is that it is persistent; (5) Denial is usually rather consistent, especially when it involves family pain such as drinking behavior. Denial is also demonstrated by a consistent minimization of problems and the use of justifications or rationalizations aimed at protecting the person from perceived or real consequences; (6) Rigidity is identified by cognitive, behavioral, moral/spiritual, and emotional inflexibility; (7) Identity development is also impaired. This is usually seen as an inability to take care of one's own emotional needs and as having an excessive need for others to validate one's self-worth. Along with this need is an obsessive concern about how one is perceived by others; (8) Confusion about what is normal and what is real is another behavioral pattern. Confusion is also indicated by one's gullibility and indecisiveness.

Clinical Characteristics of Codependency

Kitchens (1991) has identified what he refers to as "clinical features" of codependence. Kitchens' approach differs from that of Potter-Efron and Potter-Efron in two distinct ways: Kitchens focuses his work on "adult children" and identifies types of codependent personalities (which encompass many of the same characteristics discussed above). The term *adult children* is a popular term (see Chapter 11) used to describe adults who were raised in homes where codependent behaviors were the rule and whose identity development was thwarted as a result. According to Kitchens, codependent personalities are founded upon an "overemphasis of a normal trait" (p. 61). The six characteristics of codependent personalities are overresponsible, compulsive, schizoid/avoidant, paranoid, histrionic, and antisocial/narcissistic. When describing codependent personality disorders, Kitchens focuses on three domains: normal traits, internal feelings, and the outward manifestation. The overresponsible personality disorder contrasts the normal trait of sensitivity and care for others with the more maladaptive (codependent) internal experiences of the individual and includes feelings of self-doubt, inadequacy, and shame. What others often see in the overly responsible individual is overachievement, heightened sensitivity to others, being overly accepting of others, and always being reliable. According to Kitchens,

> *Individuals who fall into this category show extreme dependence on the acceptance and approval of other people . . . they build their lives around other persons and willingly sacrifice their needs to keep the other person involved with them . . . They have no self-confidence and do not work well alone . . . they feel helpless and may actually experience panic when threatened with the loss of the person on whom they depend (p. 63).*

The schizoid/avoidant personality disorder is based on one's excessive need for privacy. The internal experience of these individuals is typified by feelings of being unloved, having a need to escape, and anger and loneliness. In social situations, these individuals are probably withdrawn, aloof, demonstrate little need for friends and avoid stressful situations. The same author points out that these individuals usually "lead a life that is characterized by its barrenness in interpersonal experience despite their carefully hidden desire for affection and acceptance" (p. 65). Schizoid/avoidant individuals originate from one of two kinds of families: those coming from homes where there was emotional and/or spiritual rigidity and those coming from homes where there was physical or sexual abuse. Kitchens maintains that these individuals often experience a great deal of guilt, have difficulty expressing anger, have a difficult time with their own sexuality, and, in extreme cases of this disorder, may approach schizophrenia. The paranoid codependent personality is seen as having difficulties trusting others. Rather than having a healthy need for self-protection, these individuals are generally persistent in their suspiciousness of others and guard themselves accordingly. Individuals with this disorder are critical, judgmental, chronically jealous, pessimistic, constantly comparing themselves with others, and are generally dissatisfied with life. The histrionic codependent is seen as pushing one's natural need for attention and for caring for others to the extreme by trying to please everyone through entertaining behaviors such as joking, being super-cute, or by being hyperactive. These behaviors, according to Kitchens, mask real feelings of anxiety, feelings of rejection, and anger. The author points out that these individuals will often fluctuate between optimism and depression. Moreover, histrionic individuals will vacillate between extremes such as being friendly one day and rejecting others the next or as being prudish one minute and promiscuous the next. The antisocial/narcissistic codependent personality disorder is demonstrated through excessive competitiveness, through the need to belong to powerful groups, through the need to make a great deal of money, and through the need to appear confident and in control of all situations. Underlying these behaviors are feelings of anger, rejection, and insecurity (Kitchens, 1991). These feelings will also be accompanied by outward aggressiveness and hostility. Other people are seen as being less-than and are to be used to the advantage of the narcissistic codependent. Similar to the overresponsible personality disorder is the compulsive codependent disorder that is based on one's need for structure and organization. When there is an excessive focus on structure and organization, one experiences self-doubt, inadequacy, shame, and guilt. Individuals with this disorder will often demonstrate perfectionistic tendencies, compulsive behaviors, and obsessive thoughts. According to many in the field, the compulsive codependent person is closely akin to an addict (Kitchens, 1991). This disorder is the one that has the broadest implications and is a likely source of the controversy surrounding the term *codependence.*

Quotations were used in the preceding paragraphs to specifically illustrate the language used by many authors in the field. This illustration is important because, as you can see, much of the writing about codependency uses informal language that has the tenor of a fortune cookie. That is, authors writing about codependency tend to categorize individuals into broad categories. Moreover, the language itself denotes a less scientific approach to personality typology. In this Age of Science, when epistemology is founded upon the scientific method, informal language and labels such as "people pleaser" used to describe mental disorders are not well favored among professional circles and can be seen as cause for criticism. Second, clients who use the term *codependent* may not have a clear understanding of what the term means and can mislabel their problems. Another problem with use of the term *codependent* is that it may be unconsciously or consciously used by clients as a defense mechanism that can mask other problems needing professional attention.

Criticisms of Codependency

Criticism of *codependency* comes from professionals and nonprofessionals alike. From the popular circles, criticism is focused on assertions of the incidence and prevalence of codependency in the general population. Popular authors state that the incidence of codependency in the "normal" population is upward of 95% (Schaef, 1986; Weigscheider-Cruse, 1985). Popular critics are also reacting to the ideas purported by many who say that our whole culture is codependent. For example, Schaef writes about how our culture reinforces codependency in government, in our families, in our workplace, in our communities, and in our schools.

Anderson (1987) spends considerable time in his book *When Chemicals Come to School* talking about the insidious process of denial (and codependency) operating in our communities and in our schools (see Chapter 8). He maintains that ridding schools of drug-related problems requires support from all levels. This approach includes an awareness and a commitment to break the cycle of denial, from the school district itself all the way down to each student's decisions about drug involvement, and includes similar exhortations to the school's administration, staff, student body and community. These authors and others like them depict codependency as a community-wide disease not relegated simply to those affected directly or indirectly by alcohol and other drugs. Such broad social statements do create their own difficulties, because they cut so deeply into the American psyche.

Interestingly, though, commentaries upon the American psyche such as those just described have appeared in the professional literature as well—although the term *codependency* was not used. For example, the well-known neo-Freudian Karen Horney identified characteristics similar to those described by authors writing about codependency in her book *The Neurotic Personality of Our Time* (Horney, 1937). In discussing our culture's obsession with competition, Horney differentiates healthy from sickly ambition, and the ideas in her presentation appear very similar to those ideas advanced by current authors writing about codependency. The common ground between Horney and contemporary authors is found in the emphasis upon the compulsive reaction to anxiety or sickly ambition, in which one strives to be not just better but the best—a reaction that actually reinforces one's sense of mistrust and powerlessness. Codependency is also predicated upon a deep-seated mistrust of others. When applied to codependency, mistrust is seen as operating in one's adult life, among other things, by excessive competition in which one needs to be "the best." This need to be the best is based upon the belief that equates being less than the best with failure, rejection, and with the belief that one will not get one's needs met (see Chapter 15). So the concept of codependency, as such, is not new in professional circles, nor is it the first to make broad social statements. However, the term *codependency* itself is relatively new. The rejection of this term may also emanate from use of the term *dependent*, which runs antithetical to the American value of independence. While the scope of the definition of codependency may create some problems and ensuing criticism that could partially be explained away historically, other areas of concern do remain.

Criticism from nonprofessional circles is echoed by some professionals who maintain that the term *codependent* is too watered down to mean anything. They believe that, if 95% of the population is codependent, then being codependent is the norm, and the term *codependency* offers little in the way of new information about us or about the world. Other professionals take a more pedantic approach in discussing codependency, and maintain that, although these characteristics may exist, they do so without continuity across populations. Moreover, these characteristics lack identifiable behaviors that could be used to diagnose individuals. For example, Cermack (1986) identifies diagnostic criteria for codependency and differentiates personality traits from personality disorders. He believes that acceptance of the term would require that

> *1) a definition of codependency with objective criteria for the diagnosis [be] developed on a level of sophistication at least equal to other diagnostic categories in* (sic) *DSM III-R; and 2) research using adequate diagnostic criteria [be] undertaken to verify the existence of codependency as a reliable and valid entity (p. 16).*

This same author believes that codependency can be collapsed into the Personality Disorder Not Otherwise Specified (301.9) category of the *DSM IV* (APA, 1994).* Cermack addresses critics of the concept of codependency by noting that many critics have attempted to invalidate the concept because of its ubiquity but have failed to understand the differences between personality traits and personality disorders. The former are enduring patterns of perceiving oneself and the world, while personality disorders generally occur when there is inflexibility in social, occupational, or intrapersonal functioning. Cermack maintains that, while codependent traits may be widespread, a diagnosis pointing to a personality disorder would need to result in an "identifiable dysfunction resulting from excessive rigidity or intensity associated with these traits" (p. 16). In other words, he says, "If narcissism can be a universal human trait, but Narcissistic Personality Disorder (Axis II, *DSM-IV*) only exists in the face of objective dysfunction, the same could be true for codependency as well" (p. 16).

Gierymski and Williams (1986) criticize the concept of codependency because of the lack of systematic studies pointing toward its clinical presence. They maintain that much of the knowledge base about codependency is "bare assertions, intuitive statements, overgeneralization and anecdotes" (p. 7). Although skeptical, these same authors do believe that proponents of the term are well-meaning. In addition, the policies and practices of local treatment centers are often influenced by public opinion such as that surrounding the concept of codependency. Therefore, regardless of whether the concept will be recognized as a diagnostic category or a clinical syndrome, there is an immediate and pragmatic application of the term. The popularity of the concept "may mean a growing acceptance of the body of knowledge that has emerged from the modern family movement" (Gierymski & Williams, 1986, p. 12). Moreover, these same authors believe that

> *[a] closer look should be taken at other issues of human dependency and interrelatedness in similar problems faced by the families of other severely stressed persons, especially those with chronic illnesses. The understanding of alcoholism would benefit greatly from such comparisons (p. 12).*

As far as the controversy is concerned, the mental health profession has the last word for now: The *DSM IV* does not include codependency in its nomenclature on personality disorders. This may or may not dissuade others from adhering to the concept of codependency, but this omission does make a clear statement that may

---

*According to the *DSM IV,* a Personality Disorder Not Otherwise Specified (301.9) is given when one's behavior crosses several personality disorders but does not fit neatly into one specific disorder.

intensify the chasm that exists over the use of the term between mental health practitioners and those practitioners in the chemical dependency field.

A close examination of the concept of codependency and the criticism surrounding the term and its corollaries will likely indicate that much of the argument involves degrees of acceptance. Even though little empirically based research has been conducted on the subject *per se*, Gierymski and Williams maintain that

> *It would be a mistake to deny that living or even working side by side with a drug dependent person causes stresses and problems or that wives and children as well as other members of families of drug dependent individuals undergo deprivations and stresses, that they suffer indignities, that such problems deserve help, and that help should be offered. However, the authors wonder if the term "codepedency" has not been given connotations far exceeding justification, whether or not the implications (systematic, theoretical, and practical) at the level of the delivery of needed services have been sufficiently examined and the consequences considered (p. 7).*

In this sense, the very least that can be said about the concept of codependency is that it has helped to describe a variety of interpersonal and intrapersonal dynamics in a language that many can understand. In that alcohol and other drugs are rampant in our society across every economic and social line, the concept of codependency may currently be best operating as a paradigm attempting to make sense out of the confusing, paradoxical and often deleterious effects of one's extended drug involvement and its impact on others. Whether intuitively understood or empirically proved, it is safe to say that the characteristics identified as codependent operate in almost all of us at one time or another. Differences between individuals exist in incidence, degree, and persistence. Our society is based upon competition and achievement. You, as a reader of this book, might be termed an *overachiever*, but, it is often overachievers who are in positions to help others. The need for belonging to powerful groups, identified as indicative of an antisocial/narcissistic personality disorder (Kitchens, 1991), can be functional, and decisions that affect us all are made by groups of powerful people. We all need humor in our lives, so the histrionic personality identified as maladaptive is necessary for us to have perspective on our lives. Compulsivity is almost a given in undergraduate and graduate school, isn't it? Does that mean you are maladaptive for choosing to go to college or graduate school? The point we are making here is that codependent characteristics, *per se*, are not inherently good or bad. Sometimes behaving codependently is appropriate, very adaptive, and can lead to satisfaction with oneself and others. Sometimes these same characteristics can lead to problems. An inflexible adherence to codependency as well as an inflexible avoidance of it may become problematic. The advice given here is for you to remain open to the client and to employ an understanding of codependency as it relates to the well-being of that client. Categorically disregarding the presence of codependent behaviors may limit the amount and kind of information being presented by clients and can lead to less than efficacious results in counseling. At the same time, "creating a codependent client" by adhering rigidly to the tenets of codepedency may not only be ineffective (to say nothing of inappropriate), it may increase your own codependency because inflexibility is one of the pervading themes of codependent personality disorders.

Two Case Examples

When reviewing these authentic case examples the reader should remain aware of the delineation between the clinical impression of codependency and the formal and recognized diagnostic criteria. Under the current diagnostic criteria of the *DSM IV*, which does not include codependency, both of these clients could be assigned a diagnosis of personality disorder. The purpose in presenting these particular cases is twofold. First, each case illustrates the controversy surrounding the construct of codependency in terms of the criticism leveled about definition. Second, both cases depict clients whose behaviors meet many, if not all, of the characteristics described previously as codependent. These cases will demonstrate how such an understanding of codependency can be helpful in assessment and treatment. A brief psycho-social history of both clients will precede an analysis of their codependent characteristics.

Becky's Case

At the time of the intake, Becky (not her real name) was a 42-year-old, Caucasian female, married for twenty years to Jim, a Vietnam veteran. They had two children, both girls. He worked the graveyard shift as a delivery truck driver for a local firm. She was a full-time student taking courses to finish up her undergraduate degree, and, at the time of her first session, she had one-and-one-half years remaining in her studies. Becky told the author that she and her husband had only had sex "twice in the past three months." She had been working part-time for a dozen or so years at a local casino as a blackjack dealer. However, she claimed that her husband had "taken away her credit cards" because she was "so irresponsible." Becky had been seeing a psychiatrist who had determined that she had a history of conversion reactions, diagnosed her as depressed, and had prescribed 100 mg. of Elavil. She had been taking this medication for five years and had little desire to cease. Reasons for her insistence on medication included her having had episodes of "deep depression three times a year—even when I am on Elavil."

Her psychosocial history revealed that she was the first born of "three Catholic-raised children" (her words). Her mother was reported to have been "extremely strict, controlling, and emotionally abusive." Becky's mother's drinking was underplayed and rationalized as "not being a problem." Her parents divorced when she was six. She was molested by her father for several years prior to the divorce, and Becky said that as a result she remained afraid of the dark. She also revealed that she had been in counseling on several occasions, sometimes with her husband. Becky stated that the "two precious counselors were female and ended up taking my husband's side after 12 sessions. The last counselor, Frank, was too nice, and after three sessions started liking me too much."

Becky had a history of numerous extra-marital affairs, although all were reported to have stopped short of intercourse. Most of the relationships were characterized as nonsexual, but involved intimate discussions, dating, and recreating. At the time of her sessions, she was involved with two men aside from her husband. She stated that she "was obsessed" with one of the men, Rick. Becky said that she "was always thinking of him, wondering if he was thinking of her." She reported that she volunteered at the firm where he worked "just so I could see him weekly." She also stated that she would "dress for him" on every occasion that she anticipated seeing him. Interestingly, Becky claimed that Rick had "no interest" in her. Upon the closing of the first session, Becky said that she had not told her husband that she was coming "because he would forbid it." As a result, she paid cash so he "would not have any record or indication that I am coming here."

During the course of counseling, Becky presented herself as dissociated from her feelings, especially from that of anger. Although she exuded a great deal of anger, she refused to acknowledge that she was, in fact, angry. Her dissociation was seen when she described the men with whom she was involved. When describing these men, Becky remained aloof, distant, and focused exclusively upon attributes, such as being good looking, confident, athletic, or intelligent. These descriptions were in contrast to the possibility of describing the men being described as compassionate, passionate, sensitive, considerate, or respectful. Moreover, all of the men whom Becky had befriended were "unavailable" because they were either already married and not willing to divorce, already involved in other significant relationships, depressed and therefore emotionally unavailable, or themselves were interested only in a casual relationship.

In addition, Becky did not like to allow others to know how she was feeling. For example, on many occasions she came into the session relating how her husband (and perhaps others) had left her very angry, yet she consistently chose to shy away from any confrontation or share any aspect of her anger with them. Instead, she chose to depress her feelings and to withdraw emotionally. On a few occasions, Becky mentioned that she had broached the subject of divorce with her husband, but had found out that he "loves me too much, so I agreed to live with him peacefully. So, things are okay." When confronted with her need to "survive" rather than flourish, Becky stated that she, "did not want to repeat what my mother went through in divorcing my father. She was vulnerable and got screwed." Moreover, Becky claimed that she needed to "take care of Jim. He needs me. I don't think he can live without me."

Counseling lasted several months. Toward the end of counseling, Becky gathered up the courage to seek a separation and moved herself and her two children into a rented home. She followed up with a phone call a few months later to let the counselor know that she had divorced and was currently enjoying time to herself.

Dave's Case

Dave (also not his real name), a 45-year-old Caucasian male who was married with ten children (nine adopted), referred himself for counseling. At the initial session, his first words were, "I abuse my children." To avoid legal issues, a "release of information" was obtained, and a letter requesting a summary of the case was sent to Social Services to insure that the abuse had been reported. The social services investigator reported that she had been unable to prove or disprove the allegations, since none of the children would substantiate the accusations. Dave, however, readily acknowledged that, "I abuse my children by calling them stupid, dumb, hitting them on their arms, and swearing at them regularly."

At the time of the first session, Dave had been asked to leave his home by his wife, Madeline. She also prohibited him from seeing his children—something he reported as devastating. He reported to the counselor that he needed to have a note saying it was okay for Dave to be admitted back into his home. Dave reported that his wife "wears the pants in the family." While exploring the issue of his needing the counselor to write a "permission slip" to be able to go back home, Dave denied being angry at his wife for taking his children away from him, for kicking him out of his house, or for being verbally abused by her when she went on a drinking binge.

A family history revealed that, when Dave's father got mad or was drinking heavily, his mother would "get in Dad's face." Dave and his wife repeated that same pattern. This helped to explain why Dave would say to himself, "I can't get angry or I'll go back to what I did before (become abusive and/or drink again)." His lack of expressed anger was also reflected in his having had four extra-marital affairs, for which the timing of two was directly related to his passive-aggressive manner of dealing with anger. He recalled that one of the affairs took place when his wife was in the hospital having elective surgery that he had opposed. One of the other affairs took place when his wife was visiting her mother even after Dave had requested she stay at home.

In the fourth weekly session, Dave reported that he had gone over and seen his children while his wife was out of town. He presented himself as jovial with little or no concern for the consequences, which by now involved Madeline's filing for a divorce against his wishes and her request that he not see the children unless she were there to supervise. The following week, Dave stated that Madeline was attempting to obtain a temporary restraining order (TRO) that would prohibit his seeing his children and Madeline. Dave did not demonstrate motivation to pursue legal advice in defense of her actions, was not even aware of whether his presence at the hearing was voluntary or mandated, did not have any plans to call the judge to determine appropriate protocol, and said that "he was resigned to let her do what she wants." All of this was in the face of his categorical declarations that his children meant everything to him. When asked for clarification, Dave stated, "I have come to accept over the years that my wife's word is law."

An accomplished artist, Dave revealed that he had given up his art for another career because his wife did not like New York, where he had attempted to show his art. He claimed that he had never really had any friends and that his social life was focused solely upon his wife and family. Even though he was a middle-school math teacher and therefore had ample opportunity to make friends, Dave shied away from intimate or much collegial contact, saying that he didn't have much faith in others and felt as though he didn't fit in.

Throughout the sessions, Dave looked to the counselor for approval while hiding many of his authentic emotional experiences. His manner of presentation was rigid in terms of his belabored speech and lack of spontaneity. He kept time during the session, and, before being confronted on the matter, would draw the sessions to a close at the appropriate time. He claimed to feel depressed most of the time, but stated that "it is not enough to make me want to kill myself or anything." Finally, it should be noted that the counselor's experience was one of fascination over how this grown man of 45 appeared so naive about the world. His affect was restricted even when confronted with a TRO and an impending divorce, while his use of intellectualization as a defense mechanism reinforced a sense of dissociation from his experience.

Dave was seen for 15 sessions before he left the state for his summer vacation. He never made another appointment, although plans had been made to do so. He did contact a lawyer for advice regarding the TRO and, as a result, was granted joint visitation rights for six months. He did report in the fourteenth session that he had begun to paint again and had befriended another male teacher whose company he enjoyed.

Analysis of Becky's and Dave's Cases

Both Becky and Dave could be conceptualized as codependent. Although quite different in terms of their presenting problems, both had a history of parental alcohol abuse. Both had come from homes where there was sexual and/or physical abuse. Both had been raised in homes where they had been taught to control their emotions. Both had, themselves, issues of substance abuse: Becky was relying upon a prescription drug, and she self-medicated often, whereas Dave had stopped drinking, although admitting that he "usually drank too much for my own good."

The characteristics of both indicated an excessive reliance upon others' approval. Becky projected her own fears of being alone onto her husband and remained in the relationship ostensibly because of her husband's inability to live without her. Dave had given up his passion for art in order to satisfy the geographical needs of his wife. Rather than simply moving and resuming his dream to become an accomplished artist, he moved while giving up his dream and thus resented his wife for taking away his dreams. Becky prided herself on "getting any man she wanted," as if her conquests would satiate some hidden need to feel powerful.

Both were manipulative, although the concept of manipulation is somewhat different in codependency than it is usually understood to be. Both Becky and Dave attempted to manipulate their spouses by giving up their own goals with the hopes that, by doing so, their partners would never leave. In Becky's case, she attempted to be, in her own words, "the perfect wife who would take care of the children, the home, and her husband." In doing so, she had given up much of herself and had remained emotionally distant from her husband for "at least a dozen years." Even though she would accompany him to social events, Becky stated that she was always on the hunt for an interesting man while her husband was conversing at the parties.

In their own ways, both had assumed too much responsibility for the actions of others. Dave believed that he was solely responsible for the problems in his marriage. He portrayed his wife as being "independent and together" while believing himself to be dependent upon her. Becky also felt completely responsible for the problems in her marriage. Both were angry and resentful at giving their power away to their spouses, which contributed to statements that there was no love left in their respective marriages. Leaving the marriages, however, was so terrifying that Becky and Dave denied having any substantial marital problems. Becky and Dave had resigned themselves to lives void of spontaneous emotion. Becky believed that she was being punished by God for being a bad child, which she defined as resulting from her father's molestation, and she saw little hope for resolution to her low-level depression. Dave had also given up hope for feeling better—resigning himself instead to being dependent upon his wife and living a life according to her dictates. Although both were quite successful in their academic and professional pursuits, neither believed themselves to be adequate at their job. Becky worked compulsively and received A-minus grades, but she minimized this feat, claiming that the tests were easy and that she was older and knew more. Dave continually played down his ability to teach effectively. Instead, he focused upon his shortcomings as a teacher: his perceived lack of social skills and his fears about not being able to answer every question. In both Becky and Dave's case, boundaries were blurred. Becky and Dave were enmeshed in their relationships and demonstrated difficulty in determining their own needs, instead focusing almost exclusively upon the needs of their spouses. Finally, both individuals were engaging in behaviors that left them with a great sense of shame. Dave abused his children and felt shame, while Becky engaged in adulterous affairs that left her also with a deepened sense of shame and guilt.

Therapist's Focus in the Cases

The focus in each case was to identify and address the client's diminished sense of self. While this focus is not new to the mental health field, the techniques used in therapy with codependent clients can differ. One of the presumptive foundations upon which codependency rests is the sense of having had a "lost childhood" (Whitfield, 1989). Addressing this in therapy may take the form of "re-parenting," where the goal is to have clients learn how to parent themselves. That is, clients learn how to nurture themselves by giving themselves permission to feel what they feel, by acknowledging what they are thinking, and by practicing the skills that allow them to talk more openly about their experiences. One of the popular techniques used in this endeavor is "inner-child work" (Miller, 1981). This technique includes having the client keep a journal that records a dialogue between "the Parent" and the "Little Child" within. So that the writing will appear more childlike, the client writes to his or her "Little Child" using the nondominant hand to help contact this childlike dimension of self. First, the "Parent" writes and asks how the "Little Child" is doing. In Becky's case, she wrote, "Hi, Becky. I love you and was wondering how you were doing?" Then taking the pencil in her nondominant hand, she replied, "I am sad and hurt." Then the Parent would respond, and the dialogue could continue for as long as the client wants. It is important, however, that when closing, the "Parent" should assure the "Little Child" that he or she is loved and does not have to hurry and finish his or her feelings—something likely to have been advocated in his or her home of origin. The essential message to the "Child" is that it is okay to feel a feeling—any feeling—for as long as he or she wants to do so.

In Dave's case, another approach was used. Although it was believed that he had a less than desirable upbringing, the counselor assessed that inner-child work would have been met with resistances—partly because of Dave's views of his masculinity (which did not leave much room for emotion) and partly because his emotional nature was rather rigid and could have precluded an attempt to help him become more flexible. The counselor believed that inner-child work might create too much cognitive dissonance and would result in increasing Dave's resistance to counseling. Instead, the counselor used a "parenting" approach. The counselor regularly assessed his own nurturing dimension and was more guiding than with other clients. Therapist's suggestions were more frequent with the belief that this approach allowed Dave to experience a "parent" who was nurturing, caring, sensitive, and loving. Although Dave did not return for therapy after his summer break, the course of help would have been to gently, yet firmly, begin to reintroduce Dave' own ability to nurture himself. This would have been accomplished through gentle confrontation once the bond between counselor and client (between "parent" and "child") had been sufficiently strengthened.

Note that in such confrontations, the counselor would have needed to demonstrate a caring for the client that approximates what should have been there for the client in his or her own family of origin. That is, the counselor would have needed to demonstrate both a pulling together attitude and a pushing away attitude with the client in much the same way that a parent might leave his or her child at preschool. Both parent and child experience grief, loss, and fear. However, it is loving to allow one's child to interact with others in the real world. Thus, the child gradually learns to accept that he or she can be independent. In fact, he or she can experience how exciting it is to be independent. In this technique, it is crucial for mental health professionals to be flexible in drawing the client closer to demonstrate nurturance while at the same time pushing the client out into the real world to demonstrate another dimension of caring.

Implications for Mental Health Professionals

Usefulness of the Codependency Concept

In reviewing the cases presented, a question remains as to why the concept of codependency is needed when it appears that another diagnostic category could suffice. The potential benefit is reflected in one's conceptualization and in the ensuing treatment approach. In both case examples, the focus of counseling was upon the clients' self-esteem and the attempt to help both see their world for what it really was. Both clients presented with relationships that were not thriving. Although couples therapy was suggested, both remained firm in their rejection of such intervention. Hence, a codependency paradigm allowed for a relationship-oriented intervention to be used without the presence of their respective partners. It is important to note that it is still preferable to have both partners involved in therapy when relationship issues are presented. However, if one cannot directly access the client's partner for one reason or another, the mental health professional might focus upon the client's need to control self and significant others in the environment. This focus can be useful in helping the client gain insight into reasons why the relationships are not working, while diminishing the need to be overresponsible. Accessing the client's emotional experience allows him or her to gain some self-esteem because a fundamental principle in codependency is that cutting oneself off from feelings initiates manipulative, controlling, and irresponsible behaviors. All of these behaviors are seen as leading to a diminished sense of self.

Another benefit to using codependency as a framework concerns the clients themselves. These days, labeling oneself as codependent when (according to some authors) almost everyone is codependent, allows for clients to gain a sense of comfort with having the same problems as everyone else. This subtle but potentially profound sense of inclusion may help a client's self-esteem by allowing him or her to feel more normal than abnormal. Moreover, as Gierymski and Williams point out, whether one believes or doesn't believe in the concept of codependency, millions of Americans are familiar with the term, so clients will likely bring some awareness (and perhaps some disdain) of the concept into therapy.

Mental health professionals' understanding of such a popular term can allow them to gain different insights with clients. However, professionals should be cautioned about the limitation of labeling a client as codependent. It might be more useful to regard a client as demonstrating codependent behaviors to a greater or lesser degree. A further important point is related more to the generic helping process: At times, clients will ask professionals whether they are aware of codependency or will ask the therapist's thoughts on the subject. It would be very important to view this request for information as a "test" as it has been the authors' experience that clients may use the mental health professional's response as a yardstick for continued counseling. If the client has some disdain for the concept and professionals admit their preference for it, resistances will likely occur. The same is true in reverse: Clients may appreciate the tenets of codependency and can terminate therapy if professionals present doubts. The rule of thumb is for mental health professionals to treat the query as they would treat any other question. A middle-of-the-road approach would suggest that mental health professionals simply demonstrate respect for the client's views of the concept and perhaps suggest to the client that some interesting ideas are contained in the concept of codependency. In this sense, practitioners may find the concept more useful than researchers in the field do. It is important for mental health professionals to remain aware that, while their clients may believe in the concept of codependency, the jury is still out on its being a discrete and identifiable construct.

Assessing for Codependency

As mentioned earlier in this chapter, there is presently no formal recognition of codependency as a discrete diagnostic category. It is helpful if codepedency is thought of as a cluster of behaviors that lie on a continuum ranging from "mildly codependent" to "severely codependent." In this manner, mental health professionals can determine the significance of codependent behaviors as they relate to the person's functioning. Specifically, mental health professionals should determine the severity of codepedency as well as determining how much pain codependency is causing the client.

Because of the lack of formal acknowledgment, assessing codependency in clients is relatively informal, relying upon subjective clinical impressions or using nonstandardized assessment procedures. For example, Friel (1985) developed a test for codependency called the "Friel Codependent Assessment Inventory," which contains sixty true/false items. The total score is measured by tabulating the number of "True" responses. Scores can range from "Few Codependent Concerns" (less than 20 "True" responses) to "Severely Codependent" (more than 60 "True" responses). Kitchens (1991) developed "A Codependence Test" that has 25 Likert-type questions, and scores can range from "Healthy" (a score of less than 25) to "Severe Codependence" (a score greater than 75). Gossett (1988) and a staff of graduate students, at the Institute for the Study of the Family and Addictive Disorders at the University of North Texas, developed the "Orientation to Life Inventory." The authors state that the 50-item instrument, although unpublished, measures a client's internal consistency or denial of codependence through the use of a type of validity scale as well as measuring three different aspects of codependence: cognitive rigidity, emotional disintegrity, and extreme normative expectations. As with other instruments, scores on this scale range from "Healthy" to "Severe Codependence." Unfortunately, none of the instruments mentioned above report reliability or validity coefficients. Thus, should you, as a mental health professional, choose to administer an instrument, you are advised to use these instruments with extreme caution. Probably the best use of these assessment devices is for the mutual identification of problematic areas occurring in the client's life. Asking the client to share his or her impressions of the assessment results can help focus on areas that might need attention.

Aside from the structured paper and pencil tests, Kitchens discusses subjective methods for assessing codependence. In fact, Kitchens states that it is imperative that mental health professionals combine subjective and objective assessment procedures. According to Kitchens, there are seven indicators that can help determine the severity of codependence: (1) the extent to which the client equates performance with self-value; (2) the extent to which the client equates self-worth with taking care of others' needs; (3) the extent to which the client believes he or she is helpless to control what happens in life; (4) the extent to which the client attempts to feel more powerful or more in control of life than is actually the case; (5) the extent to which the client ruminates about dysfunctional family of origin behavior; (6) the extent to which the client continues to protect or defend against any criticism of his or her parents in the face of contradictory information; (7) the extent to which the client experiences unexplained or overwhelming anger; and (8) the extent to which the client feels stuck in his or her relationships.

Using Codependency in Family Assessment

According to Kitchens (1991), "The codependent family is clearly an appropriate target for therapy..." (p. 150). The premise of this statement lies in the notion that adult children grew up in dysfunctional families and will likely create another dysfunctional family when they marry or engage in other intimate relationships. Kitchens believes that each family practices and passes on rules for its behaviors and ways of thinking so that a codependent family pattern can run for generations.

Often, clients will come in alone but will present issues that involve other family members or significant others. Mental health professionals can assess the extent of the individual client's codependency and generalize, with some fair degree of accuracy, that codependency exists in the client's family or relational system. Friel, Subby and Friel's (1984) list of eight rules that exist in every codependent family can help with an assessment of codependence in the family. These rules are (1) It's not okay to talk about problems; (2) Feelings should not be expressed openly; (3) Communication is best when it is indirect and when one person acts as a messenger between two others; (4) One should be strong, good, right, perfect, and one should make the family proud; (5) One should not be selfish; (6) One "should do as I say, not as I do;" (7) It is not acceptable to play or be playful; (8) One should never rock the boat.

From a systems approach, codependency is a family problem. Therefore, unless there is some family intervention, the client may return to dysfunctional behaviors upon returning to the codependent system. Kitchens alludes to three types of interventions for the codependent family: information-oriented, action-oriented, and affective-oriented. Information-oriented interventions can include psychoeducation, exercises, and/or a question-and-answer format. The aim is to have family members recognize dynamics that are dysfunctional. For example, individual family members may be asked to write out impressions of past experiences in the family while the mental health professional offers analysis, comments, and suggestions for the family's understanding. Action-oriented interventions may involve having the family re-enact a problem while the mental health professional attempts to restructure each family member's role in the problem. For example, the professional may ask family member, who has played the role of messenger, to be silent, while encouraging direct communication between the two dissenting family members. Affective-oriented interventions are aimed at getting family members in touch with their feelings. Professionals can focus upon current or past problematic situations in the family and/or can focus upon feelings as they are experienced in the therapy session. For example, a woman, who is indirect in her communication, might be encouraged to get in touch with her emotional response to her spouse's disparaging remarks and be urged to share her feelings with him.

Mental Health Professionals' Own Codependency

The authors conducted a preliminary study (Fisher & Harrison, 1993) assessing codependent characteristics of graduate students in a masters degree counseling program. We found that these prospective mental health professionals reported more codependent characteristics than did students in other graduate programs. Moreover, the graduate students in the mental health profession were more likely to have come from an alcoholic home. This preliminary study suggests that mental health professionals' codependency may be a potential problem in a counseling relationship.

Recall Potter-Efron and Potter-Efron's list of codependent behaviors that were described earlier. They identified codependent behaviors as including a preoccupation with the problems of others, utilizing manipulative attempts to change another's behaviors, rigidity, and attempts to have others validate one's self-worth. Although these behaviors lie on a continuum, it can certainly be seen how a proclivity may exist for those of us in the helping profession to engage in one or more of these codependent behaviors. Should any mental health professional have a history of family dysfunction, the inclination to engage in one or more dysfunctional behaviors with clients could increase. For the mental health professional, this proclivity might increase when clients, themselves, are working on codependent issues.

Professional ethics (see Chapter 17) will obviate many codependent behaviors in mental health professionals. Prohibiting personal relationships with clients is one example. However, as you would expect, professionals can exhibit many more subtle forms of codependency that fall within the realm of professional practice. For example, accepting phone calls after hours at home from clients is not precluded in the ethics of our profession. However, taking calls at home instead of directing them to your answering service may be symptomatic of your need to be accepted by clients. It may also suggest that the client's needs are more important than your needs are. If you allow these after-hours calls to be fairly regular, you may experience resentment that would certainly impact your relationship with the client. These after-hours phone calls may also serve to blur the boundaries between you the helper and your client. Consistently accepting more clients on your caseload than you can reasonably handle could also be detrimental to clients: You may become too tired to give undivided attention to each client. In this case, the workaholic (see Chapter 15, "Other Addictions") professional may be ignoring his or her own needs by focusing excessively upon work.

Professional Enabling

The dynamics that transpire between client and mental health professional in sessions may also reflect the professional's codependent behaviors and may result in a type of professional enabling of your client's maladaptive behaviors. Weigscheider (1981) sees attempts to keep an alcoholic from experiencing logical or natural consequences as enabling (see Chapter 10). Miller (1989) believes that enabling reinforces another's dysfunctional behavior. Thus, your attempts to keep clients from experiencing the natural consequences of their actions can be framed as professional enabling and can reinforce maladaptive client behaviors. You might perceive a client's desire to return to a dysfunctional relationship as reflecting your failure to effect client change. By personalizing the client's progress, you might strongly advise the client to avoid returning to the dysfunctional relationship and become angry with the client if the advice is not heeded. You might also over-identify with the experience of the client, resulting in an enmeshed relationship with the client. The loss of these interpersonal boundaries can diminish the effectiveness of the helping process, or at least confound the process. For example, you might identify with the client's feelings of helplessness in changing an alcoholic partner's behaviors. Rather than recognizing and working with the enabling aspects of the client's behaviors, you might prematurely attempt to steer the client into solutions rather than helping him or her gain insight into how his or her behaviors actually enable or reinforce the partner's alcoholism. In this manner, the client is kept from experiencing the consequences of his or her own behaviors.

We could continue with protracted examples of mental health professionals' potential codependent behaviors. Suffice it to say that codependency in the profession can be problematic. Training programs go a long way in helping mental health professionals understand the parameters of interactions with clients. Yet, if you come from a home where there was alcoholism or other family dysfunction, you may be more prone at times to behaving codependently with clients. Personal work can increase awareness of your codependent behaviors and can help you arrive at some strategies and solutions. It may well be that our profession attracts those who have experienced much of the same pain that clients will have experienced. Your experiences with your own pain and codependency can significantly increase the potential for accurate empathy with your clients and, therefore, can be of potential benefit. The extent of the benefit to clients will likely be related directly to the amount of your own work on codependency issues.

Summary

Until further empirical can establish discrete criteria for the construct, codependency will not likely be included in future editions of the *DSM* as a diagnosis. The debate surrounding codependency is a heated one, and each side of the debate has good points. Nevertheless, an understanding of codependency can help mental health professionals conceptualize behavioral patterns that are problematic for clients and can aid in the development of therapeutic interventions.

It may be particularly useful to subscribe to the notion of codependency as lying on a continuum from functional to dysfunctional behaviors. Also important will be your own self-exploration of codependency. This will be especially true when you comes from an alcoholic family or one in which there was other dysfunction.

Chapter 13

Relapse Prevention

A few years ago, we met a 16-year-old girl named Anna. Anna was in an intensive outpatient treatment program for polydrug use problems, with her drugs of choice including tobacco, alcohol, marijuana, LSD, and methamphetamine. She was court-ordered to treatment following a variety of status offenses and crimes and a psychological assessment. On the basis of the assessment, Anna was diagnosed as Alcohol Abuse, Amphetamine Abuse (see Chapter 5), and post-traumatic stress disorder (PTSD). The diagnosis of PTSD was related to a history of sexual molestation by Anna's step-father that began when she was 8 and ended when she was 13 when her biological mother discovered the molestation and divorced the perpetrator. The crime was reported, but Anna had never been in therapy. Shortly after the molestation began, Anna began to demonstrate a series of problems in school including deteriorating academic performance, fighting, and noncompliance with teachers. These problems continued until she entered treatment. Anna's biological father left the family when Anna was two and was an active alcoholic who had been in two treatment programs. He maintained sporadic contact with his daughter. Anna was slightly obese and had an acne problem. On an IQ test, she scored 88 (low average), and her academic skills were at the sixth to seventh grade level (she was a sophomore). Anna's mother was 33 years old, did not complete high school, and worked in a service position at a hotel/casino. She used alcohol and marijuana on an infrequent basis. She and Anna had a volatile relationship with a great deal of conflict. The mother noted a strong similarity between Anna and her biological father. She also expressed guilt over not discovering the sexual molestation sooner.

Anna completed her treatment program in three months. She was initially resistant and defiant. However, she bonded with a female counselor in the program and, for the first time, found support and consistency from both adults and peers. She maintained abstinence for the last two months of her program. Her mother participated in the program and began to learn about the disease of chemical dependency (which was the orientation of the program) and about her own enabling. Anna and her mother had four family counseling sessions and made a little progress. There was still a lot to do, so they were referred to a marriage and family therapist. The school counselor was invited to the discharge conference and encouraged to assist Anna in readjusting to school. She had earned just two credits in high school (that means, she had passed only two classes). Anna began attending AA meetings and was encouraged to go to four to five meetings a week. She was scheduled to attend a weekly, two-hour, aftercare meeting at the treatment program.

Need for Generalist Training in Relapse Prevention

Imagine that you are the marriage and family therapist whom Anna and her mother contact. Or, let's say that you are the school counselor at Anna's high school. We hope that you can identify some of the issues that might lead Anna to return to alcohol and other drug use and would require attention in family therapy or at school. First, there is the history of sexual molestation, which we have discussed as a frequent issue for women in substance-abuse treatment programs. Some of the other issues include academic problems at school, conflict with mom, physical appearance (We are not making a judgment here. Just remember what it was like when you were in high school for a kid who was overweight and had lots of zits.), and contact with an actively drinking father. There are also problems that, although not explicitly stated, might be logically assumed to exist. For example, we would expect that Anna's social group involved kids who use alcohol and other drugs. If she returns to the same school, how will she handle her peer group? She may have some deep-seated emotional issues involving abandonment by her father and anger at her mother for not protecting her from her step-father. Finally, given her intellectual ability and academic achievement, school may be challenging.

In Chapter 1, we gave examples of how social workers, school counselors, and marriage and family therapists work with clients with alcohol and other drug problems whether or not these helping professionals work in treatment programs. The area of relapse prevention is a clear illustration of this. In Anna's case, the marriage and family therapist and school counselor would probably have more intensive and a longer duration of contact with Anna than the staff at the treatment program. Therefore, the therapist and counselor are critically important in Anna's success in recovery. She could also have a probation officer and contact with social service professionals (i.e., through vocational training programs). Their work could also impact Anna's abstinence.

Although it would be nice if there were a formal discharge staffing that included all relevant parties and a formal relapse prevention plan, our experience is that these are not the norm. The mental health professional usually has sketchy information from the client and/or treatment program and is left to develop his or her own relapse prevention plan. That is why we will spend considerable time in this chapter acquainting you with the specifics of relapse prevention.

Definition of Slip *and* Relapse

As we shall see, a need exists to differentiate a *slip* from a *relapse*. A slip is an episode of alcohol or other drug use following a period of abstinence, while relapse is the return to uncontrolled alcohol or other drug use following a period of abstinence. Usually, a slip or slips precede relapse, and there is some evidence (e.g., Polich, Armor, and Braiker, 1981) that slipping is the rule rather than the exception for those clients who receive alcohol or other drug treatment.

The disease model of addiction and AA slogans (an alcoholic is always "one drink from a drunk") can promote the idea that a slip inevitably leads to relapse. The depiction of addiction as a progressive, chronic disease that can be managed only through abstinence may create a sense that a slip means complete deterioration to pre-treatment levels of functioning (Lewis, Dana, & Blevins, 1994). The result of clients' adopting this point of view is that, when a slip occurs (as it is likely to), the client may experience guilt, anxiety, or hopelessness. These negative emotions may lead to further, heavier use. The cognitive process of the client may go something like this: "Well, I used again. Since that means I'm back to square one, I might as well do it up right."

Regardless of the model of addiction or orientation to treatment, alcohol and other drug treatment providers will tell you that a return to some level of use is a frequent occurrence (shortly, we will examine data on how frequent). Although we believe that abstinence is the safest and healthiest "level" of use, we also believe that it is foolish to ignore the reality of slips, and it is poor practice to leave clients unprepared to prevent a slip from escalating to a relapse. As we discussed in Chapter 3, there is no evidence that addiction proceeds in an inevitable progression. Therefore, there is no reason to treat a slip as a catastrophe and every reason to view a slip as a signal to the client, treatment providers, and other mental health professionals to reexamine the aftercare plan (see Chapter 7) in order to prevent slips from occurring in the future and to prevent the current slip from escalating.

Frequency of Slips and Relapse

Regardless of the researcher, drug or drugs of choice, and population studied, a consistent finding from studies is that lots of people who receive treatment for alcohol and other drug problems use again after leaving treatment. For example, Miller and Hester (1980) examined 500 alcohol treatment outcome studies. They concluded that

> *With regard to "average" outcome rates from treatment programs, it appears that 1/3 abstinent and 1/3 improved (but not abstinent) represent reasonable estimates of at least short-term response to treatment. A review restricted to studies with one-year follow-up data, however, suggests that 26% is a representative figure for successful outcome (abstinent plus improved) 12 months after treatment (p. 15).*

Hunt, Barnett, and Branch (1971) reported that 65 to 70% of alcoholics, heroin addicts, and smokers relapsed (defined as any level of use following treatment) within the first year and most of these occurred in the first 90 days. Finally, Hoffman and Harrison (1986) followed more than 1,900 adults from five private inpatient alcohol and other treatment programs. Two years after treatment, 54% achieved total abstinence, 18% had slips and returned to abstinence, and 28% had multiple relapses. Clients who came from high socioeconomic groups and had good social stability had the lowest relapse rates. As would be expected, stereotypic "skid row" alcoholics had the poorest prognosis.

We are not presenting this data to generate an argument (which is important from a research point of view) regarding the many factors that influence these research results. Certainly, the length of time following treatment, the type of treatment setting and methods, the method of defining *relapse*, the drug or drugs of choice, the client and the environmental characteristics, and other variables influence the data. Our point is that many, if not most, clients return to use at some point following treatment. Therefore, the issue of return to use must be a focus of treatment and aftercare.

Models of Relapse Prevention

The Cenaps Model

The Cenaps Model was developed by Terence Gorski (president of the Cenaps Corporation) and articulated in a variety of articles and books (e.g., Gorski, 1988, 1989, 1990, 1992, 1993; Gorski & Miller, 1986). The disease concept is the underlying philosophy of the model, although the methods used are eclectic. In Gorski's words, the Cenaps model "integrates the fundamental principles of AA and the Minnesota Model Treatment (see Chapter 7) to meet the needs of relapse-prone patients..." (Gorski, 1990, p. 126). The model is proposed as a formal program within alcohol and other drug treatment programs.

With the disease concept as a guiding philosophy, chemical dependency is viewed as a biopsychosocial disease. This means that the disease affects biological or physical, psychological, and social functioning. Although there is a complex interaction among these areas, Gorski (1990) stated that "The physical consequence of chemical dependence is brain dysfunction... [that] disorganizes the pre-addictive personality and causes social and occupational problems" (p. 126). Since the disease is chronic and affects the brain (causing psychological and social problems), total abstinence is necessary. However, this is not the exclusive goal of the model. Personality, lifestyle, and family functioning are also areas that require change for biopsychosocial health. For example,

> *Being raised in a dysfunctional family can result in self-defeating personality traits or disorders. These traits and disorders do not cause chemical dependence; however, they can cause a more rapid progression of the chemical dependence,*

making it difficult to recognize and to seek treatment.... Self-defeating personality traits and disorders also increase the risk of relapse. As a result, family-of-origin problems need to be appropriately addressed in treatment. (Gorski, 1990, p. 126–127)

Gorski (1990) differentiates clients who have completed the "primary goals" of treatment from those who have not completed these goals. These primary goals are

(1) the recognition that chemical dependency is a biopsychosocial disease, (2) the recognition of the need for lifelong abstinence from all mind-altering drugs, (3) the development and use of an ongoing recovery program to maintain abstinence, and (4) the diagnosis and treatment of other problems or conditions that can interfere with recovery (p. 127).

If a client has not completed the primary goals, then, in Gorski's view, a relapse prevention program is inappropriate. The relapse prevention program outlined in the Cenaps Model is for clients "who believe that they have the disease, require abstinence, and need to use recovery tools, but are unable to maintain abstinence" (Gorski, 1990, p. 127). As can be seen from the primary goals of treatment, this would limit the number of clients who would be seen as appropriate for a relapse prevention program.

According to Gorski (1990), recovery and relapse are related processes. Recovery follows a sequence of six steps that are as follows:

(1) abstaining from alcohol and other drugs; (2) separating from people, places, and things that promote chemical use and establishing a social network that supports recovery; (3) stopping compulsive self-defeating behaviors that suppress awareness of painful feelings and irrational thoughts; (4) learning how to manage feelings and emotions responsibly without resorting to compulsive behaviors or the use of chemicals; (5) learning to change addictive-thinking patterns that create painful feelings and self-defeating behaviors; and (6) identifying and changing the mistaken core beliefs about self, others, and the world that promote the use of irrational thinking (p. 128).

The relapse process begins at step 6 and proceeds upward. For example, let's take a look at Anna's situation and see how a relapse might occur based on Gorski's model. Remember that she was sexually molested by her step-father. Anna starts thinking about the molestation and how unfair it is that this happened to her. She believes that she must have encouraged this behavior to get attention and affection from her step-father and blames herself for the molestation (mistaken core belief about herself, step 6). She ponders this and feels guilty, embarrassed, and victimized (painful feelings, step 5). Anna becomes sexually involved with a 22-year-old who is initially kind and attentive. When she is with this man, she feels worthwhile and does not experience the feelings of guilt, embarrassment, and victimization (managing feelings in an irresponsible manner, step 4). However, the man becomes verbally abusive and openly sees other women. Anna's painful feelings return but she tries desperately to hang on to the relationship (self-defeating behavior, step 3). The man uses alcohol and other drugs, as do his friends (people, places, and things that promote chemical use, step 2). In an effort to impress the man and cope with her feelings, she returns to use (step 1).

The Cenaps Model uses a variety of procedures in relapse prevention, including client self-assessment of problems that might result in relapse, education about relapse, identification of the signs of the relapse progression, strategies to manage or modify the signs, and the involvement of others, such as family members. Techniques from cognitive, affective, and behavioral therapies are used (Gorski, 1993). Therefore, while the Cenaps Model is based on the disease concept of addiction, eclectic treatment strategies are utilized. Furthermore, techniques have been developed for involving the family and the employee-assistance counselor, and procedures have been adapted for adolescents (Bell, 1990).

A Cognitive-Social Learning Model

In contrast to the Cenaps Model, cognitive-social learning approaches to relapse prevention do not have a prerequisite requirement that the client achieve "primary goals" of treatment. Therefore, the strategies of relapse prevention in this model could be used with any client who wants to maintain a behavior change. This change may involve abstinence from alcohol and other drugs or a moderation in use.

The cognitive-social learning model of relapse prevention has been presented by Alan Marlatt (e.g., Marlatt and Gordon, 1985) and Helen Annis (e.g., Annis, 1986, 1990; Annis and Davis, 1988). Marlatt (1985) views addictive behaviors as "overlearned *habits* that can be analyzed and modified in the same manner as other habits" (p. 9, italics in original). This model of addiction was discussed in Chapter 3. With regard to relapse prevention, Marlatt (1985) states that those who believe in this model

> "*are particularly interested in studying the* determinants *of addictive habits, including situational and environmental antecedents, beliefs and expectations, and the individual's family history and prior learning experiences with the substance or activity. In addition, there is an equal interest in discovering the* consequences *of these behaviors, so as to better understand both the reinforcing effects that may contribute to increased use and the negative consequences that may serve to inhibit the behavior. . . . [A]ttention is paid to the social and interpersonal reactions experienced by the individual before, during, and after engaging in an addictive behavior. Social factors are involved both in the initial learning of an addictive habit and in the subsequent performance of the activity once the habit has become firmly established (p. 9–10, italics in original).*

Although the language is different from that used by Gorski, there is a similarity between the steps of recovery and relapse delineated by Gorski and Marlatt's determinants and consequences of addictive behaviors. Both emphasize the need to attend to behavior, thoughts, and feelings (Marlatt uses the terms "social and interpersonal reactions" for feelings and "beliefs and expectations" for thoughts). As we will see later in the chapter, the similarities are probably the reason for the overlap in relapse prevention techniques between the two models.

Annis (1990) criticizes traditional solutions to relapse that emphasize

> *"Booster" sessions of the same treatment . . . added over time to reinforce the initial effects of treatment . . . intensify and broaden the number of treatment components offered . . . [or] adoption of a model of lifelong treatment, such as that embodied in Alcoholics Anonymous (AA) and other self-help groups (p. 117).*

Rather than focus on a model of addiction, Annis argues that the principles that guide the maintenance of a behavior change may be different from the principles that determine the initiation of a change. In other words, a person may enter treatment under coercion, be exposed to and accept the disease concept of addiction, and discontinue his or her use of alcohol and other drugs as a result. However, this same individual may be unable to maintain abstinence. This is the population who Gorski believed was appropriate for the Cenaps Model. However, Annis (and Marlatt) conceptualize this inability to maintain the "habit" change through self-efficacy theory:

> *when a client enters a high risk situation for drinking, a process of cognitive appraisal of past experiences is set in motion which culminates in a judgment, or efficacy expectation, on the part of the client of his or her ability to cope with the situation. The judgment of personal efficacy determines whether or not drinking takes place . . . (Annis and Davis, 1989, p. 170).*

For example, let's say Anna returns to school after treatment. One day after school, she sees a group of students with whom she previously used. They invite her to "party." She says, "no" and the kids make fun of her. In this model, Anna makes a judgment about her ability to cope with the peer pressure. If she decides that she can handle the situation and does so (i.e., asserts herself appropriately and has a social support system), her self-efficacy is enhanced. If she does not believe she can handle the situation or does not have the skills, her self-efficacy is threatened. Annis (1990) reported a high correlation between a client's situation-specific self-efficacy ratings and relapse episodes. Using self-efficacy theory, Marlatt developed a model of relapse that involves the coping strategies that an individual utilizes in high-risk situations. A high-risk situation is defined as "any situation that poses a threat to the individual's sense of control and increases the risk of potential relapse" (Marlatt, 1985, p. 37). These high-risk situations may be either unexpected or covertly planned.

Unexpected high-risk situations are similar to the situation in which Anna runs into her former using friends. She did not plan to encounter this situation; it just happened. In Marlatt's conceptualization, if Anna does not possess an appropriate coping response to the high-risk situation, she will experience decreased self-efficacy that may result in a slip. The slip may have associated thoughts and feelings such as conflict, guilt, and blame, which Marlatt termed the "abstinence violation effect (AVE)." The probability of a slip's progressing to a relapse is related to the intensity of the AVE, which, in turn, is related to factors such as the length of sobriety, the commitment to abstinence, and the knowledge of the slip by significant others.

Anna does not have an effective coping mechanism to use. To stop the teasing, she goes with the group and smokes a little pot. Unfortunately, at aftercare the next night, she has a random urinalysis. Anna's counselor calls her to discuss her "positive" drug test. Anna has an intense AVE. She is disappointed in herself for not resisting her friends and embarrassed that her counselor found out. Due to these painful feelings, Anna begins a relapse.

If Anna did have an effective coping response to the high-risk situation, Marlatt's model predicts that she will experience increased self-efficacy and a resulting decreased probability of slipping. Let's say that Anna asserts herself appropriately with her friends and goes to aftercare that night and reports the incident to her group. She is praised and supported by her peers and her counselor. Anna feels proud of herself and her renewed confidence in her ability to remain abstinent.

High-risk situations can also be encountered due to the covert planning of the individual. This occurs when the person has a "life style imbalance." Marlatt defines this as having "shoulds" that are greater than "wants." Let's use Anna again to illustrate. She is trying to make up lost credits at school, attending four to five AA meetings a week, going to aftercare, trying to get along with her mother, going to counseling, and meeting with her probation officer. She is a busy young woman. Anna is 16 years old and has the same goals as most 16-year-olds—have friends and have fun. But her "shoulds" eat up all her time. Anna starts to feel resentful and victimized. When she has felt this way before, she has used alcohol and other drugs because using helps her forget (at least temporarily) her painful feelings. Also, she starts thinking that she deserves a little fun and relaxation. Although she thinks about using, Anna also has pangs of guilt when she imagines herself doing so. So, instead of simply getting alcohol or another drug and using it, she covertly makes decisions that will place her in a high-risk situation. For example, Anna decides to go to Dorothy's house on Friday to get back some CDs that she loaned Dorothy before going to treatment. Dorothy is a former using friend, and Anna knows that there are usually kids there on Friday after school getting high. Anna gets there, sees everyone loaded, and joins in. Marlatt calls Anna's decision to go to Dorthy's house an "apparently irrelevant decision (AID)." An AID is covertly planned to result in a high-risk situation. In isolation, it seems unrelated to alcohol or other drug use.

Annis and Marlatt describe a variety of interventions to prevent slips and also to prevent slips from escalating into relapse. Some of the interventions are designed to teach coping strategies in high-risk situations, and others are directed toward global life-style changes. Consistent with the model, the strategies are cognitive and behavioral. Many of these will be described in the following section.

For those who are interested in school counseling, Fisher and Harrison (1993) have applied Marlatt's model and strategies to adolescents in the school setting.

Essential Components to Relapse Prevention

As we have seen from the discussion of models of relapse prevention, differences exist between the two models with regard to the definition of client readiness for relapse prevention programming. In the Cenaps Model, a client must have completed the primary goals of treatment (which involve acceptance of the disease model of addiction) to be appropriate for relapse prevention. Annis and Marlatt do not discuss prerequisite conditions for relapse prevention. However, regardless of whether the Cenaps or a cognitive-social learning model of relapse prevention is the choice, the strategies employed to prevent relapse are quite similar. Therefore, we want to describe the strategies of relapse prevention that seem to be necessary in either model. Certainly, some strategies are associated to a larger extent with a particular model, which will be highlighted. However, our goal is to emphasize the techniques that a mental health professional may have to utilize in helping clients with alcohol and other drug problems to remain abstinent or avoid relapse. Keep in mind that these strategies often must be developed by generalists in schools, agencies, and private practice settings, since mental health professionals in these settings usually have the most contact with clients after formal alcohol and other drug treatment has ended.

Assessment of High Risk Situations

The first step in a relapse prevention program must be to determine the specific situations for each client that may lead to a slip. Calling these situations *high risk* denotes a high probability of use based on past experience. The type of situations that are risky varies from client to client, although Cummings, Gordon, and Marlatt (1980) found that 75% of the relapses by alcoholics, smokers, and heroin users were due to negative emotions, interpersonal conflict, and social pressure.

In Gorski's (1990) model, the first step in determining high-risk situations is a client self-assessment that "involves a detailed reconstruction of the presenting problems, the alcohol and other drug use history as well as the recovery and relapse history to identify the past causes of relapse" (p. 129). Next, an examination of the client's life history helps identify any life-style issues that are associated with relapse. Finally, the client's recovery and relapse history is analyzed, with the goal being to "examine each period of abstinence to identify the recovery tasks that were completed or ignored, and to find the sequence of warning signs that led back to chemical use" (p. 130).

In the cognitive-social learning model, there is a "highly individualized analysis of a client's drinking behavior over the previous year to determine the high-risk situations for heavy drinking experienced by that particular client" (Annis, 1990, p. 118). For this purpose, Annis (1982) developed a 100-item self-report questionnaire called the Inventory of Drinking Situations. Obviously, the same type of assessment would occur for clients who use drugs other than alcohol.

Anna, our 16 year old with polydrug problems, has a number of high-risk situations. Negative emotions, such as guilt, shame, and embarrassment related to her history of sexual molestation, have resulted in alcohol and other drug use in the past. She also feels unattractive and unintelligent. Interpersonal conflicts with her mother and with teachers have also been identified as high-risk situations. Finally, in the past, Anna used when she experienced social pressure from her peers. Anna's current life-style involves a lot of time alone, because she has not established a non-using social group. She watches a lot of TV and movies, and she has been using food as a substitute for alcohol and other drugs.

Coping with High-Risk Situations

Once the high-risk situations have been identified, it is necessary for the client to have strategies to deal with these situations effectively. Education and information sharing may be useful to clients. "Relapsers need accurate information about what causes relapse and what can be done to prevent it. This is typically provided in structured relapse education sessions and reading assignments that provide specific information about the recovery and relapse process as well as relapse prevention planning methods" (Gorski, 1990, p. 130).

Daley and Marlatt (1992) recommend that clients be taught that relapse is a process and an event by reviewing the common relapse warning signs identified by recovering clients: "it [is] helpful to have relapsers review their experiences in great detail so that they can learn the connections among thoughts, feelings, events, or situations, and relapse to substance use" (p. 537).

As we saw in the Chapter 7 discussion on methods of treatment, education is rarely sufficient for long-lasting change. Individualized strategies for high-risk situations are usually needed. Gorski (1990) recommends managing high-risk situations on situational-behavioral, cognitive-affective, and core issue levels. On the situational-behavioral level, the client often must avoid the people, places, and things that are high risk and learn to modify his or her behavioral response if a high-risk situation were to occur. For example, Anna identified peer pressure as a high-risk situation. She should avoid her friends with whom she previously used. She might attend a different school following treatment, but, because this is not always possible, she may not be able to avoid these peers. Anna may need assertiveness skills training to learn how to respond to the peer pressure she encounters.

Since Annis (1990) focuses on self-efficacy as the critical component of relapse prevention, a situational-behavioral intervention from this orientation "focuses on having the client engage in homework assignments involving the performance of alternative coping responses in high-risk situations..." (p. 119). A hierarchy of progressively riskier situations is developed, and coping behaviors in these situations are planned, imagined, and used when needed. The underlying rationale is that the most powerful way to change thinking about self-efficacy is behavioral performance. For Anna, this hierarchy might begin with a chance meeting with one of her using friends in the hall at school, then progress to having a group of these friends sit down with her at lunch, and finally to encountering the group on Friday afternoon on their way to "party."

On the affective-cognitive level, the irrational thoughts and intense feelings that emerge in high-risk situations may need to be challenged. For those clients in Twelve Step recovery programs, the acronym HALT is used to advise recovering people to avoid getting too hungry, angry, lonely, or tired. The term "stinking thinking" is used to challenge irrational thoughts, and members are told to get off the "pity pot" when they are immobilized by their feelings. Daley and Marlatt (1992) recommend a worksheet that lists the relapse-related thought, a statement or statements that dispute the thought, and a new, rational thought. As an example, Anna forgets to do her homework in math one day. Her teacher points this out in front of the class and tells her that she will fail unless she "gets with the program." Anna becomes angry and tells the teacher to "shut up." She is told to leave class. On the way to the office, Anna is consumed with her anger and has an inner dialog with statements such as "Mr. C. (the teacher) hates me. He's always picking on me." "I should just get loaded. No one cares anyway." Fortunately, Anna goes to see her school counselor, who listens to her, lets her emotions reduce in intensity, and then confronts her about her responsibility in completing her homework and also the fact that she is allowing Mr. C. to control her recovery program. While not condoning the public reproof by a teacher, the counselor points out the irrationality of Anna's thinking: "I should have done my homework. It embarrassed me to have it pointed out in front of the class. I conclude that the teacher hates me, nobody cares about me, and therefore, I have an excuse to use." A more rational sequence of thoughts would be: "I need to remember to do my homework and ask for help if I'm stuck. I don't like to be embarrassed and would prefer Mr. C. handle the situation differently. None of this has anything to do with people caring about me or using."

The school counselor might also conceptualize that Anna's decision not to complete her homework was part of a covert relapse plan and constitutes the "apparently irrelevant decision" we discussed in the cognitive-social learning model. In other words, Anna covertly planned a relapse by deciding not to complete her homework in a class in which the teacher often reacts with a public reprimand. Since interpersonal conflict with teachers is a high-risk situation that Anna has identified, she has an excuse to create a conflict, thus giving her an excuse to use. In this case, it would be useful to determine how much of Anna's thoughts and feelings involve her "shoulds" being greater than her "wants" and, if this is the case, to help her to modify this disparity. In addition, the AID needs to be confronted.

On the core issue level, the psychological issues that lead to high-risk situations need to be identified. Anna has identified guilt, shame, and embarrassment as negative emotions that are high risk for her. As these feelings originate from her history of sexual molestation, there is an obvious need for therapeutic attention to this issue. Low self-esteem, depressive and anxiety disorders, and codependency are examples of other psychological issues that can result in high-risk situations.

An additional issue in coping with high-risk situations involves urges and cravings. Marlatt (1985) defines a craving as the degree of desire for the positive effects a person expects as a result of use and an urge as the intention to engage in use to satisfy the craving. As Anna leaves her math class and is experiencing intense anger, she has an urge to smoke pot to satisfy a craving for the calming effect and the dissipation of her anger. In a high-risk situation, clients often report that the cravings and urges are so powerful that they lose focus on other aspects of relapse prevention. Therefore, strategies specific to coping with urges and cravings are necessary.

Daley and Marlatt (1992) suggest a variety of strategies to cope with urges and cravings. For example, intentional cognitive strategies such as changing thoughts or self-talking through the cravings can be used. Let's say you are mulling over a conflict you had at work and are having trouble falling asleep. You say to yourself, "I'm going to stop thinking about that and think about something more pleasant." Self-talking through the craving might involve an internal dialog such as, "OK, I know what is happening. I'm upset and I'm thinking that a drink will make me feel better. It's happened before and it will probably happen again. I can get through it." It is often helpful for the client to combine this self-talk with an inner dialogue about the negative consequences of use and the positive benefits of not using (e.g., "If I drink, I'll blow nine months of sobriety and feel terrible about myself. If I don't, I'll feel really strong and proud of myself.") For some clients, calling their AA or NA sponsor or attending a meeting is helpful, while others find that getting involved in a strenuous or pleasant activity takes their thinking away from the urges and cravings.

Support Systems

As Gorski (1990) has stated, "Relapse-prone patients cannot recover alone. It is the therapist's responsibility to involve significant others in the structured process of relapse prevention planning. Family members, 12-step sponsors, and employee-assistance program counselors are significant resources who need to be involved" (p. 132). We would expand on Gorski's statement in several ways. First, the "therapist" may be you—school counselor, marriage and family therapist, social worker, mental health counselor, or rehabilitation counselor. Many treatment programs do not have a formal, structured relapse-prevention program that coordinates the necessary services and people for successful relapse prevention (one reason we want you to be familiar with relapse prevention strategies). Second, Gorski says "therapist" as if the assumption is that all clients will have such a person. If you have been attending to the discussion in this chapter, you can see that it is essential that recovering individuals be involved with a mental health professional. The behavioral, cognitive, and affective strategies we have mentioned require the expertise of trained "helpers." Although Twelve Step meetings are a wonderful form of support in recovery, they are not designed to individually address the needs of recovering individuals. The "core psychological issues" that may lead to relapse require the involvement of mental health professionals. Finally, for adolescents, support involves more than just family members and Twelve Step meetings and sponsors. Imagine that Anna returns to school after treatment. As a 16 year old, her primary goals in life are to have friends and have fun. She also sincerely wants to remain abstinent. If she does not have a school-based support group of nonusing peers and no organized activities are available that do not involve the use of alcohol and other drugs, it is highly probable that she will relapse, in spite of her good intentions. We believe school personnel have an obligation and a challenge to help recovering adolescents such as Anna develop school-based support.

The involvement of the family in relapse prevention is certainly critical. "Numerous studies have substantiated a positive correlation between abstinence... and the presence of family and social supports" (Daley & Marlatt, 1992, p. 537). Furthermore, "Families of the chemically dependent are more likely to support rather than sabotage an addict's recovery if they are involved in the recovery process and have an opportunity to heal from the emotional pain they experienced" (Daley & Marlatt, 1992, pp. 537–538). This is not as simple a process as it may seem. As we saw in Chapter 10, although family therapy may be necessary in many cases, constellations and dynamics of families are very complex. For example, Anna and her mother are in family therapy. But, what about her actively alcoholic biological father? He's not involved and may have some investment in Anna's returning to use in order to justify his own use pattern. In a family in which the child with an alcohol or other drug problem plays the "scapegoat" role, the family "hero" may subtly sabotage recovery to maintain the family roles (see Chapter 10).

Life-Style Changes

At the risk of beleaguering poor Anna, let's look at other aspects of her life that require some attention. We have already mentioned the history of sexual molestation that needs therapeutic attention. In addition to the negative emotions that have been generated, implications arise with regard to her sexual behavior, choice of partners in relationships, and more. She is obese and has problems with acne, indicating a need for nutritional and hygiene advice. Her IQ is low average and her academic skills are below grade level, so she needs remediation and vocational guidance. She also needs to work on her social skills, her conflict with her mother, her relationship with her father, developing support systems at school, and more.

Does this seem like a lot of "stuff" to work on? It certainly is, and each area can lead to relapse. Now imagine a 47-year-old man who has been abusing alcohol for 25 years. Due to his use, he has physical, legal, financial, family, and vocational problems, all of which causes stress and conflict—high-risk situations for relapse.

As you can see, successful relapse prevention does not simply involve a client's ability to cope with high-risk situations. Many high-risk situations result from the life-style of the client and the client's inability to modify this life-style. Many such modifications are difficult and require significant investments of time and resources. Let's examine some of these life-style areas and the modifications necessary for relapse prevention.

Leisure Time

What do you do in your spare time? (We know. You are a student and you don't have spare time. Just pretend). Do you read, exercise, have a hobby? Many people with alcohol and other drug problems have had only one leisure time activity—using. When you remove alcohol and other drugs, these people don't know what to do with themselves. They become bored, but are avoiding their only known method to relieve boredom. We have had clients become intense workaholics after treatment to alleviate the fear of having any free time. We also find clients attending one AA meeting after another because they don't know what else to do. We recently worked with a middle-aged man who had completed an alcohol treatment program at the Salvation Army. Each day, he would work at the Salvation Army, attend an AA meeting, and then wander around the casinos in town. Not surprisingly, it wasn't long before he started to use again.

Support Systems

We have already mentioned the importance of support systems. This is certainly related to leisure time. If a recovering person has a circle of friends, he or she has something to do with his or her free time and will become involved with the interests and activities of friends. However, many recovering people have not had contact for years, if at all, with people who are nonusers. Furthermore, recovering clients are often advised during treatment to discontinue contact with friends who use but, as we will discuss, may not have developed the social and communication skills needed to develop new friends. If the recovering person does not develop an alternative social support system, the options may be isolation or the resumption of the old relationships that involved alcohol and other drug use. Certainly, Twelve Step meetings provide a structure to meet nonusing people. However, it is essential to assist in the development of healthy support systems and to not rely solely on Twelve Step meetings, particularly with adolescents.

Social and Communication Skills

If a client does not have appropriate social and communication skills, he or she can attend all the Twelve Step meetings available and still not be able to develop a social network. Many people with alcohol and other drug problems have not had to rely on social or communication skills to have "friends". Simply having money and alcohol or other drugs probably created a social network. They may have never been in a social situation without being under the influence. Clients might need training in listening skills, asking people questions about themselves, or practice in "small talk". We have found the lack of social skills to be a particular problem with adolescents, who normally feel awkward in new social situations. But many adult clients feel like adolescents too, because their social skill development has been truncated by their alcohol and other drug use. In addition, assertiveness training and stress and anger management may be needed. Clients may have simply used alcohol and other drugs in situations in which stress was encountered. In the absence of using alcohol or other drugs, these clients may demonstrate passive or aggressive responses to conflict.

Self-Care

Anna needs advice on nutrition and hygiene in a caring and supportive way. If her self-esteem improves, she might pay more attention to this area, but she simply may not know how to eat, dress, or even wash to make herself look better. She may need an adult's help in making the best of what nature has given her. Self-care is a relapse issue because people tend to tease or reject those who are inattentive to their appearance and hygiene. Teasing and rejection can certainly elicit negative emotional states, which we discussed earlier as a significant cause of relapse. While self-care is a sensitive area and may be embarrassing to discuss, the following case illustrates the importance of this area in relapse prevention. We worked with a man who was recovering and trying to find employment. He was quite obese, sloppily dressed, and had halitosis and body odor. Needless to say, he was not having much luck in interviews. We would not have been doing a good job if we had not been honest with him about his self-care issues, especially since his discouragement over his lack of a job was a high-risk situation.

Advice on nutrition, dress, and hygiene are not the only self-care issues with which clients may need assistance. Exercise might have been neglected during the time the clients were using, and they may need guidance with the development of an exercise program. Clients may also need assistance with the discontinuation of other unhealthy addictions such as tobacco use. In addition to the health hazards of tobacco use, smoking has an effect on energy level, and the growing intolerance of smoking can have social ramifications.

Educational and Vocational Guidance

It is common for school and jobs to be affected by alcohol and other drug problems. Also, these areas can be high-risk situations for many different reasons. As we saw with Anna, her scholastic aptitude and poor academic achievement contributed to making school an unpleasant experience. An unsatisfying or unpleasant job can also elicit negative emotions. Frequently, a client may be reluctant to return to the same school or to the job he or she had before treatment because the people and/or the situation there may be associated with use. With adult clients, community colleges and vocational rehabilitation can be resources for educational and vocational guidance. For school-aged clients, high schools generally have vocational counselors and school psychologists who may be of assistance with low achieving or low scholastic aptitude youngsters.

Financial Planning

Clients may need financial guidance for two reasons. The first is that they may have financial problems because of their alcohol and other drug use. Second, the client may have little experience with budgeting, since the priority for money was to secure the drug(s) of choice. Financial issues may require attention because they can be a source of stress, negative emotions, and interpersonal conflict. For example, a client goes through treatment and is working on remaining abstinent. For the first time in a long time, the client is taking his responsibilities seriously. Whereas creditors were ignored when the client was using, now he is making an attempt to clear up his debts, but he has no idea how to negotiate with creditors and budget his current income. Creditors are making harassing phone calls, he can't get his car fixed, and he has no money for recreation. Does this sound like a set-up for relapse?

Relationships

A few years ago, we worked with a 37-year-old client named Gene who had been sober for 18 months. Gene had been using alcohol and other drugs since he was 14. The longest relationship he had ever been in had lasted six months. Due to the length of time he had been using, emotional attachment, commitment, and inter-dependence were all unfamiliar to Gene. He sought therapy when he slipped after the end of a short relationship with a woman he met in AA. After a couple of dates and sex, he had proposed to the woman and she had dumped him. Clearly, Gene needed some help with many aspects of relationship development and management.

Although Gene may seem to be an extreme case, relationship problems are a cause of many relapses. Recovering adults may have virtually no experience in relationships while drug free. They may not be able to make logical decisions in the face of the intense emotions that romantic relationships can generate. They may not have a basis for making decisions about potential partners. In many ways, working with adult recovering clients can be like counseling an infatuated adolescent who is "in lust" for the first time. The emotional roller coaster of relationships can be high risk for many clients.

Balance

In reading this section, you may have experienced some sense of being overwhelmed with all the areas that may need attention. Clients can have this experience as well. As a mental health professional, you might contribute to a client's frustrations if you list all the life-style changes a client must make to prevent relapse. Presenting a recovering client with all of these life-style changes at once would probably result in an immediate relapse. Certainly, these areas must be prioritized and then be worked on in increments. As we discussed in the section on covert relapse planning, if a client perceives a great imbalance between "shoulds" and "wants," this perception alone can lead to relapse. It is usually easy for clients and mental health professionals to develop long lists of "shoulds." But it is also important to help clients achieve a balance in their lives so they can have some fun and pleasure. It takes most people a number of years to mess up their lives with alcohol and other drugs. So in spite of a client's desire to repair everything quickly, it will probably take a number of years to clear up their lives as well.

Preventing Slips from Escalating

Earlier in the chapter, we discussed the frequency of slips and relapses. Given the fact that it is more common than not for a client to return to use following treatment, it makes sense to develop strategies to reduce the likelihood of a slip's progressing to a relapse. However, this is a sticky issue in the treatment field. Since most treatment programs are abstinence based, you might feel a hesitancy to introduce such strategies, since doing so may provide an excuse to a client to use again. The alternative to withholding these techniques is not attractive either because, if a client does slip, he or she has no "weapons" to use to prevent the slip from escalating. In fact, without the knowledge that slips are common, the client's feeling of failure might contribute to further use. As we stated earlier, the conflict, guilt, and shame a client may experience after a slip has been termed the *abstinence violation effect* (AVE) by Marlatt (1985), and "The AVE involves perceived loss of control that undermines self-efficacy and increases expectations of continued failure" (Annis, 1990, p. 121). In our own experience, we have found it useful to discuss slips, AVE, and strategies to limit slips in the context of an expectation that the client will remain abstinent. We believe that it is important to attempt to limit a client's guilt and blame if a slip occurs, so that the client will be more likely to discuss the slip with a mental health professional.

Marlatt (1985) describes strategies to limit slips. One such strategy is a relapse contract. "The purpose of this procedure is to establish a working agreement or therapeutic contract to limit the extent of use should a lapse occur" (p. 59). The contract includes an agreement to "time out" if a slip occurs. In other words, the client agrees to leave the situation when this happens. Clients can also carry reminder cards that contain specific steps, including people to call if a slip occurs. The cards also have cognitive and behavioral reminders such as "Remember, you are in control," "This slip is not a catastrophe. you can stop now if you choose," and "Imagine yourself in control." Clients may also carry a decision matrix they have developed with a counselor. The decision matrix contains the immediate and delayed consequences of use and, hopefully, would be reviewed after a slip, reminding the client of the consequences of continuing to use. Clearly, these strategies rely on pre-planning that would convince a client to use the techniques immediately following a slip. If the slip continues, the cognitive impairment resulting from use would impact the effectiveness of these strategies.

Summary

Relapse prevention is a critical component of recovery and often involves mental health professionals other than alcohol and other drug counselors. Since return to use following treatment is a common occurrence, it is important for comprehensive relapse prevention planning to occur. Although there are different models of relapse prevention, the strategies employed have much in common. These include assessment of high-risk situations; strategies for coping with high-risk situations including education, individualized strategies, dealing with urges and cravings, and support systems; life-style changes; and strategies for preventing slips from escalating to relapse. Since there are so many areas requiring attention, as a mental health professional, you must be cautious to avoid overwhelming clients.

Chapter *14*

HIV/AIDs

According to Primm (1992), five cases of *Pneumocystis carinii* pneumonia were reported to the Centers for Disease Control (CDC) in Atlanta in May, 1981. In December of that same year, more than 100 cases of Kaposi's sarcoma (a form of cancerous skin lesion) were reported in homosexual men. The unusual occurance of these two maladies caused suspicion and spawned further investigation, so that in September, 1982, the Centers for Disease Control identified and labeled the acquired immunodeficiency syndrome (AIDs) as resulting from HIV infection. Although the White House Conference for a Drug Free America barely mentioned HIV in 1988, the Presidential Commission on the Human Immunodeficiency Virus Epidemic issued a separate report calling for increased research into treatment modes, increased treatment capacity, strengthening of primary and secondary prevention and early intervention programs, and an aggressive outreach program in HIV-related prevention and education.

In the time it took you to read the above page, one more American has been infected with HIV. By the time you finish reading this chapter, three more will have died from AIDs. By the end of the day, 212 more Americans will be diagnosed with full blown AIDs (Primm, 1992).

Prevalence and Incidence

In spite of efforts to curtail the spread of AIDs, approximately 4 million people have contracted HIV (the precursor to AIDs) in the United States, and over 325,000 cases of diagnosed AIDs have been reported to the Centers for Disease Control. Over 200,000 deaths have occurred (Needles, 1994). These deaths have resulted from diagnosed AIDs, and estimates of undiagnosed AIDs cases may reach 1 million (Primm, 1992). Worldwide, there are 10 million people with HIV, and by the year 2000 it is estimated that between 30 and 110 million people will be infected with HIV (Primm, 1992).

HIV was first identified among gay and bisexual men, and men who have sex with men still constitute the majority of AIDs cases in the United States (Battjes, 1994). However, cases of AIDs among women are on the rise. O'Leary (1994) reports that of the 28,000 cases of AIDs among females reported by December, 1992, roughly half were reported during 1991 and 1992 alone. The World Health Organization (WHO) estimates that 3 million women and children will die from AIDs in the 1990s—more than six times the number that died in the 1980s (Primm, 1992). In addition, several million children will become orphans in this decade due to parental death from AIDs. There are over 4 million infants born to American women infected with HIV, and, as a result, about 1 million babies themselves are infected with HIV (Primm, 1992). The incidence of HIV in children of African American or Latino intravenous (IV) drug using women living in New York City suggests that this population is particularly vulnerable: Of the AIDs infants in that city, about 77% contracted the virus either because the mother herself was an IV drug user or she was a sex partner of an IV drug user (Primm, 1992).

As of 1992, heterosexual contact accounted for only 3% of all reported AIDs cases in the United States (Inciardi, 1994). While comprising only a small proportion of AIDs cases in the general population, heterosexuals are over-represented among IV drug users with AIDs. According to Needles (1994), about 30% of AIDs cases in the United States involve IV drug users, and 80% of these reported cases are among heterosexuals. The same author states that male IV drug users constitute about 75% of the AIDs cases among all heterosexual IV drug users. Again, however, IV drug-using women and their children are increasingly at risk. This is reflected in geographic as well as ethnographic studies.

For women between the ages of 20 and 40 living in the city of New York, AIDs is the leading cause of all deaths. Moreover, according to this same author, of the 2,380 cases of pediatric AIDs in the United States reported to the Centers for Disease Control within the first six months of 1990, 28% of this total were found in New York City (Primm, 1992), and 91% of those pediatric cases involved a mother who was either African American or Latino.

Since first diagnosed, an association between HIV infection, drug use, and sexually transmitted diseases (STDs) has been found. According to Des Jarlais and Friedman (1987), although many drug users are practicing safer drug-use behaviors (presumedly to reduce risk of HIV transmission), they are not practicing safer sex behaviors. The presence of anal and genital ulcerations often present in STDs have been found to be a "strong independent risk factor for HIV infection in both men and women" (Selwyn, 1992, p.753). Aside from STDs, a growing number of cases of serious bacterial infections (e.g., bacterial pneumonia, endocarditis, and bacterial sepsis); hepatitis B virus (HBV), and tuberculosis (TB) have been found among those diagnosed with HIV (Selwyn, 1992). Recent reports from sub-Saharan Africa indicate an alarming rise in the co-infection of *Mycobacterium tuberculosis* and HIV (Selwyn, 1992). In the United States, the co-occupance of TB and HIV sounds a similar alarm, especially for minority population IV drug users living in the northeastern and southeastern cities. Studies have found that 40% of the patients in those cities who were treated for TB also had HIV (Centers for Disease Control, 1989).

The higher incidence of AIDs among African Americans and Latinos in these cities is partially explained by Schoenbaum, Hartel, and Selwyn (1989). They maintain that the higher incidence of AIDs in these minority groups may be due to behavioral and environmental factors resulting from living in poor, overcrowded inner cities. In addition, a higher concentration of IV drug use occurs among those living in those United States cities.

AIDs is found throughout the world. As a result, beliefs and stereotypes about the typical AIDs victim has changed dramatically. For example, until recently intravenous (IV) drug use was considered essentially an American disease, and AIDs was seen as a disease spread sexually by homosexual men in industrialized countries (Des Jarlais, Friedman, Woods, & Milliken, 1992). While IV drug use continues to be associated with a greater number of HIV cases in the Unites States, IV drug use is now related to an increase in HIV infection in the populations of countries in southern Europe and Latin America, and in Australia, Thailand, and Myanmar (formerly called Burma) (Sato, Chin, & Mann, 1989; Selwyn, 1992). Of the total cases of AIDs in the United States and Europe alone, about 30% involved IV drug use as a risk behavior (Des Jarlais et al., 1992).

Myths and Facts about HIV and AIDs

Because of the severity of the AIDs epidemic, rumors and misinformation about the disease abound. In general, three areas of interest and of potential misinformation can be identified. One area is information about HIV itself—what it is, what it does, and how an individual infected with HIV will appear to others. Another area of concern relates to how HIV is transmitted, and the third area focuses on the workplace—what employers can and cannot do regarding a worker with HIV or AIDs.

The HIV Virus

Human immunodeficiency virus is known as HIV. The virus attacks a person's immune system, thereby damaging the individual's ability to fight off other opportunistic diseases such as pneumonia or cancers. Once an individual is infected with HIV, it may take years for acquired immunodeficiency syndrome (AIDs) to develop. Individuals infected with HIV develop a characteristic serum antibody response that can usually be detected between 2 weeks and 6 months following exposure (Selwyn, 1992). However, it is possible for as much as 6 months to 2 years to pass before one's body begins producing detectable HIV antibodies (Pimentel & Lamendella, 1988).

Testing for HIV
The HIV antibody test reflects only exposure to the AIDs virus, but this exposure does not mean that the person will develop the AIDs disease syndrome. It is possible for a person to test positive for HIV antibodies and suffer no detectable immune system damage, feel healthy, and not develop the full AIDs disease

syndrome. The incubation period between HIV infection and AIDs is 7 to 10 years (Selwyn, 1992). However, once individuals have been infected with HIV, there is a great likelihood they will develop AIDs—the only unknown factor is when this will occur, since the progression of illness is unpredictable. Approximately 50% of people with HIV will develop AIDs within 6 years of exposure (Pimentel & Lamendella, 1988). Although early detection of HIV and medical treatment can slow the progression of AIDs significantly, medical treatment cannot stop AIDs from developing.

Diagnosis of AIDs and AIDs Related Complex

AIDs and AIDs Related Complex (ARC) are medical diagnoses indicating a specific set of characteristic symptoms. A diagnosis of AIDs is made when any of twelve opportunistic infections (e.g., *Pneumocystis carinii* pneumonia) and/or any of three malignancies (e.g., Kaposi's sarcoma) are reliably diagnosed in the absence of any other known cause for immunodeficiency (CDC, 1986). AIDs Related Complex refers to the condition of those individuals who have damaged immune systems and some specific symptoms, which include night sweats, weight loss, and lymphoma, but who do not have any of the opportunistic infections associated with AIDs. An individual may be diagnosed as having AIDs Related Complex and be sick some of the time with less serious opportunistic infections than those found in AIDs cases. Individuals with AIDs or AIDs Related Complex may show signs of a disease, but they will not always be sick. Thus, an individual may test antibody positive but show no signs of opportunistic diseases. On the other hand, an individual may have full-blown AIDs where any number of opportunistic infections may be present.

To date, there is no known vaccine currently available that can prevent HIV infection. There is also no known cure for AIDs. Although new information is being discovered every day, at present a cure is not in sight (Selwyn, 1992).

Transmission of HIV

The Avenues of Transmission

There is consensus and certainty about how AIDs is transmitted, and no new information regarding this issue is expected. Anyone infected with HIV can infect others. According to the World Health Communication (1988), "HIV is transmitted primarily during sexual contact through parenteral exposure to blood and blood products, and from mother to child during the perinatal period" (p. 10). Hence, "The virus must be transmitted from the blood stream of a person with AIDs to the blood stream of another person" (Pimentel & Lamendella, 1988, p. 42). However, needles used by individuals with HIV to take drugs intravenously can transmit the infection to others sharing the same needle. Contaminated blood can also transmit HIV when used for transfusions. This is especially true for individuals (including hemophiliacs and persons with sickle cell disease) who received blood transfusions or blood product transfusions between 1978 and 1985 and for recipients of organ transplants prior to 1985 (U.S. Department of Health and Human Services, 1993). Since that time, however, safeguards regulating blood transfusions and organ transplants have greatly decreased, but not entirely eliminated, the likelihood of this occurring (World Health Organization, 1988). Similar safeguards protect blood donors from risk of HIV since hypodermic needles used for drawing blood are now discarded after use. Another avenue of transmission is the breast milk of HIV-infected mothers who may pass the infection to their babies.

Some of the popular fears surrounding the transmission of HIV concern working or living with someone who has HIV. In the workplace, no known risk of nonsexual infection exists in most of the standard working situations. Obviously, medical health care workers are more at risk than others, but protection is now generally provided for dentists, physicians, their assistants, and others who might come into contact with a patient's blood. Therefore, one is not at risk simply because he or she works alongside an individual infected with HIV or one who has full-blown AIDs.

Living with a Person with HIV

With some precautions, living with a person infected with HIV or AIDs is known to be safe because it is a safe conclusion that AIDs cannot be transmitted via casual contact. Practicing safer sex techniques by restricting sexual acts to those in which no bodily fluids are exchanged is recommended (Pimentel & Lamendella, 1988). Included in such sexual relations would be a restriction on French kissing, with "dry kissing" the recommendation. Unprotected oral sex increases the risk of transmission. Using latex (as opposed to natural membrane) condoms offers a degree of protection, but the use of condoms alone during intercourse is not recommended because of potential condom misuse. Proper use of condoms concomitant with a foam containing nonoxynol-9 is recommended because nonoxynol-9 kills the AIDs virus. No evidence suggests that eating utensils, drinking glasses, telephones, swimming pools, toilet seats, or computer keys are conduits for transmitting HIV or AIDs (Pimentel & Lamendella, 1988). Touching, hugging, shaking hands, or being in the same proximity with an HIV infected individual who sneezes or coughs does not pose any risk for transmitting HIV. Moreover, insects cannot transmit HIV, nor can a person get AIDs from being bitten or spit on by someone with AIDs (Pimentel & Lamendella, 1988).

Living with an HIV-infected person may pose a threat in the case of co-occurance of tuberculosis (Selwyn, 1992). Because of the risk of TB infection to household members, it is recommended that all who live with an HIV-infected individual be screened for TB and follow-up.

Issues in the Workplace

An employer cannot force an individual to have a test for HIV. Moreover, a person having HIV is not required to disclose the information to his or her employer. If, however, an infected individual who is symptom free chooses to disclose the information to his or her employer, the employer cannot tell anyone without both a compelling reason and the infected employee's permission. (This is based upon the fact that casual contact with a HIV-infected individual is not a venue of transmission.) It is not legal for an employer to attempt to decrease insurance coverage, avoid paying insurance, or cancel benefits for an infected individual. An employer cannot fire someone from their job once it is certain that the person has HIV "because persons with infectious diseases are officially considered disabled, and AIDs is treated legally just as any other disability (Pimentel & Lamendella, 1988, p. 44). Nevertheless, any employee, including an individual with AIDs, may be fired if the individual is absent so much that it affects productivity. If an individual infected with AIDs is showing symptoms of the opportunistic diseases that result from a damaged immune system, "then issues of reasonable accommodation in the workplace apply (Pimentel & Lamendella, p. 15). Essentially, this suggests that an employer will not be able to make accommodations for a person with a disability unless the employer is made aware of the disability. Therefore, it may help both the person with AIDs and the employer if the latter were made aware of the condition.

Risk Factors and High-Risk Populations

General Risk Factors

Although the IV drug users living in the northeastern and southeastern U.S. cities continue to account for the heaviest concentration of AIDs cases, HIV infection has been increasing among all drug users outside of this geographical location (Hahn, Onorato, Jones, & Dougherty, 1989). Simply using drugs increases one's risk for HIV (Primm, 1992). Because of this fact, heterosexuals are not immune to HIV infection, and HIV is being passed from one HIV-infected, drug-using partner to the other partner during traditional heterosexual relations in greater frequency than before (Des Jarlais et al., 1992). For example, more than two-thirds of all AIDs cases among U.S. women involve their drug use or the drug use of their male partners. Based on this information, Selwyn (1992) maintains that "AIDs and drug use are virtually inseparable" (p. 744). Reasons given for this strong association are varied, but a main reason may be the effect of drug use upon one's judgments and decisions about sex. For example, while under the influence of drugs, individuals can often become more careless about practicing safer sex (i.e., using condoms), may be less willing to assert themselves with their partners, and may not discuss sexual histories that might influence one's decision to engage in sex. In fact, even without drug use, most single Americans have not changed their sexual habits (Pimentel and Lamendella, 1988). These same authors state that "Approximately 50% of single people are not modifying their behavior in ways that will actually protect them from AIDs" (p. 48).

Barthwell and Gibert (1993) have identified behavioral and other risk indicators for HIV infection. In reviewing records of HIV cases, they found that having unprotected oral, vaginal, or anal sex with an HIV-infected individual or with anyone who is at risk for HIV increases one's risk. This is also true for individuals who have multiple sex partners. These authors also found that a man having anal sex with another man also increases risk. Moreover, a history of prostitution also increases risk as does a man having sex with a man during incarceration. In terms of specific geographical locations, Barthwell and Gibert (1993) state that having lived in, or having a sexual partner from, the Caribbean basin—especially Haiti and sub-Saharan Africa where HIV is endemic—increases one's risk for contracting HIV.

High-Risk Groups

Gay and Bisexual Males
As stated earlier, this group continues to be over-represented among those who are at high risk for HIV-infection. According to Battjes (1994), 60% of the reported AIDs cases have occurred in men who reported having sex with men. Moreover, the group of gay and bisexual males who use nonmedically prescribed psychoactive drugs are at an increased risk (Ostrow, 1994).

Gay and Bisexual Male IV Drug Users
Based on data from AIDs cases, Battjes (1994) maintains that gay and bisexual male IV drug users are considered to be in a dual risk group and "are at substantially increased risk for AIDs compared with persons reporting either risk behavior alone" (p. 83). Part of the reason for the increased risk among this population is that this group reports more high-risk sexual activity than their non-IV drug-using counterparts (Stall & Ostrow, 1989).

Female Partners of HIV-Infected Males
It is now believed that heterosexual transmission has become a prominent source of female infection (O'Leary, 1994), and women who have unprotected sex with HIV-infected males appear to be at a higher risk for infection. In addition, those women who become sexually involved with a male IV drug user are also at a high risk (Selwyn, 1992). For example, Brown and Primm (1988a) found that the female AIDs clients in their study revealed that 63% of their sexual partners were IV drug abusers.

Reasons for increased risk among women in general has been associated with the fact that HIV transmission to women is apparently more efficient when the partner is male (O'Leary, 1994). Other factors include poverty, cultural factors, personal characteristics, beliefs and attitudes regarding condoms, and partner relationship issues (O'Leary, 1994). For example, the increased risk for women in general is exacerbated when women do not insist upon safer sex practices (i.e., the use of latex condoms concomitant with nonoxynol-9). However, not insisting upon safer sex is a complicated issue. DeBruyn (1992) found that some women do not insist upon condom use because it may suggest to a partner that he has been unfaithful; it may suggest that she, herself, has been unfaithful; and it may suggest that she has been infected with HIV. Nevertheless, the lack of safer sex practices coupled with other risk factors does put women at an increased risk.

African Americans and Latinos

Whereas AIDs accounted for 3% of the deaths of Euro-American women between the ages of 25 and 34 in 1988, it accounted for 11% of the deaths of African American women in the same age bracket during the same year. Latino women, Latino men, and African American males do not fare much better. In fact, although comprising 18% of the U.S. population, African Americans and Latinos of both sexes account for 39% of the AIDs cases (Brown & Primm, 1988b). The overwhelmingly high incidence of HIV in minority populations may be partly explained by the concentration of IV drug abuse in those populations. However, because of the paucity of research into minority drug abuse (see Chapter 4), one can really only surmise reasons for this remarkably high incidence. Another factor identified as being associated with a higher incidence of HIV infection among minorities is the general distrust of the health care system by these groups—especially minority women—that may heighten resistance for preventive help (O'Leary, 1994). Magana and Magana (1992) believe that many Latino women are at risk because of the behavior of their husbands who are allowed by their norms to engage in male extramarital affairs and have frequent sex with men—both high-risk factors for HIV infection.

Adolescents

Studies examining adolescents' and young adults' attitudes and knowledge regarding HIV/AIDs, alcohol and other drug use, sexual behavior, and sexually transmitted diseases suggests that this group is at substantial risk for HIV infection. This is especially true for minority adolescents, who are over-represented among persons with AIDs relative to the general population (CDC, 1993). In the general adolescent population, risk of HIV infection is due to a variety issues. For example, Smeriglio (1994) and Boyer and Ellen (1994) identified that adolescents begin sexual intercourse at earlier ages than ever before, and many do not protect themselves from diseases. Moreover, these same authors point out that sexually transmitted diseases and pregnancy rates among this population are high and that the use of substances, especially alcohol, is common. It is for these reasons that Boyer and Ellen (1994) are able to report that most adolescents with AIDs were infected as a result of high-risk sexual behaviors or IV drug use. Poverty also contributes to the risk of HIV infection in adolescents, especially among poor, inner-city African American and Latino youth under age 18. Because adolescence is the period when the search for self-identity is strongest, experimentation with a variety of behaviors is to be expected; therefore, this group will likely remain at risk until a cure is found.

Clients in Drug Treatment Centers

Because research suggests that drug use increases one's risk for HIV, it should not be surprising that the incidence and prevalence of HIV/AIDs among patients in drug treatment centers is high. However, only a small minority of drug abusers are in treatment programs, and, by the time they enter treatment, their HIV-related problems "may be largely beyond the reach of most human services" (Sorensen & Batki, 1992). This most likely means that the large majority of drug users infected with HIV are not in treatment centers and may not even know they are infected with HIV.

Those in the Penal System
Some infected individuals are also in the prison system, where a survey of 70 state, federal, and local correctional centers revealed a cumulative total of 1,964 confirmed cases of AIDs (Primm, 1992). However, criminals with HIV who are on probation and parole may be undetected. This is due partially to the fact that much of the educational information disseminated by probation and parole departments is aimed at those believed to be at high risk for HIV, but, according to Primm (1992), "such programs may miss many drug abusers (and their sexual partners) because criminal justice records and arrest or conviction charges are poor indicators of drug abuse" (p. 617). Moreover, because of the extensive overcrowding in the nation's jails, criminals charged with minor infractions—many of whom may have drug-abuse problems putting them at high risk for HIV infection—are routinely released back into the community.

The Homeless
The homeless present another population at high risk for HIV because of their high incidence of drug abuse. Currently, it is estimated that there are three million homeless people in the United States, and about one million of these individuals are drug abusers (Primm, 1992). In addition, communicable diseases, especially tuberculosis and hepatitis, are also rampant among the homeless population because of poor hygiene, inadequate nutrition, a lack of medical care, crowded shelters, and the unsanitary conditions that prevail among this population (U.S. Department of Health and Human Services, 1993).

Other Groups
Other groups at high risk for HIV and/or other infectious diseases include homeless adolescents, individuals with a history of sexually transmitted diseases, people living in public housing or poor urban dwellers, and young babies who are breastfed by HIV-infected mothers.

Assessment of Clients for HIV and AIDs: Signs and Symptoms

As you saw earlier in this chapter, early detection and medical treatment can forestall the onset of AIDs and ARC, although to date nothing can eliminate the probability of AIDs once a person has been infected with HIV. Although the diagnosis of HIV can be made only by testing positive for the HIV antibody, several indicators might suggest the presence of the infection in clients who have not undergone medical testing for the virus. Therefore, it is important that you, as mental health professionals, be aware of issues that suggest the presence of HIV in order to urge high-risk clients to be tested and, hopefully, to receive appropriate medical intervention if they show early stages of infection. When risk factors are coupled with other signs and symptoms, it is crucial that every attempt be made to refer the client for assessment of HIV infection. These other signs and symptoms include physical anomalies and neuropsychiatric disturbances.

Physical Signs and Symptoms

It is customary for mental health professionals to initially elicit a psychosocial, drug, and brief medical history from their clients. In the course of that interview, clients may mention many symptoms that, to them, may seem unrelated to the risk of HIV infection. These signs and symptoms may include complaints of fever, unexplained weight loss or loss of appetite, night sweats, general malaise, coughing and/or shortness of breath, swollen lymph nodes, recurrent or persistent sinusitis, abdominal pain, diarrhea, and visual changes such as visual field defects (Barthwell & Gibert, 1993). Other symptoms that should alert you to the possibility of HIV may be dermatological conditions such as genital warts, rashes, herpes zoster (shingles), and psoriasis (U.S. Department of Health and Human Services, 1993). Although these symptoms are not diagnostic nor unique to HIV, these coupled with a history of substance abuse may help guide your efforts in evaluating the possibility of HIV infection.

HIV-Related Neuropsychiatric Signs and Symptoms

Aside from a psychosocial, drug, and medical history, a mental status examination may also reveal clinically significant signs and symptoms of HIV infection. If clients present themselves with the following organic issues, you would need to refer them for further medical work-up.

Delirium

Fernandez and Ruiz (1992) state, "Of all the organic mental disorders associated with HIV infection, delirium is the most prevalent" (p. 781). According to these same authors, delirium may also be the most underdiagnosed of all organic disorders. Common symptoms of delirium in HIV-infected individuals include difficulty in thinking, restlessness, irritability, insomnia, or interrupted short periods of sleep containing vivid nightmares. Delirium fluctuates throughout the day, and typically worsens at night.

AIDs Dementia Complex

It was once thought that severe cognitive impairment occurred in those patients who were in the more advanced stages of AIDs. However, it is now recognized that cognitive impairment can occur at any time during the course of the infection (Fernandez & Ruiz, 1992). Known as AIDs dementia complex, HIV-infected individuals may exhibit impairment of verbal memory, attention and retention, information processing, psychomotor speed, cognitive flexibility, nonverbal problem-solving, visuospacial integration and construction, and nonverbal memory

(Fernandez & Ruiz, 1992). Van Gorp, Miller, Satz, and Visscher (1989) found that, in the early stages of AIDs, the areas of cognitive impairment will likely include problems with psychomotor tasks, memory tasks, and delayed recall. Other early manifestations of dementia include general memory loss, impaired concentration, apathy, agitation, depressive mood, psychotic features, unsteady gait, tremors, clumsiness, and motor weakness (Fernandez & Levy, 1990). It is important to note that, "The profound dementia that is part of AIDs dementia complex [that] occurs in the absence of opportunistic infections or neoplasia [tumors] . . . is now accepted as diagnostic of AIDs" (Fernandez & Ruiz, 1992, p. 777). That is, a diagnosis of AIDs can now be made when there is severe dementia without the presence of any of the usual co-occurring opportunistic infections.

Depression

According to some researchers, close to 85% of HIV-infected individuals will exhibit some form of mood disturbance (Fernandez and Ruiz, 1992; Perry & Tross, 1984). Although depression is the most common form of mood disturbance, manic and hypomanic disturbances have also been reported (Fernandez & Ruiz, 1992). In general, depression in HIV-infected persons is more common than in the general population of mentally ill individuals or in the general population itself (Fernandez & Ruiz, 1992). This observation has lead some to suggest that there may be certain features of HIV infection that contribute to a depressive syndrome (Fernandez & Ruiz, 1992). In addition, these same authors point out that it is difficult to formulate an accurate diagnosis of depression in HIV disease "because the usual diagnostic indicators of depression are also common to both HIV-systemic disease and to HIV-related impairment" (p. 783).

The gravity of this last statement is reflected in concern for the suicidal ideation that will likely also be present in HIV-infected individuals. There is consensus among mental health professionals that clinical depression and/or stress impairment are usual precipitating factors in patients who complete suicide, so a determination of the origin of depression may be key in the intervention process.

Helping HIV-Infected Clients

Clients with HIV can manage only the disease process and the disease itself. So, once a client is diagnosed with HIV or AIDs, your concern as a mental health professional will be to focus on helping the client attempt to manage and cope with the disease. The World Health Communications (1988) has published a handbook addressing the management and treatment of HIV-infected clients. In general, helping the HIV-infected client focuses on assisting the client in understanding and accepting the changes that are occurring and will occur in their lives. Educating the client about the disease and treatment is also important, as is the emphasis on the fact that AIDs is not necessarily fatal. This last statement is critical because general misconceptions about the disease are held by the public and by many HIV-infected individuals. For example, one of the authors' HIV infected clients stated during the second group therapy session, "Having HIV is like living with a time bomb. The only thing you know is that the bomb will go off. You never know when or where you'll be in life when it goes off. All you know is just that it will explode someday and you'll die." Helping clients identify and evaluate their existing supportive networks and develop strategies to invoke further help is also an important focus for counselors (World Health Communications, 1988). Finally, this organization recommends that counselors assist HIV-infected clients cope with the multiple effects of the disease, which will include psychosocial issues, in some cases drug treatment issues for drug-abusing clients, psychological issues, and issues regarding medical treatment.

Psychosocial Concerns of HIV-Infected Clients

Vital in the approach to helping drug-abusing clients with HIV is a coordinated effort between the psychological, medical, social services, legal, pastoral and religious, peer support groups, significant family members, and other community-based service networks (Selwyn, 1992). The plethora of services required by these clients is due to the myriad tasks needing attention once the individual has AIDs. Selwyn (1992) purports that, for the young heterosexual HIV population, there will be issues surrounding childbearing, child support and custody, and orphanhood that will need to be addressed. These family issues will likely require the assistance of social and legal services. Legal services may also be needed in helping to determine a person who will be designated as having power of attorney (POA) for the client; also, this necessity should be addressed before the onset of delirium or AIDs dementia complex that can leave the client adjudicated as incompetent. The HIV-infected client may be reluctant to ask for help in seemingly unimportant areas of his or her life. This neglect can impact surviving loved ones, so the term *coordinated effort* takes on special significance. Such coordinated effort can also help to identify the services needed to avoid a duplication of services—an issue that might increase client reluctance in asking for assistance.

Another area of concern is the client's sexuality and the risk of HIV transmission. Understanding the sexual aspects of the disease is of paramount importance, and frank communication between you as the mental health professional and your client is essential. Human touch is essential to everyone, and the client should be encouraged to hug his or her loved ones as well as to engage in safe sex. However, if an individual has already been exposed to HIV infection and has unprotected sexual relations with another infected individual, an acceleration of the disease process may be experienced. So it is important to emphasize the importance of safer sex practices among already infected HIV clients (World Health Communications, 1988). Clients should also be made aware of their own capacity to transmit the HIV infection.

Clients tend to do better and remain longer in the home setting when they have a caretaker (World Health Communications, 1988). Therefore, home health care and other supportive systems should be explored. Often these supportive networks are nontraditional, therefore some exploration of community resources may be indicated. Identifying individuals and services that the client can access during a time of crisis can help allay fears regarding how he or she will be cared for. One of the goals of this identification is to help the HIV client avoid isolation, and many community, volunteer-based support systems are available for assistance. Ideally, these systems allow the client to live freely within his or her physical limitations.

Treatment Concerns for Drug-Abusing HIV-Infected Clients

Des Jarlais, Friedman, Woods, and Milliken (1992) report that, although it is clear that drug abuse treatment has helped prevent the spread of HIV infection in many individuals, the effectiveness of drug treatment in preventing the spread among IV drug users has yet to be demonstrated. Preventing the spread of HIV among IV drug users defies several drug treatment issues. For example, Des Jarlais et al., (1992) point out that many IV drug users are not motivated to enter treatment. Moreover, these same authors maintain that the current treatment programs are equipped to deal only with approximately 15 to 20% of IV drug users. Finally, Des Jarlais et al. (1992) believe that the low (15%) success rate (i.e., no reported relapse) in treating IV drug users underscores the need for repeated admissions for the vast majority of IV drug users to treatment. It is believed that the cost of expanding treatment for them is high and would constitute considerable time and effort.

Drug-abuse treatment for HIV-infected clients requires greater flexibility than generally exists in drug treatment programs (Sorenson & Batki, 1992). These same authors point out that it has also become necessary to be more flexible in addressing the duration of treatment of these individuals. The main reason for this concern is that, aside from drug-abuse issues, a frequent co-occupance of psychiatric disorders associated with HIV-infected clients may require therapeutic intervention (Batki, 1990; Sorenson, Costantini, & London, 1989).

Educating HIV-infected drug-abusing clients about the disease is imperative and is seen as departing from the usual drug treatment counseling. Families of HIV-infected clients may need strategies and skills to cope with the impact of the disease and will likely require help with their grieving process as well (Sorenson & Batki, 1992). In addition, clients, themselves, will probably need help with grieving. This process of letting go will take on special implications if they have friends who also have died or are dying of AIDs, because grieving will focus upon grief for themselves as well as for the loss of their friends. Selwyn (1992) maintains that during times of grieving, clients may relapse as a means of coping with these multiple losses.

The impact of simultaneously using drugs and being infected with HIV is unclear, and questions focus on the extent to which this dual existence is deleterious to the disease process. Some research suggests that alcohol and other drugs may exert adverse effects upon the lymphocyte function or on different elements of the immune system of HIV-infected clients, while other studies demonstrate no association between alcohol and other drug use and the suppression of the disease (Ginzburg, Weiss, MacDonald, & Hubbard, 1985; Kaslow, Blackwelder, & Ostrow, 1989). Regardless of the outcomes of these studies, it is generally believed that heavy involvement with alcohol and other drug use will eventually interfere with the primary medical care of HIV-infected individuals (Selwyn, Feingold, & Iezza, 1989).

In spite of the low rates of efficacy in treating IV drug abusers, including those with HIV infection, some individuals will respond to the disease with great inner strength and find resources that may have previously been unnoticed. Therefore, it is important that you maintain an open and informed mind when treating the drug-abusing HIV-infected client.

Emotional Concerns

Certainly, client reactions to having a catastrophic illness will be of paramount importance to mental health professionals working with this group of clients. This work likely will include helping clients prepare for death. In the *Treatment Handbook* (World Health Communications, 1988), it is suggested that using the grief process identified by Elizabeth Kubler-Ross (1969) can be helpful, while remembering that there are long-term AIDs survivors—those who have survived longer than five years. It is also important to help clients examine their quality-of-life-issues, with a focus on establishing a philosophical understanding about what is acceptable in terms of work and disability status. Regardless of the extent to which one can work or one wants to work, delaying hospitalization as long as possible is recommended (World Health Communications, 1988).

Clients who have HIV may present a number of emotional reactions that can include anxiety, stress-distress syndrome, panic reactions, suicidal ideation, rumination, depression, and a plethora of defense mechanisms such as denial, anger, guilt, and isolation (World Health Communications, 1988). These reactions have been gleaned from clinical impressions in working with HIV-infected clients as well as from studies on opiate addicts with AIDs or ARC. For example, Batki, Sorensen, Faltz, and Madover (1988) and Rounsaville, Weissman, Kleber, and Wilbur (1982) have identified that addicts with AIDs or ARC use denial as a defense mechanism and are also angry, isolated, and depressed.

Denial would certainly be a component of any client's grieving process when confronted with HIV. In HIV-infected, drug-abusing clients, however, denial about drug abuse as well as about having HIV may become more pronounced (Sorensen & Batki, 1992), and, as a result, clients and counselors can face a double-whammy of denial. However, it can be helpful for mental health professionals to understand that denial may only be a component of a larger construct of ambivalence: ambivalence about drug abuse and/or ambivalence about having HIV. In Chapter 6, we discussed the motivational interviewing techniques of Miller and Rollnick. One premise used in these techniques is that clients may be more accurately described as being ambivalent rather than being in denial about drug abuse. The client may actually sense that drugs may be a problem but may not be sure of the extent of the problem—or even if a problem truly exists. While this concept was originally intended for application to drug abusers, Miller and Rollnick's notion of ambivalence can apply as well to both HIV-infected drug-abusing clients and to those infected clients not abusing drugs. So, rather than being in denial about HIV infection *per se*, clients may be seen as experiencing ambivalence, and the techniques to reduce ambivalence described in Chapter 6 can be helpful and easily adapted to working with HIV-infected individuals. It should be noted, however, that denial and/or ambivalence can also be present in clients who are at high risk for HIV, and, if issues of denial and ambivalence are mishandled, it could be that they would refuse to be tested or refuse medical treatment or counseling interventions.

Anger displayed by people with HIV is to be expected, and in many cases is a sign of healthy adaptation to having been infected. However, it is possible that infected individuals could inappropriately displace their anger onto health care workers, family members, significant others, and at their healthcare management. Covert expression of this anger may be seen in individuals' missing appointments, in their refusal to comply with medical or counseling interventions, in their continued drug abuse, and/or in the selling of their medications. Some of this anger may be due to fear and mistrust of the system and of the care providers. This is exemplified by one of the author's own experiences: When running therapy groups for HIV-infected clients, a few group members attended only sporadically. Attendance became more stable only after the author had been "checked out" (clients' words) by other group members who passed the information along.

Mood disturbance such as depression, a phenomenon already common among drug abusers, is exacerbated in HIV-infected individuals (Sorensen & Batki, 1992). Moreover, isolation is characteristic of drug-abusing, HIV-infected individuals. According to Sorensen and Batki (1992), isolation occurs in two ways: First, if the person's drug abuse already places him or her outside of mainstream society, HIV only pushes him or her further away; and, second, if the individual already has difficulty in initiating and maintaining healthy social contacts (as is rather common in drug abusers) then this difficulty may be a significant barrier to treatment. Because of the isolation factor, outreach programs designed to identify high-risk individuals for testing and counseling need to be aggressive and skillfully handled.

Medical Concerns

Currently, Retrovir (AZT) is seen as the first anti-HIV agent indicated for the treatment of HIV disease, because the vast majority of clients appear to improve markedly within the first six to twelve months of administration (Barthwell & Gibert, 1993). Mental health professionals may hear their clients refer to other antiretroviral therapies such as ddC-zalcitabine (HIVID) and ddI-didanosine (Videx) that are used for the treatment of HIV. In addition to these antiretroviral agents, the U.S. Public Health Service recommends the use of prophylaxis for the prevention of the two common opportunistic infections, *Pneumocystis carinii* pneumonia (PCP) and *Mycobacterium avium* complex (Pimentel & Lamendella, 1988). PCP has been estimated to develop in 85% of HIV-infected persons.

Unfortunately, side effects are associated with antiretroviral agents (Barthwell & Gibert, 1993). These same authors state that many of the side effects of AZT will occur at the outset of chemotherapy and can include anemia, nausea, vomiting, headaches, fatigue, and mystosis. Oral ulcers, peripheral neuropathy, rash, pancreatitis, and bone marrow suppression have been identified as side effects of HIVID (ddC-zalcitabine), and hepatitis, headaches, diarrhea, acute pancreatitis, and peripheral neuropathy are side effects of Videx (Barthwell & Gibert, 1993).

Although all questions concerning medical therapy should be referred to the proper medical personnel, mental health professionals will most likely be confronted with complaints of side effects by their HIV-infected clients who are prescribed any of the above anti-HIV agents. These side effects may increase client resistance to treatment and should be explored with clients who can be reminded that early intervention with these chemotherapies have been shown to slow the disease process (Selwyn, 1992). Moreover, doses of AZT are usually taken every four hours around the clock, a schedule that can be seen as significantly interrupting the client's normal activities. Therefore, even in the absence of significant side effects, treatment compliance may be a problem that needs to be addressed by mental health professionals. It is also important to warn the client against self-medication with certain over-the-counter drugs such as acetaminophin, which is used to control headaches. This drug has been associated with bone marrow suppression when taken concurrently with AZT (Selwyn, 1992).

Pain management might also be a potential problem, because HIV-infected clients frequently require analgesia for the pain syndrome that often accompanies the opportunistic infections (Selwyn, 1992). Drug-abusing HIV-infected clients probably have access to illegal drugs that can be used to numb the pain, one issue counselors need to keep in mind when and if their clients talk about pain. With the drug-abusing HIV-infected client, self-medication with AZT and antibiotics may also be a problem, since both can be purchased on the street. Again, clients should be warned of the dangers of self-medicating.

HIV-Related Issues Specific to the Helping Professional

Hopefully, you can sense the complexities in working with HIV-infected clients or with clients whose behaviors put them at risk for infection. As a mental health professional, many of the issues facing you as you work with this population will be the same issues when working with any clients: helping build self-esteem, helping clients gain a greater sense of responsibility, and other issues. Some concerns are indigenous to working with HIV-infected clients, however, because these concerns touch on issues of confidentiality complicated by the variety of state laws that protect confidentiality—particularly in reporting test results, contact tracing and partner notification, record-keeping, and "Duty to warn." For a review of ethical and legal guidelines covering work with HIV-infected clients, you should refer to Chapter 17, "Ethical and Legal Issues."

Certain issues of HIV testing warrant special consideration. Although some states have resolved the issue of mandatory HIV testing for certain personnel, such testing remains the subject of heated debate in other states (Barthwell & Gibert, 1993). Essentially, the debate centers on mandatory versus voluntary and anonymous versus confidential testing for HIV. Anonymous testing assigns a unique identifiable code to each person tested, so that the results are not traceable to an individual. Confidential testing links an individual by name to the test result, so that the laws protecting confidentiality protect the test results. According to Barthwell and Gibert (1993), the Centers for Disease Control and Prevention and many other professional health care associations that represent the public interest strongly urge voluntary and confidential or anonymous testing for individuals at high risk for HIV infection.

The confidentiality of testing is not an issue when it comes to sexually transmitted and other communicable diseases such as TB. However, because of the strong co-occurance of these diseases among the HIV-infected population (Selwyn, 1992), you should assess for the presence of these diseases during the assessment phase of your work with clients who are at high risk for HIV infection and urge your clients to be tested. According to Selwyn (1992),

> With a greater density of HIV infection and tuberculosis cases, and hence growing numbers of infectious individuals, the risk of transmission to household members, health care providers, and other close but not necessarily intimate contacts would be expected to increase (p. 753).

Currently, federal law requires all who enter the military to be tested for HIV as well as requiring testing for HIV of all organ and tissue donors, all blood donors, persons seeking immigration to the United States, and federal prisoners (U.S. Preventive Task Force, 1989). According to Gostin (1989), some states may require mandatory testing for all marriage applicants, mentally ill or mentally retarded patients, IV drug users, and sex offenders. Because of the varied laws concerning mandatory testing, reporting, and confidentiality concomitant with the issues surrounding the catastrophic effects of the disease itself, mental health professionals should take great care in becoming informed of these issues with their clients and learn to handle such clients delicately.

Needle Exchange

Another issue that can confront you as a mental health professional relates to the controversial issue of needle exchange in which drug-injecting addicts can receive clean needles so as to diminish the risk of sharing needles that might be carrying HIV. Alan Marlatt believes that "we will never get ahead of AIDs and our drug problems. People think that the solution, a softer drug policy or legalization, is worse than the problem. Our ways of handling these problems are not working and they may be making them worse" (Manisses Communication Group, Inc., 1994, p. 1).

The more moderate approach advocated by Marlatt is based upon a European approach called *harm reduction*. Taking a middle-of-the-road approach between prohibition and legalization, the harm reduction approach would include legalized needle-exchange programs as well as including "a more humane approach to drug problems and [would] begin to soften criminal penalties for drug use" (Manisses Communication Group, Inc. p. 5). Marlatt believes that a harm reduction

approach offers the at-risk populations simple behavioral solutions that can dramatically reduce the danger associated with high-risk activities, and these simple
behavioral skills can help prevent the spread of AIDs (through needle-exchange
programs and safe-sex and condom-use programs). A harm reduction approach
would also include methadone programs for heroine addicts and nicotine replacement therapy for tobacco users, and would attempt to control such addictive or excessive behaviors as drinking and overeating.

As a final note, we need to state that working with HIV-infected clients can be
a very rewarding undertaking. You will be confronted with your own views of
mortality that can help you along your own journey toward discovery. From our
own experience, we know that the work is both exhilarating and exhausting. Seeing clients persevere in the face of death truly reveals the essence of the human
condition, and, as mental health professionals, we are privileged to witness such
inspiring struggles. In our own work, we have been indescribably moved by these
clients, and of one thing we can assure you: Anyone who works with this population will never be the same again.

Chapter 15

Other Addictions

You have probably heard someone refer to "chocaholics" or know someone who claims to be addicted to a television show, such as a soap opera. Usually, such comments are made in an amusing or self-deprecating context. However, some people have serious problems as a result of excessive participation in behaviors such as overeating, gambling, work, and sex. Is this excessive participation addiction?

It is important for mental health professionals to formulate an opinion about whether behaviors other than alcohol and other drug use can be classified as addictions. Because of the content in many popular magazines, books, and television talk shows, it is quite likely that you will encounter clients who believe they are addicted to gambling, food, work, or relationships. While there is little disagreement among professionals that excessive engagement in these and other behaviors can result in a variety of problems, there is controversy about whether these behaviors can be classified as addictions. We believe that it is important for you to be informed about the different arguments in this controversy so that you can develop your own view. After outlining the arguments "pro" and "con" regarding the existence of other addictions, we will describe pathological eating, gambling, sex and love, and work behaviors. Next, we will present four theoretical paradigms that can help explain or broaden your understanding of "other addictions." These paradigms include the disease model of addiction, psychodynamic theories, social learning theory, and family systems theory. These are not the only explanations for the development and maintenance of these problematic behavioral patterns. However, similar to our discussion of the differing models of alcohol and other drug addiction (Chapter 3), these paradigms may be helpful to you in formulating your opinion about so-called other addictions.

Two Points of View about Other Addictions

In preparing to write this book, we submitted a prospectus that included a proposed table of contents. One reviewer was particularly impressed with the fact that we had included a chapter on other addictions. This reviewer commented that this area was usually neglected in books in the alcohol and other drug field. Another reviewer was quite critical of our inclusion of this topic and chastised us for creating the impression that behaviors such as overeating, excessive gambling, and other behaviors were addictions. This was a clear demonstration to us that there are different points of view on the topic of other addictions and that these perspectives are expressed with considerable fervor.

Critics of Other Addictions

There are three groups who discount the notion that behaviors such as problematic eating, gambling, and sex can be addictions. One group claims that classifying compulsive behaviors as *addictions* is inappropriate because these behaviors are already well defined in the mental health field. The debate is similar to the one regarding codependency that was discussed in Chapter 12. It can be argued that compulsions involving sex are already identified in the DSM-IV. For example, the sexual disorders called *paraphilias* include many of the sexual behaviors often referred to as *addictive* (e.g., exhibitionism, fetishism, voyeurism). Furthermore, the criteria for "Histrionic Personality Disorder" includes "interaction with others [that] is often characterized by inappropriate sexually seductive or provocative behavior" (APA, 1994, p. 657), suggesting that those who are "addicted" to sex may have a personality disorder. Therefore, no new diagnostic category of sex addiction is necessary. For other interpersonal relationship problems, such as the compulsive need for love and attention, critics of other addictions point out that these symptoms may also be characteristic of a personality disorder, such as "Dependent Personality Disorder", "Narcissistic Personality Disorder", or "Histrionic Personality Disorder" or may be classified as an "Other Condition that May Be a Focus of Clinical Attention" (e.g., "Partner Relational Problem"). Similarly, "Pathological Gambling" is already classified as an "Impulse-Control Disorder Not Elsewhere Classified," and there is an "Eating Disorders" category in the DSM-IV.

A second group of critics of "other addictions" are the same people who view alcohol and other drug problems as bad habits or willful misconduct. These conceptualizations have been described in Chapter 3 and may be held by professionals promoting a certain theoretical model of addiction or by lay people who see addictive behaviors from a moral model. For example, Alan Marlatt has written extensively regarding a social learning model of addictive behaviors (see Chapter 3 and 13). In his words, "addictive behaviors represent a category of 'bad habits' including such behaviors as problem drinking, smoking, substance abuse, overeating, compulsive gambling, and so forth" (Marlatt, 1985, p. 9).

Finally, there are "purists" who see addiction from a medical model and restrict this label to those who are dependent on alcohol or other drugs. From this point of view, the demonstration of tolerance and withdrawal (see Chapter 2) in an individual who uses alcohol and/or other drugs is indicative of addiction. Since physiological tolerance and withdrawal cannot be shown in regard to behaviors such as overeating, gambling, and sex, these behaviors cannot be thought of as "addictions". Purists see the use of the term *addiction* when applied to behaviors other than alcohol and other drug use as diminishing the disease model of addiction.

Proponents of Other Addictions

The proponents of other addictions point out the similarities between alcoholics and drug addicts and those who excessively engage in behaviors other than alcohol and other drug use. For example, Moran (1975) observed that a close relationship exists between the signs and symptoms of pathological gambling and those of alcoholism. Wray and Dickerson (1981) described disturbances in mood and/or behavior when clients stopped gambling that closely resemble the withdrawal symptoms demonstrated by alcoholics. If you go back to Chapter 5 and review the criteria for Substance Dependence from DSM-IV, you will see that only three of the criteria are necessary for the diagnosis. Even if we ignore the first two criteria, since they involve the controversial topics of tolerance and withdrawal, it is still easy to see that a client who overeats, gambles too much, or has constantly changing sex partners would meet the criteria for dependence if that behavior were substituted for the word *substance*. For example, Steve, a compulsive gambler with whom we worked, often gambled more money than he intended and tried to cut down on his gambling on many occasions. His marriage and job were adversely affected by his gambling. With these symptoms, it could be argued that Steve was dependent on gambling.

A less scientific argument to support the similarity of other addictions to alcohol and other drug addictions is the development of twelve step support groups for over-eaters, gamblers, and "sex addicts" (see Chapter 8). Because twelve step groups are based on the principles of Alcoholics Anonymous, and because these groups have helped many people with problem behaviors in many areas other than alcohol and other drugs, it is argued that these "other" behaviors should be seen as addictions. It is clear that someone can feel powerlessness over eating, gambling, or sex, which is consistent with the first of the twelve steps (see Chapter 8).

Finally, proponents of other addictions contend that adoption of this concept has resulted in organized efforts to help people with these problems. Popular books and talk shows, the heightening awareness of mental health professionals, and the development of support groups have all helped people label their problems. While some people believe that the labeling process is used as an excuse for problematic behavior, the opposite may be true. For example, if you have some troubling physical symptoms that you cannot explain, it is often comforting to receive a diagnosis of the condition, even if there is no cure. Perhaps you find out that you are hypoglycemic. You will always have the condition, but you can modify dietary habits to reduce the unpleasant symptoms. Similarly, if Steve identifies himself as a gambling addict, he may believe that he will always be a gambling addict but that he also has some resources for help (e.g., Gamblers Anonymous). Therefore, the open discussion about problems involving eating, gambling, and sex has resulted in many people acknowledging that they have one of these problems, that many people share their problem, and that there is help for those with these problems.

Food Addiction: The Eating Disorders

We eat to survive. We eat for a variety of other reasons as well, such as in celebration, for enjoyment, for social acceptance, or to relieve boredom. We also eat to win affection, as reflected in the often-heard phrase, "The way to a man's heart is through his stomach." Our eating is often ritualized: hot dogs at a sporting event, popcorn at the movies, snacking in front of the television, or setting aside meals as the time when the family can meet to discuss family issues or the day's events. Ritualistic eating can likewise be reflected in a tradition of over-eating at Thanksgiving or other holidays. Eating patterns also vary: Some may eat when they feel stress or to avoid painful feelings, while others may restrict their intake under the same circumstances. It can safely be said that most of us, at one time or another, eat for reasons other than to survive.

You are probably most familiar with the eating disorder anorexia nervosa, described by Bruch (1986) as the relentless pursuit of thinness, and bulimia nervosa, binge-eating followed by purging. These two disorders are cited in the DSM-IV under the section "Eating Disorders" (p. 539). Our preoccupation with food and its relationship with success has been cited as a cause of the increase in the incidence of eating disorders—especially among women (Schwartz, Thompson, & Johnson, 1983). However, there are other aberrant eating patterns such as chronic obesity, binge-eating, and chronic over-eating that are not cited in the DSM-IV. These eating behaviors can eventually become problematic as well.

Chronic Obesity

Obesity occurs when one is over 20% of the desirable weight for one's height (Burrows, 1992), and chronic obesity occurs when individuals are at least 20% overweight for prolonged periods of time. There are mild, moderate, and severe degrees of obesity. According to researchers in the field, obesity in American males and females of all ages and ethnic backgrounds is on the rise (e.g., Agras, 1987; Bray, 1989; Burrows, 1992).

Serious health complications can arise from chronic obesity. For example, Burrows cites increased cardiovascular risk problems, increased risk of diabetes, and increased respiratory problems resulting from obesity. Emotional distress (reactions to others' disapproval of one's weight, anxiety, depression, and lowered self-esteem) is another complication cited by this same author. It is important to note that Wadden and Stunkard (1987) believe that these side effects are consequences, not causes, of obesity. Other consequences may include job discrimination and social ostracism.

Regarding social ostracism, the models of addiction we discussed in Chapter 3 can help explain the differing views of chronic obesity. Burrows (1992) states that overweight individuals are perceived as having a weak moral character or as being lazy (the moral model), as having personality deficiencies (the sociocultural and psychological model), and/or as being out of control (the disease model).

Some research suggests that obesity has a genetic component and that obesity in childhood has a strong positive correlation with weight status in adulthood (Brownell & Stukard, 1978). However, Burrows qualifies this assertion by stating that a high fat cell count in infancy and childhood is only predictive of adult obesity when other factors such as overeating and inactivity persist. In addition to the genetic component and ensuing environmental factors leading to obesity in adulthood, two other avenues lead to this condition: a pattern of chronic binge eating or chronic over-eating. Chronic over-eating occurs when individuals routinely eat more than they need to eat in order to be healthy. Whenever you sit at a dinner table and say to yourself or to others, "I am so full, but I don't want that last piece of chicken to go to waste," you are engaging in over-eating. Imagine if you were to repeat this at every meal—that is the experience of the chronic over-eater. In contrast to chronic over-eating, binge-eating involves consumption of large and unnecessary quantities of food in one sitting and in a relatively short amount of time. Movies that depict First-century Romans lying on their couches and engaged in an eating orgy show a good example of binge-eating. Although binge-eating and obesity commonly co-occur, the relationship of one to the other is not always causal. For example, Gormally, Black, Dastrom, and Rardin (1982) estimated that only 50% of those seeking treatment for obesity indicated a pattern of binge-eating at least once per week.

Chronic Binge-eating

Since first described, the research on binge-eaters suggests that these individuals seem to have a higher incidence of low self-esteem, have problems managing stress, exhibit higher levels of anxiety when in social situations, and are relatively less assertive than nonbinge, obese individuals (Loro, 1984). In addition, binge-eating is often accompanied by difficulty in distinguishing between negative feelings and hunger, so eating becomes a response to emotional distress (Freeman, 1992). Loro maintains that binge-eating can occur in response to stressful interpersonal events such as break-ups, other losses, conflict, and perceived rejection or criticism. This same author goes on to report that binge-eating can be seen as an attempt to restock one's diminished emotional stores after other attempts to restore one's self-esteem have failed.

Chronic Over-Eating

Excessive intake of one's favorite food, intake of a food substance with a particularly high calorie count, or excessive intake of fats are forms of over-eating. However, we most often consider it to be over-eating when individuals engage in a pattern of eating large quantities of food. In general, over-eating is defined as the degree of food intake that brings in more energy than is needed for an individual to function (Striegel-Moore & Rodin, 1986).

Much of the research on over-eating involves obese individuals. This research focuses on the effects of diffuse anxiety, uncontrollable arousal, uncontrollable life stress, emotional sensitivity, and physiological bases of food preferences and their relation to obesity (e.g., Brownell & Foreyt, 1986; Slochower, 1986). In general, studies indicate that high, uncontrollable anxiety coupled with available food produces over-eating (Slochower, 1986), and, when a person eats in response to the anxiety, his or her anxiety level is lowered (Bruch, 1986). Over-eating as a means of "stuffing" feelings or to relieve painful feelings has also received some support in the professional literature. For example, Slochower found that obese individuals may have more difficulty in spontaneously describing or labeling emotional experiences. She goes on to say,

> If the obese person is relatively unable to deal with emotions via the cognitive labeling process, then his or her sense of helplessness and distress would persist until an alternative stress-reducer was found. In this sense, over-eating may represent an unconscious attempt to reassert control in the face of emotional helplessness, thereby suppressing that highly painful state (p. 98).

The issue of control is apparent in this quote on obesity. Control is also an issue when discussing more pathological forms of eating, such as anorexia nervosa and bulimia nervosa.

Anorexia Nervosa and Bulimia Nervosa

According to Goodman, Blinder, Chaitin, and Hagman (1988), there have been no extensive reports of childhood anorexia or bulimia associated with purging. However, the adolescent and adult population present a different picture. Reports show the incidence of anorexia and bulimia to be less than 5% of high school and college women, although other estimates state that 80 to 90% of adolescent and young adult women have concerns about weight or are dieting (Freeman, 1992). Cause for alarm is signaled by studies that have demonstrated that only a minority of college women have normal eating habits (Hesse-Biber, 1989; Mintz & Betz, 1988). Kashubeck, Walsh, and Crowl (1994) believe that many college campuses may promote eating-disordered behaviors by emphasizing perfection, competition, and physical attractiveness. The presence of such sociocultural pressures is at least partially responsible in the development of eating disorders during adolescence, and researchers in the field generally agree. However, early childhood trauma and other factors also influence the pressures leading to the final development of the illness (Hsu, 1988; Kashubeck, Walsh, & Crowl, 1994).

Bulimia Nervosa

Bulimia nervosa features cyclical binge-eating, or eating more food than one would normally eat under similar circumstances, followed by compensatory methods preventing weight gain (APA, 1994). According to the *DSM IV*, specific diagnostic criteria for bulimia nervosa include recurrent episodes of binge-eating, recurrent inappropriate compensatory behavior aimed at preventing weight gain, binge-eating and inappropriate compensatory behaviors occurring on the average two times per week for three months, the over-influence of body shape and weight upon one's self evaluations, and that the disturbance does not occur exclusively during periods of anorexia nervosa.

The incidence of bulimia nervosa in males comprises only 10% of the total bulimic population (Mitchell & Pyle, 1988). Subsequently, most researchers consider bulimia nervosa to be a woman's disease. Freeman (1992), profiles the bulimic: a young, single, Caucasian woman with a college education. Once the pattern of purging sets in, it takes about five years for the individual to seek help. Purging itself does not begin until about a year after the individual begins to binge-eat. In these bulimic women, eating is seen as fulfilling an emotional need, and it tends to be rather a secretive and solitary compulsion (Kirkley, 1986).

Interestingly, whereas obesity can occur in both men and women across their lifespan, the "window of opportunity" for anorexia and bulimia nervosa opens generally between the ages of 18 and a woman's early thirties (Freeman, 1992). According to Mitchell and Pyle (1988), the usual age of onset for bulimia nervosa is between 16 and 19 years of age, and the average age of initial treatment is about 24. Dally (1984) states that it would be unusual for a woman over the age of 25 to have bulimia nervosa, and no incidences of bulimia have been reported in the elderly (Morley & Castele, 1986). In their study, Mintz and Betz (1988) report that subthreshold bulimia (purging less than two times per week) was the most frequent type of disordered eating (occuring 17 to 27% the time), and full-blown bulimia was seen as occuring 3 to 6% of the time. According to Mitchell and Pyle (1988), the frequency of compensatory methods used by bulimics include diuretic abuse (33.1%), excessive use of enemas (7%), and chewing and spitting out food without swallowing (64.5%).

Striegel-Moore, Silbertstein, and Rodin (1986) and McDougall (1989) found that women with bulimia generally have a diminished ability to regulate tension, have lowered impulse control, have a need for immediate gratification, and have a lowered sense of self. Brouwers and Wiggum (1993) consider bulimia and perfectionism to be highly associated. These same authors maintain that perfectionism is made up of unrealistic expectations and the utilization of dichotomous (all-or-none) thinking. Bulimics are seen as holding unrealistic expectations and dichotomous thinking as related to their physical appearance. Bulimics also typically believe that they should be thin and could accomplish this by eating "good" foods all of the time, by being able to exercise vigorously, and by always demonstrating self-control—one form of which is demonstrating control over food (Brouwers & Wiggum, 1993). Failure to control their weight leaves bulimics feeling weak and worthless.

As stated previously, bulimia in males is rare. Nevertheless, the clinical characteristics of male bulimics are comparable to those of female bulimics. Some male bulimcs report being preoccupied with weight control (Gwirtsman, Roy-Byrne, & Lerner, 1984). These same authors also indicate that male bulimics tend to feel more cultural pressure related to performance in sports, fashion, and music than do nonbulimic males.

Brouwers and Wiggum (1993) see conflicts as abounding within the bulimic population. An individual with bulimia often gets caught up in a psychic "no-win" situation, in which one side of her insists that she must eat only the right foods and the other side begs for spontaneity with food and a natural acceptance of herself. The classic case of this conflict is the binge-purge cycle, in which the person eats a large quantity of food spontaneously (the "all") followed by purging ("the nothing"), or is seen when she tells herself that she can eat anything and everything since she can always purge (Neuman & Halvorson, 1983).

Anorexia Nervosa

According to Garfinkel and Kaplan (1986),

> Anorexia is an increasingly common and complex disorder...that overrides the patient's physical and psychological well-being...Pursuing a thin body becomes an isolated area of control in a world in which the individual feels ineffective; the dieting provides an artificially dangerous sense of mastery and control. As the weight loss progresses, a starvation state ensues, which eventually develops a life of its own, leading to features of anorexia nervosa (p. 266).

Interestingly, anorexics do not suffer from a loss of appetite. Rather, they are "frantically preoccupied with food and eating...[they] deliberately, seemingly willfully, restrict their food intake and overexercise. These girls are panicky with the fear that they might lose control over their eating..." (Bruch, 1986, p. 331). The literature reflects two distinct patterns of anorexia: restrictive anorexia (those restricting intake through dieting) and bulimic anorexia (those using purging as a means to control weight). Restrictive anorexics are characterized by greater social isolation (Freeman, 1992) and are also found to be sexually inexperienced, often to fear dating, and often to stress the importance of grades. As well, restrictive anorexics often reflect "model" or "A" students (Garfinkel, Moldofshy, & Garner, 1980). These same authors estimate that 40 to 50% of restrictive anorexics develop bulimic behaviors at some time during the course of the disorder.

In contrast to restrictive anorexics, bulimic anorexics control their weight level by vomiting and/or laxative abuse following episodes of binge-eating. Bulimic anorexics often display histrionic personality traits and tend to be more socially and sexually active than restrictive anorexics. Bulimic anorexics also tend to display a variety of other compulsive behaviors including alcohol and other drug abuse, stealing, and self-mutilation (Garfinkel et al., 1980). Given these other psychiatric disturbances, Freeman (1992) suggests that bulimic anorexics have a longer history with the disorder and a poorer prognosis than restrictive anorexics.

The DSM-IV cites four diagnostic criteria for anorexia nervosa. The first is a refusal to maintain body weight at or above a minimally normal weight when controlled for age and height. Secondly, the anorexic has intense fears of gaining weight or becoming fat (even though underweight). The intense fears reflect the fact that anorexic women usually have disturbed perceptions in how they experience their body and will usually ascribe inappropriate meanings to body weight or shape. Finally, anorexic females experience amenorrehea (the absence of at least three consecutive menstrual cycles).

The incidence of anorexia nervosa in males is approximately 6% of the total number of reported cases of anorexia (Goodman, Blinder, Chaitin, & Hagman, 1988). So the incidence of anorexia nervosa and bulima nervosa in males is approximately the same. The age range for males with anorexia nervosa parallels that range for females: approximately 17 to 24 years of age. Clinical manifestations for male anorexics is also similar to that of females—although some minor differences have been noted. In general, male anorexics display perfectionism (Anderson & Michalide, 1983) and obsessional, passive/dependent and antisocial characteristics (Vandereycken & Van den Broucke, 1984).

It would be unusual for anorexia nervosa to be found in a woman over the age of twenty-five, and the same can be said for the incidence of anorexia nervosa in African Americans and Latino/Hispanic populations. For example, Goodman, et al., (1988) found that only 5% of the reported cases of anorexia nervosa were reflected in these ethnically diverse populations. Regarding anorexia in women over the age of twenty-five, Dally (1984) maintains that these anorexics tend to come from upper-middle-class families. Other researchers found anorexic women over the age of twenty-five to have had multiple surgical procedures or illnesses (Ryle, 1936), stress secondary to childbirth or marriage (Kellett, Trimble, & Thorley, 1976), or death of a spouse (Price, Giannini, & Colella, 1985). Although rare, Morley and Castele have reported some cases of anorexia nervosa in elderly women. These same authors believe that a diminished sense of smell, appetite disorders, and impaired taste sensation may contribute to anorexia nervosa in the elderly. Moreover, Goodman et al. state that a spectrum of anorexia occurs in the elderly in the absence of overt depression. In this population, bereavement can precipitate a diminished appetite or a cessation of eating altogether as well as producing a distortion of body image.

Gambling Addictions

When you think of gambling, you probably think of the betting that occurs between friends or around sporting events, horse-races, and the various state lotteries. If asked to imagine what a professional gambler would look like, you would likely think of poker players or someone who spends all his or her time at the race track. You probably do not think of stockbrokers as professional gamblers in the same way you consider professional poker players. But are these two groups really different? Both "play" everyday: The stockbroker wagers money in the market and the poker player wagers money on cards. In addition, both individuals can develop problematic behaviors surrounding their occupations. Moran (1975) refers to the syndrome of problematic gambling as reflecting

> concern on the part of the gambler and/or family about the amount of gambling . . .
> an overpowering urge to gamble so that the individual may be intermittently or
> continuously preoccupied with thoughts of gambling . . . [a] subjective experience
> of the inability to control the amount once gambling has started . . . [and] distur-
> bances of economic, social and/or psychological functioning of the gambler and/or
> family as a result of persistent gambling (p. 418).

Although there are no accurate statistics on the number of compulsive gamblers in the United States, Gamblers Anonymous estimates that there are roughly 4.2 million Americans gambling compulsively (Gaudia, 1992). This number includes a growing population of adolescent gamblers. Lesieur and Custer (1984) estimate that the typical compulsive gambler affects between 10 and 15 persons directly or indirectly. The average debt for gamblers is also unknown, but one treatment center revealed that the average debt of those in their treatment center was $54,662 (Blackman, Simone, & Thomas, 1986).

In 1980, the American Psychiatric Association recognized that some gamblers cannot control their gambling and thereby formalized compulsive gambling as an impulse disorder. The inclusion of gambling into the DSM-IV not only underscored the progressive nature (i.e., phases of compulsive gambling) of this disorder but also formally supplanted the moral model (see Chapter 3) of compulsive gambling. Compulsive gamblers, as a result, were no longer seen as responsible for the urge to gamble but were still responsible for what they did with that urge.

Phases of Gambling

Gaudia (1992) identifies three phases of gambling. In the first phase, the gambler experiences the excitement, stimulation, and enjoyment of winning. Inevitably, the gambler will sometimes lose. Two characteristics differentiate a problematic from recreational gambler: the attributions made when they lose and the failure to quit while they are ahead. For example, when losing, gamblers make attributions in attempting to understand the nature of their loss. Those gamblers making internal attributions ("everybody loses sometimes") as opposed to external attributions ("I have incredibly bad luck") tend to get back on a winning streak (Downing and Harrison, 1991; Rosecrance, 1986). The external attributions ("I have incredibly bad luck") may be important in maintaining the addictive behavior once it has been set in motion in that external attributions almost require the compulsive gambler to prove that he or she does not, in fact, have incredibly bad luck.

In the second phase, gambling becomes a dominant force in the gambler's life. The gambler's sense of identity becomes centered on his or her identity as a gambler (Matinez, 1983). Also characteristic of this phase is an increase in betting and mounting losses. Being "in the action" is paramount (Gaudia, 1992). One's obsession is this phase centers on attempting to recapture what has been lost, and betting becomes reckless and desperate. In the third phase, called the "desperate phase," losses have impacted the gambler to such an extent that he or she has begun lying to relatives and friends about where the money has gone. Gambling has continued in spite of severe family and financial consequences. The excitement is gone, only to be supplanted by depression, thoughts of suicide, threats of divorce, incarceration, possible job loss, and a remarkable loss of self-worth (Gaudia, 1992).

Addiction to Sex and Love

Sex and love addiction is seen by many as really comprising three addictions: addiction to love, addiction to sex, and addiction to sex and love. No doubt you have heard about the O. J. Simpson case in which the prosecution attempted to portray Mr. Simpson as addicted to love and as having murdered his former wife and another man because of jealous rage. Some of the popular views in this case maintain that Nicole Simpson was herself addicted to love and was thereby unable to fully extricate herself from O. J.'s abusive patterns. Do you remember seeing or hearing about the movie, *Fatal Attraction,* where love turned into an obsession? Or, you have likely heard about various movie stars who complain of having been stalked by people they do not even know. Among other things, stalkers can be viewed as addicted to love. Less serious than the alleged acts in the Simpson case are individuals who are abused in their primary relationships and continue to remain in these relationships because leaving is thought to be impossible. Griffin-Shelley (1991) writes that our physical and psychological identity is made up in part by sex and love, and "Letting go of sex and love, even for a short amount of time, seems [to addicts] like giving up [their] whole identity" (p. 19).

Addiction to sex can reflect individuals who masturbate compulsively (perhaps 10 to 15 times per day), who are preoccupied with pornography, and/or individuals who engage in prostitution or the purchase of such sexual services. Some addicted individuals can spend thousands of dollars on pornography or on prostitutes. Having sex numerous times a day is another example of an individual addicted to sex.

Historically, compulsive behavioral problems in interpersonal relationships focused on excessive sexuality, such as nymphomania, and focused mainly upon women's behaviors (Logan, 1992). Recently, however, others have identified sexual addictions as gender free and maintain that these compulsions cut across all socioeconomic lines and across sexual orientations (Forward, 1986; Norwood, 1985).

Sex and love addiction combines sex and love and can reflect individuals who involve themselves in numerous affairs in spite of promises to the contrary. More often than not, these individuals may use sex in attempting to get the love they feel they need. In many of these cases, sex is only the enticer, or the avenue through which other emotional, intellectual, or spiritual needs are met. But the act of sex does not characterize all individuals addicted to sex and love. Being in a primary relationship and compulsively fantasizing about others is also characteristic of those addicted to sex and love. Constantly fantasizing about someone other than the one to whom a person is making love also reflects a sex and love addiction.

Even without sexualizing the relationship, many sex and love addicts maintain that they compulsively engage in emotional affairs. For example, one of our clients told us of a time when she was paralyzed at a traffic light on a busy street trying to decide whether she should drive by her fantasy lover's office "just to see him, not to talk to him." She remained immobilized for an entire light cycle, with cars honking on both sides of her while she engaged in an internal debate about whether to drive straight ahead or whether to turn and drive by his office. (She drove straight ahead).

Symptoms

The symptoms of a person with an addiction to sex and love are varied but usually center on several issues. According to Griffin-Shelley (1991), the "high" or "fix" for sex and love addicts is found in "cruising" (looking for another), "intriguing" (fantasizing) and "chasing" (attempting to initiate a relationship). An individual is regarded as sex and love addicted when they engage in behavior that is experienced as disgusting, demeaning, and against their better judgement; when the behavior is ritualized, obsessive, and causes duress if interrupted; and behavior that is void of joy and emotions (Hunter 1988; Peele 1975; Schaeffer 1985; Sex and Love Addicts Anonymous, 1985). Regarding the obsessive/compulsive component, Griffin-Shelley writes,

> *The habit of thinking or fantasizing and then having to compulsively act out is like the binge/purge cycle of the bulimic. As thoughts fill the addict with excitement, anticipation, and energy, he or she feels closer and closer to losing control. When the rush into action takes place, it consumes the person with the passion of the moment, and all reason and rationality are lost in the explosion. What a 'rush.' What a release. What an orgasm. The guilt, shame, remorse come later. For the time being, the addict feels fulfilled. The pattern of riding the wave of sexual and romantic excitement to the crash on the beach is worth the ride and is difficult to give up. Ordinary life pales in comparison to the highs and lows of the obsession/ compulsion routine (p. 80).*

Consequences

Logan (1992) points out that a pattern of negative emotional, social, physical, financial, and legal consequences associated with sex and love addiction often exists and is not consequential enough to deter the behavior. For example, financial losses may be incurred as a result of individuals spending large sums of money on seductive clothes or jewelry. Other financial losses may include being fired from a job for sexual harassment or relocation due to break-ups of significant relationships. Kasl (1989) adds health, education, parenting, safety, and spiritual issues to the list of consequences. She cites individuals who became involved in relationships for which they gave up their educational aspirations or individuals who would leave their children unattended so they could go to a motel with a lover.

Some would avoid medical check-ups for years in spite of having had numerous partners. Other consequences might be sexually transmitted diseases (STDs), self-mutilation, abortions, abrasions, or HIV infection. Sex-and-love-addicted individuals can put themselves in dangerous situations by picking up strangers at a bar and going with them to remote places. Sexualizing relationships can also lead to guilt and resentment, suicidal ideation, depression, self-loathing, fear, and a diminished sense of self-worth (Kasl, 1989).

Addiction to Work: Workaholism

According to Oates (1971), a workaholic is

A person whose need for work has become so excessive that it creates noticeable disturbance or interference with his (sic) bodily health, personal happiness, and interpersonal relations, and with his (sic) smooth social functioning (p. 4).

There are other definitions of workaholism. For example, Minirth, Meier, Wichern, Brewer, and Skipper (1981) define the workaholism as occurring when there is "a noticeable disturbance on the rest of his [or her] life" (p. 28). Morris and Charney (1983) describe withdrawal symptoms, such as anxiety and depression, that characterize the workaholic when he or she lacks work to do. Klaft and Kleiner (1988) maintain that the workaholic is addicted to work itself rather than to the results of one's work efforts.

As a student, you probably have engaged in compulsive work behaviors. These behaviors will most often occur around exam time or when assignments are due. If you are also a homemaker, you probably understand clearly the meaning of the cliché, "A woman's work is never done." Remember the phrase, "The early bird catches the worm?" Many of us have subscribed to the tenets of these phrases. However, some believe these phrases to be rules to follow and believe these dictums to be essential to one's very own sense of well-being or survival.

Unfortunately, American culture tends to favor a workaholic ethic, and Spruell (1987) agrees by saying that workaholism is "the addiction most rewarded in our [American] culture" (p. 44). Paradoxically, while workaholism appears to be revered in the American culture, the workaholic individual can create chaos in the workplace. For example, Machlowitz (1980) sees that the workaholic can be a detriment to the work environment by being difficult to work with, by being excessively competitive, demanding a great deal from others while, at the same time, being critical of them, and can avoid delegating tasks and responsibilities to others. Aside from the impact of workaholism in the workplace, Seybold and Salomone (1994) report that workaholism also affects physical health, life style, and family life. Franzmeier (1988) believes that workaholics who attempt to lighten their work load might find that they suffer from anhedonia—the inability to feel pleasure after pleasure has been postponed too long. Franzmeier maintains that the workaholic can experience a type of pleasure atrophy similar to the atrophy of an unused muscle. Kiechel (1989) agrees by saying that the workaholic is not able to enjoy leisure time.

Phases of Workaholism

Oates (1971) describes two phases through which the workaholic goes: the prodromal or early phase and the crucial phase. Each phase has its own set of symptoms. In the prodromal phase, the first expression of a workaholic will likely be no different from that of all who work. Oates says that initially the individual enjoys the work, finds meaning, and social relationships. Eventually, workaholics believe that they must work in order to be happy or that they must work in order to find significance in their lives. In the cases of some female workaholics, they may work so as to become too tired or too busy to become pregnant. Or, some female workaholics may simply find work preferable to raising children. In any case, when work becomes the central and exclusive focus in one's life, workaholism has likely set in.

Oates points out that one of the telltale signs of a compulsive worker in the prodromal phase will be reflected in the individual's disclosure about how early he or she got up in order to go to work or how late he or she stayed up working. A subtle implication lies in how little sleep one is getting as a result of rising early or staying late, and the workaholic is "forced to use the hours other people use for parties or sleeping to catch up on work left undone during the day" (Oates, 1971; p. 7). A homemaker may be a workaholic as well when he or she spends several hours during the day on the telephone and then needs to burn the midnight oil to catch up on the work that was not done. In contrast to the female workaholic who may be unconsciously attempting to avoid pregnancy, a woman may become compulsive about childbearing when she attempts "to achieve the full experience of motherhood by begetting a new child again and again" (Deutsch, 1945, p. 269).

Another symptom in the prodromal phase concerns the amount of work that is accomplished. Workaholics tend to boast about the amount of work they do in contrast to others or boast how they carry the load for others (Oates, 1971). According to Oates, a third symptom of the prodromal phase is the inability to say "no" to those requesting services. One might take on more speaking engagements, more clients or sales accounts, more chairships, more committee memberships, or more administrative responsibilities. Critical to this process, however, is the idea that while this additional workload is often driven by economics, in many cases the workaholic "never knows at what point to level off one's budget or how to live within that line" (Oates, p. 8). For example, the typical nine-to-five job can turn into a seven-to-eleven job when the workaholic takes on work after hours. Thus, "moonlighting" can become a way of life. These attitudes of not saying "no" and/or of taking on extra work are formed within the "second or third decade of life when physical health and energy are at a high point" (Oates, p. 9).

The crucial phase of workaholism begins when the individual first experiences significant consequences in the form of emotional, physical, or interpersonal collapse. A person may suffer a heart attack, excessive anxiety and/or panic attacks, depression, or other problems. Oates (1971) claims that, after one or two of these episodes, "the person comes to the impasse: They can work harder or they can learn to work at rehabilitation" (p. 10). Choosing to work more chronically is the addictive pattern in which the individual considers work as a way of life. Family values may go by the wayside and friendships can soon follow, as can spiritual associations. Oates describes this individual as "an ascetic who enjoys nothing except an occasional good meal, constant supplies of work, and a good bed to fall into from sheer exhaustion" (p. 10).

Theoretical Paradigms and Other Addictions

Although the preceding sections are not comprehensive, they are intended to give you a fairly sound knowledge base of the other addictions. It is interesting to note that the compulsive behaviors we discussed have similar consequences. In each case, the consequences might often include a deterioration of the emotional, financial, spiritual, and physical aspects of the lives of those with other addictions.

As mentioned in Chapter 3, there are several explanations or models of addiction. Proponents of the disease model of "other addictions" emphasize them as primary diseases that are progressive, chronic, irreversible, and potentially fatal and that need to be treated by total abstinence. Psychodynamic and object relations theorists emphasize early childhood trauma and its relation to adult narcissism as fundamental to the development of other addictions. Family systems and social learning theorists place less emphasis upon early childhood development and, therefore, less emphasis upon the etiology of adult narcissism. Instead, those theorists focus upon the reinforcing effects of pathological family interactions and the overt and covert reinforcing effects of compulsive behaviors.

The Disease Model

A thorough explanation of the disease model has been presented in Chapter 3. Proponents of the disease model of addiction would see eating disorders, pathological gambling, compulsive sex and love, and workaholism as primary diseases and would assert that these behaviors are chronic and progressive. However, disease model theorists believe that the individual, instead of needing to abstain from food, needs to abstain from the compulsive behaviors surrounding food, including taking laxatives, binging, purging, restricting diet, and ritualistic eating practices. Failure to abstain from these compulsive behaviors will result in serious medical conditions and/or eventual death.

For proponents of the disease model, compulsive gambling is a disease, and the adult who demonstrates compulsive gambling behaviors will always have the urge to gamble. So, for recovery, the compulsive gambler would need to abstain from gambling. Blume (1988) has concluded that the addiction model of gambling that appears to have the largest following is the disease model because it "is conducive to the fostering of treatment techniques, encourages funding for treatment and research, and provides a framework for formulating social and legal policies related to the disorder" (Freeman, 1992, p. 238).

Griffin-Shelley (1991), in writing about the disease model of sex and love addiction, maintains that these addicts present the same symptoms as other addicted persons, which include experiencing a tolerance to the craving for sex and love (so that there is not ever enough sex or love), dependence, craving, withdrawal, obsessions, compulsions, secrecy, and personality changes as a result of their addictions. In addition, this same author sees sex and love addicts as experiencing "enslavement, loss of power and control, imbalance, centrality and inability to shift focus and priorities, chronicity, progression, and potential lethality..." (p. 47) more powerfully than their need for love and sex. Although symptoms vary, Logan (1992), points out that sex and love addicts will engage in the behavior in spite of severe consequences.

Engaging in behaviors in spite of severe consequences is also characteristic of workaholism. In the crucial phase of workaholism, the individual can experience emotional, physical, or interpersonal collapse, but may still continue to work compulsively (Oates, 1971). In this sense, workaholism is seen as chronic and progressive. Oates asserts that workaholics also undergo withdrawal symptoms that include excessive anxiety when unable to answer or return every phone call, anxiety associated with leaving work at the office, and anxiety at leaving the office after working only an eight-hour day. Oates also identifies, as a consequence, ego-deprivation in which the workaholic feels as though he or she is no longer important to others.

Psychodynamic and Developmental Theories

Psychodynamic Theory

In psychoanalytic theory, an emphasis is placed upon the intrapersonal tension occurring between the ego states of an individual. Advocates of this theory believe that adult compulsions result from a lack of resolution of the oral, anal, and phallic stages that occur in childhood.

In general, psychoanalytic theorists maintain that the conflicts that arose in the early periods of attachment and separation cause impairment in the individual's ability to regulate tension and anxiety, which places him or her at risk for affective instability during adolescence and adulthood. A quote from Bruch, in her book *Eating Disorders: Obesity, Anorexia Nervosa and the Person Within* (1973) might help explain the theoretical implications of a psychodynamic interpretation of eating disorders:

> *Food may symbolically stand for an insatiable desire for unobtainable love, or as an expression of rage and hatred; it may substitute for sexual gratification or indicate ascetic denial; it may represent the wish to be a man and possess a penis, or the wish to be pregnant or fear of it. It may provide a sense of spurious power and thus lead to self-aggrandizement, or it may serve as a defense against adulthood*

and responsibility. Preoccupation with food may appear as helpless, dependent clinging to parents, or as hostile rejection of them (p. 44).

Although Bruch was writing about anorexia, you can see how this quote applies to the various forms of eating disorders such as binging and compulsive over-eating.

Psychoanalytic theorists would support Moran's (1975) view that compulsive gamblers are eventually controlled by the urge to gamble and that these individuals may have unresolved issues surrounding the pre-genital phases of psychosexual growth and development. Compulsive gambling can also be seen as an expression of the desire to annihilate others who are projected as parental figures. Compulsive work, in psychoanalytic theory, can be interpreted as one's unconscious desire to overthrow one's parents by attempting to accumulate more wealth than the parents. Compulsive work can also mirror the unconscious desire to work oneself to death, in which case anger at one's parents is retroflected into self-destructive behaviors. In traditional psychodynamic theory, a heterosexual male's engaging in compulsive sex can be seen as his attempt to re-enter the womb, a place of safety and maternal nurturance. This excessive dependence upon a partner implies that the man has not fully separated from his maternal figure. Though seen as quite charming, this male may actually be covering up his unconscious rage toward women. A woman who focuses excessively upon sex with men can be seen as an unconscious attempt to possess a penis.

Object Relations Theory

According to object relation theorists, individuals have a basic need for nurturance, support, protection, and containment from parents. These four functions are initially taken on by an environmental mother, who provides a type of holding environment for the child (Hawkins, 1986; Winnicott, 1965). Traumatic anxiety can result when a disruption of this holding environment occurs. According to these theorists, the environmental mother is of central concern to infants until they reach an age at which their behavior is subjected to shaping by an object mother who is seen by the infant as the object or the one telling the child what is acceptable behavior—what one can and cannot do or what one must and must not do. At this juncture, the environmental mother moves more to the peripheral vision as the object mother becomes of central focus.

Because of the child's primitive cognitive development at this stage, the child cannot comprehend how its love object (environmental mother) can be both loving and punitive. Thus, the child "splits" the mother into the environmental mother and the object mother. In object relations theory, love is associated with gratification-attachment (environmental mother) and hate is associated with deprivation and abandonment (object mother). According to Hamilton (1989), the primary problem of the individual child rests in how he or she will maintain continuity of relationships in the presence of contradictory feelings of love for the environmental mother and hate for the object mother. When there is an over-preponderance of "object mother" setting up conditions of worth for the child, the child can come to experience a traumatic sense of loss and a diminution of one's self-esteem, which would subsequently be reflected in a growing lack of trust in self and others. When a significant disruption of basic trust occurs, the child may have great difficulty rectifying the parental relationship, and adult narcissistic disorders can result (Mahler, 1975).

Regarding eating disorders, object relations theorists focus upon the female's early childhood ambivalence when faced with an aggressively protective, unresponsive, domineering, and controlling mother. Szyrynski (1973) sees the refusal to eat to be an expression of hostility, control, and aggression toward the family. Bruch (1973) identifies anorexia nervosa as a struggle for a self-respecting identity in the failure of parents to transmit a sense of identity, competence, and self-value to their children. The notion of perfectionism, identified in the study of bulimics by Brouwers and Wiggum (1993), is often traced by object relations theorists to parent-child interactions in which the object mother was a dominant and overpowering force during a female's early development. Object relations theorists would point out that over-eating and binging result from the individual's unconscious attempts to find the environmental mother believed to be lost during childhood. During infancy, eating is a time of mother-child interaction. For object relation theorists, over-eaters and binge-eaters are attempting to recreate an environment of nurturance, albeit inappropriate.

Compulsive gambling can also be framed in object relations theory as one's attempt to find the environmental mother. In gambling, stability is established through the rituals surrounding the activity. Wearing lucky clothes, always going to the same race track, casino, bingo parlor, or store to buy lottery tickets, and other behaviors become rituals that occupy the compulsive gambler's thoughts. Out of control gambling is seen as resulting from one's grandiose beliefs about being all-powerful. The development of private rules and rituals, such as carrying a specified amount of money in one's pocket at all times or betting the same amount of money at the outset of every game, may be interpreted as symbolic of the dualistic thinking or the unresolved "split" between one's environmental mother and object mother. In compulsive gambling, rituals initially thought to bring good luck eventually change to rules (object mother) governing what they must do and/or how they must always bet.

According to object relations theory, abandonment experienced in one's family of origin can be reflected in one's compulsive looking outside of him- or herself for worth and may be manifested in an adult's over-preoccupation with sex, love, and work. For example, compulsivity in interpersonal relationships is, theoretically, a drive to find the security and acceptance perceived as absent in one's early years. Such preoccupation also may serve to defocus individuals from their original pain of abandonment. Overzealous attempts to meet potential partners or to "score" sexually can become of such concern that little time remains to think or feel the impact of rejection (felt both in one's family of origin as well as that experienced when adult relationships do not work out). The need for approval, perceived as lacking in one's early childhood, may be seen in the workplace where the workaholic attempts to gain acceptance from supervisors and employers by selling more than anyone else, by consistently attempting to be more loyal to the company than anyone else, or by volunteering to do the lion's share of work.

Social Learning and Stimulus-Response Theories

We have already described a social learning explanation of addiction in Chapter 3. Recall Marlatt's (1985) belief that addictive behaviors really represent a category of bad habits. Wolpe (1969) and Eysenck (1957) would agree with Marlatt in saying that individuals suffering from neurotic anxiety will often develop responses, such as gambling, excessive work patterns, and over-preoccupation with sex and eating habits that, at least temporarily, either relieve the tension or allow the individual to escape unpleasant emotions. However, Wolpe and Eysenck maintain that a result of such stimulus-response association does not always have the benevolent effect of reducing anxiety, and it may actually increase anxiety. Here, you can see how a compulsive gambler would need to gamble increasingly more in an attempt to relieve the escalating cycle of anxiety. Addictive work patterns operate the same way: to relieve the escalating cycle of the fear of losing one's security.

In contrast to those theories focusing exclusively upon early childhood experiences, a social learning orientation focuses upon cognitions and behaviors that can explain aspects of the illness (Garner & Bemis, 1982). In eating disorders, the outcome of exposure to the modeling effect, i.e., the media portrayal of the ideal woman, and pressures experienced by women on college campuses to be perfect, competitive, and attractive (Kashubeck, Walsh, & Crowl, 1994) are believed to reinforce the so-called benefits of being thin. As mentioned in the section on "Food Addiction," the immediate effects of purging serve to reinforce the beliefs that the woman is in control of her eating since food can be expelled at will. So, in social learning theory, a woman's proclivities towards aberrant eating habits is seen as a result of the reinforcing effects of modeling in society as well as from the more immediate effects of reinforcing behaviors (e.g., purging) aimed at self-control. One's views about body size, shape, and weight are also influenced by the reinforcing effects of the images, beliefs, thoughts, behaviors, and feelings associated with a woman's fear of gaining weight and having a less than perfect appearance (Brouwers & Wiggum, 1993). These same authors do borrow from psychodynamic theory when they state that anorexia nervosa is the final common pathway that results from a pathological sequence of events beginning with the introverted, sensitive, and isolated adolescent who believes that weight loss will alleviate her distress and dysphoria. Dieting is seen as a paragon of ascetic control, and this perception is reinforced by a gratifying sense of success, as well as by the approval and concern received from significant others (Hsu, 1988). The negative reinforcement of food avoidance gradually supersedes the rewards of eating and increases the individual's isolation while decreasing the adolescent's responsiveness to other considerations.

Reinforcement theory also applies to compulsive behaviors surrounding gambling, sex and love, and work. Addicted persons are seen as having a history of dependent relationships occurring in their families, in schools, at work, and with alcohol or other drugs (Logan, 1992). Patterned interactions that take place in these relationships are seen as having historically powerful and reinforcing effects upon the maintenance of one's lack of self-worth. Immediacy of feedback in gambling and, in some cases, work serves to reinforce the current addictive behavior. More-over, in those cases of immediate success (i.e., winning big the first time one gambles or selling at a record rate directly after being hired), one's initial self-esteem may be impacted positively. The intermittent and variable ratio of reinforcement occurring in gambling, in interpersonal relationships, and in work is seen as serving to strengthen and maintain the compulsive behavior. In the addictive phases of these behaviors, one's anxiety about losing weight, money, affection and sex, and the rewards gained from work is believed to increase to the point at which the person is left with an escalating fear of failure unless the behavior is continued. When anxiety and fear reach this point, the individual experiences a "loss of control." Behavioral interventions might help individuals regain their sense of self-efficacy.

Family Systems Theory

Although a more comprehensive discussion of family systems has already been presented in Chapter 10, we will outline basic family systems theory as it relates to other addictions. In family system approaches to other addictions, the emphasis is on pathological interactions occurring in a family.

Children grow up with conscious and unconscious views of self and others. Perceptions about gender roles, ways to communicate, strategies of relating, and views of the world result from what Beavers (1985) refers to as "absorbing the family experience, its rules and assumptions expressed in action" (p. 29). Important to family systems theory are the nature, role, and function of relationships among all family members. Repeated patterns of interactions are seen as resulting in family rules and boundaries or in what Minuchin (1974) refers to as *subsystems*. The purpose and function of these subsystems or boundaries is to maintain family homeostasis, or family balance. Families also have underlying family themes that influence the ways in which the family goes about conducting its business. For example, in Chapter 10, we noted that alcoholic families have unresolved mourning and often collude with other family members to maintain alcohol dependence. In the anorexics's family, an underlying theme might be the family's need to appear strong, cohesive, and competent at all times in spite of problems. The fact that this appearance may be a cover-up leaves the family mourning for honesty, integrity, and relief from the pressures of having to be perfect.

Anorexia nervosa and bulimia nervosa, from a family systems viewpoint, may reflect a woman's acting out the unexpressed hostility felt toward her parents when the underlying family theme did not allow for the direct expression of such anger. So, to keep the family in balance, anger in the eating-disordered client is expressed indirectly through eating habits. Early investigations into the area of family interaction and its relationship to the development of anorexia nervosa all emphasized the family pathology in terms of having anorectic mothers or fathers, having a facade of happiness and stability that kept the real competitive nature of the parents hidden, parental over-preoccupation with appearance, rejecting communication patterns, parental rigidity, and parental over-protectiveness (Hsu, 1988).

Interestingly, families of bulimics have been reported to have greater problematic interactional styles than do those of restrictive anorexics (Ordman & Kirshenbaum, 1984). Strober, Salkion, and Burroughs (1982) found that families of bulimics had disturbances in affect, unmodulated expression of hostile impulses, weak internal controls, and an absence of satisfying intrafamilial ties. According to Humphrey (1989), bulimics perceive less affection and affiliation in their families than do both restrictive anorexics and those with no history of eating disorders. Similar to anorexics, however, bulimics also perceive problems with their parents. For example, Humphrey reported that bulimics described their relationships with parents as lacking warmth, trust, affection, affirmation, and nurturing.

Gaudia (1992) points to the dearth of empirical research into the area of family systems and gambling. However, some research adheres to the view that gambling is an addiction and stresses that gambling addiction is a family problem. Because compulsive gamblers are likely to believe that money is both the cause and the result of personal and interpersonal problems (APA, 1994), it can be seen that compulsive gambling may be seen as an inappropriate attempt to cope with seemingly insurmountable problems at home. For example, a compulsive gambler might attempt to disengage from the family rather than deal directly with issues of intimacy between the gambling and nongambling partners. Compulsive gambling may also be perceived as one's attempts to keep the family in such conflict that the family cannot change. Moreover, families may cover up problems resulting from gambling addiction. This potential cover-up may underscore why gambling is referred to as an invisible illness (Gaudia, 1992, p. 244) as well as reflect underlying family communication dysfunction surrounding marital problems, child-rearing problems, and/or vocational issues. Many such problems can go unresolved in these families and the resulting anxiety may be displaced onto an individual's gambling addiction.

From a family systems point of view, Logan (1992) believes that individuals addicted to sex, love, and work feel isolated and that this isolation characterizes the histories as well as the current familial experiences of these persons. In addition, sibling rivalries, perceived special treatment or behavior, feelings of not being understood by a significant other, traumatic events such as a death or divorce, and parental or spousal role modeling of inappropriate interpersonal behaviors all significantly impact the addictive process. Logan also believes that where strong feelings of separateness exist in relationships, the tendency might be to seek solutions through addictive activities such as sex and love and work, the purpose of which is to help individuals overcome feelings of isolation. Implied here, then, is the notion that poor communication exists in relationships in which one partner is demonstrating sex and love addiction or workaholism. In this fashion, compulsions involving extra-marital affairs or workaholism, for example, could be seen as one's repeated attempts to ward off the pain associated with loneliness in a primary relationship. As the anxiety associated with the increasing guilt becomes more severe, so does one's sense of being helpless to negotiate the tension. So, the workaholic addresses the tension by working harder to earn more money, status, and prestige and the sex-and-love-addicted individuals feel temporary relief in their preoccupation with the next affair. The cycle is repeated as one's attempts to feel connected or to have enough money or status consistently fall short of the desired outcome.

Assessment and Treatment Issues

As we stated in Chapter 5, assessment is crucial in planning for treatment. Individuals with other addictions will probably reflect problems in a variety of areas such as physical health, psychological and social functioning, reproduction and sexuality, cross-addictions, and family relationships. However these same problems may also exist in individuals whose behaviors are not addictive. For example, the client who comes in to work on grieving the intense feelings of a lost relationship may or may not be a sex and love addict. Such a determination will result from exploring thematic patterns in the client's various relationships. Clearly, questions addressing an individual's eating, gambling, sex and love issues, and work habits should be included in your routine psycho-social history. The nature and extent of information gathering in these areas will, of course, depend on the presenting problem. However, as you gather such data, facts disclosed about a client's family of origin or a client's current behavioral patterns may suggest areas for further exploration. For example, in listening to a bright, thin, college-aged, woman with a family history of perfectionism and conflict, you might want to ask her about her eating patterns or about her attitudes regarding eating.

Assessment

With regard to eating disorders, Sibley and Blinder (1988) state that it is characteristic of anorexics to minimize symptoms and medical complications. Quite often, seeking professional help comes only after the individual has experienced pressure from family members and cohorts at work or school. Behavioral and attitude changes often accompany anorexia nervosa and bulimia nervosa and include an increased interest in cooking, nutrition, and concomitant increase in exercise. Sibley and Blinder also believe that until family members become fully aware of the extent of the problem, they often will reinforce the individual's interests in these three areas. Mental health professionals will want to examine the client's family for evidence of enmeshment, overprotectiveness, rigidity, lack of conflict resolution, and the involvement of the client in unresolved marital and family conflicts. In addition, information about weight loss is critical in assessing the severity of anorexia nervosa and bulimia nervosa.

When clients present difficulties in the areas of chronic marital strife, financial problems, and financial management mental health professionals should consider completing a gambling history (Gaudia, 1992). Moreover, Ciarrochi (1987) reviewed self-reports of compulsive gamblers and found that a substantial number (up to 45%) had severe problems with alcohol or other drugs. Pathological gamblers are also likely to come from families in which there is a higher than normal incidence of parental gambling and alcohol dependence (APA, 1994). So assessing for addiction to gambling should include attention to a family history of addictive behaviors as well as to the individual's demonstration of other abusive behaviors or cross-addictions.

We stated in Chapter 5 that a simple rule for determining whether a behavior is problematic is to ask yourself the question, "Does a normal drinker drink like this client?" For sex and love addiction, the mental health counselor can assess the normality of the client's relationship with a spouse or companion, the client's past and present extended family environment, other intimate relationships both present and past, and the client's relationships with strangers (Logan, 1992). The question of normality should also guide the mental health professional's assessment of workaholism. Workaholism can be assessed by using Oates' (1971) phases and by helping clients to describe their symptoms. In addition to these symptoms, workaholics may also present problems with intimacy, tying one's self-worth to accomplishments at work, feelings of isolation, and depression even after completing a work task.

Treatment Considerations

Because the notion of other addictions is controversial, treatment considerations will also vary, as you would expect. Similar to our discussion in Chapter 7, various treatment modalities are used for these other addictions. Addiction counselors who believe in the Minnesota Model (Cook, 1989) may view the treatment of other addictions to be similar to the treatment of alcohol and other drug addiction and use this model, which includes individual, family, and group treatment modalities with an emphasis upon abstinence. Other mental health professionals may treat these other addictions through the use of classical and operant conditioning techniques. Regardless, recall from Chapter 7 that treatment efficacy depends on the length and type of treatment and that matching clients with appropriate treatment strategies is very important. For example, Sibley and Blinder (1988) point out that short-term therapies focusing on one area of concern will not produce efficacious outcomes for these other addictions.

In general, a treatment plan for other addictions should have similar considerations of those used in treating alcohol and other drug addiction, such as identifying problematic behaviors, identifying goals, helping clients initiate change, following up, and making plans for relapse prevention. In Chapter 7, we discussed issues surrounding the choice of treatment setting. Nace (1987) stated that these issues include client motivation, an ability to discontinue the problematic behavior, social support, employment considerations, and the client's medical condition, psychiatric status, and past treatment history. Mental health professionals should consider these issues when choosing a treatment modality for other addictions.

There are some differences among professionals regarding the treatment of eating disorders. The more pathological disorders, anorexia nervosa and bulimia nervosa, require medical attention, because these conditions are life threatening. So it would be important for a mental health professional to arrange for medical consultation with a physician familiar with eating disorders who can help monitor the medical complications that accompany anorexia nervosa and bulimia nervosa. Because of the complex nature of these eating disorders, it is also important for mental health professionals to undergo additional training in the assessment and treatment of anorexia and bulimia.

For eating disorders, Freeman (1992) recommends "a multicomponent approach to treatment by a multi-disciplinary treatment team..." (p. 157). Freeman asserts that the treatment approach should include individual, family, and group psychotherapy and should include the more directive techniques of psycho-education, nutritional counseling, and self-monitoring techniques. As we pointed out in Chapter 7, it is critically important for mental health professionals to determine the client's learning style or learning capacity before initiating psycho-educational approaches. In addition to individual, family, and group psychotherapy, Twelve Step support groups, such as Overeaters Anonymous (OA), may be of some help to clients whose problems include binge-eating and over-eating. These support groups can be especially helpful with relapse prevention, since clients with full-blown anorexia nervosa and bulimia nervosa will probably have problems in other areas of functioning. Specifically, support groups may help with important issues related to the initiation of pathological eating behaviors. For example, clients with eating disorders may demonstrate codependent behaviors or complain of other family dysfunction, factors that trigger compulsive eating behavior. Learning how to identify these triggers concomitant with hearing about how others deal with them may help to prevent a relapse.

Relapse prevention is also an important consideration for compulsive gambling, regardless of the type of treatment approach. As we pointed out in Chapter 13, the supposition that a relapse means a return to full-blown gambling or some other addictive behavior is not an accurate assumption to make. As we also mentioned, it is important to use these slips to educate clients about their gambling behaviors.

Another means of educating clients is through conducting gambling histories, which is usually done in conjunction with a psychosocial history. Freeman (1992) believes that it is crucial for mental health professionals to gather this data before determining a course of treatment for compulsive gambling, because different treatment considerations depend on whether the client is actively gambling or in a period of recovery. Regardless of whether the mental health professional uses a behavioral approach, psychotherapy, family therapy, group therapy, or some other treatment venue, "treatment should focus on the connection between the client's inability to regulate tension and the accustomed pattern of discharging tension by gambling" (Freeman, p. 241). Moreover, Freeman believes that the initial task of any treatment plan should focus on abstinence or on disruption of the gambling pattern.

Taber, McCormick, Russo, Adkins, and Ramirez (1987) suggest that compulsive gambling is treatable in terms of abstinence and general behavior improvement. In addition to individual, family, and group psychotherapy, support groups such as Gamblers Anonymous (GA) can help clients who have this disorder maintain abstinence. It should be noted that one of the goals of GA is to have the addicted gambler make full restitution wherever possible (Gamblers Anonymous, 1989), which can be a formidable task for some clients. Clients may need some additional support from mental health professionals when attempting to make financial amends.

In treating sex and love addiction and work addiction, we recommend an approach similar to that for eating disorders and emphasize a multifaceted approach. In the case of sexual acting-out, medical consultation might be indicated for the detection and treatment of sexually transmitted diseases or HIV infection. It is also important to conduct an extensive history to determine where the client is in a recovery process. Obviously, abstinence from sex, love, or work is not a goal, so treatment plans should focus on the client's acknowledgment of repetitive and self-defeating interaction patterns and focus as well on understanding the impact of social and family functioning as it relates to compulsive sex, love, or work behaviors. Although there is no formal support group for workaholism, such groups do exist for sex and love addiction. Many members of Sex and Love Addicts Anonymous have reported this Twelve Step program to be effective in helping them identify this addiction, exert self-control measures, and maintain abstinence. Therefore, mental health professionals might want to consider a support group as part of the treatment plan.

Peele (1975) suggests that the most effective approaches to use with sex and love addiction include behavior modification and group therapy. The same can be said for workaholism. In treating both sex and love addiction and workaholism, approaches should include the client's self-examination of his or her attitudes and beliefs about compulsive behaviors as well as paying attention to his or her views of the world in general. Freeman (1992) maintains that self-examination requires establishing goals with baselines, timelines, and plans for evaluating the over-all effectiveness of the treatment approach. Clients can be asked to maintain a written log used to identify events at work or in relationships, happenings, and feelings associated with the compulsion. In addition to such a process-oriented approach, Freeman suggests that treatment for sex, love, and work addictions involves significant others. Mental health professionals should take care in determining the timing and who to include in such treatment. When including other family members, the mental health professional might use a genogram (McGoldrick & Gerson, 1985). This tool is designed to help clients identify a history of sex, love, or compulsive work patterns in their families or origin. In addition, the genogram helps bring to the surface family communication or transmission patterns, family role assignments, secrets, and projections. Specific to sex and love addiction, Freeman suggests the use of the Halpern's (1982) relationship review. A review can identify patterns of the type of people with whom clients have a tendency to become involved. The review can also identify repeated patterns of interaction and the types of relationships that have been formed. Mental health professionals might adapt the relationship review to assess the client's relationships at work as well. It has been our experience that workaholics often attempt to avoid stressful relationships at home by pouring themselves into their work. So identifying relationship patterns at work can assist the mental health professional in helping to lead the client more easily toward dealing with problematic relationships at home. By dealing with family-of-origin patterns and looking at their home and work arenas, workaholics are more likely to gain a better understanding of their need to work so hard and can begin to identify triggers that propel them into a cycle of compulsive work.

Summary

Setting aside the debate over whether there are other addictions, each of the disorders we described results from a complex system of multiple interacting determinants and can serve numerous personal functions for individuals ((Orford, 1985). Whether you as a mental health professional subscribe to the traditional view of addictions or to a broader view of compulsive behaviors as being other addictions, you will need to be aware of the theories attempting to explain the etiology and maintenance of these disorders. The disease model offers some support for the concept of other addictions. Early childhood experiences, interpreted through psychoanalytic or object relations theory, are certainly significant components of compulsive behaviors and can help explain one's proclivities to initiate compulsive behaviors. Hsu (1988) believes these theories have a great deal of explanatory power but are difficult to research empirically. More accessible to empirical research are interpretations based upon social learning theory with its emphasis upon overt and covert reinforcement and modeling. Family systems theory also lends itself more easily to empirical investigations.

Assessment and treatment considerations for other addictions remain similar to those we outlined in Chapter 7. Although some debate remains about the best approach in treating these disorders, it is well established that any treatment should include a thorough psycho-social assessment as well as attention to gathering specific histories of food, gambling, sex and love, or work patterns. Matching appropriate treatment with individuals is critical. In cases of anorexia nervosa and bulimia nervosa, medical consultation and additional training for mental health professionals should be sought. A medical consultation may also be indicated when the client presents a history of sexual acting-out. In most cases, mental health professionals should utilize individual, family, and group therapy whenever possible. Finally, these clients with other addictions may also benefit from the use of support groups.

Chapter 16

Prevention

Most of this text is concerned with the problems caused by the abuse of alcohol and other drugs, reflecting our view of mental health professionals' need for this information and the frequency of alcohol and other drug abuse in our society. Although it is probably inevitable that humans will use and abuse drugs, we believe that the number of individuals who encounter problems as a result of alcohol and other drug use is related to the success of prevention efforts. Therefore, please do not conclude that prevention is less important than other topics in this book because only a single chapter is devoted to this topic. We believe that prevention is critically important both from a policy and a program standpoint. In particular, those of you who are planning to work in public schools as counselors or social workers should go beyond the information in this chapter. The reference list would be a good place to start looking for further information.

Policy Issues in Prevention

Drug Free?

On a surface level, it might seem that prevention (which we will define shortly) hardly needs a policy discussion. After all, most people would agree that preventing alcohol and other drug misuse, especially by young people, is positive and that's all the policy necessary. Clearly, the issues are more complicated. For example, federal agencies set drug-free goals. The Center for Substance Abuse Prevention publishes booklets to help create drug-free communities (e.g., Office for Substance Abuse Prevention, 1989) and the Department of Education developed the Drug Free Schools and Communities Program. The Department of Education's goal is to have drug- and violence-free schools by the year 2000. However, *drug-free* does not include alcohol, which ignores the fact that alcohol is the most widely used drug by young people and adults and causes more harm to society than any illegal drug. Also, the goal of drug-free schools and communities, while admirable, is unrealistic. Maintaining such a goal may divert efforts and resources from achieving more realistic, reduction goals.

Gateway Drugs

Related to this issue is the fact that federal prevention efforts have not focused on so-called gateway drugs as much as they should. Gateway drugs are those drugs that precede the use of other drugs and are usually considered to be alcohol, tobacco, and marijuana (Kandel, 1989). In fairness, more recent publications from the Center for Substance Abuse Prevention now refer to "alcohol, tobacco, and other drug problems," but this has not always been the case. As we will discuss, the reasons for the lack of focus on tobacco and alcohol probably is related to political pressure as opposed to best practice. It makes sense to focus on gateway drugs in prevention programs because it is rare that a drug user begins with drugs such as cocaine or heroin (New York State Division of Alcoholism and Alcohol Abuse, 1989). A young person usually begins drug use with tobacco or alcohol, since these drugs are readily available and their use is perceived as dangerous, exciting, and adult-like. Once a young person "takes the plunge" (begins use), it is much easier to go on to the next class of drugs. Furthermore, Hawkins, Catalano, and Miller (1992) have shown that the age of first use of any drug is related to later drug abuse by adolescents. Finally, alcohol and tobacco cause more health and related problems than other drugs. For example, in 1989, there were 500,000 deaths associated with tobacco and alcohol as opposed to 9,000 deaths from all of the currently illegal drugs combined (Jonas, 1992).

For all these reasons, it makes sense to focus on preventing the initiation of use of gateway drugs. However, the alcohol and tobacco industries have powerful lobbies that present constant barriers to prevention efforts. To give you one simple example, the tobacco industry is allowed to market a product that has no medically useful purpose, is highly addicting, and kills 400,000 people a year. A product with these characteristics would never be allowed to be introduced today, and the failure to ban the promotion of tobacco is unconscionable. Obviously, alcohol is also marketed widely. For example, Madden and Grube (1994) found that there were 1.5 alcohol commercials for each hour of televised sports, and Grube and Wallack (1994) found a significant association between awareness of beer advertising and the drinking intentions, beliefs, and knowledge of children. Therefore, any efforts designed to prevent young people from initiating alcohol or tobacco use is directly countered by the marketing of these products. Legislators are heavily lobbied and receive campaign contributions from the alcohol and tobacco industries and have little motivation to pass laws that restrict or prohibit advertising. So research indicates that we need prevention efforts that focus on the gateway drugs, but federal and state government officials do not want to upset the tobacco and alcohol industries. Furthermore, prevention efforts are sabotaged by the sophisticated marketing of tobacco and alcohol. Can you see how policy effects prevention?

Supply versus Demand

Public policy regarding allocation of resources and prevention focus is also a contentious issue. How much emphasis should be placed on reducing the supply of illegal drugs and how much on reducing the demand? Reducing supply implies an allocation of resources to law enforcement, while reducing demand requires community-based prevention programs. A review of federal spending for the War on Drugs illustrates federal policy.

> *Of the $1.7 billion authorized to implement the War on Drugs legislation in 1987, approximately $1.2 billion was allocated to law enforcement and "supply reduction" strategies targeting illicit drugs.... The funds have been spent almost exclusively on expensive paramilitary hardware and law enforcement activities. The 1988 War on Drugs legislation continued to rely heavily on law enforcement and other "supply reduction" strategies targeting illicit drug use... (American Public Health Association, 1989, p. 362).*

How effective has this strategy been? According to the House of Representatives Government Operations Committee report in 1990 regarding the supply of cocaine:

> *The Committee's investigation revealed little evidence to suggest that supply reduction programs in source countries have affected the supply or use of cocaine in the United States. Compelling evidence was presented to the Committee that even successful source-country supply reduction efforts can have only a negligible impact on cocaine prices and consumption in the U.S.: the costs of producing cocaine are so low that even a fifty percent reduction in supply would add less than three percent to the retail price. (p. 7)*

According to Grinspoon and Bakalar (1994), the war on drugs is actually a war on drug users:

> *The federal budget for the control of illicit drugs has increased more than eightfold since 1981, and more than two-thirds of the total is devoted to the enforcement of increasingly harsh criminal laws.... Of the 1 million drug arrests each year, about 225,000 are for simple possession of marijuana, the fourth most common cause of arrest in the United States.... Largely because we imprison so many drug users and petty drug dealers, the United States has a higher proportion of its population incarcerated than any other country in the world for which reliable statistics are available. (p. 357)*

With regard to prevention, if a large percentage of federal dollars were put into efforts to reduce the supply of illicit drugs and the arrest and incarceration of drug offenders, then there are fewer dollars for demand reduction.

Responsible Use

Another policy issue involves the acceptable level of alcohol use for young people. Advocates of "no use" argue that alcohol use by minors is illegal and that any effort to educate young people about responsible use is, in fact, irresponsible and enabling. On the other side are those who propose that modeling moderate use of alcohol will prevent alcohol abuse. Also, providing safe transportation for intoxicated minors is preferable to drunk driving. Organizations such as Mothers Against Drunk Driving (MADD) frequently organize free transportation on prom and graduation nights. This is an extremely difficult policy issue. The prevention of drunk driving is obviously important but a community may unintentionally encourage alcohol abuse by making it easy for minors who are intoxicated to get safely home. Modeling and encouraging moderate use of alcohol by minors ignores the legal prohibition on use by minors and also fails to acknowledge that certain individuals will progress to abuse and dependence in spite of being cautioned to drink moderately.

The policy issues that we have discussed involving reduction goals, gateway drugs, supply vs. demand reduction, and responsible use have a major impact on the funding as well as on the form of prevention activities. We encourage you to consider these issues carefully and to attempt to appropriately exert your influence on public policy decision makers at whatever level of government you choose.

Levels of Prevention

Prevention is often conceptualized as primary, secondary, and tertiary. Primary prevention involves attempts to dissuade an individual from initiating tobacco, alcohol, and other drug use. When one considers that 22% of fifth graders reported using alcohol (Benson, Williams, & Johnson, 1987), primary prevention must begin at an early age. Primary prevention activities occur in schools and through community organizations such as Boy and Girl Scouts, religious institutions, and park and recreation departments. Secondary prevention may be viewed as early intervention. These prevention efforts involve identifying individuals who have already begun to use tobacco, alcohol, or other drugs and are at risk for further involvement. Secondary prevention efforts are designed to halt the progression of use. As we mentioned in Chapter 4, prevention programs may have both a primary prevention and secondary prevention focus, depending on the individuals in the program. For example, imagine that a program designed as primary prevention is started in a fourth-grade class. Part of the program involves teaching the children to assertively refuse when peers pressure them to use tobacco. But, one girl in the class has already smoked several times with her older sister. After learning the assertive skills, she is able to resist smoking in the future. Technically, this would be secondary prevention. The more common examples would be programs for young people who have been caught using tobacco or alcohol at school or have become involved with the legal system for minor offenses and show evidence of alcohol or other drug use. Secondary prevention programs may take a variety of forms including education, social skills development, drug-free recreational activities, mentoring by drug-free adults, or others. Educational efforts designed to convince pregnant women to discontinue the use of tobacco, alcohol, and other drugs are also secondary prevention.

Tertiary prevention is usually considered treatment and is designed to prevent the future use of alcohol or other drugs by an individual who has been identified as an abuser or as being dependent. These strategies have been described in Chapter 7.

The remainder of this chapter is devoted to a discussion of primary and secondary prevention efforts. A public health model will be described to help you conceptualize prevention. We will also discuss research involving those individuals who have been able to resist alcohol and other drug involvement in spite of possessing risk factors for substance abuse.

A Public Health Prevention Model

According to Jonas (1992), a public health approach to prevention

> *uses epidemiological, pharmacological, and toxicological science to define the substance abuse problem. . . . It identifies the real causes of the problem and then develops interventions directed at those causes. . . . Some of the interventions are of a classically "public health" nature. . . . These include improved school and public health education and strengthened regulation, such as limitations on advertising and promotion of the currently legal recreational mood-altering drugs. Other elements are political, such as shifting the antisubstance abuse message of the national leadership from one that emphasizes punishment for bad behavior to one that emphasizes a healthy life-style. All of the public health interventions focus on helping people change their behavior in a positive way (p. 929).*

The public health model to prevention uses epidemiology to conceptualize tobacco, alcohol and other drug use problems (this model is also used with other public health problems such as communicable diseases). Imagine a triangle in which one angle represents the tobacco, alcohol, and other drug user (the host), the second angle is the substance used (the agent), and the third angle is the social and physical context of use (the environment). Problems related to tobacco, alcohol, and other drug use arise as a result of relationships and interactions among the host, the agent, and the environment. Therefore, the public health model of prevention involves all three elements.

The public health approach to tobacco, alcohol, and other drug prevention has been used with many other health issues. For example, the public health approach to preventing heart disease combines education regarding proper nutrition, exercise, and life-style with regulations on nutrition and fat content labeling on food products and warnings on heart-disease-causing products, such as cigarettes. Efforts are made to convince high-risk individuals or hosts (e.g., obese smokers) to modify their behaviors before heart disease occurs and to prevent individuals from adopting high-risk behaviors.

A similar approach is taken to the problem of tobacco, alcohol, and other drug abuse. At the national level, public health organizations such as The Centers for

Disease Control and the American Public Health Association provide research and statistics that can be used in planning prevention programs. Information is disseminated through the news media and government publications. For example, the National Institute on Drug Abuse and the Center for Substance Abuse Prevention (both part of the Public Health Service in the U.S. Department of Health and Human Services) have numerous publications, pamphlets, videos, etc. on research, prevention programs, community planning, and a variety of other topics. Public service commercials about drug use are also a part of this information dissemination. Obviously, the Public Health Service is also actively involved in the dissemination of information regarding prevention of AIDs, tuberculoses, hepatitis, and other communicable diseases related to drug use.

Public policy is also influenced through a public health approach to prevention. For example, former Surgeon General Koop recommended restrictions on alcohol and tobacco advertising as a result of information gathered by the Public Health Service. Taxation of drug products (alcohol and tobacco) and warning labels on tobacco are two results of public health prevention efforts. However, the Public Health Service is part of the federal government, and, as we've shown, politics influence policy. As the American Public Health Association (1989) stated:

> *Alcohol, tobacco, and other drug problems represent one of the most pressing public health issues in the United States today. Despite numerous assaults on these problems, including the current "War on Drugs," they remain intractable— continuing at epidemic levels and unresponsive to a variety of strategies and public policy initiatives. This intractability is in part a result of a fundamental misunderstanding of and blindness to the nature of alcohol, tobacco, and other drug problems and the degree to which they are integrated into our society (p. 360– 361).*

As Jonas (1992) points out, the current "OK/not-OK" drug dichotomy (alcohol and tobacco are "OK" and illegal drugs are "not-OK") is illogical based on the health, economic, and human costs of "OK" drugs. This national policy has "created barriers to the development of an effective drug abuse prevention program" (p. 935).

At a local level, prevention services at public health departments include the dissemination of information through classes and publications, drug testing, prenatal care, health promotions, health care referrals, nutritional guidance, family planning, home visits from health or social service workers, and social support for new mothers. All of these have produced significant differences in high-risk families and individuals (Hawkins, Catalano, & Miller, 1992).

Prevention Strategies for Youth

Clearly, prevention efforts at national, state, and local levels are primarily directed toward young people. This makes sense, since minors are less likely than adults to have initiated their own use, are more easily influenced, and are at great risk for future problems from tobacco, alcohol, and other drug use.

How great is the need for prevention strategies for young people? In other words, does extensive tobacco, alcohol, and other drug use exist among young people? At the risk of "number numbing" you, we will give you the latest figures from the National Institute on Drug Abuse, which sponsors a yearly study of use patterns of minors and young adults called "Monitoring the Future." Based on the most recent results available (Johnston, O'Malley, & Bachman, 1994), the percentage of 8th graders who reported using cigarettes, alcohol, marijuana, and cocaine in the last 30 days[1] were as follows: 16.7%, 26.2%, 5.1%, and 0.7% respectively. For 12th graders, the percentages were cigarettes, 29.9%; alcohol, 51.0%; marijuana, 15.5%; and cocaine, 1.3%. Clearly, tobacco and alcohol are the primary drugs of choice, and the number of users of tobacco, alcohol, and cocaine nearly doubles between 8th and 12th grade. Reports of marijuana use in the last 30 days triples. Since the survey was begun in 1975, the 30-day prevalence for the following drugs for 12th graders has decreased significantly: cigarettes are down 6.8%; alcohol, 17.2%; marijuana, 11.6%; and cocaine, .6%. The data on cocaine is distorted, since the percentage of 30-day users was 1.9% in 1975 but reached a high of 6.7% in 1985. The direction of these data is certainly encouraging. However, recognize that the rates of use by 13 and 14 year olds, particularly with regard to tobacco and alcohol, is alarming. Furthermore, 30-day prevalence of drugs such as cigarettes, marijuana, and hallucinogens increased from 1992 to 1993. These data also indicate that, contrary to the belief of many adolescents that "everybody is doing it," the majority of adolescents are not doing it. Even in the case of alcohol, nearly half of 12th graders reported abstaining in the last month.

At the federal level, the Center for Substance Abuse Prevention (Public Health Service, Substance Abuse and Mental Health Services Administration, U.S. Department of Health and Human Services) and the Drug-Free Schools and Communities Program (U.S. Department of Education) have funded a variety of prevention programs and activities at state and local levels and provide many printed materials about prevention that are usually available at no cost. In each state, the agency responsible for alcohol and other drug treatment services will have a designated prevention coordinator. These resources may help you in determining prevention activities and programs in your area or in finding out what is working in other areas.

As can be expected, many different approaches to prevention for young people have been developed. Until recently, the sense was that prevention programs were not effective in reducing drug-use behavior. In fact, some approaches were associated with increased drug use by participants (Botvin, Baker, Dusenbury, Tortu, & Botvin, 1990). However, comprehensive literature reviews and meta-analysis (Botvin and Botvin, 1992; Tobler, 1992) have identified some successful prevention programs. We will describe the types of prevention approaches and activities that have been used and their outcomes, the essential components for successful prevention programs, and some examples of prevention programs.

---

[1] The "Monitoring the Future" study surveys the use of a variety of drugs over a respondent's lifetime, annually, in a 30-day period, and daily. Respondents are 8th, 10th, and 12th graders; young adults; and college students. We are providing only a small portion of the reported data.

Why Do These Kids Use Drugs?

In talking to various groups of parents, teachers, and community leaders, this question invariably arises. First, we make sure that adults understand that tobacco and alcohol are also drugs before responding to this question. Second, rather than quoting research to answer the question, we ask the adults to develop a comprehensive list of reasons for adolescent tobacco, alcohol, and other drug use. This list usually includes the euphoric effect of alcohol and other drugs (people feel good when they use), boredom, desire for excitement and danger, need to experiment, rebelliousness, peer pressure, desire to feel adult-like, desire to fit in with a social group, difficulty in coping with negative emotions, lack of information, modeling by influential peers and adults (including family members), and societal messages that there is a chemical solution for every human problem. (After developing this list, we point out that adults use alcohol and other drugs for the same reasons). Notice that these reasons for adolescent use can be categorized under the components of the public health model. For example, the host (or adolescent) may not have skills to deal with negative emotions. The agents (tobacco, alcohol, and other drugs) are available and produce euphoria (except for tobacco). The environment (e.g., advertisements) shows use by influential adults (e.g., athletes, attractive people). Some reasons for adolescent use can be conceptualized as fitting into more than one category as well. For example, peer pressure is an environmental factor but the ability (or lack thereof) to resist such pressure is a host (or individual) factor. Because the public health model of prevention assumes that tobacco, alcohol, and other drug use results from interactions between the host, agent, and environment and because the reasons for adolescent use involve all three elements, it is reasonable to assume that prevention efforts must involve the host, agent, and environment. As we shall see, this is not always the case.

Types of Prevention Approaches

Botvin and Botvin (1992) divide prevention approaches into five categories: information dissemination, affective education approaches, alternatives approaches, social resistance skills approaches, and competency enhancement approaches. Information dissemination involves didactic instruction, discussions, and printed materials. Audio-visual materials and displays of drugs (or representations of drugs) may be used. In schools, specific curriculum on tobacco, alcohol, and other drugs may be presented by specially trained teachers or health professionals. Public information is disseminated through printed materials, public service announcements, and special programs. The information dissemination approaches are based on the assumption that individuals will make good choices if they have accurate information and that poor choices are the results of ignorance. Botvin and Botvin also include scare tactics in the information dissemination approach. The use of scare tactics is designed to provoke fear in students by dramatizing the negative effects of tobacco, alcohol, and other drugs.

It is not surprising that information dissemination methods have been unsuccessful in impacting tobacco, alcohol, and other drug use. As Botvin and Botvin (1992) state:

studies have rather consistently indicated that informational approaches do not *reduce or prevent tobacco, alcohol, or drug use; they indicate quite clearly that increased knowledge has virtually no impact on substance use or on intentions to engage in tobacco, alcohol, or drug use in the near future (p. 914, italics in original).*

Similarly, Tobler (1992) found that prevention programs that only presented information did increase knowledge of participants but had no effect on attitudes and drug use. If you will recall the public health model that involves the host, agent, and environment, information dissemination only impacts the cognitive understanding of the host. Since there is no attempt to intervene with the agent or the environment, the public health model of prevention would predict that information dissemination methods would, if isolated from other interventions, be ineffective. Consider an analogy with the prevention of heart disease. Most Americans know that quitting smoking, regular aerobic exercise, reducing fat in one's diet, etc., will reduce the risk of heart disease. However, this information alone is usually insufficient to result in a significant behavior change for most people. Similarly, simply learning about the negative consequences of using tobacco, alcohol, and other drugs does not affect the reasons for use by most young people. However, as we will discuss later, information dissemination should be a component of a comprehensive prevention program.

While the goal of information dissemination approaches is cognitive change in students, affective education prevention approaches focus on personal and social development. According to Botvin and Botvin (1992):

Affective education approaches focus on increasing self-understanding and acceptance through activities such as values clarifications and responsible decision making; improving interpersonal relations by fostering effective communication, peer counseling, and assertiveness; and increasing students' abilities to fulfill their basic needs through existing social institutions (p. 914).

The results from Tobler's (1992) meta-analysis show that prevention programs that used only affective education were ineffective in impacting knowledge, attitudes and values, self-reported drug use, or decision-making, assertive, and refusal skills. Furthermore, drug incident reports, school grades and attendance, and achievement test scores also were unaffected. Approaches that combine cognitive (information dissemination) and affective approaches did have a positive effect on knowledge of participants but a negligible effect on the other outcomes.

Prevention approaches that utilize alternative activities have typically involved the school and community groups in a partnership. Conceptually, if adolescents use alcohol and other drugs because of boredom and/or the need for excitement and danger, then they will be less likely to engage in use if there are sufficient activities available that are fun and exciting. Community youth centers have been established that include video games, sports, crafts, etc. The popular midnight basketball concept, in which school and community gyms are open and supervised late at night, was designed to give adolescents an alcohol and other drug-free, healthy, fun activity during the hours that many adolescents typically get involved in use and other criminal activity. Community and school centers often combine academic tutoring and mentoring by responsible adults to counter other possible causes of use. The *Outward Bound* program, in which high-risk youth participate in a wilderness experience, is another example of an alternatives program. In addition to providing a healthy, exciting alternative to young people, the program also encourages cooperation, team work, and self-confidence (a complete description of Outward Bound can be found in Boldt and Miner, 1981).

Botvin and Botvin (1992) indicate that entertainment, vocational, and social alternatives programs have been associated with more rather than less substance use, although academic, religious, and sports activities are associated with less use. They report that evaluations of alternatives programs have failed to demonstrate an impact on adolescent use. In contrast, Tobler's (1992) meta-analysis of alternatives programs for high-risk youth showed positive effects on skills and behavior, including school grades, school attendance, and independent reports of observed drug use.

Another approach to prevention is based on the environmental influences on young people that result in the initiation of tobacco, alcohol, and other drug use. Family use patterns (including parents and siblings), peer pressure, and media all may influence young people to use (or not to use). Social resistance skills approaches (also called *social influence* or *refusal skills* approaches) have been developed to counter-act environmental influences. According to Botvin and Botvin (1992):

> *these interventions were designed to increase students' awareness of the various social influences to engage in substance use. A distinctive feature of these prevention models is that they place more emphasis on teaching students specific skills for effectively resisting both peer and media pressures to smoke, drink, or use drugs. (p. 916)*

According to Botvin and Botvin (1992), social resistance skills approaches generally contain the following components: recognizing situations in which there is a high probability that a young person will experience peer pressure to use, formulating strategies to avoid these high-risk situations, teaching students what to say and how to say it when confronted with peer pressure, and developing awareness of techniques used by the media to encourage use by young people. Peers are frequently used in implementing these programs, since peers, particularly older adolescents with perceived status, may be more influential than teachers or other adults. Information dissemination, with a focus on prevalence of use by young people, is used to counter the argument that "everyone is doing it."

In evaluating social resistance skills approaches, Botvin and Botvin (1992) report that these programs have been associated with reductions in tobacco, alcohol, and marijuana use for up to three years. However, long-term follow-up studies have shown that these reductions are not maintained over time. Tobler (1992) found that programs using peers as implementors had a positive impact on knowledge, attitudes, self-reported drug use, and skills. However, no beneficial effect was noted on drug incident reports or on indirect measures of use such as school grades and attendance. The age group of the students, number of training sessions, use of booster sessions, instructional materials, and characteristics of the students may all impact evaluation of these programs, and Botvin and Botvin suggest that additional research is necessary to clarify the variables that are important for success.

Competency enhancement approaches are more comprehensive than the other approaches and focus on the interaction between the individual and environment in the prevention of substance use by young people. Competency enhancement approaches emphasize the development and use of personal and social skills that are directly related to substance use but that are also applicable to many other adolescent problems. According to Botvin and Botvin (1992), competency enhancement approaches

typically teach two or more of the following:

1. *General problem-solving and decision making skills*
2. *General cognitive skills for resisting interpersonal or media influences*
3. *Skills for increasing self-control and self-esteem*
4. *Adaptive coping strategies for relieving stress and anxiety through the use of cognitive coping skills or behavioral relaxation techniques*
5. *General social skills*
6. *General assertive skills*

These skills are taught using a combination of instruction, demonstration, feedback, reinforcement, behavioral rehearsal (practice during class), and extended practice through behavioral homework assignments (p. 320).

Evaluation studies of competency enhancement approaches seem generally positive. In a summary of these studies, Botvin and Botvin (1992) report reductions in initiating use of tobacco, alcohol, and marijuana. Effectiveness has been demonstrated using many types of trainers (e.g., peers, teachers, project staff) as well as with ethnically diverse groups. With booster sessions, the effects have been maintained for up to three years.

Elements of Successful Prevention Programs

As can be seen from the preceding discussion, the prevention approaches that focus on the host (individual), the environment, and their interaction seem to be the most effective. From a public health perspective, prevention efforts would be enhanced if public policy were more effective in limiting the marketing and availability of agents, such as tobacco and alcohol. However, school-based and community-based prevention programs generally do not include public policy efforts with regard to availability and marketing.[2] Keeping in mind that this aspect of a public health model of prevention is usually missing, we want to discuss some of the elements of successful prevention programs.

---

[2]An exception is the Partnership for a Drug-Free America, a coalition of advertising and media associations who donate their time to produce and direct anti-drug advertising. Unfortunately, the partnership focuses on marijuana, cocaine, and crack and tends to ignore tobacco and alcohol.

As we mentioned earlier, information dissemination is not, in isolation, an effective prevention approach. However, information is important as a component of a comprehensive prevention effort. The facts that are presented to students should be accurate and up-to-date. Scare tactics are unlikely to be effective, since the programs will usually include students who have personally used or know others who have used without adverse consequences. As Botvin and Botvin (1992) pointed out, it is helpful to present young people with prevalence statistics, since these numbers dispel the idea that "everyone is doing it." Local data is particularly useful in such presentations.

As we discussed in the social resistance skills and competency enhancement approaches to prevention, successful programs emphasize the development of life skills for use in resisting peer pressure. These skills are also generalizable to a variety of situations and enhance the young person's satisfaction with life. These skills include the ability to set goals, make decisions, solve problems, think critically, cope with negative emotions, communicate effectively, make friends, and assert oneself appropriately. We will discuss some prevention programs that include the development of these skills.

The method of implementing a prevention program is critically important. A six-year study by the Institute for Prevention Research at Cornell University (reported by Western Regional Center for Drug-Free Schools and Communities, 1994) found that prevention programs must be taught at least throughout junior high school and must exceed one year with several booster sessions in order to produce lasting reductions in drug use. In addition, it is suggested that prevention programs be taught throughout the school year rather than in short, concentrated sessions. Teachers or other trainers should also be formally trained and receive consultation and support from experts. However, some evidence (summarized by Hawkins, Catalano, & Miller, 1992) shows that student or peer-led prevention programs achieve greater reductions in drug use than those led by teachers.

Prevention programs that go beyond the presentation of lessons in the classroom are also most likely to impact a wide range of host and environmental factors that may lead to use. For example, improving the classroom management skills of teachers, developing cooperative learning strategies, using shared decision making and management policies, and increasing opportunities for student-teacher-community interaction and involvement are school-based strategies that may be associated with reducing the risk for substance abuse (Hawkins, Catalano, & Miller, 1992). At the community level, there is a need for increased crisis intervention, referral, and other mental health services; parent education; other social and health services (e.g., child care, medical services); and organized drug-free recreational activities.

Examples of School-Based Prevention Programs

The following examples of school-based prevention programs are meant to illustrate the philosophy and content of widely used prevention programs. Please note that we are describing, not endorsing, these programs.

Drug Abuse Resistance Education (DARE)

The DARE program is unique among school-based prevention programs with its use of police officers as instructors. The program was developed by Daryl Gates, former Los Angeles Chief of Police. DARE officers are trained in child development, classroom management, teaching techniques, and communication skills prior to classroom instruction. The program consists of 17 lessons delivered to fifth- and sixth-grade students offering information about alcohol and other drugs, refusal skills, decision making, alternatives to drug use, resistance to peer pressure, and self-esteem enhancement (DARE America, 1991). There are ten follow-up lessons in junior high and an additional nine lesson in high school.

According to DARE America (1991), the non-profit organization that coordinates DARE, over five million children a year participate in the program. Ennett, Rosenbaum, Flewelling, Bieler, Ringwalt, & Bailey (1994) report that DARE is the most widely used prevention program in the United States. However, in a long-term evaluation study in 36 schools in Illinois, they found limited support for DARE's impact on drug use immediately following the program and no support for continuing impact on drug use one to two years following the program. There was a positive effect on self-esteem but no effect on peer resistance skills. A meta-analysis of eight evaluation studies of DARE found the program less effective than more interactive prevention programs on measures of drug knowledge, drug attitudes, social skills, and drug use (Ennett, Tobler, Ringwalt, & Flewelling, 1994).

Here's Looking at You, 2000

This kindergarten through 12th grade curriculum was originally developed in 1975 and has been revised twice since then. The curriculum addresses the risk factors for substance abuse identified by J.D. Hawkins and his associates (e.g., Hawkins, et al., 1992) (these risk factors will be discussed later in the chapter). For example, living in a chemically dependent family, early first use of drugs, and having drug-using friends are some of the risk factors addressed.

Here's Looking at You, 2000 focuses on gateway drugs and has a clear "no use" message. The curriculum contains video tapes, posters, books, cards, filmstrips, games, puzzles, hand puppets, reference materials, costumes, charts, and scripts to engage students in a variety of learning activities. School personnel are expected to implement the curriculum, and training is available from Roberts, Fitzmahan, and Associates, developers of the curriculum. There are 14 to 31 lessons per grade level, with some lessons requiring more than one day. The content of the curriculum varies by grade level and includes alcohol and other drug information as well as lessons regarding self-control, living in a chemically dependent family, refusal skills, consequences of use, resisting peer pressure, making friends, alternative activities, and self-esteem enhancement.

An outcome evaluation of Here's Looking at You, 2000 was conducted by Kim, McLeod, and Shantzis (1993) with 463 students in North Carolina. No changes were noted in attitudes or use patterns by students exposed to the program. However, attrition and methodological problems may have contributed to these results.

Life Skills Training (LST)

This social skill competence enhancement approach to prevention was developed as a research and demonstration program at Cornell University Medical College by Gilbert Botvin in 1983. According to Botvin, et al. (1990):

> The main purpose of the LST program is to facilitate the development of personal and social skills, with particular emphasis on the development of skills for coping with social influences to smoke, drink, or use drugs. The LST program teaches students cognitive-behavioral skills for building self-esteem, resisting advertising pressure, managing anxiety, communicating effectively, developing personal relationships, and asserting one's rights. These skills are taught using a combination of teaching techniques including demonstration, behavioral rehearsal, feedback and reinforcement, and behavioral "homework" assignments for out-of-class practice.

In addition to teaching skills for the enhancement of generic personal and social competence, the LST program teaches problem-specific skills and knowledge related to smoking, drinking, and drug use (p. 439).

The curriculum consists of 12 units that are taught in 15 class periods to seventh grade students. Booster sessions are provided to students in eighth and ninth grades. There is a one-day training workshop for teachers before implementation.

Botvin and his associates have conducted several well-designed evaluation studies of LST. Some of these results have been referred to earlier in the chapter. In a three-year follow-up (Botvin, et al., 1990), significantly lower rates of smoking, marijuana use, and excessive drinking were found in the group of students who had been trained. There were no significant differences found in frequency of alcohol use or amount of alcohol used. Similarly, positive effects were seen on nearly all knowledge and attitude variables. However, the effects on skill and personality variables were less pronounced. A six-year follow-up (reported by Western Regional Center for Drug-Free Schools and Communities, 1994) indicated that the positive effects on drug use were maintained by the end of the twelfth grade.

Evaluation of Prevention Programs

Attempts to measure the success of prevention programs has resulted in some controversy. The prevailing attitude regarding prevention programs is summarized in a statement made by Botvin and Botvin (1992): "Until recently, virtually all efforts to develop effective substance abuse prevention approaches have failed" (p. 910). However, this perceived failure may be due to the evaluation problems in this area as opposed to (or in addition to) the prevention approaches themselves.

Several issues need to be considered in evaluating prevention programs. Clearly, local, state, and federal government entities are interested in evaluating the success of prevention programs because of the money spent on the programs. As you might imagine, the typical method for evaluating success is the implementation of a prevention program in classrooms or schools and to later see whether the kids who were involved in the program use alcohol and other drugs to a lesser extent than kids who were not involved in the program. One problem is that the initiation of use by young people depends on a complex interaction of personal, familial, cultural, and societal variables. To expect a school-based prevention program to singularly impact a behavior influenced by so many variables is unrealistic. Second, we know that attitudes and behavior can be influenced by a consistent, long-term, and comprehensive effort. For example, when many of us were young, cars did not have seat belts. Seat belts were then made optional, but we still never used them. Today, they are standard features in all cars, and many states have legislation requiring their use. So, our children don't even think about it. When they get in the car, they put on their seat belts. We do, too. However, this change in attitude and behavior in adults who grew up with seat-belt-free cars was accomplished through a long-term process involving public policy (legislation) and public awareness. Similarly, school-based prevention programs should be viewed as a part of long-term, consistent, comprehensive prevention efforts and not as isolated "cures" for the problem of tobacco, alcohol, and other drug use by young people. If the contradictory messages (e.g., marketing of alcohol and tobacco) are eliminated, prevention programs may become more effective. At this point in time, the prevention message is not consistent or comprehensive. Finally, school-based prevention programs are often viewed in a similar manner to other programs in a school. If you want to evaluate a new reading program, you compare the reading performance of the children in the new program with the performance of children in another program. However, we would argue that prevention programs are different. For example, imagine that you begin a prevention program that costs $10,000 in materials and training. In the entire school, only one student, who would have become dependent on tobacco, alcohol, or other drugs, is impacted and avoids use. You will have more than made up for the money invested in the program by preventing the financial and societal impact on health care, work productivity, the legal system, and family members that this person would have caused. We are not arguing that prevention programs should be purchased and implemented without careful evaluation. We are arguing that prevention programs should not be blamed for failing to solve a complex and multi-faceted problem.

High-Risk and Resilient Youth

There has been considerable research interest in the factors identified in childhood and adolescence that are associated with the development of alcohol and other drug problems later in life. The purpose of this research is twofold. First, the identification of groups who have these risk factors can assist in targeting such groups for intervention. The term *high risk* is now commonly used to describe such children and adolescents, and the Anti-Drug Abuse Act has defined "high risk youth" as the primary target group for the Center for Substance Abuse Prevention (Center for Substance Abuse Prevention, 1993). Second, once a risk factor is identified, it may be possible to ameliorate or reduce the influence of the risk factor. The *Here's Looking at You, 2000* prevention curriculum described earlier is partially based on the desirability of reducing the influence of certain risk factors.

David Hawkins and his colleagues at the University of Washington have done considerable work in the area of identifying the risk factors associated with alcohol and other drug problems in adolescence and early adulthood. In a comprehensive review of literature in this area, Hawkins, Catalano, and Miller (1992) have categorized and listed these risk factors, which are identified as either societal and cultural or intra and interpersonal.

Societal and Cultural Risk Factors

Societal and cultural risk factors include the laws and public policy related to tobacco, alcohol, and other drugs. For example, one effect on tobacco use is related to the taxation of this drug. If the United States were to adopt the heavy tobacco taxation policy of Canada, the number of smokers would probably decrease because the price of cigarettes would be prohibitive for some people. Alcohol use can be manipulated in the same way. Laws regarding the legal age of drinking also have affected use patterns. When we were in college, the legal drinking age was 21 in Washington state and 19 in Idaho. Our friends who went to a school near the Washington/Idaho border would go to Idaho on weekends and drink legally. The possibility that taxation and laws limiting availability may affect the age that a person begins use is directly related to the age of first use, which is an intrapersonal risk factor.

Availability may also depend on cultural and societal values rather than laws. If a family does not have tobacco, alcohol, or other drugs available because of religious or cultural beliefs, their availability to the children is limited. Alternatively, if there is easy access and availability, initiation of use is greatly simplified. Certainly, as we will see in the next section, this easy access and availability is also related to the modeling of alcohol and other drug use.

Other social and cultural factors, such as extreme economic deprivation and neighborhood disorganization, may have a relationship to later alcohol and other drug problems. Extreme poverty combined with childhood behavior problems has been associated with alcoholism and drug problems. Neighborhood disorganization has also been found to be related to problems that are related to later drug abuse (e.g., poor parental supervision).

Intra and Interpersonal Risk Factors

In Chapter 3, we reviewed some of the evidence for a genetic predisposition for alcoholism. An individual cannot modify this risk factor if it does exist. However, the increased risk for chemical dependency for children of alcoholics and addicts may be important information to teach, since it may impact such a person's decision with regard to use.

The use of alcohol and other drugs by family members and the attitudes communicated about substances are important risk factors. As Hawkins et al. (1992) state, "family modeling of drug using behavior and parental attitudes toward children's drug use are family influences related specifically to the risk of alcohol and other drug abuse" (p. 82). Other family factors associated with adolescent drug abuse include poor and inconsistent family management practices, family conflict, and low bonding to the family. This latter factor involves a lack of closeness in the family and low parental involvement in the children's activities.

School factors related to adolescent substance abuse include early and persistent behavior problems, academic failure, low degree of commitment to school, and peer rejection in elementary grades. The implications of these risk factors are clear. Students who begin school with behavior and social problems and have poor preparation for academic leaning are at risk.

The other risk factors in this category identified by Hawkins et al. (1992) include association with drug-using peers, alienation and rebelliousness, attitudes favorable toward use, and early onset of use. For any of you who have raised adolescents, it should come as no surprise that peers have a great influence on adolescent behavior. An alienated and rebellious young person will seek out others with similar attitudes, and favorable attitudes toward drugs are certainly at odds with the traditional norms. These young people tend to begin their use at an early age.

The interaction between these intra- and interpersonal risk factors should be obvious. Families in which there are substance abuse problems will have availability of certain drugs and tend to have more conflict and less closeness (see Chapter 10). These problems can lead to problems in school, alienation, and association with others who share the same experience. However, before you are overwhelmed with discouragement at the prognosis for high-risk children, let's look at those high-risk children who *don't* develop problems.

Protective Factors and Resiliency

A few years ago, we came into contact with a young man named Frank, a high school junior. Frank was in one special education class for learning disabled students. He had had fairly serious reading problems in elementary school but had improved considerably. Frank's father was an active alcoholic who had left the family when Frank was 12 but had maintained periodic contact with the family. The father had been physically abusive to the mother and the children. Frank earned good grades, worked 20 hours a week, and was a very positive influence on his siblings and peers at school. He was involved in a drug prevention program in which he worked with younger children and was a peer counselor. Frank did not display the characteristics of a family "hero" (see Chapter 10), as he took care of his own needs, knew how to have fun, and occasionally acted rowdy. In short, except for his minor learning problem, he was a well-adjusted, relatively happy adolescent. Considering all his risk factors, how could this have come about?

In the prevention literature, Frank would be referred to as *resilient*. In spite of having a number of risk factors for substance abuse and other problems, he seems OK. There has been considerable research interest in young people such as Frank and in identifying those factors that are associated with resiliency. These factors are called *protective factors* and, as you might expect, are the antithesis of risk factors. Bonnie Benard (1991) from the Western Regional Center for Drug-Free Schools and Communities has done an excellent review of literature and a summary of protective factors, which have been categorized as individual personality attributes, family factors, and environmental factors.

Individual Personality Attributes

The intrapersonal characteristics of resilient children include social competence, problem solving skills, and autonomy. Social competence includes responsiveness, flexibility, empathy, caring, communication skills, and a sense of humor. Problem solving skills involve the ability to think abstractly, reflectively, and flexibly and to be able to attempt alternative solutions for problems. Autonomy refers to a sense of identity, the ability to act independently, and the perception of control over the environment. Resilient children seem to be able to adaptively distance themselves from dysfunctional relationships. Adaptive distancing "involves activities and relationships that allow some breathing room for reparative work and acknowledgment of the effect of family alcoholism on the sense of self" (O'Sullivan, 1992, p. 425). In other words, rather than isolating oneself and denying, the resilient individual disengages from the dysfunction but learns from it as well.

Family Factors

It is not surprising that "a caring and supportive relationship remains the most critical variable throughout childhood and adolescence" (Benard, 1991, p. 6). What may be surprising is that the caring and supportive relationship may be with someone other than a parent. Bernard's review found that resilient children had established a close bond with at least one person. This certainly has implications for teachers and helping professionals, as the close bond that adults may form with high-risk children can have a protective effect. Conceptually, it makes sense that a close bond with a supportive adult will assist the child in developing trust. As Benard states, "(a) sense of basic trust . . . appears to be the critical foundation for human development and bonding, and, thus, human resiliency" (p. 7). However, if you remember your stages of psychosocial development (Erikson, 1963), you know that trust (or mistrust) develops very early in life. Therefore, another implication is that early intervention for high-risk children is essential. If a close bond with an adult has not occurred by the time a child enters school, it may be difficult (but not impossible) to overcome the child's mistrust.

Other characteristics of families that produce resilient children include high expectations; structure, discipline, and clear rules and regulations; spiritual faith; and participation in the family. Bernard's review found that children who were at risk because of poverty but who became successful identified high parental expectations as a contributing factor to their success. Families demonstrating warmth, support, and clear rules and expectations had lower rates of adolescent alcohol and other drug use than authoritarian or permissive families. Spiritual or religious faith also characterizes many resilient children. Finally, resiliency has also been associated with opportunities to contribute to the family through chores, domestic responsibility, or part-time work. These activities may develop a sense of bonding to the family by increasing the child's value as an integral, contributing member of the family.

Environmental Factors

Protective factors in the school and community contribute to the development of resiliency. With regard to the school, "a preponderance of evidence demonstrates that schools have the power to overcome incredible risk factors in the lives of youth—including those for alcohol and drug abuse" (Benard, 1991, p. 14). Similar to the findings regarding protective factors within the family, caring and support within the school environment is a strong predictor of resiliency. Teachers and other school personnel who bond with high-risk children significantly impact the development of resiliency. Furthermore, caring peers and friends are also related to resiliency. Finally, high expectations and participation and involvement in school are related to resiliency. The school may be conceptualized as a "surrogate" family for some high-risk youth, and the same protective factors associated with resiliency can exist in the school environment.

Similarly, Benard found the same protective factors within the community as a whole. That is, caring and support, high expectations, and participation in the community are all associated with resiliency. As Benard states,

> [The] characteristic of "social cohesiveness" or "community organization" has probably been the most frequently examined community factor affecting the outcome for children and families. The clear finding from years of research into crime, delinquency, child abuse, etc. is that communities and neighborhoods rich in social networks—both peer groups and intergenerational relationships—have lower rates of these problems . . . (p. 15).

Community caring and support may be evidenced through the availability of resources such as health care, child care, housing, education, job training, employment, and recreation. The community's expectations of young people may be demonstrated through valuing young people as resources rather than as problems. In addition, the community's values and norms regarding alcohol use create an expectation regarding use by minors. A community that has a high tolerance for public intoxication, drunk driving, and alcohol use at community functions can expect youth, particularly high-risk youth, to begin alcohol use at an early age. As we have previously seen, early alcohol use is a predictive factor for later alcohol and other drug problems. Finally, a sense of belonging and bonding to the community is enhanced by opportunities to participate in the life of the community. Youth service (e.g., tutoring, child care, elder care) communicates a community expectation that young people are valuable resources and also contribute to development of individual worth and community bonding.

Summary

The public health model of prevention involves an interaction between the agent, host, and environment. We have seen that public policy relates to prevention in that such policies may work in opposition to prevention efforts. For example, there are numerous efforts to prevent young people from using tobacco, alcohol, and other drugs, and yet we allow the tremendous marketing efforts of the tobacco and alcohol industries. Therefore, public policy involving the agents (tobacco, alcohol, and other drugs) can aid or sabotage prevention efforts.

The most effective school-based prevention programs seem to focus on both the host (individual) and the environment. Social resistance skills and competency enhancement approaches to prevention have shown more promise than other approaches. These programs tend to emphasize the development of personal skills and resistance to environmental influences that may lead to alcohol and other drug use. Research on risk factors, protective factors, and resiliency all point in the same direction: a variety of individual and environmental factors contribute to the involvement of youth in tobacco, alcohol, and other drug use. Children with social competency who are bonded to the family, school, and/or community are more likely to successfully survive dysfunction than are those who lack social and problem solving skills and are alienated from their family and environment.

The complex interaction of host, agent, and environment can result in difficulties in evaluating school-based prevention programs. A school-based prevention program that is implemented in a community that tolerates a high level of alcohol use will have less impact than the same program in a community with opposite expectations.

There is an inherent implication in the public health model of prevention that it would be nonproductive to place the burden for prevention on any one segment of society. Attempts to blame the failure of prevention efforts on public policy, law enforcement, families, schools, or communities are without foundation. All are involved in prevention and all contribute to the success or failure of prevention efforts. While research has been useful in identifying the methods, processes, and components of successful prevention efforts, barriers to implementation do exist. For example, it is unlikely that the marketing of tobacco and alcohol will be eliminated in the near future. The difficulty in developing families, schools, and communities that demonstrate caring and support, high expectations, and opportunities for active participation creates obvious barriers to success in preventing alcohol and other drug abuse and can seem overwhelming at times. However, individual impact is possible. We have seen how the bonding of an adult to a high-risk child can facilitate the development of resiliency. This caring and trustworthy adult could certainly be a teacher, counselor, or social worker. Finally, each individual can examine his or her own use patterns and enabling behavior and can advocate for sensible public policy.

Chapter *17*

Confidentiality and Ethical Issues

A high school counselor has been working with a student referred through the school's student assistance program (see Chapter 9). After being caught with marijuana, the student had been referred to an alcohol and other drug treatment center for an assessment. The treatment program determined that the student was not in need of formal treatment but did recommend that the school counselor work with the student on some social skills and minor family issues. During a discussion, the student tells the counselor that he is selling LSD at school. What should the counselor do?

A licensed clinical social worker works in a nonprofit, mental health agency. The agency does not provide alcohol and other drug treatment but does provide aftercare services for recovering clients. This social worker has been working with a recovering intravenous drug user on life skills, such as hygiene, appearance, work behaviors, and leisure time activities. The client tells the social worker that he is HIV positive and has been having unprotected sex with a number of partners. What should the social worker do?

A marriage and family therapist is in private practice. She has been seeing a woman for depression. The woman works in a management position for a large company. The company has a self-funded insurance plan that pays for the woman's treatment. The personnel manager of the company contacts the therapist, reports that evidence has surfaced that the woman is using cocaine and tells the therapist that the company is considering termination. She asks the therapist for guidance. What should the therapist do?

A very large corporation has an employee assistance program counselor (see Chapter 9) on staff. Any employee can see the counselor for three sessions, after which the counselor must develop a plan that, depending on the employee's problem, usually involves a referral to a private therapist or treatment program. This counselor has been contacted by the CEO of the corporation and told to see one of the vice presidents of the company who the CEO believes is alcoholic. After talking to the vice president, the counselor believes that a referral to an alcohol treatment program is appropriate. However, the vice president refuses to follow the recommendation and tells the counselor that she will sue the counselor if he reveals any information to the CEO. The vice president claims that the discussions they have had are confidential. What should the counselor do?

In these four hypothetical situations, we have illustrated some confidentialilty issues in the alcohol and other drug area for mental health professionals. In the remainder of the chapter, we will discuss confidentiality laws that can assist mental health professionals in deciding on the appropriate course of action in such situations, provide guidance for helping professionals in documenting their work with clients, and will bring up some of the ethical issues for helping professionals related to the alcohol and other drug field.

Confidentiality: 42 Code of Federal Regulations, Part 2 (42 CFR)

Confidentiality for mental health professionals is always problematic, since many federal and state laws are often complex and confusing, as are the ethical guidelines developed by professional organizations. As a future mental health professional, you may become familiar with confidentiality guidelines in your training program and then, once in the field, be faced with specific situations that do not fit the general guidelines and legal parameters presented in courses and workshops.

In the alcohol and other drug area, federal regulations exist to govern confidentiality. We will discuss these regulations in some detail, because, even if mental health professionals are not providing alcohol and other drug treatment services in their work setting, the regulations usually still apply. However, these regulations can be complex and an infinite number of situations related to confidentiality can develop. We suggest the following in situations in which you might be unsure of the appropriate action to take:

1. Consult your supervisor and/or legal counsel.
2. Contact your state Attorney General's office regarding state laws on privileged communication and mandatory reporting.
3. Contact the Legal Action Center,[1] an organization that specializes in legal and policy issues in the alcohol and other drugs area.

---

[1]The Legal Action Center provides direct legal services to individuals, and publications, training, technical assistance and education to agencies. The Legal Action Center can be reached at 236 Massachusetts Avenue NE, Suite 505, Washington, D.C. 20002, (202) 544-5478, FAX: (202) 544-5712.

Does 42 CFR Apply to You?

Issued in 1975 and amended in 1987, 42 CFR contains the regulations issued by the Department of Health and Human Services related to the confidentiality of alcohol and drug abuse patient records (terminology used in the regulations). These regulations supersede any local or state laws that are less restrictive than the regulations. Federal regulations in this area were seen as necessary, because individuals with alcohol and other drug problems might be hesitant to seek treatment if their confidentiality could not be guaranteed. This was particularly true when treatment for illegal drug abuse was separate from alcohol treatment and, therefore, simply contacting a drug treatment program became an admission of illegal activity.

Before you conclude that these regulations are irrelevant because you will not be providing alcohol or other drug treatment, please read further. 42 CFR defines a *program* as any person or organization that, in whole or in part, provides alcohol/drug abuse diagnosis, treatment, or referral for treatment and receives federal assistance. Federal assistance is defined as receiving federal funds in *any* form, even if the funds do not directly pay for alcohol or other drug services. This includes tax exempt status by the IRS, authorization to conduct business by the federal government (e.g., Medicaid provider), or conducting services for the federal government or for branches of state government that receive federal funds. This means that, if you work in a school district that has a free lunch program and also has a student assistance program that refers students to treatment, 42 CFR applies. If you work for a mental health agency that accepts Medicaid or CHAMPUS (Civilian Health and Medical Program for Uniformed Services) and diagnoses substance use disorders, 42 CFR applies. If you are an EAP counselor who works for or has a contract with a company that does business with state or federal government, 42 CFR applies. In fact, the only scenario we can imagine in which 42 CFR would not apply to readers of this text would be a counselor or therapist in private practice who does not accept Medicaid or CHAMPUS or any other state or federal insurance reimbursement and does not refer, diagnose, or treat clients with alcohol or other drug problems. This scenario is unlikely.

The General Rule

The general rule in 42 CFR regarding disclosure of records or other information on alcohol or other drug clients (42 CFR uses the term *patients*) is: *don't*. Except under the conditions we will describe later, you are prohibited from disclosing *any* identifying information regarding clients who receive any service from a program as defined in the regulations. Clients who never enter treatment but inquire about services or are assessed to determine whether they need services are also included, as is information that would identify someone as a client. Lastly, this includes information that a person (other than the patient) may already have or may be able to obtain elsewhere, even if the person is authorized by state law to get the information, has a subpoena, or is a law enforcement official.

Let's make this general rule more concrete. You work in a community mental health center that accepts Medicaid and provides a variety of mental health services, including group counseling for alcohol and other drug abusers. You do an intake on a self-referred client (Frank) and recommend he join the group. Frank says, "No thanks" and leaves. A week later, you receive a visit from a detective from another state. He is looking for Frank and has reason to believe that you have seen him. He has a subpoena for any records on Frank. You must say, "Federal confidentiality regulations require that I neither confirm nor deny my contact with clients." You must not provide any records to the detective. If you fail to maintain Frank's confidentiality, you are subject to a fine of up to $500 for the first offense and up to $5,000 for subsequent offenses. Ironically, you could legally tell the detective that Frank had never come to the mental health center, since this would mean that Frank had never been a client (had not applied for, requested, or received services) and, therefore, you are not bound by 42 CFR.

As with any good rule, there are exceptions (which we will discuss) to the general rule against disclosure. However, we want to caution you that it is best to seek advice if you are unsure about disclosure, because these exceptions can be complex and difficult to interpret in practical situations.

Written Consent

The first exception to the confidentiality rule is that disclosure can be made if the client gives written consent for the disclosure. 42 CFR specifies that the written consent must include the name of the program making the disclosure; the name of the individual or organization receiving the disclosure; the name of the client; the purpose or need for the disclosure; how much and what kind of information will be disclosed; a statement that the client may revoke the disclosure at any time; the date, event, or condition upon which the disclosure expires; the signature of the client and/or authorized person; and the date the consent is signed. A separate consent form must be signed for each individual or organization receiving information on the client. The consent form must also include a written prohibition against the redisclosure of the information to any other party.

In the case of a minor client, a parent or guardian signature is necessary only if state law requires parental consent for treatment. If parental consent is required, the parent or legal guardian and the minor client must both sign the consent. If a minor contacts a treatment program in a state in which parental consent for treatment is required, the program cannot disclose the contact to the parent(s) unless the program director believes the minor lacks the capacity to make a rational choice or represents a substantial threat to his or her life or well-being. Clearly, these decisions can be subjective.

The regulations regarding written consent for disclosure allow treatment providers to release information to third-party payers and employers. However, the release of this information also provides an opportunity for the misuse of such information. Third-party payers and employers are prohibited from redisclosing this information. Equally important is the stipulation regarding how much and what kind of information will be disclosed. Treatment providers must be careful to limit disclosure to information necessary to accomplish the disclosure's purpose. In the case of a third-party payer, this might be limited to the diagnosis, estimated duration of treatment, and services needed. Employers may need only a general statement regarding participation in treatment and progress.

Clients who enroll in treatment programs that use addictive drugs (e.g., methadone) as part of the treatment program are required to consent to disclosure to a central registry. The purpose of this disclosure is to prevent a client from enrolling in multiple programs that use such drugs. Thus, programs may confer about the client if multiple enrollment is detected. The consent remains in force as long as the client is in a treatment program that utilizes addictive drugs.

The only situation in which an irrevocable consent is allowed is in the case of criminal justice referrals. If treatment is a condition of any disposition of criminal proceedings (e.g., dismissal of charges, parole or probation, sentence), the disclosure can be made irrevocable until the client's legal status changes. For example, if a probationary status has been completed, the client may then revoke consent.

It should be noted that written consent does not mandate the program to disclose. There may be situations in which the program believes that disclosure is not in the best interests of the client. This may present an ethical dilemma for the program, which we will discuss later in this chapter. We advise you to seek legal counsel in any situation in which you believe that disclosure in accordance with a valid written consent would be contrary to the client's welfare.

Other Exceptions to the General Rule

In addition to clients' written consent for disclosure, another exception to the prohibition would be communication among staff within an organization, if such communication is necessary to provide services. For example, staffings occur in which clients are discussed among staff members who have either direct and indirect contact with the client. Also, in a multi-service agency (e.g., a hospital), information on clients can be provided to central accounting departments for billing purposes.

This exception can be delicate in public schools. Can or should disclosure of information on a student be made to the student's teachers? The regulations state that the recipient must need the information in connection with duties that are related to providing alcohol or drug abuse diagnosis, treatment, or referral. Let's say that the SAP refers a student to a treatment program and the student is admitted for inpatient treatment. The student is in a special education program, and the teacher is asked to provide some assignments for the student during the time he or she is not in school. Does the teacher need to know where the student is to fulfill this responsibility? Probably not. After treatment, the student returns to school and the teacher is asked to report weekly on the student's behavior and academic performance. Again, the teacher probably does not need to know the reasons for this request. However, the teacher may be better able to help if he or she knows the purpose of monitoring the student. In such cases, the best practice is to request a written consent to disclose to necessary teachers or other school personnel. Having such knowledge will also prevent teachers from innocently asking students where they have been. The problem in schools, as well as other large organizations, is that information is often disclosed to individuals who should not receive it. Therefore, confidentiality education for staff is often needed.

Program staff may discuss clients with people outside of the program as long as the communication does not identify the person as an alcohol or other drug abuser and does not verify the client's receiving alcohol or other drug treatment services. For example, case histories may be discussed as long as the client cannot be identified from the history. A treatment program may tell a newspaper reporter that 37% of its clients are cocaine users. A hospital that provides a variety of services and has an alcohol and other drug treatment program can say that John Smith is a patient in the hospital, as long as John is not identified as receiving alcohol or other drug treatment.

A medical emergency is another exception to the prohibition on disclosure. A medical emergency is defined as a situation that poses an immediate threat to the health of an individual and requires immediate medical intervention. The disclosure must be made only to medical personnel and only to the extent necessary to meet the medical emergency. The name and affiliation of the recipient of the information must be documented, along with the name of the individual making the disclosure, the date and time of the disclosure, and the nature of the emergency. Such an emergency might arise in social detoxification programs, when clients are withdrawing from central nervous system depressants without medication or medical supervision. If a client begins to seizure and requires medical attention, emergency medical personnel clearly need to know where the client is and why the seizures are occurring. Other situations considered medical emergencies include drug overdoses and suicide threats or attempts.

Earlier in the chapter, we gave the example of a detective with a subpoena for records on a client of a mental health center. As we discussed, the program must not provide records, since a subpoena alone is not sufficient for disclosure according to 42 CFR. However, a subpoena *and* a court-order *are* sufficient. Usually, the court notifies the program and client regarding the application for a court-order and provides an opportunity for a response from the program and/or client, but this is not the case when a subpoena is issued. Since these issues involve legal proceedings, we suggest you seek legal counsel if you are served with a subpoena or a court-order is issued for client information.

Another exception involves disclosure to an organization with a contract to provide services to programs. These contracts are called Qualified Service Organization Agreements (QSOA). For example, in contracting for drug-testing or accounting services, a program must disclose identifying information. This disclosure is allowed as long as the QSOA documents comply with the confidentiality regulations.

Another exception to disclosure includes the commission of a crime by a client on the premises of the program or against program personnel. In such an instance, the crime can be reported to the appropriate law enforcement agency and identifying information on the client can be provided.

Identifying information regarding clients can also be disclosed for research, audit, or evaluation purposes. Although the research exception does allow programs to disclose confidential client information to individuals with a proper research protocol, the researcher is prohibited from redisclosing the information. Similarly, regulatory agencies, third-party payers, and peer review organizations may have access to client information for audit and/or evaluation of the program, but the information can be used only for these purposes.

Finally, an exception to disclosure occurs in cases of actual or suspected child abuse or neglect. Confidentiality does not apply to initial reports of child abuse or neglect, as when a client is suspected or admits to child abuse or neglect or when a minor client is the victim. After the initial report, any follow-up reports or contacts do require consent. For example, an adolescent female in an inpatient program reports that she has been sexually molested by her step-father. The program must make an initial report to the appropriate county or state office of children's protective services. However, any follow-up visits by law enforcement officials or child welfare workers require the client's written consent.

One caution regarding the report of child abuse or neglect: A client with children will not be charged with abuse or neglect simply because he or she has abused alcohol or other drugs. A danger to the child must exist before authorities will take action. Child abuse and neglect frequently occur but are not inevitable or always readily apparent when parents abuse alcohol and other drugs.

Other Confidentiality Issues

Mental health professionals often ask about reporting past crimes of clients or clients' threats to commit future crimes. 42 CFR is clear regarding the exception to disclosure when a crime is committed on program premises or against program personnel. If a proper court-order is issued, disclosure can also be made without client consent. Crimes may be reported as well if the report can be worded in such a way that the client is not identified as a client in an alcohol or other drug program (remember the broad definition of program). However, state laws regarding privileged communication vary by state and by profession. Psychologists may have one set of guidelines, social workers another, and licensed professional counselors another. It is essential that you become familiar with the state laws regarding privileged communication in your profession. However, remember that, unless the state laws regarding disclosure of clients in alcohol and other drug programs are more restrictive, they are superseded by the federal regulations.

Does a mental health professional have the duty to warn a potential victim if an alcohol and other drug client threatens to harm the person? In Tarasoff *v.* Regents of the University of California [17 Cal. 3d 425 (1976)], a case often used as a precedent, the court found a counselor negligent for failing to warn a person whom the client had threatened and did harm. However, this case applies only in California (Brooks, 1992). Because a conflict may occur between the duty to warn and 42 CFR, Brooks suggests that mental health professionals warn potential victims in such a way that the client is not identified as an alcohol or other drug program client.

Finally, the question of disclosure of communicable diseases, particularly HIV, has become a sticky confidentiality issue. All states mandate health care providers to report cases of communicable diseases to local public health authorities (Lopez, 1994). Lopez suggests several strategies that would allow compliance with such mandates as well as with 42 CFR. Clearly, the simplest strategy is to secure the client's written consent for the mandated report and for follow-up by public health authorities. If the client provides consent, public health officials would have no problem locating the client for examination (that is extremely important in the case of diseases such as tuberculosis (TB) and hepatitis), interviewing to identify partners and contacts, counseling, and monitoring compliance.

If the client does not provide written consent, program personnel could make an anonymous report. However, the client's location could not be provided if this information identified the client as an alcohol or other drug client, as would be the case in in-patient settings. Also, most states require the person making the report to identify him- or herself, which could also violate 42 CFR. An alternative suggestion (Lopez, 1994) is for the program to enter a QSOA with the local public health authority, who would screen clients for communicable diseases and could then legitimately follow-up with clients.

According to Lopez (1994), the "medical emergency" exception to 42 CFR would not apply in cases of sexually transmitted diseases and HIV/AIDS. In both instances, no immediate threat to life is apparent, and, in the case of HIV/AIDS, emergency medical intervention would not impact the condition. However, TB is transmitted by casual contact, is difficult to confirm, and is potentially deadly. Therefore, suspected or confirmed TB may constitute a medical emergency and, therefore, be an exception to disclosure. Although Lopez does not mention hepatitis, the same situation would probably apply.

Program personnel may feel a "duty to warn" sexual partners of and those who have shared needles with an HIV/AIDS client. Again, the best practice is to attempt to convince the client to provide written consent to disclose, but, failing this, anonymous reporting can be considered. The wording in 42 CFR would probably not justify using the medical emergency exception to disclosure.

The Family Educational Rights and Privacy Act (FERPA) and The Hatch Amendment

School counselors and school social workers should be aware of two federal laws that may affect their work with students in a school setting. The first of these laws, FERPA, requires that educational agencies provide information contained in student records to parents or legal guardians and prohibits the disclosure of this information to a third party without parental permission. This requirement may cause a dilemma in states in which a minor can request and receive alcohol and other drug treatment without parental permission. For example, a school counselor could refer a student to a treatment program, but FERPA would prohibit providing any student records to the program without parental consent. Furthermore, any notes made by the school counselor about the student and placed in the student's record would be available to the parent. Thus, a conflict between 42 CFR and FERPA would exist, with FERPA requiring that the information be made available to the parent while 42 CFR prohibits the disclosure of the information without the minor client's consent. School counselors, school social workers, and SAP personnel who work in states that allow minors to seek and receive treatment without parental permission are advised to consult with legal counsel for the state's department of education and/or the attorney general before disclosing or refusing to disclose information to parents.

The Hatch Amendment requires parental consent for a student to participate in programs involving psychiatric or psychological testing or treatment or programs designed to reveal information pertaining to personal beliefs, behavior, or family relationships (Western Regional Center, 1995). Although schools do not (and should not) provide treatment for alcohol and other drug problems, schools may have a variety of support groups (e.g., Alateen) on school grounds and during school times. If a student wants to participate in such a group but does not want his or her parent(s) notified or if the parent refuses permission, legal counsel should be obtained to determine the appropriate action in that particular state. If it is determined that the student cannot participate without parental permission, school personnel can certainly help students gain access to support groups outside the school environment.

Documentation

All mental health professionals must be particularly attentive to the issue of written documentation. As Marion (1995) reported:

> *By keeping good records, counselors can ensure that their clients and their own best interests are served.... Without proper records there is no way another counselor can intervene when the assigned counselor is not available, no way to defend themselves in a lawsuit and no way to verify a payable service (p. 8).*

In the alcohol and other drug treatment field, accrediting bodies and state agencies often have regulations that specify the form and content of treatment plans and progress notes and the frequency with which written documentation must be made. For the mental health professional working in an agency or institutional setting, there may also be a structure to guide written documentation. However, many school counselors, private therapists, and EAP counselors must depend on their own experiences and judgment. For those mental health professionals who are uncertain about the form and content of their progress notes on clients, the guidelines developed by Roget and Johnson (1995) for alcohol and other drug counselors may be helpful. These authors recommend that progress notes should be written with the idea that they could potentially be used in a legal proceeding. Therefore, the entries should be brief and largely factual. Opinion and conclusions should be clearly labelled as such. Terms not commonly recognized in the professional vernacular (e.g., toxic codependency, wounded inner child) should be avoided. Any reports of child abuse and neglect should be clearly documented, including the name and title of the person who received the report. The person making case notes should be especially careful to document any incidents in which the health, safety, or security of the client is an issue. For example, any threat or attempt at suicide should be documented, along with the actions taken by the mental health professional.

Ethics

Professional organizations, such as the American Psychological Association, American Counseling Association, National Association of Social Workers, and the American Association of Marriage and Family Therapists, have ethical standards for their members. Many alcohol and other drug counselors belong to the National Association of Alcoholism and Drug Abuse Counselors, which also has published ethical standards. You are obligated to become familiar with both the ethical standards of your profession and the state laws relating to ethical practice for licensed or certified professionals in your field. While most ethical issues are common to all mental health professionals and you will probably receive information about these ethical standards in your training program, we want to mention several areas that present particular problems in the alcohol and other drug field.

Scope of Practice

Most mental health professionals recognize that their training and expertise is insufficient for an actively psychotic client and would refer such a client to an appropriate treatment setting, which would include medical personnel. However, in the alcohol and other drug area, there is often a perception that any licensed or certified mental health professional is competent to treat such clients. For example, in our state, licensed psychologists can diagnose and treat alcohol and other drug problems, but the state has no training requirement in this area for licensure. In most cases, it is up to the professional to determine his or her own areas of competence, and an ethical professional will refer clients who fall outside these areas of expertise to the appropriate person and/or agency. We hope that the information in this book will help you make the determination regarding whom to refer. As we stated in Chapter 5, you should have specific training in the diagnosis of Substance Use Disorders before making a diagnosis in this area. Furthermore, it is our belief that a client with a DSM-IV Substance Dependence Disorder diagnosis should be referred to an alcohol and other drug treatment program rather than being seen by a mental health generalist. We strongly recommend consultation with a specialist in the field regarding appropriate treatment settings and planning if a client is diagnosed with a Substance Abuse Disorder.

Scope of practice is also an issue for alcohol and other drug counselors who do not have other counselor training. Although training in the field is changing, many alcohol and other drug counselors have minimal formal training and their training may be specific to alcohol and other drug treatment. Therefore, the counselor may be unprepared to treat clients with dual disorders (see Chapter 7) or may be unable to differentiate substance use disorders from other disorders. The ethical practice would be to consult with licensed mental health professionals and refer when there is any question regarding the client's diagnosis.

Client Welfare

The mental health professional has a primary responsibility to the welfare of the client. Therefore, if a counselor, social worker, or marriage and family therapist is seeing a client who is not benefiting from treatment, the mental health professional is obligated to terminate treatment and refer the client. This may mean that a client with an escalating pattern of alcohol or other drug use may need a referral to a treatment program in spite of the rapport you have established, the client's great insurance benefits, or your own conceptualization of alcohol and other drug problems. For example, if most of the programs in your area operate on the basis of the disease concept (see Chapter 3) and your point of view differs, you are not relieved of your responsibility to refer clients who need treatment. Conversely, you should not refer all clients to the same type of treatment program because you have a professional or personal relationship with a specific treatment program.

Earlier in this chapter, we discussed the fact that written consent for disclosure does not mandate that a program disclose information. Instances may occur in which the client would be harmed by disclosure. Of course, clients can revoke consent at any time (in all instances except criminal justice situations), but they may be reluctant to do so. For example, imagine you are a licensed professional counselor working at a mental health center where you are providing relapse prevention services for a recovering polydrug abuser. The client has provided a written consent to disclose treatment compliance and relapses to the client's company. One day, the client admits to a slip that you believe is an isolated event. In your opinion, the client has actually learned a great deal from the slip. On one hand, the client does not want to revoke consent because it is a condition for continued employment, while, on the other hand, you believe that reporting the slip would cause harm to the client, since termination would result. Ethically, you should not disclose the slip even though you have written consent to do so. But, we should add that it would be unethical to lie to the employer. Your best course of action would be to refuse to provide information about slips.

If a client insists that you disclose information that you believe would result in harm to the client, you should seek legal advice. However, instances may occur in which legal advice and ethical practice are in conflict. Remember, your primary responsibility is the welfare of your client.

Application of Confidentiality Regulations

Now that you are familiar with the confidentiality regulations, let's see how they apply to the situations presented at the beginning of the chapter. In the first case, a high school counselor is working with a student who was referred through the school's SAP, and the student disclosed that he had been selling LSD on campus. The counselor is covered under 42 CFR because the school district receives federal support and the SAP does refer students to treatment. However, this situation would be an exception to confidentiality since it concerns a crime that is committed on the premises. In some states, the discussion between the counselor and the student may be protected as privileged communication, in which case the counselor would not have the option of reporting the crime. In such a state, the state law is actually more restrictive than 42 CFR and therefore takes precedence. If the state has no privileged communication law, the counselor is not obligated to report the crime but could legally report it under the provisions of 42 CFR. In this case, the counselor must decide the course of action that is in the best interests of the client.

In the second case, a social worker is providing aftercare services in a mental health agency. The client is a recovering IV drug user who reports being HIV positive and admits to having unprotected sex with a variety of partners. Again, the social worker must comply with 42 CFR. The social worker is providing treatment services and the agency is nonprofit and, therefore, federally supported. If the client is aware of being HIV positive, he or she has probably already been reported to public health officials. However, the social worker can probably make a report without violating 42 CFR. Since the agency provides a variety of services and the social worker does not provide alcohol and other drug services exclusively, the report can be made without identifying the client as an alcohol or other drug treatment client. Of course, the social worker should attempt to get written consent for disclosure from the client. However, if the client lives in a halfway house for recovering addicts, the social worker cannot give the client's address to the public health authority because to do so would identify the client as an alcohol or other drug client.

Since the social worker is able to make a report to the public health authority without violating 42 CFR, the issue of warning sexual partners of the client's condition would best be left to public health officials. If the social worker has the names of sexual partners but the client would not give written consent for disclosure, the social worker can make anonymous reports to the partners. However, the social worker would probably not have names. Of course, we would hope that the social worker would counsel the client regarding his or her sexual behavior.

In the third situation, whether a marriage and family therapist in private practice falls under 42 CFR is questionable. Marriage and family therapists are generally not eligible for Medicaid or CHAMPUS payments, but the therapist may be a preferred provider for a state-funded insurance plan. In such an instance, she would have to comply with 42 CFR. When the personnel manager contacts the therapist to inquire about the employee who is seeing her, the first issue to address is consent. If the client has not given written consent for the therapist to disclose information to the personnel manager, she should neither confirm nor deny that the woman is in therapy. If written consent has been provided, the therapist has several options for handling the suspicion of cocaine use. Since depression has been the focus of treatment, we would hope that alcohol and other drug use has been assessed and ruled out as a problem. However, the therapist may feel that this issue exceeds her scope of practice, and so she refers the client for a more thorough assessment. Drug testing may also be needed. Clearly, if a therapeutic relationship has been developed, the therapist should discuss the issue of cocaine use with the client.

The EAP counselor for the large corporation will have to comply with 42 CFR if the company does any business with state or federal government. In the situation described, the counselor would have a problem if he or she did not obtain a written consent for disclosure from the vice president *before* providing services. Once the counselor interviews the vice president, the vice president becomes a client and the information discussed is confidential. The CEO has no right to be informed, regardless of who is paying the bill or the fact that the counselor is an employee of the company. However, if the company does not meet the criteria in 42 CFR for federal support, then the counselor has an ethical dilemma. The EAP counselor first needs to clearly establish the parameters of reporting before providing any services and, ethically, must then ensure that anyone who sees the counselor understands these parameters.

When an employer insists that an employee see the EAP counselor as a condition of avoiding an adverse action, such as suspension or termination, the employee must give written consent to disclose before any services are provided. However, the disclosure is limited to a report of the EAP counselor's recommendation(s) and a report about whether the employee followed the recommendation(s). Clearly, a less restrictive disclosure would inhibit most employees from being open with the counselor. However, EAP counselors should warn clients that, if employees sue employers or file workman's compensation claims, all records of contacts with EAP counselors and other mental health professionals may be disclosed during legal proceedings (Schultz, 1994).

Summary

The intent of 42 CFR is to ensure that individuals who seek alcohol and other drug services are in no more legal jeopardy than individuals who do not seek such services. Most mental health professionals will have to comply with these federal confidentiality regulations. Since the regulations can be complex and difficult to understand and generalists may have only sporadic need to remember them, the best advice is to keep all identifying information on alcohol and other drug clients confidential, including a confirmation or denial about whether an individual is a client. In situations in which the mental health professional has questions about exceptions, legal counsel should be obtained.

All mental health professionals should conform to the ethical standards of their professional association and licensing board. In the alcohol and other drug area, the mental health professional should be particularly sensitive to the scope of practice and client welfare issues.

References

AA Grapevine (1985). New York: Alcoholics Anonymous Grapevine, Inc.

Abrams, R. C., & Alexopoulos, G. (1987). Substance abuse in the elderly: Alcohol and prescription drugs: Over-the-counter and illegal drugs. *Hospital and Community Psychiatry, 39,* 822–823.

Abadinsky, H. (1993). *Drug abuse: An introduction* (2nd ed.). Chicago: Nelson-Hall.

Ackerman, R. J. (1983). *Children of alcoholics. A guidebook for educators, therapists, and parents.* New York: Simon & Schuster, Inc.

Ackerman, R. J. (1987). *Same house, different homes: Why adult children of alcoholics are not all the same.* Deerfield Beach, FL: Health Communications.

Adelman, S. A., & Weiss, R. D. (1989). What is therapeutic about inpatient alcoholism treatment. *Hospital and Community Psychiatry, 40,* 515–519.

Agras, W. S. (1987). *Eating disorders: Management of obesity, bulimia, and anorexia nervosa.* New York: Pergamon Press.

Alateen: Hope for children of alcoholics (1973). New York: Al-Anon Family Group Headquarters.

Alcohol (in Korean). (1978). *Fifty-nine authors, fifty-nine essays.* Gi So Rhim Publishing Company.

Alcoholics Anonymous (3rd. Ed.) (1976). New York: Alcoholics Anonymous World Services.

Alcoholics Anonymous: Twelve steps and twelve traditions (1981). New York: Alcoholics Anonymous World Services, Inc.

American Psychiatric Association. (1994). *Diagnostic and statistical manual of mental disorders* (4th ed.). Washington, D.C.: Author.

American Temperance Union, (n.d.). *Temperance tract for the freedman.* New York: Author.

American Public Health Association. (1989). A public health response to the war on drugs: Reducing alcohol, tobacco, and other drug problems among the nation's youth. *American Journal of Public Health, 79,* 360–364.

Ananth, J., Vandewater, S., Kamal, M., Brodsky, A., Gareal, R., & Miller, M. (1989). Missed diagnosis of substance abuse in psychiatric patients. *Hospital and Community Psychiatry, 40,* 297–299.

Andersen, A. E., & Mickalide, A. D. (1983). Anorexia nervosa in the male: An underdiagnosed disorder. *Psychosomatics, 24,* 1066–1069, 1072–1075.

Anderson, G. L. (1993). *When chemicals come to school.* Greenfield, WI: Community Recovery Press.

Anderson, J. Z. (1992). Stepfamilies and substance abuse: Unique treatment considerations. In E. Kaufman & P. Kaufman, P. (Eds.), *Family therapy of drug and alcohol abuse* (2nd ed., pp. 172–189) Boston: Allyn & Bacon.

Andre, J. M. (1979). *The epidemiology of alcoholism among American Indians and Alaska Natives.* Albuquerque: U.S. Indian Health Services.

Annis, H. M. (1986). A relapse prevention model for treatment of alcoholics. In W. R. Miller & W. Heather (Eds.), *Treating addictive behaviors: Process of change.* (pp. 407–433). New York: Plenum.

Annis, H. M. (1990). Relapse to substance abuse: Empirical findings within a cognitive-social learning approach. *Journal of Psychoactive Drugs, 22,* 117–124.

Annis, H. M., & Davis, C. S. (1988). Relapse prevention. In R. K. Hester & W. R. Miller (Eds.), *Handbook of alcoholism treatment approaches: Effective alternatives.* (pp. 171–182). New York: Pergamon.

Archambault, D. L. (1992). Adolescence: A physiological, cultural, and psychological no man's land. In G. W. Lawson & A. W. Lawson (Eds.). *Adolescent substance abuse: Etiology, treatment, and prevention* (pp. 11–28). Gaithersburg, MD: Aspen Publications.

Armor, D. J., Polich, J. M., & Stambul, H. B. (1978). *Alcoholism and treatment.* New York: John Wiley & Sons.

Arnold, M. S. (1993). Ethnicity and training marital and family therapists. *Counselor Education and Supervision, 33,* 139–147.

Attneave, C. (1982). American Indians and Alaska Natives families: Emigrants in their own homeland. In M. McGoldrick, J. K. Pierce, & J. Giordano (Eds.), *Ethnicity and family therapy.* (pp. 55–83). New York: Guilford Press.

Bachman, J., Wallace, J., O'Malley, P., Johnston, L., Kurth, C., & Neighbors, H. (1991). Racial/ethnic differences in smoking, drinking and illicit drug use among American high school seniors. *American Journal of Public Health, 81,* 372–377.

Baekeland, F., & Lundwall, L. (1975). Dropping out of treatment: A critical review. *Psychological Bulletin, 82,* 738–783.

Baker, S. P., O'Neil, B., & Karpf, R. (1984). *The injury fact book.* Lexington, MA: Lexington Books.

Bandura, A. (1977). *Social learning theory.* Englewood Cliffs, NJ: Prentice-Hall, Inc.

Barnard, C. P. (1981). *Families, alcoholism, and therapy.* Springfield, IL.: Charles C. Thomas.

Barnes, G. M. (1983). Clinical and prealcoholic personality characteristics. In B. Kissin & H. Begleiter (Eds.), *The pathogenesis of alcoholism: Psychosocial factors,* (vol. 6, pp. 113–196). New York: Plenum Press.

Barnes, G. M., Farell, M. P., & Cairns, A. (1986). Parental socialization factors and adolescent drinking behaviors. *Journal of Marriage and the Family, 48,* 27–36.

Barthwell, A. G., & Gibert, C. L. (1993). *Screening for infectious diseases among substance abusers. Treatment improvement protocol (TIP) series,* No. 6. Rockville, MD: U.S. Department of Health and Human Services.

Batki, S. L. (1990). Drug abuse, psychiatric disorders, and AIDS: Dual and triple diagnosis. *Western Journal of Medicine, 152,* 547–552.

Batki, S. L., Sorenson, J. L., Faltz, B., & Madover, S. (1988). Psychiatric aspects of treatment of intravenous drug abusers with AIDS. *Hospital and Community Psychiatry, 39,* 439–441.

Battjes, R. J. (1994). Drug use and HIV risk among gay and bisexual men: An overview. In R. J. Battjes, Z. Sloboda, & W. C. Grace, (Eds). *The context of HIV risk among drug users and their sexual partners* (pp. 82–87). National Institute of Drug Abuse Research Monograph. Rockville, MD: U.S. Department of Health and Human Services.

Beattie, M. (1987). *Codependent no more: How to stop controlling others and start caring for yourself.* Center City, MN: Hazelden.

Beavers, W. R. (1985). *Successful marriage: A family systems approach to couples therapy.* New York: W. W. Norton & Company.

Beckman, L. J., & Amaro, H. (1984). Patterns of women's use of alcoholism treatment agencies. In S. C. Wilsnack & L. J. Beckman (Eds.). *Alcohol problems in women: Antecedents, consequences, and intervention* (pp. 319–348). New York: Academic Press.

Beidler, R. J. (1989). Adult children of alcoholics: Is it really a separate field for study? *Drugs and Society, 3,* 133–141.

Bell, T. L. (1990). *Preventing adolescent relapse: A guide for parents, teachers, and counselors.* Independence, MO: Independence Press.

Benard, B. (1991). *Fostering resiliency in kids: Protective factors in the family, school, and community.* Portland, OR: Northwest Regional Educational Laboratory.

Bennett, L. A. (1988). Problems among school-age children of alcoholic parents. DATA, *Brown University Digest of Addiction Theory and Application,* July, 9–11.

Bennett, L. A., Wolin, S. J., & Reiss, D. (1988a). Deliberate family process: A strategy for protecting children of alcoholics. *British Journal of Addiction, 83,* 821–829.

Bennett, L. A., Wolin, S. J., & Reiss, D. (1988b). Cognitive, behavioral, and emotional problems among school-age children of alcoholic parents. *American Journal of Psychiatry, 145,* 185–190.

Benson, P., Williams, D., & Johnson, A. (1987). *The quicksilver years: The hope and fears of early adolescence.* San Francisco: Harper & Row.

Berenson, A. B., Stiglich, N. J., & Wilkenson, G. S., and Anderson, P. J. (1991). Drug abuse and other risk factors for physical abuse in pregnancy among white non-Hispanic, Black, and Hispanic women. *American Journal of Obstetrics and Gynecology, 164,* 1491–1499.

Berkowitz, A., & Perkins, H. W. (1988). Personality characteristics of children of alcoholics. *Journal of Consulting and Clinical Psychology, 56,* 206–209.

Bettes, B. L., Dusenbury, L., Kerner, J., James-Ortiz, S., & Botvin, G. L. (1990). Ethnicity and psychosocial factors in alcohol and tobacco use in adolescence. *Child development, 61,* 557–565.

Blackman, S., Simone, R., & Thomas, D. (1986). (Letter to the editor). *Hospital and Community Psychiatry, 37,* 404.

Blau, M. (1990). Adult children: Tied to the past. *American Health, 9,* 56–65.

Blum, K., Noble, E. P., Sheridan, P. J., Montgomery, A., Ritchie, T., Jagadeeswaran, P., Nogami, H., Briggs, A. H., & Cohn, J. B. (1990). Allelic association of human dopamine D_2 receptor gene in alcoholism. *Journal of American Medical Association, 263,* 2055–2060.

Blume, S. (1988). Compulsive gambling and the medical model. Special issue. Compulsive gambling: An examination of relevant models. *Journal of Gambling Behavior, 3,* 237–247.

Botvin, G. J. (1983). *Life skills training: Student guide.* New York: Smithfield Press.

Botvin, G. J., Baker, E., Dusenbury, L., Tortu, S., & Botvin, E. M. (1990). Preventing adolescent drug use through a multimodal cognitive-behavioral approach: Results of a 3-year study. *Journal of Consulting and Clinical Psychology, 58,* 437–446.

Botvin, G. J., & Botvin, E. M. (1992). School-based and community-based prevention approaches. In J. H. Lowinson, P. Ruiz, R. B. Millman, & J. G. Langrod (Eds.). *Substance abuse: A comprehensive textbook.* (2nd ed., pp. 910–927). Baltimore: Williams & Wilkins.

Bourne, P. G. (1973). Alcoholism in the urban Negro population. In P. G. Bourne & R. Fox (Eds.), *Alcoholism: Progress in research and treatment.* (pp. 211–226). New York: Academic Press.

Bowen, M. (1971). The use of family theory in clinical practice. In M. J. Haley (Ed.), *Changing families: A family therapy reader.* (pp. 159–192). New York: Grune & Stratton.

Boyer, C. B., & Ellen, J. M. (1994). HIV risk in adolescents: The role of sexual activity and substance use behaviors. In R. J. Battjes, Z. Sloboda, & W. C. Grace, (Eds.) *The context of HIV risk among drug users and their sexual partners.* (pp. 135–154). National Institute of Drug Abuse Research Monograph. Rockville, MD: U.S. Department of Health and Human Services.

Bradshaw, J. (1988). Compulsivity: The black plague of our day. *Lears Magazine, 42,* 89–90.

Bratter, T. E. (1985). Special clinical psychotherapeutic concerns for alcoholic and drug addicted individuals. In T. E. Bratter & G. G. Forrest (Eds.), *Alcoholism and substance abuse: Strategies for clinical intervention* (pp. 523–574). New York: The Free Press.

Bray, G. A. (1989). Obesity: Basic considerations and clinical approaches. *Dissertation Monographs, 35,* 449–537.

Brook, D. W., & Brook, J. S. (1992). Family processes associated with alcohol and drug use and abuse. In E. Kaufman & P. Kaufman, (Eds.), *Family therapy of drug and alcohol abuse.* (pp. 15–33), Boston: Allyn & Bacon.

Brooks, M. K. (1992). Ethical and legal issues of confidentiality. In J. H. Lowinson, P. Ruiz, R. B. Millman, & J. G. Langrod (Eds.). *Substance abuse: A comprehensive textbook.* (pp. 1049–1066). Baltimore, MD: Williams & Wilkins.

Brouwers, M., & Wiggum, C. D. (1993). Bulimia and perfectionism: Developing the courage to be imperfect. *Journal of Mental Health Counseling, 15,* 141–149.

Brower, K. J., Blow, F. C., Young, J. P., & Hill, E. M. (1991). Symptoms and correlates of anabolic-androgenic steroid dependence. *British Journal of Addiction, 86,* 759–768.

Brown, F., & Tooley, J. (1989). Alcoholism in the black community. In G. W. Lawson & A. W. Lawson (Eds.), *Alcoholism & substance abuse in special populations.* (pp. 115–130). Rockville, MD: Aspen Publishers, Inc.

Brown, L. S., & Alterman, A. I. (1992). African Americans. In J. H. Lowinson, P. Ruiz, R. B. Millman, & J. G. Langrod (Eds.), *Substance abuse: A comprehensive textbook.* (2nd ed., pp. 861–867). Baltimore, MD: Williams & Wilkins.

Brown, L. S., Jr., & Primm, B. J. (1988a). Sexual contacts of intravenous drug abusers: Implications for the next spread of the AIDS epidemic. *Journal of the National Medical Association, 80,* 651–656.

Brown, L. S., Jr., & Primm, B. J. (1988b). Intravenous drug abuse and AIDS in minorities. *AIDS and Public Policy Journal, 3,* 5–15.

Brown, S. (1988). *Treating children of alcoholics: A developmental perspective.* New York: John Wiley & Sons.

Brownell, K. D., & Foreyt, J. P. (1985, November). Unpublished Obesity Workshop conducted at Association for the Advancement of Behavior Therapy Convention, Chicago.

Brownell, K. D., & Stunkard, A. J. (1978). Behavioral treatment of obesity in children. *American Journal of Diseases in Children, 132,* 403–412.

Bruch, H. (1973). *Eating disorders: Obesity, anorexia nervosa, and the person within.* New York: Basic Books.

Bruch, H. (1986). Anorexia nervosa: The therapeutic task. In K. D. Brownell & J. P. Foreyt (Eds.), *Handbook of eating disorders.* (pp. 328–332). New York: Basic Books, Inc., Publishers.

Brunswick, A. F. (1979). Black youths and drug use behavior. In G. M. Beschner & A. S. Friedman (Eds.), *Youths drug use: Problems, issues, and treatment.* (pp. 443–490). Lexington, MA: Lexington Books.

Burgess, D. M., & Streissguth, A. P. (1992). Fetal alcohol syndrome and fetal alcohol effect: Principles for educators. *Phi Delta Kappan, 74,* 24–26.

Burk, J. P., & Sher, K. J. (1988). The "forgotten children" revisited: Neglected areas of COA research. *Clinical Psychology Review, 8,* 285–302.

Burk, J. P., & Sher, K. J. (1990). Labeling the child of an alcoholic: Negative stereotyping by mental health professionals and peers. *Journal of Studies of Alcohol, 51,* 156–163.

Burns, C. M., & D'Avanzo, C. E. (1993). *Alcohol and other drug abuse in culturally diverse populations: Hispanics and Southeast Asians. Faculty resource.* Washington, D.C.: Cosmos Corporation.

Burrows, B. A. (1992). Research on the etiology and maintenance of eating disorders. In E. M. Freeman (Ed.), *The addiction process: Effective social work approaches.* (pp. 149–160). White Plains, NY: Longman.

Buss, A. H., & Plomin, R. (1984). *Temperament: Early developing personality traits.* Hillsdale, NJ: L. Erlbaum Associates.

Cabaj, R. P. (1992). Substance abuse in the gay and lesbian community. In J. H. Lowinson, P. Ruiz, R. B. Millman & J. G. Langrod (Eds.), *Substance abuse: A comprehensive textbook.* (2nd Ed.) (pp. 852–860). Baltimore: Williams & Wilkins.

Caetano, R. (1990). Hispanic drinking in the U.S.: Thinking in new directions. *British Journal of Addictions, 85,* 1231–1236.

Callahan, E. J. (1980). Alternate strategies in the treatment of narcotic addiction: A review. In W. R. Miller (Ed.), *The addictive behaviors: Treatment of alcoholism, drug abuse, smoking, and obesity.* (pp. 143–168). New York: Pergamon Press.

Callan, V. J., & Jackson, D. (1986). Children of alcoholic fathers and recovered alcoholic fathers: Personal and family functioning. *Journal of Studies on Alcohol, 47,* 180–182.

Cantwell, D. P., Sturzenberger, S., & Borroughs, J. (1977). Anorexia nervosa: An affective disorder? *Archives of General Psychiatry, 34,* 1087–1093.

Centers for Disease Control. (1986). Classification system for human T-lymphotropic virus type III/lymphadenopathy-associated virus infection. *Morbidity and Mortality Weekly Report, 35,* 334–339.

Centers for Disease Control. (1989). Motor vehicle crashes and injuries in an Indian community. *Journal of the American Medical Association, 262,* 2205–2206.

Centers for Disease Control. (1989). *National HIV seroprevalence surveys: Summary of results, data from serosurveillance activities through 1989.* Atlanta: U.S. Department of Health and Human Services, Public Health Service, Centers for Disease Control, HIV/CID 19-90/006/.

Centers for Disease Control and Prevention. (1993). *HIV/AIDS surveillance report, July 5*, 10–11.

Center for Substance Abuse Treatment. (1993). *Substance abuse services and state health care reform.* Report of a meeting of the Center for Substance Abuse Treatment, September 9–10, Kansas City, Missouri. Prepared by Johnson, Bassin, & Shaw, Inc. for the Treatment improvement Exchange, Contract #270-90-0001.

Center for Substance Abuse Prevention. (1993). *Prevention primer: An encyclopedia of alcohol, tobacco, and other drug prevention terms.* Rockville, MD: National Clearinghouse for Alcohol and Drug Information.

Center for Substance Abuse Research. (1994). National survey shows over 220,000 women use drugs during pregnancy. *CESAR FAX, 3*(43), November 7.

Cermak, T. L. (1984). Children of alcoholics and the case for a new diagnostic category of codependency. *Alcohol, Health and Research World, 8,* 38–42.

Cermak, T. L. (1985). *A primer on adult children of alcoholics.* Pompano Beach, FL: Health Communications.

Cermak, T. L. (1986). *Diagnosing and treating codependence: A guide for professionals with chemical dependents.* Minneapolis: Johnson Institute.

Chafetz, M. E. (1964). Consumption of alcohol in the Far and Middle East. *New England Journal of Medicine, 271,* 297–301.

Charuvastra, V. C., Dalali, I. D., Cassuci, M., & Ling, W. (1992). Outcome study: Comparison of short-term vs. long-term treatment in a residential community. *International Journal of the Addictions, 27,* 15–23.

Chasnoff, I. J. (1992). Cocaine, pregnancy, and the growing child. *Current problems in pediatrics, August,* 302–321.

Chasnoff, I. J., Griffith, D. R., Freier, C., & Murray, J. (1992). Cocaine/polydrug use in pregnancy: Two year follow-up. *Pediatrics, 89,* 284–289.

Chassin, L., Mann., L. M. & Sher, K. J. (1988). Self-awareness theory, family history of alcoholism, and adolescent alcohol involvement. Special issue: Models of addiction. *Journal of Abnormal Psychology, 97,* 206–217.

Chi, I., Lubben, J. E., & Kitano, H. H. (1989). Differences in drinking behavior among three Asian-American groups. *Journal of Studies on Alcohol, 50,* 15–23.

Chittenden, H. (1935). *American fur trade of the far west: A history of pioneer trading posts and early fur companies of the Missouri Valley and Rocky Mountains and of the overland commerce with Santa Fe.* (Vol. 1). New York: Barnes & Noble, Inc.

Christopher, J. (1988). *How to stay sober: Recovery without religion.* Buffalo, NY: Prometheus Books.

Ciarrochi, J. (1987). Severity of impairment in dually addicted gamblers. *Journal of Gambling Behavior, 3,* 16–26.

Clark, W. B., & Midanik, L. (1982). Alcohol use and alcohol problems among U.S. adults: Results of the 1979 national survey. In *Alcohol and health monograph 1: Alcohol consumption and related problems.* (pp. 3–54). Rockville, MD: National Institute on Alcohol Abuse and Alcoholism.

Coleman, D. (1990, June 26). Scientists pinpoint brain irregularities in drug addicts. *New York Times,* Sec. C, p. 1.

Coleman, E. (1982). Family intimacy and chemical abuse: The connection. *Journal of Psychoactive Drugs, 14,* 153–158.

Coleman, P. (1989). Letter to the editor. *Journal of the American Medical Association, 261,* 1879–1880.

Collins, J. J., & Allison, M. (1983). Legal coercion and retention in drug abuse treatment. *Hospital and Community Psychiatry, 34,* 1145–1149.

Committee on Government Operations, House of Representatives. (1990). *United States antinarcotics activities in the Andean region.* (Union Calendar No. 584). Washington, DC: U.S. Government Printing Office.

Cook, C. C. (1988). The Minnesota model in the management of drug and alcohol dependency: Miracle, method, or myth? (Part I: The philosophy of the programme). *British Journal of Addiction, 83,* 625–634.

Cooney, N. L., Zweben, A., & Fleming, M. F. (1995). Screening for alcohol problems and at-risk drinking in health-care settings. In R. K. Hester & W. R. Miller (Eds.), *Handbook of alcoholism treatment approaches: Effective approaches,* (2nd ed., pp. 45–60). Boston: Allyn & Bacon.

Cooper, S. E., & Robinson, D. A. G. (1987). Use of the Substance Abuse Subtle Screening Inventory with a college population. *Journal of American College Health, 36,* 180–184.

Corbett, K., Mora, J., & Ames, G. (1991). Drinking patterns and drinking-related problems of Mexican-American husbands and wives. *Journal of Studies on Alcohol, 52,* 215–222.

Corey, G. (1990). *Theory and practice of group counseling* (3d ed.). Belmont, CA: Brooks/Cole.

Cork, M. (1969). *The forgotten children: A study of children with alcoholic parents.* Toronto: Addiction Research Foundation.

Craeger, C. (1989). SASSI Test breaks through denial. *Professional Counselor* July/August, p. 65.

Cummings, C., Gordon, J. R., & Marlatt, G. A. (1980). Relapse: Strategies of prevention and prediction. In W. R. Miller (Ed.), *The addictive behaviors: Treatment of alcoholism, drug abuse, smoking and obesity* (pp. 291–321). New York: Pergamon Press.

D'Andrea, L. M., Fisher, G. L., & Harrison, T. C. (1994). Cluster analysis of adult children of alcoholics. *The International Journal of the Addictions, 29,* 565–582.

Daley, D. C., & Marlatt, G. A. (1992). Relapse prevention: Cognitive and behavioral interventions. In J. H. Lowinson, P. Ruiz, R. M. Millman & J. G. Langrod (Eds.), *Substance abuse: A comprehensive textbook* (2nd ed., pp. 533–542.) Baltimore: Williams & Watkins.

Dally, P. (1984). Anorexia tardive—late onset marital anorexia nervosa. *Journal of Psychosomatic Research, 28,* 423–428.

DARE America. (1991). *D.A.R.E. will teach over 5 million children drug resistance skills in 1991.* Los Angeles: Author.

DeBruyn, M. (1992). Women and AIDs in developing countries. *Social and Medical Science, 34,* 249–262.

DeLeon, G. (1990). Treatment strategies. In J. A. Inciardi (Ed.), *Handbook of drug control in the United States* (pp. 115–138). Westport, CT: Greenwood.

Des Jarlais, D. C., & Friedman, S. R. (1987). HIV infection among intravenous drug users: Epidemiology and risk reduction. *AIDS, 1,* 67–76.

Des Jarlais, D. C., Friedman, S. R., Woods, J., & Milliken, J. (1992). HIV infection among intravenous drug users: Epidemiology and emerging public health perspectives. In J. H. Lowinson, P. Ruiz, R. B. Millman, & J. G. Langrod (Eds.), *Substance abuse: A comprehensive textbook* (2nd. ed., pp. 734–743). Baltimore: Williams & Wilkins.

Desire for drugs fuels crime. (1991, August 26). *Associated Press.*

Deutsch, H. (1945). *The psychology of women: A psychoanalytic interpretation. Vol II.* New York: Grune and Stratton.

DiCicco, L., Davis, R. B., Hogan, J., MacLean, A., & Orenstein, A. (1984). Group experiences for children of alcoholics. *Alcohol Health and Research World, 8,* 20–24.

DiCicco, L., Davis, R. & Orenstein, A. (1984). Identifying the children of alcoholics from survey responses. *Journal of Alcohol and Drug Education, 30,* 1–17.

DiCicco, L., Davis, R. B., Travis, J., & Orenstein, A. (1984). Recruiting children from alcoholics families into a peer education program. *Alcohol Health and Research World, 8,* 28–34.

Doctor, S. (1994). *Fetal alcohol syndrome, fetal alcohol effect, fetal drug effect: Educational implications. A training-curriculum for educators and other service providers.* Reno, Nevada: Washoe County School District.

Doering, P. L., Davidson, C. L., & LaFauce, L. (1989). Effects of cocaine on the human fetus: A review of clinical studies. *The Annals of Pharmacotherapy, 23,* 639–645.

Dole, V. P. (1989). [Letter to the editor]. *Journal of the American Medical Association, 261,* 1880.

Dole, V. P., & Nyslander, M. (1967). Rehabilitation of the street addict. *Archives of Environmental Health, 14,* 477–480.

Douglass, F. (1855). *My bondage, My freedom.* New York: Ortin and Mulligan.

Doweiko, H. E. (1990). *Concepts of chemical dependency.* Pacific Grove, CA: Brooks/Cole.

Downing, C. J., & Harrison, T. C. (1991). Parents' tough beat and the school counselor. *The School Counselor, 39,* 91–97.

Downs, W. R. (1982). Alcoholism as a developing family crisis. *Family Relations, 31,* 5–12.

DuBois, W. E. B. (1928). Drunkenness. *The Crisis, 35,* 348.

Dunst, C. J., Trivette, C. M., & Deal, A. G. (1988). *Enabling and empowering families: Principles and guidelines for practice.* Cambridge, MA: Brookline Books.

el-Guebaly, N., & Offord, D. R. (1977). The offspring of alcoholics: A critical review. *American Journal of Psychiatry, 134,* 357–365.

el-Guebaly, N., & Offord, D. R. (1979). On being the offspring of an alcoholic: An update. *Alcoholism: Clinical and Experimental Research, 3,* 148–157.

Emrick, C. (1987). Alcoholics Anonymous: Affiliation processes and effectiveness as treatment. *Alcoholism: Clinical and experimental research, 11,* 416–423.

Englehart, P., Robinson, H., & Carpenter, H. D. (1992). The workplace. In J. H. Lowinson, P. R. Ruiz, R. B. Millman, & J. G. Langrod (Eds.), *Substance abuse: A comprehensive textbook.* (2nd ed., pp. 1034–1048). Baltimore: Williams & Wilkins.

Engs, R. C. (1990). *Women: Alcohol and other drugs.* Dubuque, IA: Kendall/Hunt.

Ennett, S. T., Rosenbaum, D. P., Flewelling, R. L., Bieler, G. S., & Bailey, S. L. (1994). Long-term evaluation of drug abuse resistance education. *Addictive Behaviors, 19,* 113–125.

Ennett, S. T., Tobler, N. S., Ringwalt, C. L., & Flewelling, R. L. (1994). How effective is drug abuse resistance education? A meta-analysis of project DARE outcome evaluations. *American Journal of Public Health, 84,* 1394–1401.

Erekson, M. T., & Perkins, S. E. (1989). System dynamics in alcoholic families. Special issue. Codependency: Issues in treatment and recovery. *Alcoholism Treatment Quarterly, 6,* 59–74.

Erikson, E. H. (1963). *Childhood and society* (2nd ed.). New York: Norton.

Ewing, J. A., & Fox, R. E. (1968). Family therapy of alcoholism. In F. Messerman (Ed.), *Current psychiatric therapies.* (pp. 86–91). New York: Grune & Stratton.

Ewing, J. A. & Rouse, B. A. (1970, February). Identifying the hidden alcoholic. Paper presented at the 29th International Congress on Alcoholism and Drug Dependence, Sydney, Australia.

Eysenck, H. J. (1957). *The dynamics of anxiety and hysteria.* New York: Praeger.

Fairbairn, W. R. D. (1954). *An object relations theory of personality.* New York: Basic Books.

Falicov, C. J. (1982). Mexican families. In M. McGoldrick, J. K. Pierce, & J. Giordano (Eds.), *Ethnicity and family therapy.* (pp. 134–163). New York: Guilford Press.

Fernandez, F., & Levy, J. K. (1990). Diagnosis and management of HIV primary dementia. In D. G. Ostrow (Ed.), *Behavioral aspects of AIDS.* (pp. 235–246). New York: Plenum Publishing Company.

Fernandez, F., & Ruiz, P. (1992). Neuropsychiatric complications of HIV infection. In J. H. Lowinson, P. Ruiz, R. B. Millman, & J. G. Langrod (Eds.) *Substance abuse: A comprehensive textbook* (2nd. ed., pp. 775–786). Baltimore: Williams & Wilkins.

Fingarette, H. (1988). *Heavy drinking: The myth of alcoholism as a disease.* Berkeley, CA: University of California.

Finn, P. R., Martin, J. B., & Pihl, R. O. (1987). Alexithymia in males at high genetic risk for alcoholism. *Psychotherapy and Psychosomatics, 47,* 18–21.

Finn, P. R., & Pihl, R. O. (1988). Risk for alcoholism: A comparison between two different groups of sons of alcoholics on cardiovascular reactivity and sensitivity to alcohol. *Alcoholism: Clinical and Experimental Research 12,* 742–747.

Fisher, J. C., Mason, R. L., & Fisher, J. V. (1976). A diagnostic formula for alcoholism. *Journal of Studies on Alcohol, 37,* 1247–1255.

Fisher, G. L., & Harrison, T. C. (1992). Assessment of alcohol and other drug abuse with referred adolescents. *Psychology in the Schools, 29,* 172–178.

Fisher, G. L., & Harrison, T. C. (1993). Codependent characteristics of prospective counselors as compared to other graduate students. Paper presented at American Counseling Association National Conference, Atlanta, March.

Fisher, G. L., & Harrison, T. C. (1993). The school counselor's role in relapse prevention. *The School Counselor, 41,* 120–125.

Fisher, G. L., Jenkins, S. J., Harrison, T. C., & Jesch, K. (1992). Characteristics of adult children of alcoholics. *Journal of Substance Abuse, 4,* 27–34.

Fisher, G. L., Jenkins, S. J., Harrison, T. C., & Jesch, K. (1993). Personality characteristics of adult children of alcoholics, other adults from dysfunctional families, and adults from nondysfunctional families. *International Journal of the Addictions, 28,* 477–485.

Floyd, R. L., Zahniser, C., Gunter, E. P., & Kendrick J. S. (1991). Smoking during pregnancy: Two year follow-up. *Pediatrics, 89,* 284–289.

Forward, S. (1986). *Men who hate women and women who love them.* New York: Basic Books.

Franzmeier, A. (1988). To your health. *Nation's Business, 76,* 73.

Fredrickson, G. M. (1971). *The Black image in the White mind; The debate on Afro-American character and destiny, 1817–1914.* New York: Harper and Row.

Freehling, W. W. (1968). *Prelude to civil war: The nullification controversy in South Carolina, 1818–1836.* New York: Harper & Row, Publishers.

Freeman, E. M. (Ed.). (1992). *The addiction process: Effective social work approaches.* White Plains, NY: Longman.

Freud, S. (1926). Inhibitions, symptoms and anxiety. In J. Strachey (Ed.), (1959), *The standard edition of the complete psychological works.* (pp. 76–178). London: Hogarth Press.

Friel, J. (1985). Codependency assessment inventory: A preliminary research tool. *Focus on Family, May/June,* 20–21.

Fukuyama, M., & Inoue-Cox, C. (1992). Cultural perspectives in communicating with Asian/Pacific Islanders. In J. Wittmer (Ed.), *Valuing diversity and similarly: Bridging the gap through interpersonal skills.* (pp. 93–112). Minneapolis: Educational Media Corporation.

Galanter, M., Egelko, S., & Edwards, H. (1993). Rational recovery: Alternative to AA for addiction? *American Journal of Drug and Alcohol Abuse, 19,* 499–510.

Gamblers Anonymous. (1989). *Life line bulletin.* National Service Office. Los Angeles: Gamblers Anonymous.

Garfinkel, P. E., & Kaplan, A. S. (1986). Anorexia nervosa: Diagnostic conceptualizations. In K. D. Brownell & J. P. Foreyt (Eds.), *Handbook of eating disorders.* (pp. 266–282). New York: Basic Books.

Garfinkel, P. E., Moldofsky, H., & Garner, D. M. (1980). The heterogeneity of anorexia nervosa: Bulimia as a distinct subgroup. *Archives of General Psychiatry, 37,* 1036–1040.

Garn, S. M., & Clark, D. C. (1975). Nutrition, growth, development, and maturation—Findings from the ten state nutrition survey of 1968–1970. *Pediatrics, 56,* 306–319.

Garner, D. M., & Bemis, K. M. (1982). A cognitive behavioral approach to anorexia nervosa. *Cognitive Theory and Research, 6,* 1–27.

Gaudia, R. (1992). Compulsive gambling: Reframing issues of control. In E. M. Freeman (Ed.), *The addiction process: Effective social work approaches.* (pp. 237–248). White Plains, NY: Longman.

Gedig, U., & Gedig, G. (1977). The alcohol question in Japan. *Suchtgefahren, 23,* 97–106.

Giermyski, T., & Williams, T. (1986). Codependency. *Journal of Psychoactive Drugs, 18,* 7–13.

Gilbert, M. J. (1978). *Five week alcoholism ethnography conducted in three Spanish speaking communities.* Sacramento, CA: State Office of Alcoholism.

Gilbert, M. J., & Cervantes, R. C. (1986). Patterns and practices of alcohol use among Mexican Americans: A comprehensive review. *Hispanic Journal of Behavioral Sciences, 8,* 1–60.

Ginzburg, H. M., Weiss, S. H., MacDonald, M. C., & Hubbard, R. L. (1985). HTLV-III exposure among drug users. *Cancer Research, 45* (Suppl.), 4605–4608.

Glick, P. C. (1984). Marriage, divorce and living arrangements: Prospective changes. *Journal of Family Issues, 5,* 7–26.

Goldstein, P. J. (1989). Crack and homicide in New York City, 1988: A conceptually-based event analysis. *Contemporary Drug Problems,* Winter.

Goodman, C. (1984). The PACE family treatment and education program: A public health approach to parental competence and promotion of mental health. In B. Cohler & J. Musick (Eds.), *Intervention with psychiatrically disabled parents and their young children. New dimensions for mental health services.* (pp. 53–78). San Francisco: Jossey-Bass.

Goodman, R. W. (1987). Adult children of alcoholics. *Journal of Counseling and Development, 66,* 162–163.

Goodman, S., Blinder, B. J., Chaitin, B. F., & Hagman, J. (1988). Atypical eating disorders. In B. J. Blinder, B. F. Chaitin, & R. S. Goldstein (Eds.), *The eating disorders: Medical and psychological bases of diagnosis and treatment.* (pp. 393–404). New York: PMA Publishing Corp.

Gordis, E. (1990). *Alcohol and health: Seventh special report to the U.S. Congress.* Rockville, MD: National Institute on Alcohol Abuse and Alcoholism.

Gormally, J., Black, S., Daston, S., & Rardin, D. (1982). The assessment of binge-eating severity among obese persons. *Addictive Behaviors, 7,* 47–55.

Gorski, T. T. (1988). *The staying sober workbook: A serious solution for the problem of relapse.* Independence, MO: Independence Press.

Gorski, T. T. (1989). *Passages through recovery: An action plan for preventing relapse.* Center City, MN: Hazelden.

Gorski, T. T. (1990). The Cenaps model of relapse prevention: Basic principles and procedures. *Journal of Psychoactive Drugs, 22,* 125–133.

Gorski, T. T. (1992). Creating a relapse prevention program in your treatment center. *Addiction & Recovery,* July/August, 16–17.

Gorski, T. T. (1993). Relapse prevention: A state of the art overview. *Addiction & Recovery,* March/April, 25–27.

Gorski, T. T., & Miller, M. M. (1986). *Staying sober: Guide to relapse prevention.* Independence, MO: Herald House.

Gossett, G. (1988). Unpublished seminar report, March, 1988. Denton, TX: University of Texas.

Gostin, L. O. (1989). Public health strategies for confronting AIDS. *Journal of the American Medical Association, 261,* 1621–1630.

Griffin, J. E. (1993). *Using Faces II to predict a shelter-seeker's return to an abusive relationship.* Unpublished doctoral dissertation, University of Nevada, Reno, NV.

Griffin-Shelley, E. (1991). *Sex and love.* New York: Praeger.

Griffith, D. R. (1989). Neurobehavioral effects of intrauterine cocaine exposure. *Ab Initio.* Boston: University of Massachusetts, Amherst, and Boston Children's Hospital.

Griffith, D. R. (1990). *Developmental follow-up of cocaine-exposed infants to three years.* Paper presented at the International Society for Infant Studies Conference, Montreal.

Griffith, D. R. (1992). Prenatal exposure to cocaine and other drugs: Developmental and educational prognoses. *Phi Delta Kappan, 74,* 30–34.

Grinspoon, L., & Bakalar, J. B. (1994). The war on drugs—a peace proposal. *The New England Journal of Medicine, 330,* 357–360.

Grube, J. W., & Wallack, L. (1994). Television beer advertising and drinking knowledge, beliefs, and intentions among schoolchildren. *American Journal of Public Health, 84,* 254–259.

Gwirtsman, H. E., Roy-Byrne, P., Lerner, L., & Yager, J. (1984). Bulimia in men: Report of three cases with neuroendocrine findings. *Journal of Clinical Psychiatry, 45,* 78–81.

Hahn, R. A., Onorato, I. M., Jones, T. S., & Dougherty, J. (1989). Prevalence of HIV infection among intravenous drug users in the United States. *Journal of the American Medical Association, 261,* 2677–2684.

Haley, J. (1973). *Uncommon therapy: The psychiatric techniques of Milton H. Erickson, M.D.* New York: Ballantine Books.

Halpern, H. M. (1982). *How to break your addiction to a person.* New York: Bantam Books.

Hamilton, N. G. (1989). A critical review of object relations theory. *American Journal Psychiatry, 146,* 1552–1560.

Harper, F. D. (1978). Alcohol use among North American Blacks. In Y. Israel, F. B. Glaser, H. Kalant, R. E. Popham, W. Schmidt, & R. G. Smart (Eds.), *Research advances in alcohol and drug problems vol. 4.* (pp. 349–364). New York: Plenum Press.

Harper, F. D. (Ed.). (1976). *Alcohol abuse and Black America.* Alexandria, VA: Douglass Publishers.

Harrison, P. A., & Belille, C. A. (1987). Women in treatment: Beyond the stereotype. *Journal of Studies on Alcohol, 48,* 574–578.

Hawkins, D. M. (1986). Understanding reactions to group instability in psychotherapy groups. *International Journal of Group Psychotherapy, 36,* 241–260.

Hawkins, J. D., Catalano, R. E., & Miller, J. Y. (1992). Risk and protective factors for alcohol and other drug problems in adolescence and early adulthood: Implications for substance abuse prevention. *Psychological Bulletin, 112,* 64–105.

Hawkins, J. D., Lishner, D. M., & Catalano, R. E. (April, 1984). Childhood predictors and the prevention of adolescent substance abuse. Presented at the National Institute on Drug Abuse research analysis and utilization system meeting, etiology of drug abuse: Implications for prevention.

Hawkins, J. D., Lishner, D. M., & Catalano, R. E. (1985). Childhood predictors and the prevention of adolescent substance abuse. In C. L. Jones & R. J. Battjes (Eds.), *Etiology of drug abuse: Implications for prevention.* (pp. 75–186). Washington, DC: National Institute on Drug Abuse.

Hawkins, J. D., Lishner, D. M., Catalano, R. F., & Howard, M. O. (1985). Childhood predictors of adolescent substance abuse: Toward an empirically grounded theory. Special issue. Childhood and chemical abuse: Prevention and intervention, *Journal of Children in Contemporary Society, 18,* 11–48.

Hawley, N. P., & Brown, E. L. (1981). The use of group treatment with children of alcoholics. *Journal of Contemporary Social Work, 62,* 40–46.

Hayford, S. M., Epps, R. P., & Dahl-Regis, M. (1988). Behavior and development patterns in children born to heroin-addicted and methadone-addicted mothers. *Journal of the National Medical Association, 80,* 1197–1200.

Hegedus, A. M., Alterman, A. I., & Tarter, R. E. (1984). Learning achievement in sons of alcoholics. *Alcoholism: Clinical and Experimental Research, 8,* 330–333.

Hemfelt, R., & Fowler, R. (1990). *Serenity: A companion for twelve step recovery, complete with New Testament, Psalms, Proverbs.* Nashville, TN: Nelson Publishing.

Herd, D. (1991). The paradox of temperance: Blacks and the alcohol question in nineteenth-century America. In S. Barrows & R. Room (Eds.) *Drinking: Behavior and belief in modern history.* (pp. 354–375). Berkeley, CA: University of California Press.

Herzog, D. B. (1984). Are anorexic and bulimic patients depressed? *American Journal of Psychiatry, 141,* 1594–1638.

Hesse-Biber, S. (1989). Eating patterns and disorders in a college population: Are college women's eating problems a new phenomenon. *Sex Roles, 20,* 71–89.

Hester, R. K. (1995). Behavioral self-control training. In R. K. Hester & W. R. Miller (Eds.). *Handbook of alcoholism treatment approaches: Effective alternatives* (2nd ed., pp. 148–175). Boston: Allyn & Bacon.

Hibbard, S. (1987). The diagnosis and treatment of adult children of alcoholics as a specialized therapeutic population. *Psychotherapy, 24,* 779–785.

Hill, A. (1989). Treatment and prevention of alcoholism in the Native American family. In G. Lawson & A. Lawson (Eds.), *Alcoholism &* substance abuse in special populations. (pp. 247–272). Rockville, MD: Aspen Publishers, Inc.

Hines, P. M., & Boyd-Franklin, N. (1982). Black families. In M. McGoldrick, J. Pierce, & J. Giordano (Eds.), *Ethnicity and family therapy.* (pp. 84–107). New York: The Guilford Press.

Hispanic Health Council. (1987). *Conference proceedings: Alcohol use and abuse among Hispanic adolescents.* Hartford, CN: Hispanic Health Council.

Hoffman, N. G., & Harrison, P. A. (1986). *CATOR 1986 report: findings two years after treatment.* Minneapolis, MN: CATOR.

Horney, K. (1945). *Our inner conflicts: A constructive theory of neurosis.* New York: Norton.

Hsu, L. K. G. (1988). The etiology of anorexia nervosa. In B. J. Blinder, B. F. Chaitin, & R. S. Goldstein (Eds.), *The eating disorders: Medical and psychological bases of diagnosis and treatment.* (pp. 239–246). New York: PMA Publishing Corporation.

Hubbard, R. L., Marsden, M. E., Rachal, J. V., Harwood, H. J., Cavanaugh, E. R., & Ginsberg, H. M. (1989). *Drug abuse treatment: A national study of effectiveness.* Chapel Hill, NC: University of North Carolina Press.

Humphrey, L. L. (1989). Observed family interactions among subtypes of eating disorders using structural analysis of social behavior. *Journal of Consulting and Clinical Psychology, 57,* 206–214.

Hunt, W. A., Barnett, L. W., & Branch, L. G. (1971). Relapse rates in addiction programs. *Journal of Clinical Psychology, 27,* 455–456.

Hunter, M. (1988). *What is sex addiction?* Center City, MN: Hazelden Foundation.

Inaba, D. S., & Cohen, W. E. (1989). *Uppers, downers, all arounders: Physical and mental effects of drugs of abuse.* Ashland, Oregon: Cinemed Inc.

Inciardi, J. A. (1994). HIV/AIDs risks among male, heterosexual noninjecting drug users who exchange crack for sex. In R. J. Battjes, Z. Sloboda, & W. C. Grace, (Eds). *The context of HIV risk among drug users and their sexual partners.* (pp. 26–40). National Institute of Drug Abuse Research Monograph. Rockville, MD: U.S. Department of Health and Human Services.

Indian Health Service. (1977). *Alcoholism: A high priority health problem.* Washington: U.S. Government Printing Office.

Ivey, A. E., Bradford-Ivey, M., & Simek-Morgan, L. (1993). *Counseling and psychotherapy: A multicultural perspective* (3rd ed.). Needham Heights, MA: Allyn & Bacon.

Jackson, D. D. (1957). The question of family homeostasis. *Psychiatric Quarterly Supplement, 31,* 79–90.

Jackson, S. A. (1993). *Educating young children prenatally exposed to drugs and at risk.* Washington, D.C.: Office of Educational Research and Improvement.

Jacob, T., Ritchey, P., Cvitkovic, J. F., & Blane, H. T. (1981). Communication styles of alcoholic and non-alcoholic families when drinking and not drinking. *Journal of Studies on Alcohol, 42,* 466–482.

Jacobs, M. R., & Fehr, K. O'B. (1987). *Addiction Research Foundation's drugs and drug abuse: A reference text* (Second edition). Toronto, Canada: Addiction Research Foundation.

Jacobson, G. R. (1989). A comprehensive approach to pre-treatment evaluation: I. Detection, assessment and diagnosis of alcoholism. In R. K. Hester & W. R. Miller (Eds.). *Handbook of alcoholism treatment approaches: Effective alternatives* (pp. 17–43). New York: Pergamon Press.

James, T., & Goldman, M. (1971). Behavior trends of wives of alcoholics. *Quarterly Journal of Studies on Alcohol, 32,* 373-381.

Jellinek, E. M. (1952). Phases of alcohol addiction. *Quarterly Journal of Studies on Alcohol, 13,* 673–684.

Jellinek E. M. (1960). *The disease concept of alcoholism.* New Haven, CT: Hillhouse Press.

Jenkins, S. J., Fisher, G. L., & Harrison, T. C. (1993). Adult children of dysfunctional families: Childhood roles. *Journal of Mental Health Counseling, 15,* 310–319.

Johnson, G. M., Shontz, F. C., & Locke, T. P. (1984). Relationships between adolescent drug use and parental drug behavior. *Adolescence, 19,* 295–298.

Johnson, J. J. (1975). Alcoholism: A social disease from a medical perspective. In R. A. Williams (Ed.), *Textbook of Black-related diseases.* (pp. 639–654). New York: McGraw-Hill Book Company.

Johnson, J. L. (1988). Cognitive functioning in children from alcoholic and nonalcoholic families. *British Journal of Addiction, 83,* 849–857.

Johnson, V. E. (1973). *I'll quit tomorrow.* Toronto: Harper and Row.

Johnson, V. E. (1986). *Intervention: How to help someone who doesn't want help. A step-by-step guide for families and friends of chemically dependent persons.* Minneapolis: Johnson Institute Books.

Johnston, L. D., O'Malley, P. M., & Bachman, J. G. (1993). *National survey results on drug use from the monitoring the future study, 1975–1992.* Rockville, Maryland: National Institute on Drug Abuse.

Johnston, L. D., O'Malley, P. M., & Bachman, J. G. (1994). *National survey results on drug use from the monitoring the future study, 1975–1993.* Rockville, Maryland: National Institute on Drug Abuse.

Jonas, S. (1992). Public health approach to the prevention of substance abuse. In J. H. Lowinson, P. Ruiz, R. B. Millman, & J. C. Langrod (Eds.). *Substance abuse: A comprehensive textbook* (2nd ed., pp. 928–943). Baltimore: Williams & Wilkins.

Jones, J. W. (1985). *Children of alcoholics screening test.* Chicago: Camelot Unlimited.

Jones-Saumty, D., Hochhaus, L., Dru, R., & Zeiner, A. R. (1983). Psychological factors of familial alcoholism in American Indians and Caucasians. *Journal of Clinical Psychology 39,* 783–790.

Juliana, P., & Goodman, C. (1995). Children of substance abusing parents. In J. H. Lowinson, P. Ruiz, R. B. Millman, & J. G. Langrod (Eds.). *Substance abuse: A comprehensive textbook.* (2nd. ed., pp. 808–815). Baltimore: Williams & Wilkins.

Julien, R. M. (1995). *A primer of drug action: A concise, nontechnical guide to the actions, use and side effects of psychoactive drugs* (7th ed.). New York: W. H. Freeman and Company.

Jung, J. (1994). *Under the influence: Alcohol and human behavior.* Pacific Grove, CA: Brooks/Cole.

Kalodner, C. R., & Scarano, G. M. (1992). A continuum of nonclinical eating disorders: A review of behavioral and psychological correlates and suggestions for intervention. Special Issue: Women and health, *Journal of Mental Health Counseling, 14,* 30–41.

Kaminer, W. (1990). Chances are you're codependent too. *New York Times Book Review,* February 1.

Kandel, D. B. (1980). Developmental stages in adolescent drug involvement. In D. J. Lettieri, M. Sayers, & H. W. Pearson (Eds.), *Theories on drug abuse: Selected contemporary perspectives.* (pp. 120–127). NIDA Research Monograph 30. Washington, D.C.: Department of Health and Human Services.

Kandel, D. B. (1989). Issues of sequencing of adolescent drug use and other problem behaviors. *Journal of Drug Issues, 3,* 55–76.

Kanoy, K., & Miller, B. C. (1980). Children's impact on the parental decision to divorce. *Family Relations, 29,* 309–315.

Karacostas, D. D., & Fisher, G. L. (1993). Chemical dependency in students with and without learning disabilities. *Journal of Learning Disabilities, 26,* 491–495.

Kashubeck, S., Walsh, B., & Crowl, A. (1994). College atmosphere and eating disorders. *Journal of Counseling and Development, 72,* 640–645.

Kasl, C. D. (1989). *Women, sex, and addiction: A search for love and power.* New York: Ticknor & Fields.

Kasl, C. D. (1992). *Many roads, one journey: Moving beyond the 12 steps.* New York: Harper Collins Publishers.

Kaslow, R. A., Blackwelder, W. C., & Ostrow, D. G. (1989). No evidence for a role of alcohol or other psychoactive drugs in accelerating immunodeficiency in HIV-1-positive individuals. *Journal of the American Medical Association, 261,* 3424–3429.

Kaufman, A. (1975). Gasoline sniffing among children in a Pueblo Indian village. *Pediatrics, 51,* 1060–1065.

Kaufman, E., & Kaufman, P. (1992). From psychodynamic to structural to integrated family treatment of chemical dependency. In E. Kaufman, & P. Kaufman, P. (Eds.), *Family therapy of drug and alcohol abuse* (pp. 34–45). Boston: Allyn & Bacon.

Keller, M. (1972). On the loss-of-control phenomenon in alcoholism. *British Journal of Addiction, 67,* 153–166.

Kellett, J. Trimble, M., Thorley, A. (1976). Anorexia nervosa after the menopause. *British Journal of Psychiatry, 128,* 555–558.

Kerr, B. (1994). Review of the Substance Abuse Subtle Screening Inventory. In J. C. Conoley & J. C. Impara (Eds.) *The Supplement to the eleventh mental measurements yearbook.* (pp. 249–251). Lincoln, NB: U of Neb. Press.

Kiechel III, W. (1989, April 10). The workaholic generation. *Fortune,* pp. 50–52.

Kim, S. (1991). *Cultural competence for evaluators working with Asian American communities: Some practical considerations.* Unpublished manuscript, Database Evaluation Research, Charlotte, N.C.

Kim, S., McLeod, J. H., & Shantzis, C. (1993). An outcome evaluation of Here's Looking at You, 2000. *Journal of Drug Education, 23,* 67–81.

King, L. M. (1982). Alcoholism: Studies regarding Black Americans: 1977–1980. In *Alcohol and health monograph No.4: Special Populations Issue* (pp. 385–410). Rockville, MD: National Institute on Alcohol Abuse and Alcoholism.

Kirby, D. G. (1989). Immigration, stress, and prescription drug use among Cuban women in South Florida. *Medical Anthropology, 10,* 287–295.

Kirkley, B. G. (1986). Bulimia: Clinical characteristics, development, and etiology. *Journal of the American Dietetics Association, 4,* 468–472, 475.

Kirkpatrick, J. (1986). *Goodbye hangover, hello life: Self-help for women.* Canada: Collier MacMillan Canada.

Kirkpatrick, J. (1990). *Turnabout: New help for the woman alcoholic.* New York: Bantam Books.

Kitano, H. H. L. (1982). Alcohol drinking patterns: The Asian Americans. In U.S. Department of Health and Human Services, *Alcohol and Health, Monograph 4, Special Populations Issue.* (pp. 411–430). Rockville, MD: National Institute on Alcohol Abuse and Alcoholism.

Kitchens, J. A. (1991). *Understanding and treating codependence.* Englewood Cliffs, NJ: Prentice Hall.

Klar, H. (1987). The setting for psychiatric treatment. In A. J. Frances & R. E. Hales (Eds.), *American Psychiatric Association Annual Review* (Vol. 6) (pp. 336–352). Washington, DC: American Psychiatric Association Press.

Klaft, R. P., & Kleiner, B. H. (1988). Understanding workaholics. *Business, 38,* 37–40.

Knop, J., Teasdale, T. W., Schulsinger, F., & Goodwin, D. W. (1985). A prospective study of young men at high risk for alcoholism: School behavior and achievement. *Journal of Studies on Alcohol, 46,* 273–278.

Kofoed, L., Kania, J., Walsh, T., & Atkinson, R. M. (1986). Outpatient treatment of patients with substance abuse and coexisting psychiatric disorders. *American Journal of Psychiatry, 143,* 867–872.

Kohut, H. (1971). *The analysis of the self.* New York: International Universities Press.

Kubler-Ross, E. (1969). *On death and dying.* New York: Macmillan.

Kurtz, E. (1979). *Not-God: A history of Alcoholics Anonymous.* Center City, MN: Hazelden.

Kurtz, L. F. (1990). Twelve step programs. In T. J. Powell (Ed.), *Working with self-help* (pp. 93–118). Silver Spring, MD: NASW Press.

Landry, M. (1984). Update on cocaine dependence: Crack and advances in diagnostics and treatment. In D. E. Smith & D. R. Wesson (Eds.), *Treating cocaine dependency* (pp. 91–116). Minneapolis: Hazeldon.

Larkin, J. R. (1965). *Alcohol and the Negro: Explosive issues.* Zebulon, NC: Record Publishing.

Lawson, A. W. (1992). Intergenerational alcoholism: The family connection. In G. W. Lawson & A. W. Lawson (Eds.), *Adolescent substance abuse: Etiology, treatment and prevention* (pp. 41–70). Gaithersberg, MD: Aspen Publishing.

Lawson, G. W. (1992). Twelve-step programs and the treatment of adolescent substance abuse. In G. W. Lawson & A. W. Lawson (Eds.), *Adolescent substance abuse: Etiology, treatment and prevention.* (pp. 219–229). Gaithersberg, MD: Aspen Publications.

Lawson, G. W., & Lawson, A. W. (Eds.) (1992). *Adolescent substance abuse: Etiology, treatment, and prevention.* Gaithersberg, MD: Aspen Publications.

Lawson, G. W., Peterson, J. S., & Lawson, A. W. (1983). *Alcoholism and the family: A guide to treatment and prevention.* Gaithersberg, MD: Aspen Publications.

Lee, E. (1982). A social systems approach to assessment and treatment for Chinese Americans. In M. McGoldrick, J. K. Pearce, and J. Giordano (Eds.), *Ethnicity and family therapy,* (pp. 527–551). New York: Guilford Press.

Lee, E., & Ja, D. Y. (1982). *Migration and the Asian families: A multi-generational perspective.* Paper presented at the Second Annual Symposium on Cross-Cultural and Trans-Cultural Issues in Family Health Care. University of California, San Francisco, March.

Lemert, E. M. (1964). Forms and pathology of drinking in three Polynesian societies. *American Anthropology, 66,* 361–374.

Lesieur, H. & Custer, R, (1984). Pathological gambling: Roots, phases, and treatment. *Annals of the American Academy of Political and Social Science, 474,* 146–156.

Levinson, D. J. (1978). *The seasons of a man's life.* New York: Knopf.

Lewis, J. A., Dana, R. Q., & Blevins, G. A. (1988). *Substance abuse counseling: An individualized approach.* Pacific Grove, CA: Brooks/Cole.

Lewis, J. A., Dana, R. Q., & Blevins, G. A. (1994). *Substance abuse counseling: An individualized approach* (2nd ed.). Pacific Grove, CA: Brooks/Cole.

Lex, B. W. (1985). Alcohol problems in special populations. In J. H. Mendelson & N. K. Mello (Eds.), *The diagnosis and treatment of alcoholism.* (2nd. ed., pp. 89–187). New York: McGraw-Hill Book Company.

Lex, B. W. (1987). Review of alcohol problems in ethnic minority groups. *Journal of Consulting and Clinical Psychology, 55,* 293–300.

Lieberman, M. A., Yalom, I. D., & Miles, M. B. (1973). *Encounter groups: First facts.* New York: Basic Books.

Lipscomb, W. R., & Trochi, K. (1981). *Black drinking practices study: Report to the Department of Alcohol and Drug Programs.* Berkeley: Source, Inc.

Locke, D. C. (1990). A not so provincial view of multicultural counseling. *Counselor Education and Supervision, 30,* 18–25.

Logan, S. M. L. (1992). Overcoming sex and love addiction: An expanded perspective. In E. M. Freeman (Ed.), *The addictive process: Effective social work approaches.* (pp. 207–222). White Plains, NY: Longman.

Lopez, F. (1994). *Confidentiality of patient records for alcohol and other drug treatment.* Technical Assistance Publication, #13. Rockville, MD: Center for Substance Abuse Treatment.

Lopez-Lee, D. (1979). Alcoholism among third world women: Research and treatment. In V. Burtle (Ed.), *Women who drink: Alcoholic experience and psychotherapy.* (pp. 98–118). Springfield, IL: Charles C. Thomas.

Loro, A. D. (1984). Binge-eating: A cognitive-behavioral treatment approach. In R. C. Hawkins, W. J. Fremouw, and P. F. Clement (Eds.), *The binge-purge syndrome: Diagnosis, treatment, & research* (pp. 183–210). New York: Springer.

MacAndrew, C. (1965). The differentiation of male alcoholic outpatients from nonalcoholic psychiatric patients by means of the MMPI. *Quarterly Journal of Studies on Alcohol, 26,* 238–246.

Machlowitz, M. (1980). *Workaholics: Living with them, working with them.* Reading, MA: Addison-Wesley.

MacKenzie, T. D., Bartecchi, C. E., & Schrier, R. W. (1994). The human costs of tobacco use (part two). *The New England Journal of Medicine, 330,* 33–38.

Madden, P. A., & Grube, J. W. (1994). The frequency and nature of alcohol and tobacco advertising in televised sports, 1990 through 1992. *American Journal of Public Health, 84,* 297–299.

Mahler, M. S. (1975). *The psychological birth of the human infant: Symbiosis and individuation.* New York: Basic Books.

Malin, H., Coakley, J., Kaelber, C., Munch, N., & Holland, W. (1982). An epidemiologic perspective on alcohol use and abuse in the United States. In *Alcohol and health monograph 1: Alcohol consumption and related problems.* (pp. 99–156). Rockville, MD: National Institute on Alcohol Abuse and Alcoholism.

Manisses Communications Group, Inc. (1994). *The Addiction Newsletter, 10,* 1–5.

Manning, D. T., Balson, P. M., & Xenakis, S. (1986). The prevalence of Type A personality in the children of alcoholics. *Alcoholism: Clinical and Experimental Research, 10,* 184–189.

Marcus, A. M. (1986). Academic achievement in elementary school children of alcoholic mothers. *Journal of Clinical Psychology, 42,* 372–376.

Marino, T. M. (1995). Writing your way out of trouble. *Counseling Today, February 8,* 10.

Markides, K. S., Ray, L. A., Stroup-Benham, C. A., & Trevino, F. (1990). Acculturation and alcohol consumption in the Mexican-American population of southwestern U.S. *American Journal of Psychiatric Health, 80, (Suppl),* 42–46.

Marlatt, G. A. (1985). Relapse prevention: Theoretical rationale and overview of the model. In G. A. Marlatt & J. R. Gordon, (Eds.), *Relapse prevention: Maintenance strategies in the treatment of addictive behaviors.* (pp. 3–70). New York: Guilford Press.

Marlatt, G. A., Demming, B., & Reid, J. B. (1973). Loss of control drinking in alcoholics: An experimental analogue. *Journal of Abnormal Psychology, 81,* 223–241.

Marlatt, G. A., & Gordon, J. R. (Eds). (1985). *Relapse Prevention: Maintenance strategies in the treatment of addictive behaviors.* New York: Guilford Press.

Martinez, T. (1983). *The gambling scene: Why people gamble.* Springfield, IL: Thomas

Maslow, A. H. (1971). *The farther reaches of human nature,* New York: Viking Press.

Matuschka, E. (1985). Treatment, outcomes, and clinical evaluation. In T. E. Bratter & G. G. Forrest (Eds.). *Alcoholism and substance abuse: Strategies for clinical intervention* (pp. 193–224). New York: The Free Press.

Matuschka, P. R. (1985). The psychopharmacology of addiction. In T. E. Bratter and G. G. Forrest (Eds.), *Alcoholism and substance abuse: Strategies for clinical intervention* (pp. 49–75). New York: The Free Press.

McAdoo, H. (1979). The impact of upward mobility of kin: Help patterns and the reciprocal obligations in Black families. *Journal of Marriage and the Family, 4,* 761–776.

McCarthy, J. C. (1988). The concept of addictive disease. In D. E. Smith & D. R. Wesson, *Treating cocaine dependency* (pp. 21–30). Minneapolis: Hazeldon.

McCrady, B. S., & Irvine, S. (1989). Self-help groups. In R. K. Hester & W. R. Miller (Eds.) *Handbook of alcoholism treatment approaches: Effective alternatives.* (pp. 153–169). Elmsford, NY: Pergamon Press.

McDermott, D. (1984). The relationship of parental drug use and parent's attitude concerning adolescent drug use to adolescent drug use. *Adolescence, 19,* 89–96.

McDougall, J. (1989). *Theaters of the body: A psychoanalytic approach to psychosomatic illness.* New York: Norton.

McGinnis, J. M., & Foege, W. H. (1993). Actual causes of death in the United States. *Journal of the American Medical Association, 270,* 2207–2212.

McGoldrick, M. (1989). Ethnicity and the family life cycle. In B. Carter & M. McGoldrick (Eds.), *The changing family life cycle: A framework for family therapy* (pp. 70–89). Boston: Allyn & Bacon.

McGoldrick M., & Gerson, R. (1985). *Genograms in family assessment.* New York: Norton.

McGovern, J. P., & DuPont, R. L. (1991). Student assistance programs: An important approach to drug prevention. *Journal of School Health, 61,* 260–264.

McKearn, J. (1988). Post-traumatic stress disorder: Implications for the treatment of family members of alcoholics. *Alcoholism Treatment Quarterly, 5,* 141–144.

McLaughlin, D. G., Raymond, J. S., Murakami, S. R., & Goebert, D. (1987). Drug use among Asian Americans in Hawaii. *Journal of Psychoactive Drugs, 19,* 85–94.

McLellan, A. T., Luborsky, L., & O'Brien, C. P. (1986). Alcohol and drug abuse treatment in three different populations: Is there improvement and is it predictable? *American Journal of Drug and Alcohol Abuse, 12,* 101–120.

Miller, D., & Jang, M. (1977). Children of alcoholics: A 20-year longitudinal study. *Social Work Research and Abstracts, 13,* 23–29.

Miller, G. A. (1983). *Substance Abuse Subtle Screening Inventory.* Bloomington, IN: The SASSI Institute.

Miller, G. A. (1985). *The Substance Abuse Subtle Screening Inventory manual.* Spencer, IN: Spencer Evening World.

Miller, G. A. (1994). Personal correspondence.

Miller, W. R. (1989). Matching individuals with interventions. In R. K. Hester and W. R. Miller (Eds.). *Handbook of alcoholism treatment approaches: Effective alternatives.* (pp. 261–272). New York: Pergamon Press.

Miller, W. R. (1995). Increasing motivation for change. In R. K. Hester and W. R. Miller (Eds.). *Handbook of alcoholism treatment approaches: Effective alternatives* (2nd ed., pp. 89–104). Boston: Allyn & Bacon.

Miller, W. R., & Hester, R. K. (1980). Treating problem drinkers: Modern approaches. In W. R. Miller (Ed.), *The addictive behaviors: Treatment of alcoholism, drug abuse, smoking, and obesity* (pp. 11–141). New York: Pergamon Press.

Miller, W. R., & Hester, R. K. (1986). Inpatient alcoholism treatment: Who benefits? *American Psychologist, 41,* 794–806.

Miller, W. R., & Hester, R. K (1995). Treatment for alcohol problems: Toward an informed eclecticism. In R. K. Hester & W. R. Miller (Eds.), *Handbook of alcoholism treatment approaches: Effective alternatives* (2nd ed., pp. 1–11). Boston: Allyn & Bacon.

Miller, W. R., & Kurtz, E. (1994). Models of alcoholism used in treatment: Contrasting AA and other perspectives with which it is often confused. *Journal of Studies on Alcohol, 55,* 159–166.

Miller, W. R., & Munoz, R. F. (1982). *How to control your drinking.* (rev. ed.) Albuquerque: University of New Mexico Press.

Miller, W. R., & Rollnick, S. (1991). *Motivational interviewing: Preparing people to change addictive behavior.* New York: Guilford Press.

Miller, W. R., & Westerberg, V. S., Waldron, H. B. (1995). Evaluating alcohol problems in adults and adolescents. In R. K.. Hester & W. R. Miller (Eds.) *Handbook of alcoholism treatment approaches: Effective approaches,* (2nd ed., pp. 61–88). Boston: Allyn & Bacon.

Miner, J. L., & Boldt, J. R. (1981). *Outward bound USA: Learning through experience in adventure-based education.* New York: William Morrow and Company.

Minirth, F., Meier, P., Wichern, F., Brewer, B., & Skipper, S. (1981). *The workaholic and his family: An inside look.* Grand Rapids, MI: Baker Book House.

Mintz, L. B., & Betz, N. E. (1988). Prevalence and correlates of eating disordered behaviors among undergraduate women. *Journal of Counseling Psychology, 35,* 463–471.

Minuchin, S. (1974). *Families and family therapy.* Cambridge, MA: Harvard University Press.

Minuchin, S. (1992). Constructing a therapeutic reality. In E. Kaufman & P. Kaufman, P. (Eds.), *Family therapy of drug and alcohol abuse* (pp. 1–14), Boston: Allyn & Bacon.

Mitchell, J. E., & Pyle, R. L. (1988). The epidemiology of bulimia. In B. J. Blinder, B. F. Chaitin, & R. S. Goldstein (Eds.). *The eating disorders: Medical and psychological bases of diagnosis and treatment* (pp. 259–266). New York: PMA Publishing Corporation.

Moore, D. D., & Forster, J. R. (1993). Student assistance programs: New approaches for reducing adolescent substance abuse. *Journal of Counseling and Development, 71,* 326–329.

Moran, E. (1975). Pathological gambling. *Contemporary Psychiatry. British Journal of Psychiatry,* Special Publication No. 9. London: Royal College of Psychiatrists.

Morehouse, E. R. (1986). Counseling adolescent children of alcoholics in groups. In R. Ackerman (Ed.), *Growing in the shadow* (pp. 125–142). Pompano Beach, FL: Health Communications.

Morgenstern. J., & McCrady, B. S. (1992). Curative factors in alcohol and drug treatment: Behavioral and disease model perspectives. *British Journal of Addiction, 87,* 901–912.

Morley, J. E., & Castele, S. C. (1985). Death by starvation: The Sepulveda Grecc Method No. 6. *Geriatric Medicine Today, 4,* 76–78, 83.

Morris, A., Cooper, T., & Cooper, P. J. (1989). The changing shape of female fashion models. *International Journal of Eating Disorders, 8,* 593–596.

Morris, S., & Charney, N. (1983, June 17). Workaholism: Thank God it's Monday. *Psychology Today,* p. 88.

Nace, E. P. (1987). *The treatment of alcoholism.* New York: Brunner/Mazel.

Nace, E. P. (1992). Alcoholics Anonymous. In J. H. Lowinson, P. Ruiz, R. B. Millman & J. G. Langrod (Eds.). *Substance abuse: A comprehensive textbook* (2nd ed., pp. 486–495). Baltimore: Williams & Wilkins

National Institute on Drug Abuse. (1985). *National household survey on drug-abuse: Population estimates 1985.* DHHS Pub. No. (ADM) 87-1539. Washington, DC: Superintendent of Documents, U.S. Government Printing Office, 1987.

National Institute on Drug Abuse (1990). *National Household Survey on Drug Abuse,* Washington, DC: National Institute on Drug Abuse.

National Institute on Alcohol and Alcoholism (1980). *Facts about alcohol and alcoholism.* Washington, DC: U.S. Government Printing Office.

Needle, R. H. (1994). HIV risk behaviors of heterosexual male drug users. In R. J. Battjes, Z. Sloboda, & W. C. Grace, (Eds). *The context of HIV risk among drug users and their sexual partners.* (pp. 5–8). National Institute of Drug Abuse Research Monograph. Rockville, MD: U.S. Department of Health and Human Services.

Neuman, P. A., & Halvorson, P. A. (1983). *Anorexia nervosa and bulimia: A handbook for counselors and therapists.* New York: Van Nostrand Reinhold.

New York State Division of Alcoholism and Alcohol Abuse. (1989). *The gateway to other drug use.* Buffalo, NY: Research Institute on Alcoholism.

Noone, R., & Reddig, R. (1976). Case studies in the family treatment of drug abuse. *Family Process, 15,* 325–332.

Norwood, R. (1985). *Women who love too much: When you keep wishing and hoping he'll change.* New York: Pocket Books.

Oashi, K., & Nishimura, H. (1978). *Alcoholic Problems in Japan.* Paper presented at the 9th World Congress of Sociology, Uppsala University, Sweden.

Oates, W. (1971). *Confessions of a workaholic.* New York: World Publishing.

O'Brien, C. P., Alterman, A., Walter, R., Childress, A. R., & McLellan, A. T. (1989). Evaluation of treatment for cocaine dependence. In L. S. Harris (Ed), *Problems of drug dependence* (pp. 78–84). Rockville, MD: National Institute on Drug Abuse.

O'Farrell, T. J. (1995) Marital and family therapy. In R. K. Hester & W. R. Miller (Eds.), *Handbook of alcoholism treatment approaches: Effective alternatives* (2nd ed., pp. 195–220.) Boston: Allyn & Bacon.

Office for Substance Abuse Prevention. (1989). *Drug-free communities: Turning awareness into action.* Rockville, MD: Author.

Office for Substance Abuse Prevention. (1990b). *Alcohol and other drug use among Hispanic youth: Technical report no. 4.* Washington, D.C.: U.S. Department of Health and Human Services.

Ohlms, D. L. (1983). *The disease concept of alcoholism.* Belleville, Illinois: Gary Whiteaker Co.

O'Leary, A. (1994). Factors associated with sexual risk of AIDs in women. In R. J. Battjes, Z. Sloboda, & W. C. Grace (Eds). *The context of HIV risk among drug users and their sexual partners.* (pp. 64–81). National Institute of Drug Abuse Research Monograph. Rockville, MD: U.S. Department of Health and Human Services.

Ordman, A. M., & Kirschenbaum, D. A. (1984). Bulimia: Assessment of eating, psychological and family characteristics. Unpublished manuscript. In E. M. Freeman (Ed.), *The addiction process: Effective social work approaches.* White Plains, NY: Longman.

Orford, J., & Guthrie, S. (1976). Coping behavior used by wives of alcoholics: A preliminary study. In G. Edward, R. D. Hawks, & M. MacCafferty (Eds.), *Alcohol dependence and smoking behavior* (pp. 136–143). Lexington, MA: The Haworth Press.

Ostrow, D. G. (1994). Substance use and HIV-transmitting behaviors among gay and bisexual men. In R. J. Battjes, Z. Sloboda, & W. C. Grace, (Eds). *The context of HIV risk among drug users and their sexual partners.* (pp. 88–113). National Institute of Drug Abuse Research Monograph. Rockville, MD: U.S. Department of Health and Human Services.

O'Sullivan, C. M. (1992). Adolescents in alcoholic families. In G. W. Lawson & A. W. Lawson (Eds.) *Adolescent substance abuse: Etiology, treatment, and prevention* (pp. 419–427). Gaithersburg, MD: Aspen Publishers.

Palfai, T., & Jankiewicz, H. (1991). *Drugs and human behavior.* Dubuque, IA: W. C. Brown.

Parsian, A., & Cloninger, C. R. (1991, November/December). Genetics of high risk populations. *Addiction and Recovery,* 9–11.

Pattison, E. M., & Kaufman, E. (1982). The alcoholism syndrome: Definitions and models. In E. M. Pattison & E. Kaufman (Eds.). *Encyclopedic handbook of alcoholism.* (pp. 3–30). New York: Gardner Press.

Paul, N. (1967). The use of empathy in the resolution of grief. *Perspectives in Biology and Medicine, 2,* 153–169.

Peele, S. (1975). *Love and addiction.* New York: Signet.

Peele, S. (1984). The cultural context of psychological approaches to alcoholism: Can we control the effects of alcohol? *American Psychologist, 39,* 1337–1351.

Peele, S. (1988). On the diseasing of America. *Utne Reader, 30,* 67.

Peele, S. (1989). *Diseasing of America: Addiction treatment out of control.* Lexington, MA: Lexington Books.

Perry, S. W., & Tross, S. (1984). Psychiatric problems of the AIDS patients in New York Hospital: Preliminary report. *Public Health Report, 99,* 200–205.

Peteet, J. R. (1993). A closer look at the role of a spiritual approach in addictions treatment. *Journal of Substance Abuse Treatment, 10,* 263–267.

Pickens, R. W., & Svikis, D. S. (1988). The twin method in the study of vulnerability to drug abuse. In R. W. Pickens & D. S. Svikis (Eds.). *Biological vulnerability to drug abuse* (pp. 1–8). Rockville, MD: National Institute of Drug Abuse.

Pimentel, R., & Lamendella, J. (1988). *Perspectives: AIDs in the workplace.* Northridge, CA: Milt Wright & Associates, Inc.

Platt, J., & Labate, C. (1976). *Heroin addiction: Theory, research, and treatment.* New York: Wiley.

Polich, J. M., Armor, D. M., & Braiker, H. B. (1981). *The course of alcoholism: Four years after treatment.* New York: Wiley.

Polich, J. M., Ellickson, P. L., Reuter, P., & Kahan, J. P. (1984). *Strategies for controlling adolescent drug use.* Santa Monica, CA: Rand Corp.

Pomerleau, O., Pertschuk, M., Adkins, D., & Brady, J. P. (1975). A comparison of behavioral and traditional treatment for middle-income problem drinkers. *Journal of Behavioral Medicine, 1,* 187–200.

Pope, H. G., & Hudson, J. I. (1984). *New hope for binge-eaters: Advances in the understanding and treatment for bulimia.* New York: Basic Books.

Potter-Efron, R. T., & Potter-Efron, P. S. (1989). Assessment of codependency with individuals from alcoholic and chemically dependent families. *Alcohol Treatment Quarterly, 6,* 37–57.

Powell, B. J., Read, M. R., Penick E. C., Miller, N. S., & Bingham, S. E. (1987). Primary and secondary depression in alcoholic men: An important distinction. *Journal of Clinical Psychiatry, 48,* 98–101.

Price, W. A., Giannini, A. J., & Colella, J. (1985). Anorexia nervosa in the elderly. *Journal of the American Geriatric Society, 33,* 213–215.

Primm, B. J. (1992). Future outlook: Treatment improvement. In J. H. Lowinson, P. Ruiz, R. B. Millman, & J. G. Langrod (Eds.) *Substance abuse: A comprehensive textbook* (2nd. ed., pp. 612–627). Baltimore: Williams & Wilkins.

Prochaska, J. O., & DiClemente, C. C. (1982). Transtheoretical therapy: Toward a more integrative model of change. *Psychotherapy: Theory, Research, and Practice, 19,* 276–288.

Reilly, D. M. (1992). Drug-abusing families: Intrafamilial dynamics and brief triphasic treatment. In E. Kaufman, & P. Kaufman, P. (Eds.), *Family theory of drug and alcohol abuse.* (pp. 105–119). Boston: Allyn & Bacon.

Rimmele, C. T., Howard, M. O., & Hilfrink, M. L. (1995). Aversion therapies. In R. K. Hester & W. R. Miller (Eds.), *Handbook of alcoholism treatment approaches: Effective alternatives.* (2nd ed., pp. 134–147). Boston: Allyn & Bacon.

Roberts, Fitzmahan, and Associates (1985). *Here's looking at you, 2000: A drug education curriculum.* Seattle, WA: Comprehensive Health Education Foundation.

Robins, L. N., & Przybeck, T. R. (1985). Age of onset of drug use as a factor in drug and other disorders. In C. L. Jones & R. J. Battjes (Eds.), *Etiology of drug abuse: Implications for prevention* (DHHS Publication No. 85-1335, pp. 178–192). Washington, DC: U.S. Government Printing Office.

Robins, L. N., & Guze, S. B. (1971). Drinking practices and problems in urban ghetto populations. In N. K. Mello & J. H. Mendelson (Eds.), *Recent advances in studies of alcoholism* (pp. 825–842). Rockville, MD: National Institute on Alcohol Abuse and alcoholism.

Rodning, C., Beckwith, L., & Howard, J. (1990). Attachment in play in prenatally drug-exposed children. *Developmental Psychopathology, 1,* 277–289.

Roget N., & Johnson, M. (1995). *Pre and post treatment planning in the substance abuse treatment case management process.* Carson City, NV: Bureau of Alcohol and Drug Abuse.

Rohsenow, D. J., Corbett, R., & Devine, D. (1988). Molested as children: A hidden contribution to substance abuse? *Journal of Substance Abuse Treatment, 5,* 13–18.

Rone, L. A., Miller, S. I., & Frances, R. J. (1995). Psychotropic medications. In R. K. Hester & W. R. Miller (Eds.), *Handbook of alcoholism treatment approaches: Effective alternatives.* (2nd ed., pp. 267–277). Boston: Allyn & Bacon.

Rosecrance, J. (1986). Attributions and the origins of problem gambling. *Sociopolitical Quarterly, 27,* 463–477.

Rounsaville, B. J., Weissman, M. M., Kleber, H. D., & Wilber, C. (1982). Heterogeneity of psychiatric diagnosis in treated opiate addicts. *Archives of General Psychiatry, 39,* 161–166.

Royce, J. E. (1989). *Alcohol problems and alcoholism: A comprehensive survey* (Rev. ed.). New York: The Free Press.

Russell, M., Henderson, C., & Blume, S. (1985). *Children of alcoholics: A review of the literature.* New York: Children of Alcoholics Foundation.

Ryle, J. A. (1936). Anorexia nervosa. *Lancet, 2.* 893–899.

Sager, C., Brown, H., Crohn, H., & Walker, L. (1983). *Treating the remarried family.* New York: Brunner-Mazel.

Satir, V. M. (1964). *Conjoint Family Therapy: A guide to theory and technique.* Palo Alto, CA: Science and Behavioral Books.

Sato, P. A., Chin, J., Mann, J. M. (1989). Review of AIDs and HIV infection: Global epidemiology and statistics. *AIDS, 3* (suppl. 1), S301–S307.

Scanlon, W. (1986). *Alcoholism and drug abuse in the workplace: Managing care and costs through employee assistance programs.* New York: Praeger.

Scarano, G. M., & Kalodner-Martin, C. R. (1994). A description of the continuum of eating disorders: Implications for intervention and research. *Journal of Counseling and Development, 72,* 356–361.

Schaeffer, B. (1985). *Is it love or is it addiction?* Center City, MN: Hazelden Foundation.

Schoenbaum, E. E., Hartel, D., & Selwyn, P. A. (1989). Risk factors for human immunodeficiency virus infections in intravenous drug users. *New England Journal of Medicine, 321,* 874–879.

Schuckit, M. A. (1982). Anxiety and assertiveness in sons of alcoholics and controls. *Journal of Clinical Psychiatry, 43,* 238–239.

Schuckit, M. A. (1983). Alcoholic patients with secondary depression. *American Journal of Psychiatry, 140*, 711–714.

Schuckit, M. A. (1984). *Drug and alcohol abuse: A clinical guide to diagnosis and treatment* (2nd ed.). New York: Plenum Press.

Schuckit, M. A. (1985). Genetics and the risk for alcoholism. *Journal of the American Medical Association, 254*, 2614–2617.

Schuckit, M. A., Goodwin, D. W., & Winokur, G. A. (1972). A study of alcoholism in half-siblings. *American Journal of Psychiatry, 128*, 1132–1136.

Schultz, E. (1994). If you use firm's counselors, remember your secrets could be used against you. *Wall Street Journal*, May 26, 1994, C2.

Schwartz, D. M., Thompson, M. G., & Johnson, C. (1982). Anorexia and bulimia: The sociocultural context. *International Journal of Eating Disorders, 1*, 20–36.

Schwartz, R. H. (1987). Marijuana: An overview. *The Pediatric Clinics of North America, 34*, 305–317.

Selwyn, P. A. (1992). Medical aspects of human immunodeficiency virus infection and its treatment in injecting drug users. In J. H. Lowinson, P. Ruiz, R. B. Millman, & J. G. Langrod (Eds.), *Substance abuse: A comprehensive textbook* (2nd. ed., pp. 744–774). Baltimore: Williams & Wilkins.

Selwyn, P. A., Feingold, A. R., & Iezza, A. (1989). Primary care for patients with human immunodeficiency virus (HIV) infection in a methadone treatment program. *Annals of Internal Medicine, 111*, 761–763.

Selzer, M. L. (1971). The Michigan Alcohol Screening Test: The quest for a new diagnostic instrument. *American Journal of Psychiatry, 127*, 1653–1658.

Sex and Love Addicts Anonymous. (1985). Boston: The Augustine Fellowship, Sex and Love Addicts Anonymous, Fellowship-Wide Service.

Seybold, K. C., & Salomone, P. R. (1994). Understanding workaholism: A review of causes and counseling approaches. *Journal of Counseling and Development, 73*, 4–9.

Shertzer, B., & Stone, S. C. (1980). *Fundamentals of counseling* (3rd ed.). Boston: Houghton Mifflin Company.

Shields, P. (1989). The recovering couples group: A viable treatment alternative. *Alcoholism Treatment Quarterly, 6*, 135–149.

Shon, S. P., & Ja, D. Y. (1982). Asian families. In M. McGoldrick, J. Pierce, & J. Giordano (Eds.), *Ethnicity and family therapy*. (pp. 208–228). New York: Guilford Press.

Sibley, D. C., & Blinder, B. J. (1988). Anorexia nervosa. In B. J. Blinder, B. F. Chaitin, & R. S. Goldstein (Eds.). *The eating disorders: Medical and psychological bases of diagnosis and treatment*. (pp. 247–258). New York: PMA Publishing Corporation.

Slochower, J. A. (1983). *Excessive eating*. New York: Human Sciences Press.

Smerigho, V. L. (1994). HIV risk in drug-using adolescents. In R. J. Battjes, Z. Sloboda, & W. C. Grace, (Eds). *The context of HIV risk among drug users and their sexual partners*. (pp. 114–131). National Institute of Drug Abuse Research Monograph. Rockville, MD: U.S. Department of Health and Human Services.

Smith, D. E. (1986). Cocaine-alcohol abuse: Epidemiological, diagnostic and treatment considerations. *Journal of Psychoactive Drugs, 18*, 117–129.

Sobell, L. C., & Sobell, M. B. (1973). A self-feedback technique to monitor drinking behavior in alcoholics. *Behavior Research and Therapy, 11*, 237–238.

Sobell, L. C., Sobell, M. B., & Toneatto, T. (1991). Recovery from alcohol problems without treatment. In N. Heather, W. R., Miller, & J. Greeley (Eds)., *Self-control and addictive behaviors* (pp. 198–242). New York: Pergamon Press.

Soderstrom, C. A., Trifillis, A. L., Shankar, B. S., & Clark, W. E. (1988). Marijuana and alcohol use among 1023 trauma patients: A prospective study. *Archives of Surgery, 123*, 733–737.

Sorensen, J. L., & Batki, S. L. (1992). Management of the psychosocial sequelae of HIV infection among drug abusers. In J. H. Lowinson, P. Ruiz, R. B. Millman, & J. G. Langrod (Eds.), *Substance abuse: A comprehensive textbook* (2nd. ed., pp. 788–793). Baltimore: Williams & Wilkins.

Sorenson, J. L., Costantini, M. F., & London, J. A. (1989). Coping with AIDS: Strategies for patients and staff in drug abuse treatment programs. *Journal of Psychoactive Drugs, 21,* 435–440.

Spruell, G. (1987). Work fever. *Training and Development Journal, 41,* 41–45.

Stall, R., & Ostrow, S. G. (1989). Intravenous drug use, the combination of drugs and sexual activity and HIV infection among gay and bisexual men: The San Francisco Men's Health Study. *Journal of Drug Issues, 19,* 57–73.

Stampp, K. (1956). *The peculiar institution: Slavery in the ante-bellum south.* New York: Alfred A. Knopf.

Standards for Employee Assistance Program. (1990). *The Employee Assistance Professionals Association, Inc, Exchange, 20,* 31–37.

Stanton, M. D., & Todd, T. C. (1992). Structural-strategic family therapy with drug addicts. In E. Kaufman, & P. Kaufman, P. (Eds.), *Family therapy of drug and alcohol abuse* (pp. 46–62), Boston: Allyn & Bacon.

Steer, R. A., Shaw, B. F., Beck, A. T., & Fine, E. W. (1977). Structure and depression in Black alcoholics. *Psychological Reports, 41,* 1235–1241.

Steinglass, P. (1987). *The alcoholic family.* New York: Basic Books.

Sterne, M. W. (1967). Drinking patterns and alcoholism among American Negroes. In D. J. Pittman (Ed.), *Alcoholism.* (pp. 66–98). New York: Harper & Row Publishers.

Sterne, M., & Pittman, D. J. (1972). *Drinking practices in the ghetto.* St. Louis: Washington University, Social Science Institute.

Stevens, E. P. (1973). Marianismo: The other face of machismo in Latin America. In A. Pescatello (Ed.), *Female and male in Latin America: Essays.* (pp. 89–102). Pittsburgh: University of Pittsburgh Press.

Streissguth, A. P., Aase, J. M., Clarren, S. K., Randels, S. P., LaDue, R. A., & Smith, D. F. (1991). Fetal alcohol syndrome in adolescents and adults. *Journal of the American Medical Association, 265,* 1961–1967.

Streissguth, A. P., Sampson, P. D., & Barr, H. M. (1989). Neurobehavioral dose-response effects of prenatal alcohol exposure in humans from infancy to adulthood. *Annals of the New York Academy of Sciences, 562,* 145–158.

Striegel-Moore, R. H., & Rodin, J. (1986). The influence of psychological variables in obesity. In K. D. Brownell & J. P. Foreyt (Eds.), *Handbook of eating disorders.* (pp. 99–121). New York: Basic Books.

Striegel-Moore, R. H., Silberstein, L. R., & Rodin, J. (1986). Toward an understanding of risk factors for bulimia. *American Psychologist, 41,* 246–263.

Strober, M., Salkion, B., & Burroughs, J. (1982). Validity of bulimia-restricter distinction in anorexia nervosa parental personality characteristics and family psychiatric morbidity. *Journal of Nervous and Mental Disease, 170,* 345–351.

Stroup-Benham, C. A., Trevino, F. M., & Trevino, D. B. (1990). Alcohol consumption patterns among Mexican-American mothers and among children from single and dual-headed households. *American Journal of Psychiatric Health, 80* (Suppl), 36–41.

Stunkard, A. (1959). Eating patterns and obesity. *Psychiatric Quarterly, 33,* 284–295.

Substance Abuse and Mental Health Services Administration. (1994). *Annual medical examiner data, 1992 and annual emergency room data, 1992: Data from the drug abuse warning network.* Series 1, Numbers 12-A and 12-B. Rockville, Maryland: U.S. Department of Health and Human Services.

Sue, D. (1987). Use and abuse of alcohol by Asian Americans. *Journal of Psychoactive Drugs, 19,* 57–66.

Sullivan, H. S. (1953). *The interpersonal theory of psychiatry.* New York: Norton.

Super, D. E. (1990). A life-span, life-space approach to career development. In D. Brown, L. Brooks, & Assoc. (Eds.) *Career choice and development: Applying contemporary theories to practice* (2nd ed., pp. 197–261). San Francisco: Jossey-Bass.

Sutherland, D., & Cressey, R. (1974). *Criminology.* Philadelphia: Lippincott.

Szyrynski, V. (1973). Anorexia nervosa and psychotherapy. *American Journal of Psychotherapy, 27,* 492–505.

Taber, J. I., McCormick, R. A., Russo, A. M., Adkins, B. J. & Ramirez, L. F. (1987). Follow-up of pathological gamblers after treatment. *American Journal of Psychiatry, 144,* 757–761.

Tani, N., Haga, H., & Kato, N. (1975). A survey of concern for drinking and alcoholics. First report: Students of junior high school. *Japan Journal of Alcohol Studies, 10,* 35–40.

Tarter, R. E., Jacob, T., & Bremer, D. A. (1989). Cognitive status of sons of alcoholic men. *Alcoholism: Clinical and Experimental Research, 13,* 232–235.

Tarter, R. E., & Schneider, D. U. (1976). Models and theories of alcoholism. In R. E. Tarter & A. A. Sugerman (Eds.), *Alcoholism: Interdisciplinary approaches to an enduring problem.* (pp. 202–210). Reading, MA: Addison-Wesley.

Tobler, N. S. (1986). Meta-analysis of 143 adolescent drug prevention programs: Quantitative outcome results of program participants compared to a control or comparison group. *Journal of Drug Issues, 16,* 537–567.

Tobler, N. S. (1992). Drug prevention programs can work: Research findings. *Journal of Addictive Diseases, 11,* 1–28.

Torres, S. (1993). Cultural sensitivity: A must for today's primary care provider. *Advance for Nurse Practitioners, 1,* 16–18.

Towers, R. L. (1989). *Children of alcoholics/addicts.* Washington, DC: National Education Association.

Trice, H. M., & Roman, P. M. (1978). *Spirits and demons at work: Alcohol and other drugs on the job.* Ithica: New York State School of Industrial and Labor Relations, Cornell University.

Trimpey, J. (1989). *Rational recovery from addiction: The small book.* Lotus, CA: Author.

Tuchfield, B. S. (1981). Spontaneous remission in alcoholics: Empirical observations and theoretical implications. *Journal of Studies on Alcohol, 42,* 626–640.

Twerski, A. J. (1983). Early intervention in alcoholism: Confrontational techniques. *Hospital and Community Psychiatry, 34,* 1027–1030.

U.S. Bureau of the Census. (1990). Washington: U.S. Government Publications.

U.S. Bureau of Justice Statistics. (1992). *Drugs, crime, and the justice system: A national report from the Bureau of Justice Statistics.* Washington, D.C.: NCJ-133652.

U.S. Department of Health and Human Services. (1990). Pregnancy and infant health. *Health United States and Prevention profile.* Rockville, MD: U.S. Department of Health and Human Services.

U.S. Preventive Services Task Force. (1989). Screening for infection with human immunodeficiency virus. *Guide to clinical preventive services* (pp. 93–98). Baltimore: Williams & Wilkins, Eds.

Umana, R. F., Gross, S. J., & McConville, M. T. (1981). *Crisis in the family: Three approaches.* New York: Gardner Press.

Vandereycken, W., & Van den Broucke, S. (1984). Anorexia nervosa in males: A comparative study of 107 cases reported in the literature (1970 to 1980). *Acta Psychiatrica Scandinavica, 70,* 447–454.

Van Gorp, W. G., Miller, E., Satz, P., & Visscher, B. (1989). Neuropsychological performance in HIV-1 immunocompromised patients. *Journal of Clinical and Experimental Neuropsychology, 11,* 35.

Wadden, T. A., & Stunkard, A. J. (1987). Psychopathology and obesity. *Annals of the New York Academy of Science, 499,* 55–65.

Wallen, J. (1990). Issues in alcoholism treatment. In R. C. Engs (Ed.), *Women: Alcohol and other drugs* (pp. 103–109). Dubuque, IA: Kendall/Hunt.

Ward, D. A. (1990). Conceptions of the nature and treatment of alcoholism. In D. A. Ward (Ed.), *Alcoholism: Introduction to them and treatment* (pp. 4–16). Dubuque, IA: Kendall/Hunt Publishing.

Wardle, J., & Beinart, H. (1981). Binge-eating: A theoretical review. *British Journal of Clinical Psychology, 20,* 97–109.

Wegscheider, S. (1981). *Another chance: Hope and health for the alcoholic family.* Palo Alto, CA: Science and Behavior Books.

Weisner, T. S., Weibel-Orlando, J. C., & Long, J. (1984). "Serious drinking," "White man's drinking," and "teetotaling": Drinking levels and styles in an urban American Indian population. *Journal of Studies on Alcohol, 45,* 237–250.

Wermuth, B. M., Davis, K. L., & Hollister, L. E. (1977). Phenytoin treatment of the binge-eating syndrome. *American Journal of Psychiatry, 134,* 1249–1253.

Westermeyer, J., & Baker, J. M. (1986). Alcoholism and the American Indian. In N. J. Estes and M. E. Heinemann (Eds.), *Alcoholism: Develop-*

ment, consequences, and interventions (pp. 273–282). St. Louis: The C. V. Mosby Company.

Westermeyer, J. O. (1991). Cultural perspectives: Native Americans, Asians and new immigrants. In J. H. Lowinson, P. Ruiz, R. B. Millman & J. G. Langrod (Eds.), *Substance abuse: A comprehensive textbook.* (2nd. ed., pp. 890–896.) Baltimore, MD: Williams & Wilkins.

Western Regional Center for Drug-Free Schools and Communities. (1995). *Confidentiality of records in student assistance programs.* Portland, OR: Author.

Western Regional Center for Drug-Free Schools and Communities. (1994). Long-term study shows drug prevention works. *Western Center News,* June, 1, 3.

Whiteside, M. (1989). Remarried systems. In L. Combinck-Graham (Ed.), *Children in family contexts: Perspectives on treatment* (pp. 135–160). New York: Guilford Press.

Whitfield, C. L. (1980). Children of alcoholics: Treatment issues. *State Medical Journal, 29,* 86–91.

Wicker, T. (1987, May 13). Drugs and alcohol. *New York Times,* p. 27.

Williams, C. N. (1990). Prevention and treatment approaches for children of alcoholics. In M. Windle, & J. S. Searles (Eds.), *Children of alcoholics. Critical perspectives.* (pp. 187–216). New York: The Guilford Press.

Williams, M. (1986). Alcohol and ethnic minorities: Native Americans: An update. *Alcohol health and research world, 11,* 5–6.

Wilson, C. (1982). The impact on children. In J. Orford & J. Harwin (Eds.), *Alcohol and the family* (pp. 151–166). New York: St. Martin's Press.

Windle, M., & Searles, J. S. (1990). *Children of alcoholics. Critical perspectives.* New York: Guilford Press.

Winfree, L, T., & Griffiths, C. T. (1983). Youth at risk: Marijuana use among Native American and Caucasian youths. *International Journal of the Addictions, 18,* 53–70.

Winick, C. (1980). A theory of drug dependence based on role, access to and attitudes toward drugs. In D. J. Lettieri, M. Sayers, & H. W. Pearson (Eds.), *Theories of drug abuse: Selected contemporary perspectives* (pp. 225–235). NIDA Research Monograph 30. Washington, D.C.: Department of Health and Human Services.

Winnicott, D. W. (1965). *The maturational process and the facilitating environment.* New York: International Press.

Witters, W., Venturelli, P., & Hanson, G. (1992). *Drugs and society* (3rd ed.). Boston: Jones and Bartlett.

Woititz, J. G. (1983). *Adult children of alcoholics.* Pompano Beach, FL: Health Communications.

Wolpe, J. (1958). *Psychotherapy by reciprocal inhibition.* Palo Alto, CA: Stanford University Press.

Wolpe, J. (1969). *The Practice of behavior therapy.* New York: Pergamon Press.

Women's lung cancer death rate rises sharply. (1993, November 13). *Sacramento Bee,* p. A4.

World Health Communications. (1988). *Management of HIV disease. Treatment team workshop handbook.* New York: World Health Communications, Inc.

Wray, I., & Dickerson, M. (1981). Cessation of high frequency gambling and 'withdrawal symptoms.' *British Journal of Addiction, 76,* 401–405.

Wrich, J. (1982). *Guidelines for developing an employee assistance program: American Medical Association Management Briefing.* New York: American Management Association.

Wright P. H., & Wright, K. D. (1990). Measuring codependents' close relationships: A preliminary study. *Journal of Substance Abuse, 2,* 335–344.

Young, T. J. (1991). Native American drinking: A neglected subject of study and research. *Journal of Drug Education, 21,* 65–72.

Young, T. J. (1992). Substance abuse among Native American youth. In G. W. Lawson & A. W. Lawson (Eds.), *Adolescent substance abuse: Etiology, treatment and prevention.* (pp. 381–390). Gaithersberg, MD: Aspen Publishers.

Zimberg, S. (1978). Psychosocial treatment of elderly alcoholics. In S. Zimberg, J. Wallace, & S. B. Blume (Eds.), *Practical approaches to alcoholism psychotherapy.* (pp. 237–254). New York: Plenum Press.

Zimberg, S. (1978). Psychiatric office treatment in alcoholism. In S. Zimberg, J. Wallace, & S. B. Blume (Eds.). *Practical approaches to alcoholism psychotherapy.* (pp. 47–62). New York: Plenum Press.

Index